A HANDBOOK OF
CHINESE CERAMICS

A HANDBOOK OF
CHINESE CERAMICS

REVISED AND ENLARGED EDITION

SUZANNE G. VALENSTEIN

RESEARCH CURATOR
THE DEPARTMENT OF ASIAN ART

THE METROPOLITAN MUSEUM OF ART, NEW YORK
WEIDENFELD AND NICOLSON, LONDON

This publication has been made possible by the
Samuel I. Newhouse Foundation.

John P. O'Neill, Editor in Chief
Barbara Burn, Project Supervisor
Martina D'Alton and Georgette Felix, Editors
Michael Shroyer, Designer

First published in Great Britain in 1989 by
George Weidenfeld & Nicolson Limited
91 Clapham High Street, London SW4 7TA

ISBN 0 297 79577 5

All black-and-white photographs in this volume not otherwise
credited were taken by The Photograph Studio, The Metropolitan Museum of Art. All color photography was taken especially for this book by Sheldan Comfert Collins.

Typeset by U.S. Lithograph, typographers
Printed by Mercantile Printing Company, USA
Bound by Riverside Book Bindery, Inc., Rochester,
New York

FRONTISPIECE: JAR. Porcelain painted in underglaze blue.
Ming dynasty, Xuande mark and period, 1426–35. Gift of
Robert E. Tod, 1937. 37.191.1.

JACKET COVER: DISH. Porcelain painted in underglaze
blue. Ming dynasty, late 15th century, Chenghua period. Gift of
Alan and Simone Hartman, 1981. 1981.81.1. LEYS JAR.
Porcelain painted in underglaze blue. Ming dynasty, late 15th
century, Chenghua period. Purchase, Mrs. Richard E. Linburn
Gift, 1986. 1986.208.1.

CONTENTS

FOREWORD

The Chinese ceramic collection in the Metropolitan Museum was off to an impressive start in 1879 when the Museum bought over 1,300 pieces from the collection of Samuel P. Avery. Reflecting the taste of the time, the Avery purchase consisted almost entirely of porcelains dating to the seventeenth, eighteenth, and nineteenth centuries, and this wealth of Qing-dynasty ceramics was further enriched by the bequest of Benjamin Altman's large and splendid collection of Qing wares in 1913. Today, while the strength of the collection still lies in its Qing-dynasty porcelains, it spans thousands of years, with objects that range from the Neolithic period through the twentieth century in date. Now numbering more than 4,500 objects, it represents—with some lacunae—a sweeping survey of Chinese ceramic history. It includes many masterpieces that are internationally famous and is rightly regarded as one of the world's great collections.

The generosity of many discerning collectors has contributed greatly to the size and quality of this assemblage, as over the years notable gifts and bequests came from such prominent connoisseurs as Edward C. Moore, Mr. and Mrs. Isaac D. Fletcher, Mary Clark Thompson, Mrs. Samuel T. Peters, Mrs. H. O. Havemeyer, William Rhinelander Stewart, Michael Friedsam, Robert E. Tod, Mary Stillman Harkness, Robert West, John D. Rockefeller, Jr., and Edwin C. Vogel. Many extremely fine and rare objects were acquired in these and other gifts and bequests, and other important pieces have come into the collection with purchases made by the Far East Department curatorial staff.

As we approach the hundredth anniversary of the acquisition of our first Chinese ceramics, we define our goals for the future. The somewhat random accumulation of the past has given us a splendid foundation on which to build. In the years ahead we hope to concentrate not so much on quantity as quality as we fill in the obvious gaps in the collection with an aim to making it fully representative of the Chinese potter's art.

Along with the responsibility to collect, conserve, and exhibit works of art, it is the obligation of a museum to help the public appreciate and understand the treasures on view. Suzanne Valenstein is to be congratulated on having written this lucid *Handbook*. In it she offers a synopsis of the historical and technological background of Chinese ceramic art as a frame of reference against which the Museum's collection can be better enjoyed.

Wen Fong
Special Consultant for Far Eastern Affairs
1975

Suzanne Valenstein is to be congratulated again for keeping pace with the rapidly changing horizons of ceramic history and technology and for presenting this complex picture clearly and concisely. Her revised *Handbook* further enhances our enjoyment of the Museum's collection.

Wen Fong
Special Consultant for Asian Affairs
1988

PREFACE TO THE SECOND EDITION

In the years that have elapsed since the appearance of the first edition of this book, the history of Chinese ceramics has been significantly recast: our knowledge about many aspects of the subject has taken a quantum leap forward. Accelerated archaeological activity in The People's Republic of China and a deluge of data from its findings, as well as important archaeological discoveries made elsewhere, have dictated substantial changes in our chronology and attributions. Concurrently, analytic studies identifying discrete variations within the broad spectrum of Chinese ceramic technology have altered many of our basic concepts.

This edition, written in the light of such enhanced knowledge, presents a far more detailed and comprehensive picture than could have been possible only a few years ago. Writing it has been a Sisyphean task. My purpose has been to report and integrate the wealth of new information that has emerged since publication of the first edition. As in the earlier book, I have endeavored to trace the thread of tradition and innovation that winds through the entire history of Chinese ceramics and is the paramount theme in the development of the Chinese potter's art.

Most of the illustrations have been drawn from the collection of Chinese pottery in the Metropolitan Museum. Since the first edition of this book was published, I have been extraordinarily fortunate in being able to enrich the collection significantly, and many of these new acquisitions have been included. I would like to express a very special word of thanks to the generous donors who have helped to make this possible.

As in all efforts of this kind, a number of people have been of considerable help. I would like to thank, in particular, Annette Juliano Geneve, John Ayers, Margaret Medley, Linda Shulsky, Clare Le Corbeiller, Alfreda Murck, Caron Smith, Pamela Vandiver, Robert Tichane, Richard Stone, Wu Meiling, and Joseph Chang, upon whom I drew for knowledge, support, and encouragement. Thanks, too, to Shinichi Doi and Barbara Bridgers for their cooperation, and to Alexander Mikhailovich and Sheldan Collins for their fine new photographs. Susan Miller was invaluable in helping me complete the manuscript; to her, to the editors, Barbara Burn, Martina D'Alton, and Georgette Felix; to Michael Shroyer, who designed the book; to Wilhelmina Reyinga-Amrhein, who drew the maps; to Penny Jones, who helped to proofread; and to Teresa Egan, Gwen Roginsky, Jean Levitt, and Helga Lose, who saw the book through its production, goes my deepest gratitude as well.

Suzanne Valenstein
April 1988

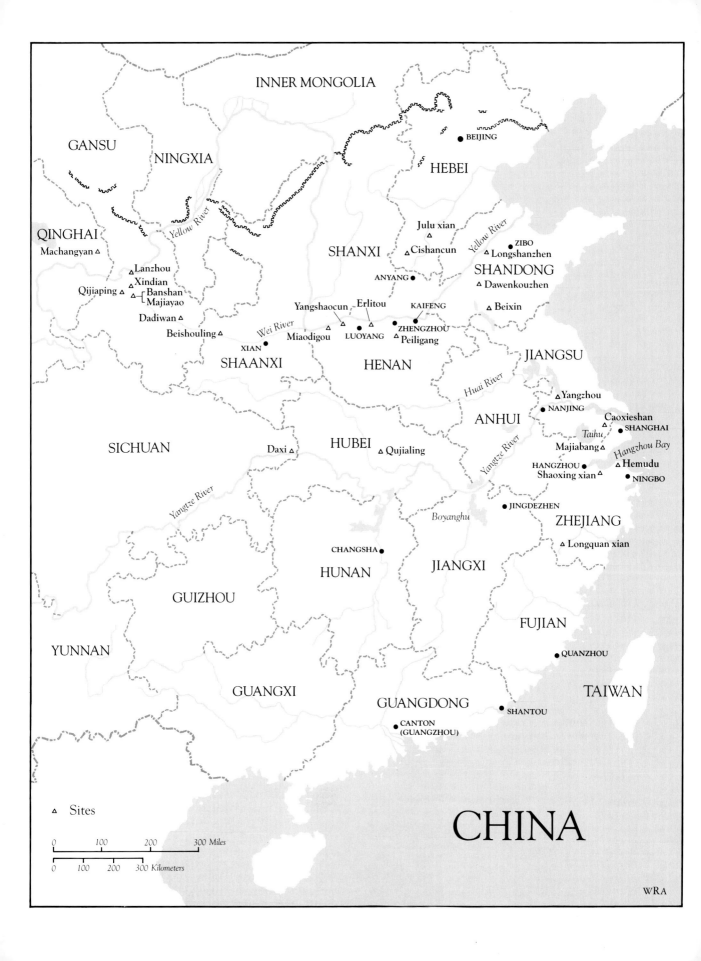

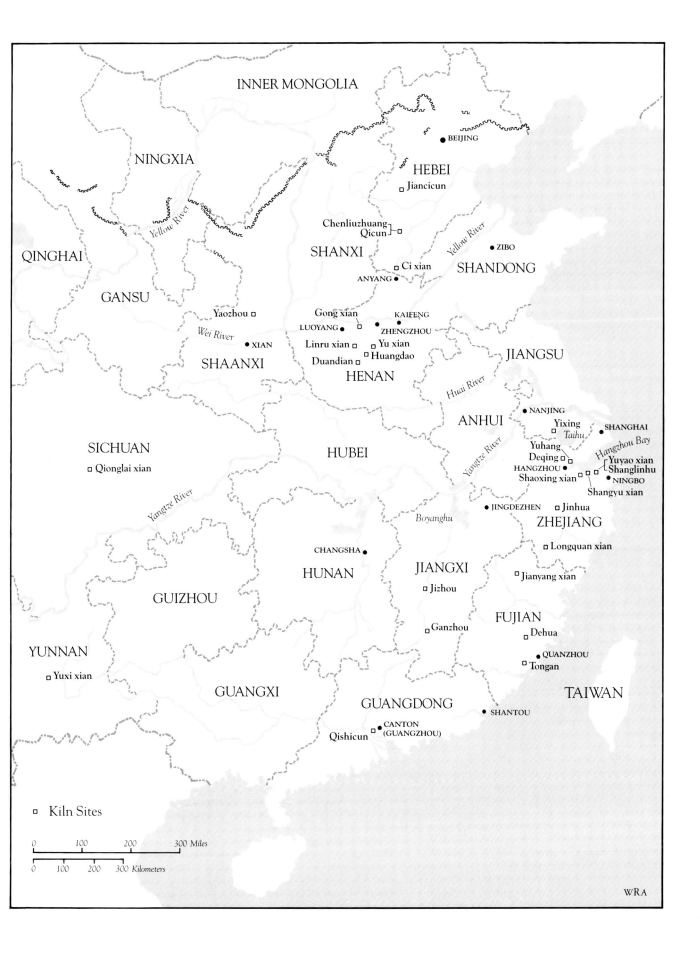

INNER MONGOLIA

NINGXIA

● BEIJING

HEBEI

□ Jiancicun

QINGHAI

Yellow River

Chenliuzhuang □
Qicun □

SHANXI

● ZIBO

SHANDONG

Ci xian □

GANSU

ANYANG ●

Yaozhou □

Gong xian
□
KAIFENG
●

Wei River

LUOYANG ●
□
ZHENGZHOU ●

● XIAN

Linru xian □
□ Yu xian

JIANGSU

SHAANXI

Duandian □
□ Huangdao

HENAN

Huai River

ANHUI

● NANJING

Yixing □
Taihu

SICHUAN

HUBEI

Yangtze River

Hangzhou Bay

□ Qionglai xian

Yuhang
Deqing □
HANGZHOU ●
Shaoxing xian □

□ Yuyao xian
Shanglinhu
● NINGBO
Shangyu xian

Yangtze River

● JINGDEZHEN

□ Jinhua

Boyanghu

ZHEJIANG

CHANGSHA ●

□ Longquan xian

HUNAN

JIANGXI

GUIZHOU

□ Jizhou

□ Jianyang xian

YUNNAN

□ Ganzhou

FUJIAN

□ Dehua

□ Yuxi xian

□ Tongan

● QUANZHOU

GUANGXI

GUANGDONG

TAIWAN

● SHANTOU

Qishicun □
□ CANTON
(GUANGZHOU)

□ Kiln Sites

0   100   200   300 Miles

0   100   200   300 Kilometers

WRA

CHRONOLOGY
Chinese Dynasties and Periods

NEOLITHIC PERIOD . . . . ? to ca. 21st century B.C.

ERLITOU (XIA) . . . . ca. 21st – ca. 16th century B.C.

SHANG . . . . ca. 16th – ca. 11th century B.C.

ZHOU . . . . ca. 11th century B.C. – 256 B.C.
    Western Zhou . . . . ca. 11th century B.C. – 771 B.C.
    Eastern Zhou . . . . 770 – 256 B.C.
        Spring and Autumn Era . . . . 770 – 476 B.C.
        Warring States Era . . . . 475 – 221 B.C.

QIN . . . . 221 – 206 B.C.

HAN . . . . 206 B.C. – A.D. 220
    Western (Former) Han . . . . 206 B.C. – A.D. 8
    Eastern (Later) Han . . . . A.D. 25 – 220

THE SIX DYNASTIES . . . . A.D. 220 – 589
    Three Kingdoms . . . . 220 – 280
        Wu 222 – 280   Shu Han 221 – 263   Wei 220 – 264
    Western Jin . . . . 265 – 317
    The Sixteen Kingdoms . . . . 304 – 439
    The Northern (386 – 581) and Southern (317 – 589) Dynasties

	North			South	
	Northern Wei	386 – 535		Eastern Jin	317 – 420
	Eastern Wei	534 – 550		Liu Song	420 – 479
	Western Wei	535 – 557		Southern Qi	479 – 502
	Northern Qi	550 – 577		Liang	502 – 557
	Northern Zhou	557 – 581		Chen	557 – 589

SUI . . . . 581 – 618

TANG . . . . 618 – 906

THE FIVE DYNASTIES . . . . 907 – 960

LIAO . . . . 907 – 1125

SONG . . . . 960 – 1279
    Northern Song . . . . 960 – 1127
    Southern Song . . . . 1127 – 1279

JIN . . . . 1115 – 1234

YUAN . . . . 1279 – 1368

MING . . . . 1368 – 1644

Hongwu	1368 – 1398	Jingtai	1450 – 1457	Longqing	1567 – 1572
Jianwen	1399 – 1402	Tianshun	1457 – 1464	Wanli	1573 – 1620
Yongle	1403 – 1424	Chenghua	1465 – 1487	Taichang	1620
Hongxi	1425	Hongzhi	1488 – 1505	Tianqi	1621 – 1627
Xuande	1426 – 1435	Zhengde	1506 – 1521	Chongzhen	1628 – 1644
Zhengtong	1436 – 1449	Jiajing	1522 – 1566		

QING . . . . 1644 – 1912

Shunzhi	1644 – 1661	Jiaqing	1796 – 1820	Guangxu	1875 – 1908
Kangxi	1662 – 1722	Daoguang	1821 – 1850	Xuantong	1909 – 1912
Yongzheng	1723 – 1735	Xianfeng	1851 – 1861		
Qianlong	1736 – 1795	Tongzhi	1862 – 1874		

REPUBLIC OF CHINA 1912

Hongxian (Yuan Shikai) . . . . 1915 – 1916

THE PEOPLE'S REPUBLIC OF CHINA 1949

COLOR PLATES

1. COVERED JAR. Earthenware with painted decoration.
Height: 22 1/8 in. (56.2 cm.). Western Han dynasty,
ca. 1st century B.C. Purchase, Mr. and Mrs. Oscar Tang
Gift, 1986. 1986.170.

2. EWER. Stoneware with celadon glaze. Height: 7 1/2 in.
(19.1 cm.). Six Dynasties, Eastern Jin dynasty, ca. second
half 4th century. Yue ware. Gift of Mrs. Richard E. Linburn,
1979. 1979.353.

3. VESSEL. Stoneware with celadon glaze.
Length: 11 7/8 in. (30.2 cm.). Six Dynasties, late
Northern Dynasties, ca. second half 6th century.
Northern ware. Harris Brisbane Dick Fund, 1960.
60.75.2.

4. BOTTLE. Stoneware with incised and impressed
designs under celadon glaze. Height: 10 in. (25.4 cm.).
Probably Sui dynasty, 581–618. Gift of Ernest Erickson
Foundation, 1985. 1985.214.130.

5, 6. TOMB GUARDIAN AND EARTH SPIRIT.
Earthenware with "three-color" glazes and pigments.
Height of tomb guardian: 35 in. (88.9 cm.). Height of
earth spirit: 30 3/4 in. (78.1 cm.). Tang dynasty, late
7th–first half 8th century. Rogers Fund, 1911.
11.83.1 and .4.

7. FLASK. Stoneware with suffused glaze. Height: 11 1/2 in. (29.2 cm.). Tang dynasty, ca. 9th century. Gift of Mr. and Mrs. John R. Menke, 1972. 1972.274.

8. DISH. Stoneware painted in underglaze green and brown. Diameter: 5 1/2 in. (14 cm.). Tang dynasty, 9th century. Changsha ware. Gift of Diane and Oscar Schafer, 1986. 1986.97.3.

10. EWER. Stoneware with applied medallions under brown-splashed glaze. Height: 6 in. (15.2 cm.). Tang dynasty, ca. 9th century. Changsha ware. Purchase, Friends of Asian Art Gifts, 1986. 1986.113.

9. WATERPOT. Stoneware painted in underglaze bluish green. Diameter: 2 1/2 in. (6.4 cm.). Tang dynasty, ca. 9th century. Changsha ware. Purchase, Gloria H. Spivak Gift, 1986. 1986.75.3.

11. BOWL. Stoneware with carved and incised design under celadon glaze. Diameter: 10 5/8 in. (27 cm.). Five Dynasties, 10th century. Yue ware. Rogers Fund, 1917. 18.56.36 [also No. 72].

12. EWER. Stoneware with incised, carved, and relief decoration under celadon glaze. Height: 8 1/4 in. (21 cm.). Northern Song dynasty, 11th–12th century. Northern celadon ware. Gift of Mrs. Samuel T. Peters, 1926. 26.292.73.

13. HEAD OF A LION. Porcelain with ivory white glaze.
Height: about 4 3/4 in. (12.1 cm.). Northern Song
dynasty, 11th–12th century. Ding ware. Gift of Ernest
Erickson Foundation, 1985. 1985.214.131.

14. VASE. Stoneware with sgraffito decoration.
Height: 13 7/8 in. (35.2 cm.). Northern Song dynasty,
11th–12th century. Cizhou ware. Gift of Mrs. Samuel T.
Peters, 1926. 26.292.61.

15. PILLOW. Stoneware painted in brownish black on white
    ground. Length: 16 1/8 in. (41 cm.). Mark: *Zhang jia zao*.
    Late Northern Song–Jin dynasty, 12th–13th century.
    Cizhou ware. Gift of Ernest Erickson Foundation, 1985.
    1985.214.132.

16. VASE. Porcelain painted in underglaze blue.
    Height: 11 1/4 in. (28.6 cm.). Yuan dynasty, ca. first half
    14th century. Gift of Irene and Earl Morse, 1984. 1984.297.

17. STEMCUP. Porcelain painted in underglaze blue.
    Diameter: 3 5/8 in. (9.2 cm.). Yuan dynasty, ca. first
    half 14th century. Gift of Diane and Oscar Schafer,
    1986. 1986.97.1 [also No. 127].

18. PLATE. Porcelain painted in underglaze blue.
Diameter: 18 in. (45.7 cm.). Late Yuan dynasty,
ca. mid-14th century. Purchase, Mrs. Richard E. Linburn
Gift, 1987. 1987.10.

19. BASIN. Porcelaneous ware with incised decoration
    under celadon glaze, and biscuit relief.
    Diameter: 12 3/4 in. (32.4 cm.). Early Ming dynasty,
    late 14th–early 15th century. Longquan ware. Purchase,
    Mrs. Richard E. Linburn and Anonymous Gifts, 1987.
    1987.157.

20. BOWL. Porcelain painted in underglaze red.
Diameter: 15 3/4 in. (40 cm.). Ming dynasty, late 14th
century. Rogers Fund, 1917. 18.56.35.

21. JAR. Porcelain painted in underglaze blue.
Height: 19 in. (48.3 cm.). Ming dynasty, Xuande mark
and period, 1426–35. Gift of Robert E. Tod, 1937.
37.191.1.

22. DISH. Porcelain painted in underglaze blue.
Diameter: 8 1/2 in. (21.6 cm.). Ming dynasty, late 15th
century, Chenghua period. Gift of Alan and Simone
Hartman, 1981. 1981.81.1.

23. LEYS JAR. Porcelain painted in underglaze blue.
Diameter: 5 1/4 in. (13.3 cm.). Ming dynasty, late 15th
century, Chenghua period. Purchase, Mrs. Richard E.
Linburn Gift, 1986. 1986.208.1.

24. CUP. Porcelain painted in underglaze blue and overglaze enamels. Diameter: 3 1/4 in. (8.3 cm.). Ming dynasty, Chenghua mark and period, 1465–87. Purchase, Mrs. Richard E. Linburn Gift, 1987. 1987.85.

25. LEYS JAR. Porcelain with incised decoration under colored glazes. Diameter: 5 7/8 in. (14.9 cm.). Ming dynasty, Zhengde mark and period, 1506–21. Gift of Mrs. Richard E. Linburn, 1981. 1981.368.1.

26. VASE. Porcelaneous ware with cloisonné-style
    decoration. Height: 14 1/2 in. (36.8 cm.). Ming
    dynasty, late 15th century. Bequest of John D. Rockefeller,
    Jr., 1960. 61.200.52.

27. BASIN. Porcelaneous ware with cloisonné-style
    decoration. Diameter: 11 1/4 in. (28.6 cm.). Ming
    dynasty, late 15th century. Bequest of John D. Rockefeller,
    Jr., 1960. 61.200.4.

28. DISH. Porcelain painted in overglaze polychrome
    enamels. Diameter: 12 in. (30.5 cm.). Ming dynasty,
    first half 16th century. Gift of Mrs. Richard E. Linburn,
    1981. 1981.368.2.

29. INCENSE BURNER. Stoneware with relief
decoration under colored glazes. Height: 17 1/8 in.
(43.5 cm.). Ming dynasty, dated in accordance with
July 1512. Gift of Mrs. Harry Payne Bingham, 1962.
62.101.1.

30. BRUSH HOLDER. Porcelain with incised decoration,
painted in underglaze blue. Height: 7 7/8 in. (20 cm.).
Transitional Period, ca. second quarter 17th century.
"Transitional" ware. Purchase by subscription,
1879. 79.2.366.

31. PLATE. Porcelaneous ware painted in overglaze
    polychrome enamels. Diameter: 16 in. (40.6 cm.). Late
    Ming dynasty, late 16th–early 17th century. "Swatow"
    ware. Gift of Dr. and Mrs. Roger Gerry, 1984. 1984.308.

32. VASE. Porcelain painted in overglaze polychrome
    enamels. Height: 14 1/4 in. (36.2 cm.). Later
    Transitional Period, ca. 1644–83. Bequest of Edmund
    Cogswell Converse, 1921. 21.175.9.

33. FIGURE, POSSIBLY THE GOD OF WEALTH IN
HIS CIVIL ASPECT. Porcelain painted in *famille verte*
enamels on the biscuit and on the glaze. Height: 23 7/8 in.
(60.6 cm.). Qing dynasty, late 17th–early 18th century,
Kangxi period. Bequest of John D. Rockefeller, Jr., 1960.
61.200.11.

34. VASE. Porcelain painted in overglaze *famille verte*
enamels and gilt. Height: 18 in. (45.7 cm.). Qing
dynasty, late 17th–early 18th century, Kangxi period.
Bequest of John D. Rockefeller, Jr., 1960. 61.200.66.

35. VASE. Porcelain with *sang de boeuf* glaze.
Height: 7 7/8 in. (20 cm.). Qing dynasty, late
17th–early 18th century, Kangxi period. Bequest of
Mary Clark Thompson, 1924. 24.80.537.

37. VASE. Porcelain with peachbloom glaze. Height: 8 in.
(20.3 cm.). Qing dynasty, Kangxi mark, late in the
period, ca. 1700–22. Bequest of Mary Stillman Harkness,
1950. 50.145.286 [also No. 231].

36. VASE. Porcelain painted in underglaze red.
Height: 7 3/4 in. (19.7 cm.). Qing dynasty, Yongzheng
mark and period, 1723–35. The Friedsam Collection,
Bequest of Michael Friedsam, 1931. 32.100.434.

38. DISH. Porcelain painted in overglaze *famille rose*
     enamels, crimson pink glaze on the reverse.
     Diameter: 8 in. (20.3 cm.). Qing dynasty, ca. 1730–50.
     Purchase by subscription, 1879. 79.2.693.

39. BOWL. Porcelain painted in overglaze *famille rose*
     enamels. Diameter: 4 1/2 in. (11.4 cm.). Qing dynasty,
     Yongzheng mark and period, 1723–35. Alfred W. Hoyt
     Collection, Bequest of Rosina H. Hoppin, 1965. 65.86.12.

40. BOWL. Porcelain with "peacock feather" glaze.
Height: 4 3/8 in. (11.1 cm.). Qing dynasty, Yongzheng
mark and period, 1723–35. Gift of Dr. and Mrs. George
Fan, in honor of J. M. Hu, 1985. 1985.389.

41. VASE. Porcelain with low-relief decoration under
celadon glaze. Height: 20 3/4 in. (52.7 cm.). Qing
dynasty, ca. middle 18th century. Gift of Mr. and
Mrs. Hugh J. Grant, 1974. 1974.223.

OVERLEAF

42. VASE. Porcelain painted in overglaze *famille rose*
enamels. Height: 20 1/4 in. (51.4 cm.). Qing dynasty,
Qianlong mark, early in the period, 1736–95. Mr. and
Mrs. Isaac D. Fletcher Collection, Bequest of Isaac D.
Fletcher, 1917. 17.120.194.

A HANDBOOK OF
CHINESE CERAMICS

5. JAR. Earthenware with painted decoration.
Height: 13 1/4 in. (33.7 cm.). Neolithic period,
ca. 2600–2300 B.C. Majiayao Yangshao culture, Banshan
phase. Purchase, Mrs. Richard E. Linburn Gift, 1980.
1980.413.

THE EARLY PERIODS

I t probably began with cupped hands. From there, at some uncharted time, the early Chinese learned to bake clay into simple vessels in which they could cook, hold, and store their food and drink. So far, the first Chinese ceramics have evaded the archaeologist's pick, and evidence of the evolution from this nascent pottery to the known accomplishments of the Neolithic era is fragmentary.

According to recent estimates, over six thousand Neolithic sites were discovered in The People's Republic of China between 1949 and 1979, and since then, other remains continue to be unearthed. As these sites have been systematically excavated and assessed, some idea of the basic structure of the Chinese Neolithic age and the nature of its individual cultures has begun to emerge. Archaeologists now perceive this period as one in which a number of diverse Neolithic societies developed simultaneously in several parts of the country, primarily in North China, along the eastern coast, and in South China. A brief examination of some of the more important of these many cultures and their representative ceramics follows.

EARLY NEOLITHIC CULTURES IN NORTH CHINA

In recent years, archaeologists working in North China, in an area reaching from Gansu Province in the west to Henan and Hebei provinces in the east, have excavated three groups of ancient settlements. These sites belong to three Early Neolithic cultures that have been named Peiligang, Cishan, and Dadiwan-I, after the eponymous sites where they were first discovered.[1] Based on carbon-14 dating, these cultures can be assigned to the seventh–sixth millennium B.C. While there are certain differences to be seen in various artifacts gathered at each of these groups of sites, at the same time the excavated material exhibits many common traits.

The Peiligang and Cishan Cultures

As of this writing, the oldest Neolithic remains excavated in North China belong to an Early Neolithic culture that is typified by the site discovered in 1977 at Peiligang, Xinzheng xian, in central Henan Province.[2] Over forty

1. BOWL. Earthenware. Early Neolithic period, ca. 6500–5400 B.C. Peiligang culture. Excavated at Peiligang, Xinzheng xian, Henan Province. From *Kaogu* 1982, no. 4.

Peiligang sites have been investigated so far; these contained the remains of houses, storage pits, and clan cemeteries. A pottery kiln has been uncovered at Peiligang itself. Excavated finds indicate that these settlements were inhabited by people with a semiagricultural economy. They cultivated crops, particularly millet; domesticated pigs and dogs; and supplemented their farming with gathering, hunting, and fishing.

Peiligang ceramics, which were constructed by hand, are fairly primitive. Generally the body is reddish colored; the clay either had been used essentially in its natural state or it had been tempered with sand. These soft-bodied earthenwares were fired at kiln temperatures of about 900–960° C. Surfaces usually are plain, but they occasionally have unsophisticated carved, combed, gouged, or nipplelike ornamentation. The most important shapes are spherical vases with two small handles; wide-mouthed, deep-bodied jars; and round-bottomed bowls that often sit on a ring base or have three small feet (No. 1).

Another Early Neolithic culture, represented by finds made in 1976 at Cishancun, Wuan xian, in southern Hebei Province, appears to have been related to Peiligang, and radiocarbon dating shows the two cultures to have been approximately contemporary.[3] Cishan earthenwares were fashioned by hand, generally of sand-tempered, reddish brown clay; however, basically unmodified, reddish-colored clay was also used. Certain shapes, such as round-bottomed bowls, three-footed bowls, and jars with wide mouths and deep bodies, are common to both Peiligang and Cishan ceramics. In Cishan ceramics, however, there are more types of vessels and a greater variety in the treatment of surfaces; surface textures include cord markings and matlike impressions. Painted decoration, which has been seen on at least one Cishan fragment, has not yet been found in Peiligang material.

Both the Peiligang and Cishan cultures exhibit many similarities to the well-known Yangshao culture in this Central Plain region, and it is fairly certain that these recently discovered cultures were the forerunners of the Yangshao and succeeding cultures in the middle Yellow River valley.

The Dadiwan-I Culture

The Dadiwan-I culture is typified by the assemblage found in 1979 at Dadiwan, Qinan xian, in eastern Gansu Province, but it is also well represented by a number of sites in Shaanxi Province. Dadiwan-I resembled the Peiligang and Cishan cultures; however, the few radiocarbon dates available at this time suggest that Dadiwan-I might have originated a little later than the other two.[4]

Archaeological reports describe Dadiwan-I pottery as handmade; it primarily consists of sand-tempered, unevenly fired, reddish earthenware. Many of these coarsely potted vessels are patterned with crisscrossed cord marks. It is thought that the cord-marked surfaces were produced when the damp clay was pressed into a cord-lined mold. In addition, there are some bowls with wide bands painted in dark red at the mouth rim and a few with simple symbols painted inside. Round-bottomed bowls, three-footed bowls, and wide-mouthed, deep-bodied jars approximate the shapes of vessels found at the Peiligang and Cishan cultural sites. The Dadiwan-I level was found under an early Yangshao cultural stratum at the Qinan xian site, suggesting that Dadiwan-I was the precursor of the Yangshao in the Wei River valley.

THE YANGSHAO CULTURE IN NORTH CHINA

The Yangshao Neolithic culture, successor to the Early Neolithic cultures in northern China described above, stretched from Qinghai and Gansu provinces in the west to Henan and Hebei provinces in the east. It can be dated from radiocarbon tests to about 5000–3000 B.C. in the middle Yellow River/Wei River valleys, although it survived about a thousand years longer in the upper Yellow River valley. This was the longest lasting and most widely diffused Chinese Neolithic culture. As such, it understandably exhibits considerable chronological and regional differences, although there is a certain uniformity of style within individual periods and areas. The Yangshao culture was named for a site discovered early on at Yangshaocun in Mianchi xian, Henan Province; however, it is now recognized that this site is scarcely representative of the entire culture.

Yangshao painted pottery. The distinctive product of most phases of the Yangshao Neolithic culture is painted pottery of remarkable refinement. These reddish- or buffish-bodied earthenware vessels were fashioned of fine-grained clay by coiling rolls of this clay into a desired form. They might then be beaten with a paddle to make the clay more compact and to strengthen the points

where sections had been joined together.[5] Although the potter's wheel does not seem to have been invented at this period, there is evidence that objects were probably finished on a slowly revolving disk. Surfaces might then be scraped and, finally, wet-smoothed. Designs chosen from a large repertoire of geometric—or, more rarely, anthropomorphic or zoomorphic—patterns were painted on the vessel, primarily in black, or black and red, pigments. Sometimes a coating of red or white slip (a fluid suspension of clay in water) was applied before the painting was executed. Finally the piece was fired at a kiln temperature of about 900–1000° C., which baked the clay into hard earthenware.

These painted wares appear to have been primarily intended for ritual use. For the most part, they have been excavated from tombs; however, some examples were recently found in dwelling areas. Although these sophisticated vessels have given the frequently used designation "painted pottery" to the Yangshao culture, they constitute, in fact, a fairly small minority of the total ceramic remains.

"Cord-marked" pottery. Most of the Yangshao ceramics that have been excavated are relatively crude, utilitarian, cooking, serving, and storage utensils with gray, red, or brownish bodies that range from comparatively fine to coarse in texture. The coarse bodies, in particular, have been noticeably tempered with sand; this would have made the clay easier to work during manufacture and prevented the vessel from cracking over a cooking fire. These common wares are either unembellished or have a simple pattern that was made in the surface while the clay was still damp. A characteristic surface treatment of deep, cordlike markings has given rise to the term "cord-marked" pottery, which, for convenience, is frequently used to refer to all types of this large family of ubiquitous everyday wares.

As has been seen, the ceramics discovered in the northern Chinese Early Neolithic cultural sites included fairly primitive, utilitarian objects of the "cord-marked" type. The tradition of "cord-marked" pottery was a persistent one: it continued through several stages of the Yangshao culture, and it can be traced through the Neolithic periods that succeeded the Yangshao into the Shang and Zhou eras. In fact, it remained on the ceramic scene in some areas of China until as late as the Han dynasty.

2. BOTTLE. "Cord-marked" earthenware. Neolithic period, ca. 4800–3600 B.C. Yangshao culture, Banpo phase. Excavated at Banpocun, Xian, Shaanxi Province. From *Zhonghua Renmin Gongheguo chutu wenwu zhanlan zhanpin xuanji*, 1973.

Beater-and-pad technique. Among the "cord-marked" type of wares are some with small groups of impressions repeated over a major portion of the body. These impressions are the signature of the beater-and-pad, also known as the paddle-and-anvil, method of ceramic construction. After the vessel was formed, its walls were beaten into a desired thickness and made denser and more uniform: the exterior of the piece was beaten with a cord-wrapped stick or a textured paddle while a wrapped pad was held against the interior surface. Evidence that the beater and pad were used in the fabrication of Yangshao pottery has been found in the remains of Yangshao kilns.

Yangshao white and black wares. In addition to these more typical ceramics, a few fragments of white-bodied wares are reported to have been found at Yangshao cultural sites such as Miaodigou in Henan Province. These finds indicate that Chinese potters were aware of the existence and possibilities of light-burning clays even at this early date. A few fragments of fine black pottery were also unearthed in the Yangshao stratum at Miaodigou; such black wares were to become an important factor in later Neolithic ceramics.

The Yangshao Culture in the Middle Yellow River/ Wei River Valleys

Beishouling. The earliest Yangshao people who lived in northern China's Central Plain are known from the remains excavated at sites in Shaanxi Province such as Beishouling near Baoji.[6] Like their Early Neolithic predecessors, they farmed, with an emphasis on cultivating millet and raising such animals as pigs and dogs. They also gathered, hunted, and fished. Their pottery was built in simple shapes; it basically consisted of sand-tempered "cord-marked" wares, and painted pottery was rare.

Banpo. By the next phase of the Yangshao culture in the middle Yellow River/Wei River valleys, the pottery industry was so important that even semipermanent villages contained a ceramic-manufacturing center as well as a dwelling area and cemetery. These early Yangshao villages are exemplified by the site of Banpocun, near Xian, in Shaanxi Province.[7] Their occupants lived a quasi-agricultural existence much like that seen in earlier periods: they grew millet and vegetables; bred pigs, dogs, and other animals; and raised silkworms. Marks of fabrics found on some pottery indicate that the crafts of spinning and weaving were well advanced. Banpo-type settlements have been excavated in other parts of Shaanxi Province, as well as in southern Shanxi, southeastern Gansu, and northern Hubei provinces. "Cord-marked" earthenwares with a variety of surface patterns (No. 2) constituted the bulk of Banpo ceramics; black-painted pottery (No. 3) formed only a small percentage of the total Banpo ceramic inventory.

Miaodigou. A later phase of the Yangshao culture in this region is typified by the remains discovered in 1953 at Miaodigou in Shan xian, Henan Province. Both archaeological evidence and radiocarbon dating have shown the Miaodigou period to be somewhat later than the Banpo.[8] The Miaodigou culture was distributed over a larger area than the Banpo; important sites have been found in eastern Shaanxi, eastern Gansu, and southern Shanxi provinces. While "cord-marked" wares still dominated the ceramics during the Miaodigou phase, painted pottery was more prevalent than before. White slip was frequently used on Miaodigou painted pottery; designs were primarily drawn in black, although some red was also used.

The Yangshao culture at Dadiwan. Recent excavations have shown that the Yangshao culture extended farther into the upper Wei River valley than was originally believed. As has been seen, the Early Neolithic Dadiwan-I cultural level found at the Qinan xian site in eastern Gansu Province lay under an early Yangshao cultural stratum. This early Yangshao cultural stratum was one of three successive Yangshao cultural layers that were found at the Dadiwan site. They are considered to belong to early, middle, and late periods.[9] The cultural assemblages of the early and middle layers were Banpo and Miaodigou types, respectively, with ceramics that were similar to other Banpo and Miaodigou wares. Material found in the late layer was related to that of the Majiayao Yangshao culture described below.

The Yangshao Culture in the Upper Yellow River Valley: The Majiayao Culture

From its earliest to its latest phase, the succeeding Majiayao Yangshao culture—sometimes referred to as the Gansu Yangshao culture—continued for about two thousand

3. BOWL. Earthenware with painted decoration. Neolithic period, ca. 4800–3600 B.C. Yangshao culture, Banpo phase. Excavated at Banpocun, Xian, Shaanxi Province. From *Historical Relics Unearthed in New China,* 1972.

4. BASIN. Earthenware with painted decoration.
Diameter: 11 in. (27.9 cm.). Neolithic period,
ca. 3200–2700 B.C. Majiayao Yangshao culture, Majiayao
phase. Lent by Mrs. Judith Ogden Bullitt. L.1986.82.

years in eastern Gansu and eastern Qinghai provinces.
Stratigraphic evidence and carbon-14 chronology have
documented the successive development of four individual
Majiayao cultural phases: the Shilingxia, Majiayao,
Banshan, and Machang.[10] It would seem that these
Majiayao cultural phases were intimately related; indeed,
objects of both the Banshan and Machang types were
recently found in the same tomb at a cemetery in the
suburbs of Lanzhou, Gansu Province.[11] As with the

ceramics of other Yangshao cultures, while several types
of Majiayao wares were produced, it is the painted pottery
that monopolizes our attention.

Majiayao. The earliest example of the Majiayao, or
Gansu, Yangshao culture illustrated in this book belongs
to the Majiayao cultural phase. It is a handsome basin
(No. 4) decorated in long, sweeping, parallel black lines
combined with dots; this design is characteristic of the
Majiayao painted earthenwares.

Banshan. A strongly potted jar with its forceful,
curvilinear black-and-red decoration (No. 5) exemplifies
the kind of painted pottery first found in a cemetery in

6. JAR. Earthenware with painted decoration.
Height: 15 1/2 in. (39.4 cm.). Neolithic period,
ca. 2300–2000 B.C. Majiayao Yangshao culture, Machang
phase. Lent by Mrs. Judith Ogden Bullitt. L.1986.22.1.

8. JAR. Earthenware with painted decoration. Height: 3 1/2 in. (8.9 cm.). Neolithic period, ca. 2300–2000 B.C. Majiayao Yangshao culture, Machang phase. Purchase, Gloria H. Spivak Gift, 1986. 1986.75.1.

7. JAR. Earthenware with painted decoration. Height: 4 1/4 in. (10.8 cm.). Neolithic period, ca. 2300–2000 B.C. Majiayao Yangshao culture, Machang phase. Harris Brisbane Dick Fund, 1950. 50.61.4.

the Banshan hills of eastern Gansu Province. The most impressive Banshan painted wares are large, thin-walled, ovoid jars that have a wide variety of designs on their upper portion. These ceramics testify to the mastery of technique achieved by the Chinese potter at a prehistoric date.

Machang. Pottery of the Machang phase of the Majiayao culture, named for a site at Machangyan in eastern Qinghai Province, is rather similar to Banshan wares; indeed, as has been seen, the two types are known to have overlapped at one stage. By and large, however, Machang vessels were not quite as carefully worked as the Banshan examples. A large, boldly painted jar (No. 6)

and two small, squattish jars (Nos. 7 and 8) illustrate the Machang group of painted Neolithic pottery.

LATER GANSU AND QINGHAI CULTURES: QIJIA AND XINDIAN

Excavated Qijia cultural assemblages in Gansu and Qinghai provinces have provided evidence of the production of both copper and bronze.[12] Qijia potters continued the tradition of "cord-marked" earthenwares inherited from the earlier Yangshao Neolithic cultures in the area; they produced various undecorated, painted, and reticulated wares as well.

Succeeding cultures in this region, such as the Xindian—which apparently was contemporary with the early Western Zhou period in the Central Plain[13]—also continued many Yangshao ceramic conventions, including the "cord-marked" and painted pottery traditions, for quite some time. Xindian painted wares are noticeably coarser than the earlier Gansu/Qinghai examples. They have frequently been covered with colored slip, and they are decorated in their own very distinctive vocabulary of motifs (Nos. 9 and 10).

THE LONGSHAN CULTURE IN NORTH CHINA

Let us return to the Neolithic cultures farther to the east. The widely spread Longshan stage of China's Neolithic period is seen by archaeologists today as two distinctive major regional cultures. One was in the middle Yellow River/Wei River valleys; it was preceded by the Yangshao culture in this area. The other was on the east coast, in the lower Yellow River valley; it was preceded by different cultures to be discussed presently. While few characteristics were universal among the many local cultures constituting these two principal regional cultures, their common life-style was based on a primarily agricultural subsistence. Archaeological remains of villages encircled by walls of rammed earth indicate a need for defense by this time. Evidence exists that some of these Late Neolithic people practiced scapulimancy (divination by observing the effects of heat applied to an animal's shoulder blade).

Longshan ceramics. Many Longshan ceramics were fashioned by hand as before; however, evidence that a potter's wheel was used can be seen on a number of vessels. There is a significant difference between the Longshan wares that have been excavated in the middle Yellow River/Wei River valleys and those found on the east coast. In the most general terms, the textured, gray "cord-marked" earthenware that has been dominant in the west has diminished in importance toward the east; and smooth-surfaced white and black pottery that characterizes the eastern regions has appeared less frequently toward the west. The shapes of vessels, too, show marked differences, and certain forms that distinguish one area have not been found in the other. Pottery of local cultures within these two major regional Longshan cultures varies considerably from area to area as well.

9. JAR. Earthenware with painted decoration. Height: 11 3/8 in. (28.9 cm.). Neolithic period, ca. 1000 B.C. Xindian culture. Lent by Mrs. Judith Ogden Bullitt. L.1986.23.2.

NEOLITHIC CHINA: CHRONOLOGICAL PROFILE

YEARS B.C.	UPPER YELLOW RIVER VALLEY	MIDDLE YELLOW RIVER/ WEI RIVER VALLEYS (THE CENTRAL PLAIN)		LOWER YELLOW RIVER VALLEY	MIDDLE YANGTZE RIVER/ HAN RIVER VALLEYS	LOWER YANGTZE RIVER VALLEY/ HANGZHOU BAY AREA
		WEI RIVER	YELLOW RIVER			
1000	• Xindian					
2000	• Qijia					
	• Machang	• Shaanxi Longshan	• Henan Longshan	• Shandong Longshan	• Qujialing (late period)	
	• Banshan			• Late Dawenkou		
3000			• Miaodigou-II			
	• Majiayao				• (?)	• Liangzhu
				• Middle Dawenkou	• Daxi (middle and late periods)	
4000	• Shilingxia		• Miaodigou		• (?)	
				• Early Dawenkou		• Majiabang/ Songze
5000		• Banpo				• Hemudu
		• Beishouling		• "Beixin"		
6000		• Dadiwan-I				
			• Peiligang • Cishan			

(vertical labels: "Majiayao Yangshao" spanning Upper Yellow River Valley; "Longshan" and "Yangshao" spanning Wei/Yellow River columns; "Dawenkou" spanning Lower Yellow River Valley)

10. JAR. Earthenware with painted decoration and cord markings. Diameter: 8 in. (20.3 cm.). Neolithic period, ca. 1000 B.C. Xindian culture. Harris Brisbane Dick Fund, 1950. 50.61.3.

The Longshan Culture in the Middle Yellow River/ Wei River Valleys

Findings at such sites as Miaodigou in Henan Province have shown that the Longshan culture in the middle Yellow River/Wei River valleys—frequently called the Central Plain Longshan—descended from the Yangshao culture in the same region. The Longshan culture in this area can probably be dated to about 2800–2000 B.C.[14] Inasmuch as this was a rather long span in China's Neolithic history, it is divided by historians into early and late stages, represented by Miaodigou-II, and the Henan and Shaanxi Longshan cultures, respectively.

Miaodigou-II. The early Central Plain Longshan, found in northern Henan, southern Shanxi, and eastern Shaanxi provinces, is typified by the cultural assemblage discovered in a stratum at Miaodigou in Henan Province.[15] Miaodigou-II–type ceramics were generally constructed

by hand and finished on a slow wheel. The preponderance of material is coarse, gray-bodied "cord-marked" ware with a basket- or cord-impressed surface. Other types of ceramics include plain-surfaced red or black earthenwares, as well as a scattering of painted pottery and some very thin black pottery.

The Henan and Shaanxi Longshan cultures. The later Central Plain Longshan culture can be further subdivided, and the two most important cultures at this time were the Henan and Shaanxi Longshan cultures. These two individual local cultures are thought to have been fairly contemporary. Material excavated at both types of sites included considerable amounts of gray "cord-marked" wares, along with a smaller proportion of red and black pottery. The shapes of vessels in the two areas,

11. JAR. Earthenware with painted decoration. Neolithic period, ca. 4300–3500 B.C. Early Dawenkou culture. Excavated at Dawenkou, Taian xian, Shandong Province. Courtesy of The Wenwu Publishing Company.

however, were notably different. Tests have shown that both the red- and gray-bodied wares were fired at kiln temperatures of about 1000° C. Ceramics were generally built by hand, although some were made in a mold; the potter's wheel was used at this time, but not extensively.

Hougang-II. Henan Longshan cultural assemblages have been found in Henan, eastern Shaanxi, southwestern Shanxi, southern Hebei, western Shandong, and northwestern Anhui provinces.[16] The culture is typified by a stratum excavated at Hougang, near Anyang, in Henan Province. While gray "cord-marked" wares with cord, basket, or check designs were an important ceramic tradition in this culture, black pottery, including some very thin black pottery, and white wares were also produced.

Kexingzhuang-II. Shaanxi Longshan cultural sites have been located for the most part in Shaanxi Province, principally along the Wei River valley.[17] A cultural layer found at Kexingzhuang, near Xian, in Shaanxi Province, characterizes the culture. The ceramic inventory is relatively simple, consisting mainly of gray or red earthenwares. Cord- and basket-marked surfaces are very common in the "cord-marked" wares; there are some painted wares, but they are rare.

NEOLITHIC CULTURES IN THE LOWER YELLOW RIVER VALLEY

Eastern Neolithic cultures can be separated into those distributed along the lower reaches of the Yellow River, and those found in the lower Yangtze River valley and Hangzhou Bay area. (It must be emphasized that here, as in the discussion of all early Chinese periods, geographical and chronological divisions are used very broadly and are not to be considered as well defined in any way.)

The "Beixin," Dawenkou, and Shandong Longshan cultures, found primarily in Shandong and northern Jiangsu provinces, paralleled the Peiligang, Yangshao, and Longshan cultures of the Central Plain area fairly closely. Probably, like those Neolithic cultures of the middle Yellow River/Wei River valleys, these cultures represent a continuous regional developmental sequence.[18]

The "Beixin" Culture

Whether the cultural assemblage excavated in 1978–79 at Beixin in Teng xian, Shandong Province, typifies a separate, established culture or is part of the Dawenkou culture that followed it is not certain; consequently, there is some indecision as to its proper name. This relatively new find is characteristic of several pre-Dawenkou-type assemblages that have been discovered in southern Shandong and northern Jiangsu provinces.[19]

The pottery found at the Beixin site was constructed by hand; for the most part it was sand-tempered, yellowish brown earthenware or untempered red earthenware. According to the archaeological reports, surfaces of the low-fired, sand-tempered wares had, more often than not, been dressed with a layer of slip. Ornamentation included applied, carved, gouged, and nipplelike patterns. A few black-bodied and painted pieces were also found.

The Dawenkou Culture

The Dawenkou culture was named for its type site at Dawenkouzhen, located between Taian xian and Ningyang xian, in Shandong Province. Radiocarbon dates of about 4300–2400 B.C. indicate that this culture continued for close to two thousand years in Shandong and northern Jiangsu provinces; in its later phase, it extended into Henan Province as well. Inasmuch as it lasted for such a long time—approximating the length of our present Christian era—the Dawenkou culture is ordinarily divided by archaeologists into early, middle, and late periods.[20] The diverse sizes and furnishings of a considerable number of tombs excavated at the Dawenkou site demonstrate that social distinctions were well established. Smaller tombs were sparsely equipped, while larger ones could contain close to one hundred objects. Large quantities of pigs' skulls found among the grave goods indicate that pig breeding played an important part in Dawenkou agriculture.

Ceramics produced during the very lengthy Dawenkou era understandably underwent substantial changes over the centuries. There is great variety in the color of the earthenware bodies, which can be red, gray, brown, yellow, black, or white. Dawenkou potters adapted their clays to the purpose of the vessel: some clays were carefully washed and used with little or no modification; others were tempered with fine- or coarse-grained sand. Surfaces of ceramics by and large are smooth and very often have been burnished. Objects have been decorated by different techniques; designs can be painted, reticulated, carved, stamped, or applied in low relief.

12. BOWL WITH RETICULATED PEDESTAL. Earthenware. Neolithic period, ca. 3500–2800 B.C. Middle Dawenkou culture. Excavated at Yediancun, Zou xian, Shandong Province. From *Wenhua dageming qijian chutu wenwu*, 1972.

13. STEMCUP. Black earthenware. Neolithic period, ca. 2800–2400 B.C. Late Dawenkou culture. Excavated at Jingzhizhen, Anqiu xian, Shandong Province. Courtesy of The Wenwu Publishing Company.

Early Dawenkou ceramics. For the most part, early Dawenkou pottery is fairly low-fired, unaltered or tempered red earthenware. There are not many types of vessels, and the shapes are relatively simple. These wares were constructed by hand, usually by the coiling method; the mouth rims were frequently finished on a slowly moving wheel.

Dawenkou painted pottery, which was manufactured in limited quantities during the early and middle periods, is quite distinctive. It has been painted in red, black, and white, sometimes over a layer of red or white slip (No. 11). There is a striking resemblance between the designs seen on some Dawenkou painted wares and those found on the Yangshao painted pottery excavated in Henan Province.

Middle Dawenkou ceramics. During the middle Dawenkou era, although most wares were still fashioned by hand and perhaps finished on a slow wheel, some small objects were made on a fast-moving potter's wheel. Both untempered red wares and sand-tempered red wares were still significant; however, gray- and black-bodied ceramics assumed new importance, and thinly potted, fine-bodied, grayish white earthenwares made their appearance. New types of vessels were produced, and some notable changes were made in the shapes of those vessels that were continued from earlier times.

Several kinds of cups and bowls have bold geometric designs pierced into their pedestals (No. 12). These reticulated wares, which were especially popular during the middle and late periods, are one of the hallmarks of the Dawenkou culture. While the precise nature of their function is not known, it is generally presumed that such dramatic ceramics were intended for ceremonial use.

Late Dawenkou ceramics. By the late Dawenkou stage, gray- and black-bodied ceramics predominated over red wares. Although it was still not employed universally, the potter's wheel was used more frequently than before. Some burnished black pottery stemcups made of fine-textured, fairly high-fired clay (No. 13) were crafted to a remarkable thinness, reflecting a high level of ceramic technology. Kaolinic clay was probably used in the manufacture of a rather large group of objects that are generally classified as white wares, although they may in fact be white, yellow, or pink in tone. These ceramics usually have thin, hard bodies that were fired at kiln temperatures of about 900° C.

The Shandong Longshan Culture

The Longshan phase of China's Neolithic period takes its name from the modern town of Longshanzhen, near Chengziyai, a type site in western Shandong Province. At one time, the cultural assemblage unearthed at Chengziyai was thought to typify the entire Longshan cultural stage. It has become clear, however, that what had been thought of as a single Longshan culture was not one but two distinctive major regional cultures. There was the one in the middle Yellow River/Wei River valleys, or Central Plain Longshan, previously mentioned, and there was what is now called the Shandong, or "Classic," Longshan culture. This Shandong Longshan culture developed after the Dawenkou culture, during the second half of the third millennium B.C.,[21] in the same general area.

While Shandong Longshan pottery basically continued the Dawenkou ceramic traditions, a more common use of the fast-moving potter's wheel resulted in an improvement in quality: vessel shapes became more uniform, and the walls of objects became more evenly potted. Shandong Longshan ceramics vary in color, and while the black pottery is outstanding, gray-, red-, yellow-, and white-bodied wares were produced.

Black wares. The Shandong Longshan culture is characterized by some black earthenwares that often have a rather angular profile. They were made of well-washed, fine-grained clay and trimmed on a wheel to extraordinary thinness: the walls of some vessels are only one millimeter thick. Surfaces were burnished to a high luster, probably with a pebble, before the clay was quite dry. These wares were fired at temperatures of about 1000° C. They were reduction fired: smoke was introduced into the kiln chamber during firing to reduce the amount of oxygen. This reduction firing affected the iron in the clay and gave the body a dark gray or black color. Because of the types of objects found, their elegant shapes, and their extreme thinness, it is believed that this black pottery was intended for ritual rather than for everyday utilitarian use.

White wares. A small percentage of white pottery has also been found in "Classic" Longshan cultural sites. These wares have a fine-grained, smooth body that was fired at temperatures of about 800–900° C.; the color is due to the relative purity of the kaolinic clays that were

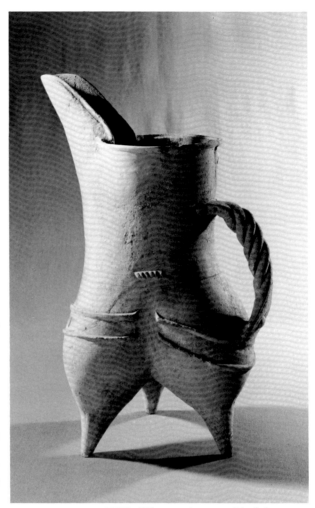

14. TRIPOD PITCHER. White earthenware. Neolithic period, ca. 2400–2000 B.C. Shandong ("Classic") Longshan culture. Excavated at Liangchengzhen, Rizhao xian, Shandong Province. Courtesy of The Wenwu Publishing Company.

used. For the most part, this light-burning clay was reserved for select objects, such as various types of elaborately constructed beaked tripods, known as *gui* (No. 14). These tripods, which are among the most attractive of the Chinese Neolithic wares, as well as the very thin black pottery described above, demonstrate the high technical skill of Shandong Longshan potters.

NEOLITHIC CULTURES IN THE LOWER YANGTZE RIVER VALLEY AND HANGZHOU BAY AREA

Concurrent with the development of the Yangshao and Longshan Neolithic cultures in the Central Plain region, another series of different Neolithic cultures with other ceramic traditions developed to the southeast. These cultures—among them the Hemudu, Majiabang, and Liangzhu—were spread over the southern Jiangsu/northern Zhejiang area during the fifth–third millennia B.C. The milder, damper climate of this region was conducive to the cultivation of rice, the principal agricultural product of these east-coast Neolithic cultures.

The Hemudu Culture

Identified by finds made at the Hemudu site in the Yuyao district of Zhejiang Province, the Hemudu culture seems to have been primarily located in the area just south of Hangzhou Bay. It is the oldest Neolithic culture found in this region to date[22] and was more or less contemporary with the Banpo phase of the Central Plain Yangshao culture. Excavations at the Hemudu site were extraordinarily fruitful; finds included some of the earliest remains of rice husks known anywhere, as well as vestiges of over forty different animals and some twenty species of vegetable.

Hemudu pottery was built by hand; while it is fairly primitive, it is not without interest. The culture is characterized by a thick-walled, black-bodied earthenware, the body of which was tempered with charcoal that was made by burning rice husks and the stems and leaves of plants. Such vegetal temper improved the working and drying properties of the clay and helped to decrease the possibility of a vessel cracking when it was fired. This charcoal-tempered black pottery was fired at the fairly low temperature of about 800–930° C. Other excavated

Hemudu ceramics included gray pottery, some of which was tempered with sand; this ware was fired at about 800–850° C. The surfaces of Hemudu vessels often exhibit dense cord markings; a few painted fragments have also been found. Certainly the most distinctive Hemudu wares are those decorated with freely incised designs of plants and animals (No. 15).

The Majiabang Culture

The 1972–73 excavations of the Caoxieshan site in Wu xian, east of Taihu (Lake Tai), in Jiangsu Province, produced stratigraphic evidence of the development of primitive cultures in the Taihu area. These cultures, which were clearly linked to the Hemudu culture, were found in successive layers, proving that the Majiabang culture—Majiabang and Songze phases—was followed by the Liangzhu culture.

Radiocarbon dating of the Majiabang culture places it reasonably close to the middle and late phases of the Central Plain Yangshao culture.[23] The early Majiabang stage is typified by the site at Majiabang, Jiaxing, in northernmost Zhejiang Province; the later stage by finds at the Songze site in Shanghai.

For the most part, the excavated Majiabang ceramics have had tempered red bodies; finer red wares, as well as gray and black pottery, were also found. Some characteristic wares had red exteriors and black cores; surfaces of many other pieces were dressed with red slip. Sand had been used to temper the clay of the earlier pottery; bits of straw, grain husks, or powdered shell had sometimes been added to the later wares. All of these wares were fired at relatively low temperatures. By and large, vessels were handmade and perhaps finished on a slow wheel; however, many of the later-period gray wares were made on a potter's wheel.

The Liangzhu Culture

The Liangzhu culture of southern Jiangsu and northern Zhejiang provinces is named for a site near Hangzhou. Certain artifacts found in Liangzhu cultural assemblages were quite similar to Shandong Longshan material; according to carbon-14 dating, the Liangzhu was fairly contemporary with the Central Plain Longshan cultures.[24] One of the distinguishing features of the Liangzhu culture is a highly developed skill in working jade.[25]

A potter's wheel was frequently used in the

manufacture of Liangzhu ceramics; appendant parts and unusually shaped vessels could be made by hand or in a mold. Liangzhu pottery includes black, gray, and sand-tempered red wares; the last were frequently dressed with a coating of reddish brown slip.

Black pottery. Some of the black pottery that is a highlight of the Liangzhu culture has a thin, fairly high-fired body reminiscent of the Shandong Longshan black wares. The more typical Liangzhu black ware, however, has a somewhat soft, low-fired, gray body; it has been covered in black slip that flakes off rather easily.

During recent excavations, such as those made in 1982–84 of a Liangzhu-culture cemetery in the Shanghai area, some black-slipped earthenware vessels decorated with finely carved designs of *chi* ("hornless dragons," or "immature dragons") and other animals have been found.[26] It is quite possible that this unusual ornamentation reflects the influence of the beautifully worked contemporary jade mentioned above.

15. RECTANGULAR CUP. Charcoal-tempered black earthenware. Neolithic period, ca. 5000–3300 B.C. Hemudu culture. Excavated at Hemudu, Yuyao xian, Zhejiang Province. From *Xin Zhongguo de kaogu faxian he yanjiu*, 1984.

NEOLITHIC CULTURES IN THE MIDDLE YANGTZE AND HAN RIVER VALLEYS

The final Chinese Neolithic cultures to be mentioned here, the Daxi and Qujialing, have been found in the middle Yangtze River/Han River valleys. They cannot be precisely dated, but they can probably be assigned to about the fourth and first half of the third millennium B.C. Daxi and Qujialing were agricultural peoples; their economy was based on the cultivation of rice, which they supplemented with some hunting and fishing. There was a close relationship among these two cultures and those in the Central Plain area to the north cited earlier.

The Daxi Culture

Archaeological assemblages of the Daxi culture have been found in eastern Sichuan, Hubei, and northern Hunan provinces; the culture takes its name from the Daxi site, Wushan xian, in eastern Sichuan. Dates of the Daxi culture approximated those of the middle and late phases of the Yangshao culture,[27] and apparently there were close ties between the two.

Most of the excavated Daxi pottery had a red body, although some gray, black, and white wares have also been found. The clay itself could be untempered, or mixed with sand or finely ground rice husks; this use of rice husks links Daxi pottery to the east-coast Neolithic wares. Daxi vessels were handmade; mouth rims were touched up on a slow wheel; and they were fired at relatively low kiln temperatures of about 600–800° C. A fine-textured, red-bodied ware with rather simple curvilinear designs that were painted in either black or black and red pigments is outstanding in the Daxi material.

The Qujialing Culture

The Qujialing culture is named for the type site at Qujialing, Jingshan, in central Hubei Province. This culture has been found for the most part in Hubei Province, extending north into southwestern Henan Province, and south into the northern part of Hunan Province. Stratification at some sites has shown that Qujialing followed the Daxi culture. Qujialing was roughly contemporary with the Central Plain Longshan culture,[28] and the people of these two cultures apparently knew each other fairly well.

The quality of Qujialing potting was somewhat higher than that of Daxi; however, ceramics were still fashioned by hand. During the early Qujialing period, black wares predominated, although a few red wares were produced;

in the later Qujialing stage, most objects had gray bodies. While the surfaces of a great many vessels were left undecorated, some ornamental surface treatments were used. The most arresting Qujialing wares are those with very thinly potted, orange yellow bodies. They have been covered in gray, black, red, or orange red slip, over which designs in either black or orange yellow pigments have been painted. Pottery spindle whorls with designs painted in one of several colors are also characteristic of this culture.

As they arrived at the threshold of the second millennium B.C., the Chinese had done much to lay the foundations of their ceramic traditions. They had learned to remove the impurities from common earthenware clay, and to use it in its natural state or to mix it with a variety of tempers to give it good working and firing properties. They had begun to take advantage of the white-burning properties of relatively iron-free kaolinic clays. They had begun to use a fast-moving potter's wheel. Construction of their kilns had greatly improved, so that firing temperatures could be increased, and they were capable of reduction firing. While the levels of technology differed in various parts of the country,[29] the way was open for the next stage in the development of Chinese ceramics.

1. An Zhimin, *Kaogu*, 1984, no. 10, pp. 936–44.

2. *Kaogu Xuebao*, 1984, no. 1, pp. 23–52. • Cai Lianzhen gives the carbon-14 dates of three samples from the Peiligang site—with corrections based on bristlecone-pine dating—as ca. 6685–5530, 6465–5305, and 6375–5395 B.C. (*Kaogu*, 1985, no. 3, pp. 279–81).

3. *Kaogu Xuebao*, 1981, no. 3, pp. 303–38. • Cai Lianzhen gives the carbon-14 dates of three samples from the Cishan site—with corrections based on bristlecone-pine dating—as ca. 6470–5525, 6320–5455, and 6110–5380 B.C. (*Kaogu*, 1985, no. 3, pp. 279–81).

4. *Wenwu*, 1981, no. 4, pp. 1–8. Zhang Pengchuan and Zhou Guangji, *Wenwu*, 1981, no. 4, pp. 9–15, 86. *Wenwu*, 1983, no. 11, pp. 21–30. • Radiocarbon testing of four samples from the Dadiwan-I layer provides a date—with corrections based on bristlecone-pine dating—of ca. 5850–5400 B.C. (*Wenwu*, 1983, no. 11, p. 22).

5. Pamela Vandiver, "The Implications of Variation in Ceramic Technology: The Forming of Neolithic Storage Vessels in China and the Near East," to be published in *Archaeomaterials*, Spring 1988. I am most grateful to Dr. Vandiver for allowing me to read an advance copy of this fascinating paper.

6. Shao Wangping gives corrected carbon-14 dates for two samples from the lower level of Beishouling as ca. 5150 and 5020 B.C. (Zhongguo shehui kexueyuan kaogu yanjiusuo [ZSKKY], comp., *Xin Zhongguo de kaogu faxian he yanjiu* [Beijing, 1984], p. 40).

Carbon-14 dates are frequently interpreted differently by various authors; in general, the dates cited in ZSKKY, *Xin Zhongguo*, 1984, are used here.

7. Carbon-14 testing dates the Banpo Yangshao phase to ca. 4800–3600 B.C. (ibid., p. 46).

8. Radiocarbon dating shows the Miaodigou phase as ca. 3900–3000 B.C. (ibid.).

9. *Wenwu*, 1983, no. 11, pp. 1–14. Ibid., pp. 15–20, 30. Ibid., pp. 21–30. Ibid., pp. 31–39. • Carbon-14 tests give these corrected dates: Dadiwan Yangshao early period, ca. 4000 B.C.; Dadiwan Yangshao middle period, ca. 3900–3600 B.C.; Dadiwan Yangshao late period, ca. 3500–2900 B.C. (ibid., chart, p. 29).

10. Gansu sheng bowuguan, ed., *Gansu caitao* (Beijing, 1979). Qinghai sheng wenwu kaogudui, ed., *Qinghai caitao* (Beijing, 1980). • Xie Duanju gives corrected carbon-14 dates for the four Majiayao Yangshao phases as follows: Shilingxia, ca. 4000–3500 B.C.; Majiayao,

ca. 3200–2700 B.C.; Banshan, ca. 2600–2300 B.C.; and Machang, ca. 2300–2000 B.C. (*Kaogu yu Wenwu*, 1985, no. 1, pp. 63–74). These vary slightly from those Xie cites in ZSKKY, *Xin Zhongguo*, 1984, p. 106.

11. *Kaogu Xuebao*, 1983, no. 2, pp. 191–222.

12. Xie Duanju gives carbon-14 dates for the Qijia culture as 2050 ± 155 years to 1915 ± 155 years B.C. (ZSKKY, *Xin Zhongguo*, 1984, p. 118).

The use of copper in this area can be traced as far back as the Majiayao culture, making Majiayao, technically, an Aeneolithic society. Fragments of bronze have been discovered in Machang sites in Gansu Province, which, in fact, places the Machang phase in the Bronze Age (Ma Chengyuan, "The Splendor of Ancient Chinese Bronzes," in *The Great Bronze Age of China*, ed. Wen Fong, exhib. cat. [New York, 1980], p. 1). However, those pre–Bronze Age cultures that are known to have used some metal are still considered "Neolithic" in recent archaeological reports.

13. Xie Duanju cites one carbon-14 date of ca. 990 ± 90 years B.C. (ZSKKY, *Xin Zhongguo*, 1984, p. 355).

14. Yang Xizhang, ibid., p. 69.

15. According to Yang Xizhang, only one radiocarbon test has been made on Miaodigou-II material, giving a corrected date of ca. 2780 ± 145 years B.C. (ibid., p. 70).

16. Yang Xizhang gives corrected dates for the Henan Longshan culture as ca. 2625 ± 145 years to 2005 ± 120 years B.C. (ibid., p. 74).

17. It is thought that the dates of the Shaanxi Longshan culture were close to those of the Henan; however, according to Yang Xizhang, there are no confirming tests at the present time (ibid.).

18. Wu Ren, *Wenwu*, 1982, no. 10, pp. 44–56.

19. Shao Wangping reports corrected carbon-14 dates of seven Beixin samples as ca. 5300–4400 B.C. (ZSKKY, *Xin Zhongguo*, 1984, pp. 95–97).

20. Shao Wangping gives dates for the individual Dawenkou periods as: early, ca. 4300–3500 B.C.; middle, ca. 3500–2800 B.C.; and late, ca. 2800–2400 B.C. (ibid., pp. 89–91).

21. Shao Wangping gives carbon-14 dates of approximately 2400–2000 B.C. (ibid., p. 100).

22. Ren Shinan gives corrected carbon-14 dates for the Hemudu culture of ca. 5005 ± 130 years to 3380 ± 130 years B.C. (ibid., p. 145).

23. Ren Shinan cites radiocarbon dating for the Majiabang culture—both the Majiabang and Songze phases—as ca. 4325 ± 170 years to 3230 ± 140 years B.C. (ibid.).

24. Ren Shinan gives calibrated Liangzhu carbon-14 dates of ca. 3100–2200 B.C. (ibid.).

25. E.g., some remarkable jades were found at the Liangzhu cultural site at Sidun, Changzhou, Jiangsu Province (*Kaogu*, 1984, no. 2, pp. 109–29, and pls. 2–4; figs. 8–12).

26. *Wenwu*, 1986, no. 10, pp. 1–25, and color pl. 1(top); pls. 1:1, 2:3; figs. 33, 34, 39.

27. Ren Shinan gives two corrected carbon-14 dates that tentatively place the middle and late Daxi periods at ca. 3990 ± 260 years to 3380 ± 145 years B.C. (ZSKKY, *Xin Zhongguo*, 1984, p. 127).

28. Ren Shinan gives the corrected carbon-14 dates for the late Qujialing period as ca. 2875 ± 220 years to 2635 ± 150 years B.C. (ibid.).

29. Tong Zhuchen discusses the many centers of development and the uneven development of the various Neolithic cultures in China (*Wenwu*, 1986, no. 2, pp. 16–30, 39).

CHAPTER TWO
THE XIA AND SHANG DYNASTIES

THE XIA DYNASTY

According to ancient literary sources, China's first hereditary dynasty, the Xia, came into power in the general area of the middle Yellow River valley about the twenty-first century B.C. While this legendary Xia dynasty still remains something of an enigma, the theory that it can be identified with what is known as the Erlitou culture has gained wide acceptance in recent years. This bronze-producing Erlitou culture is typified by the remains found at the Erlitou site in Yanshi xian, in northwestern Henan Province. Similar cultural remains have been found in other parts of the province, as well as in southern Shanxi, eastern Hubei, eastern Shaanxi, and southern Hebei provinces. Stratigraphic evidence places the Erlitou culture between the late Henan Longshan culture and the Zhengzhou phase of the Shang dynasty, and carbon-14 tests have shown that the Erlitou site itself is datable to about 1900–1600 B.C.[1]

Erlitou ceramics seem to fit quite comfortably into the segment of time between the late Henan Longshan and early Shang periods, showing an evolution from the later Longshan pottery to the early Shang material. Excavated Erlitou/Xia pottery has mainly consisted of natural clay or sand-tempered gray earthenwares. Black pottery—including black-slipped pottery—brownish, red, and white wares have been seen less frequently.

THE SHANG DYNASTY

The earliest historic civilization in China, the Shang dynasty (about sixteenth–eleventh century B.C.), was first known archaeologically from excavations of the late Shang capital, historically known as Yinxu, close to the modern village of Xiaotun, near Anyang, in northern

20. VESSEL. Earthenware with incised and relief decoration. Height: 10 in. (25.4 cm.). Late Shang dynasty, ca. 13th–11th century B.C. Harris Brisbane Dick Fund, 1950. 50.61.5.

16. JAR. Near-stoneware with primitive glaze. Shang dynasty, ca. 16th–14th century B.C. Erligang (Zhengzhou) phase. Excavated at Zhengzhou, Henan Province. From *Historical Relics Unearthed in New China*, 1972.

Henan Province. Later important excavations have included the ones at Erligang in the city of Zhengzhou, which may have been one of several early Shang capitals. These discoveries have helped to complete the portrait of a dynamic people who added many outstanding sociological and technological innovations to their late Neolithic cultural inheritance.

By the late Shang era, a sophisticated system of writing had been developed, horse-drawn chariots were being employed, ivory carving had become a fine art, and jade carving was flourishing. The practice of divination was much more advanced than in the Longshan period: tortoise shells were being used in addition to animal shoulder blades, which were more carefully prepared than before. Many of these "oracle bones" now had questions—and sometimes answers—written on them. Bronze metallurgy was the outstanding feature of this urbanized Shang society. Many of the Erlitou/Xia and earliest Shang bronzes were fashioned after ceramic

shapes that were already familiar, but the bronzes soon developed an identity of their own, and numerous new forms and decorations in a strictly metallic idiom appeared. By the Anyang phase, Shang bronzes had reached a stage of technical development difficult to surpass. As they became more splendid, they tended to overshadow all other contemporary artistic achievements, and Shang pottery became the imitator, reflecting the influence of bronzes.

Shang near-stonewares. Despite the ascendancy of metallurgy, the Shang period did contribute to the development of Chinese ceramics. Two related major innovations in the Shang potter's art founded a ceramic patrimony that is drawn upon to this day. The first innovation was the development of a kind of material that is very close to what is known in the West as stoneware: a high-fired pottery that is dense, hard, and impervious to liquid. (There are certain conflicts in methodology here. While Westerners segregate stoneware as a separate type of pottery, the Chinese and Japanese do not generally recognize this distinction and classify all ceramics as either earthenware or porcelain. Whatever designation is used, it must be remembered that the boundaries between one type of ware and another are often extremely nebulous.)

Introduction of stonewarelike pottery was made possible by the discovery of the kinds of clays, or mixtures of clays, that would become vitreous at the relatively high temperature of about 1200° C. It presupposes kilns and firing techniques adequate to produce the required high temperatures. Higher-fired stoneware vessels were a considerable improvement over those made of relatively low-fired earthenware, as the latter, being porous and permeable, were unsuitable for any prolonged storage.

Shang glazes. The second innovation, which can be documented at least as early as the Zhengzhou phase of the Shang dynasty,[2] was the use of a glaze. A glaze, in essence, is a glassy coating on the surface of a ceramic that serves the twofold function of helping to seal the clay body and decorating the object. Most glazes are predominantly composed of silica, which itself would form a glass if fired to a high enough temperature. Other materials, known as fluxes, are added to the silica, primarily to lower its melting point, and alumina is almost always added to increase the viscosity of the glaze.

Shang-period glazed vessels (No. 16) have bodies that are close to stoneware; they were generally fired at temperatures of about 1200° C. These bodies are fine textured, fairly hard, and can be grayish white, grayish brown, or white with a yellowish tinge. Chinese scholars usually classify these ceramics as primitive green wares, or primitive porcelains, indicating that they are at an early stage in the development of porcelain. Most of this pottery was coil constructed, and patterns were frequently impressed on parts of the vessel before the glaze was applied. The thin glazes are uneven and fairly primitive in appearance. A small amount of iron and titanium oxides in these glazes gave them a greenish yellow or light olive brown color. Analyses done on a few glaze samples have shown that they belong to the calcia glaze family, meaning that calcium oxide—which is generally referred to as lime—was used as the chief fluxing agent.[3] It is possible that this lime was added in the form of wood or plant ash, or as burned limestone; however, opinions differ on this matter.

Glazed pottery has constituted a very small percentage of the total Shang-period ceramic remains. It has been found in Shaanxi, Shanxi, Henan, Hebei, Shandong, Hubei, Hunan, Jiangxi, and southern Jiangsu provinces; the wares from various areas have exhibited distinct regional characteristics. Excavations of Shang-era sites in the middle and lower Yellow River valley have yielded a much smaller quantity and variety of glazed pottery than were found at sites in the middle and lower Yangtze River valley.

The appearance of these relatively high-fired glazes in the Shang period marked the beginning of a tradition of high-temperature glazes, all of which belong to the calcia glaze family, that has continued in Chinese ceramics to the present day.

Geometric-impressed pottery. A very large and widely divergent family of ceramics with a variety of impressed geometric patterns had begun to appear by this time. In classifying these ceramics, Chinese scholars rank them as hard earthenwares, noting that the brownish-toned bodies can, in fact, range from fairly soft to what would be described as stoneware in the West. Occasionally these vessels have a surface luster resembling a thin layer of glaze. Excavations of Shang- and Zhou-period sites have frequently unearthed this geometric-impressed pottery in company with contemporary glazed wares.

Geometric-impressed ceramics have been found in sites along the middle and lower Yellow River valley, the middle and lower Yangtze River valley, and the Southeast China coast. The shapes and decorations have varied somewhat from region to region. The preponderance of

17.   JAR. White earthenware. Late Shang dynasty, ca. 13th–11th century B.C. Yinxu (Anyang) phase. Courtesy of the Freer Gallery, Smithsonian Institution, Washington, D. C.

these wares was manufactured in Southeast China, where both the types of vessels and kinds of decoration have been more numerous than in the north.[4]

Shang white wares. Fabrication of white-bodied earthenwares began at an early date in China. Fragments have been discovered at Yangshao cultural sites, and a number of striking white vessels have been associated with some Longshan cultures. White wares can be traced through the Erlitou/Xia phase and into early Shang. Fairly hard, fine-bodied, white pottery has been found in sites attributed to the middle Shang era in both the Yellow and Yangtze River valleys.

The quality of white wares peaked in the late Shang period. Choice examples (No. 17) are so elegant and carefully potted that it is generally agreed they were intended for ceremonial use. These vessels show the dominance of bronzes in the hierarchy of late Shang tastes. This bronze influence is particularly true in the

been constructed in a cord-lined mold or by the beater-and-pad technique; mouths and feet have frequently been shaped on a wheel and have often been nicely finished. The bodies are either untempered or sand-tempered common clay, ranging from relatively fine to very coarse in texture; they may be gray or, less frequently, red or brown. Two *li* tripods (Nos. 18 and 19), one gray and the other with a coarse, sand-tempered, red body, are reliably reported to have been found in Shandong Province. They are honest, straightforward, utilitarian "cord-marked" pots that were designed to expose a large surface to the cooking fire.

Shang gray wares after bronzes. A widely varied family of superior-quality, gray to very dark gray earthenwares diverges from the essentially ceramic concept of the "cord-marked" type: it exhibits distinct influences of bronze vessels. Ranging from fine-bodied, well-made wares with burnished, almost black surfaces to relatively coarse-bodied, less refined, and lighter-colored vessels, this group has bronze-inspired forms and often carries carved, impressed, or relief designs corresponding to those on the metal prototypes. A particularly fine example of

18. TRIPOD. Earthenware with cord markings. Height: 7 7/8 in. (20 cm.). Late Shang dynasty, ca. 13th–11th century B.C. Gift of Dr. Benjamin Pasamanick and Dr. Hilda Knobloch, 1972. 1972.275.5.

carved or impressed designs, which can be correlated with the progression of bronze decorative styles.

Analyses have shown that the clay used in Shang white wares was very similar to kaolin (a clay that is particularly free of impurities, especially iron). These earthenwares were fired at temperatures estimated to have been about 1000–1150° C.

For some as-yet-unexplained reason, white wares do not seem to have been produced to any appreciable extent after the fall of the Shang, and they did not become an important factor in Chinese ceramics again until about the sixth century A.D.

"Cord-marked" pottery. Common "cord-marked" wares for everyday use, a tradition continued from the Longshan cultures, might be seen as the staple of Shang ceramics. Many of these vessels show evidence of having

19. TRIPOD. Earthenware with cord markings. Height: 6 3/8 in. (16.2 cm.). Late Shang dynasty, ca. 13th–11th century B.C. Gift of Dr. Benjamin Pasamanick and Dr. Hilda Knobloch, 1972. 1972.275.4.

this sham-bronze group is the late Shang vessel, known as a *zun* (No. 20), which has a very dark gray, burnished surface. The covered jar (No. 21) is analogous in shape to a bronze *hu*.

Shang lacquered pottery. Excavations in 1975 at the Xiaotun site near Anyang, in Henan Province, produced fragments of lacquer-painted, black-surfaced pottery. Some of these fragments had red-lacquer designs taken from Shang-dynasty bronze vessels.[5] While lacquered pottery was never very popular in China, its manufacture did continue at least through the Han dynasty.

Utensils for the bronze industry. Among the most important products of the Shang ceramic kilns were pottery molds and crucibles used in the bronze industry. It has been found that the bronze casters and potters lived in the type of houses usually associated with the aristocracy; this would indicate that they were especially esteemed in the Shang era.

Architectural pottery. The earliest type of architectural pottery manufactured by the Chinese seems to have been pipes to carry water. Remains of such earthenware water pipes have been found at both the Erlitou and Zhengzhou sites in Henan Province.

21. COVERED JAR. Earthenware with carved and relief decoration. Height: 12 1/8 in. (30.6 cm.). Late Shang dynasty, ca. 13th–11th century B.C. or later. Harris Brisbane Dick Fund, 1950. 50.61.7.

1. Yin Weizhang in *Xin Zhongguo de kaogu faxian he yanjiu*, comp. Zhongguo shehui kexueyuan kaogu yanjiusuo (Beijing, 1984), p. 214.

2. Fragments of glazed "primitive celadons" have recently been reported excavated from the late Longshan cultural level at Dongxiafeng, near Xia xian, Shanxi Province (*Kaogu Xuebao*, 1983, no. 1, pp. 55–92). Judgment on this find must wait until further evidence of "Neolithic glazed wares" is published.

3. Li Jiazhi, *Kaogu*, 1978, no. 3, pp. 179–88. Idem, "The Evolution of Chinese Pottery and Porcelain Technology," in *Ancient Technology to Modern Science*, Ceramics and Civilization, ed. W. D. Kingery, vol. 1 (Columbus, Ohio, 1984), pp. 135–62. Zhang Fukang, "The Origin and Development of Traditional Chinese Glazes and Decorative Ceramic Colors," ibid., pp. 163–80. Nigel Wood, *Oriental Glazes: Their Chemistry, Origins and Re-creation* (London, 1978).

4. The entire issue of *Wenwu Jikan* 3 (1981) is devoted to reports from a conference on impressed-design pottery produced south of the Yangtze River.

5. *Kaogu*, 1976, no. 4, pp. 264–72, 263, and fig. 10. • Lacquer fragments with similar decoration were excavated in 1973 at Taixicun, Gaocheng xian, Hebei Province (Hebei sheng bowuguan and Wenwu guanlichu, eds., *Hebei sheng chutu wenwu xuanji* [Beijing, 1980], pl. 55 and color pl. 55).

CHAPTER THREE
THE ZHOU DYNASTY

The exact nature of the Zhou, a people who lived in Shaanxi Province on the fringes of the Shang civilization during the later part of the Shang era, is not clear at this time. We do not know precisely when the Zhou conquered the Shang, although the eleventh century B.C. is a popularly accepted date. This conquest led to the establishment of the longest dynasty in Chinese history. During the early part of the Zhou dynasty, known as the Western Zhou, which lasted until 771 B.C., Zhou rulers essentially functioned as the feudal heads of a group of states in the North China Plain. Their most important capitals were the cities of Hao and Feng, near the modern city of Xian in Shaanxi Province.

Whatever their early character may have been, after the Zhou subjugated the Shang, they maintained and elaborated upon the basic Shang culture. For example, bronze metallurgy remained a prime industry, the writing system continued to evolve, construction of chariots was improved, techniques of spinning and weaving were furthered, and the art of jade carving was advanced.

THE WESTERN ZHOU

Western Zhou pottery provides a logical place to digress for a moment and discuss an important fact about the development of all Chinese pottery. Unlike automobiles from a Detroit assembly line, where this year's model is distinct from last year's or next year's car, Chinese ceramics exhibit a gradual, albeit constant, evolution in both style and physical characteristics, with relatively few major innovations interrupting this slow and measured pace. Throughout Chinese history, while the temper of the time certainly made itself felt in all creative efforts, changes in taste generally occurred by degrees. As might be expected from the empirical methods of manufacture

30. JAR. Stoneware with impressed and carved decoration, remnants of glaze. Height: 7 1/4 in. (18.4 cm.). Eastern Zhou dynasty, Warring States period, ca. 5th–mid-4th century B.C. Harris Brisbane Dick Fund, 1950. 50.61.10.

22. BOWL. Earthenware with carved and incised decoration.
Diameter: 8 7/8 in. (22.5 cm.). Western Zhou dynasty,
ca. 11th–10th century B.C. Harris Brisbane Dick Fund,
1950. 50.61.6.

that were used, the material qualities of fabricated objects
altered progressively as well. It is therefore axiomatic
that Chinese pottery—which on the whole developed in
barely perceptible successive stages—usually cannot be
pigeonholed in precise or narrow dates, either by Chinese
or Western calendars.

Unglazed pottery. Unglazed pottery produced after
the Zhou conquered the Shang illustrates the above point
well. It shows little dramatic change; instead, it evolved
predictably from the typical Shang style to one
characteristic of the Zhou. In fact, it is often somewhat
difficult to state with certainty whether a given piece
dates to the late Shang or early Zhou. A case in point is
the unburnished, high-footed bowl with carved and incised

decoration (No. 22) that was illustrated in the first edition
of this book as an example of late Shang-dynasty gray
wares copying the shape of bronze serving vessels. Recent
archaeological reports have shown rather convincingly
that this vessel should be attributed to the Western Zhou
period instead.

Ordinary Western Zhou unglazed wares still were
the relatively crude, gray or red "cord-marked" variety
stemming from earlier periods, and, as before, many
examples of this long-enduring type show marks from
the mold or beater. As demonstrated above, the gray
earthenwares of better quality that were produced during
the Shang dynasty continued to be made in the early
Zhou era and, like the Shang wares, this finer Zhou gray
pottery frequently shows strong bronze influences in shapes
and designs.

23. BOWL. Near-stoneware with olive brown glaze. Diameter: 3 in. (7.6 cm.). Eastern Zhou dynasty, ca. 7th–5th century B.C. Gift of Dr. Paul Singer, 1977. 1977.449.5.

24. JAR. Near-stoneware with impressed decoration. Diameter: 5 3/4 in. (14.6 cm.). Middle Western–Eastern Zhou dynasty, Spring and Autumn era, ca. 9th–6th century B.C. Gift of Diane and Oscar Schafer, 1986. 1986.97.2.

Glazed pottery. A furthering of the tradition of high-fired glazes that was inherited from the Shang era can be seen in the considerable amount of glazed pottery excavated in recent years from Western Zhou–period sites in at least ten provinces.[1] It is obvious that ceramic technology had advanced, for some of these wares correspond in every respect to what is known as stoneware in the West. An interesting group of ceramics was excavated in 1959 from two Western Zhou–period tombs in the suburbs of Tunxi in Anhui Province. Among the seventy-one glazed vessels that were found, some were fairly low fired, with porous bodies and poorly fitting brownish glazes, while others were higher fired and had much harder bodies and well-fitting, grayish green glazes.[2]

Geometric-impressed pottery. The tradition of ceramics with geometric designs stamped into the surface while the clay was still damp continued in this period, although such wares have seldom been found in Yellow River valley Western Zhou sites. On the other hand, excavations of contemporary sites farther south, in Jiangxi, Jiangsu, and Zhejiang provinces, have unearthed large quantities of this material; its manufacture can be documented in Southeast China down to Guangdong Province.

Lacquer and shell inlay. A few late Western Zhou potters appear to have made a gesture in the direction of originality by coating vessels with lacquer and/or inlaying them with pieces of shell, but apparently the use of these decorative devices was not widespread.

Architectural pottery. Both flat and cylindrical roofing tiles were in use by the Western Zhou era, and pottery rings for the construction of wells were being manufactured.

THE EASTERN ZHOU

Under pressure from nomadic tribes to the north, the royal house of Zhou was forced to move its capital farther east in 771 B.C. The capital was reestablished near the modern city of Luoyang in Henan Province; however,

25. COVERED FOOTED BOWL. Earthenware with remains
of red decoration. Height: 9 1/4 in. (23.5 cm.). Eastern
Zhou dynasty, 770–256 B.C. Harris Brisbane Dick Fund,
1950. 50.61.9.

Zhou authority thereafter was minimal. Because of the location of the new capital, this segment of the Zhou dynasty is known as Eastern Zhou, which conventionally is further subdivided into the Spring and Autumn period (770–476 B.C.) and the Warring States era (475–221 B.C.).

Despite the political weakness of the ruling house and the constant shifting of power and struggles for supremacy among various states, the Eastern Zhou was an energetic and creative era in Chinese history, and there were many technological and cultural milestones. Particularly noteworthy was the introduction of iron metallurgy—probably during the Spring and Autumn period—and both weapons and agricultural implements began to be made of this new material. It was also the great age of Chinese thought, when Confucianism, Taoism, and several other philosophies flourished. The *Five Classics*, or the *Confucian Classics*, a group of books that were to have an enormous influence on Chinese thought throughout history, originated in this period.

26. DUCK-SHAPED VESSEL. Burnished earthenware. Eastern Zhou dynasty, Warring States era, end of 4th century B.C. From the tomb of a king of the Zhongshan State. Excavated at Pingshan xian, Hebei Province.

The Spring and Autumn Era

Pottery manufactured early in the Spring and Autumn era is scarcely distinguishable from that of the late Western Zhou, but as time went on, shapes gradually changed, and new types of vessels were introduced.

Unglazed pottery. Unglazed ceramics comprise the typical, fairly coarse, "cord-marked" utility products and the finer gray earthenwares that, like their Western Zhou forerunners, frequently show the influence of bronzes. Occasionally the surface of these superior gray wares had been polished with a hard instrument while the clay was in what is known as a leather-hard state. This polishing produced burnished designs that contrast with the duller, dark-surfaced body. A softer-bodied gray earthenware also came into being at this time. It is assumed that these lower-fired ceramics, which would have been less expensive to produce than other wares, were used exclusively as mortuary pottery.

Painted unglazed pottery. Two tombs belonging to members of the ruling family of the state of Ju, of the late Spring and Autumn period, were excavated near Junan xian, Shandong Province, in 1975. Among the tomb furnishings were a number of gray-bodied earthenwares that had been dressed with black slip, over which various designs had been painted in red pigment.[3]

27. OVOID TRIPOD. Earthenware with remnants of tinfoil. Eastern Zhou dynasty, Warring States era, 475–221 B.C. Courtesy of the Yale University Art Gallery, Gift of Mrs. William H. Moore.

While this type of material was somewhat rare in the Spring and Autumn era, painted gray pottery would later become quite popular.

Glazed pottery. During the Spring and Autumn period, the quality of high-fired glazed pottery continued to improve; some objects now show evidence that a wheel was used in their construction. Bodies are fairly fine and hard; they can be grayish white, yellowish white, or dark brown. The green glazes frequently lean toward a yellow or gray tone. The olive-toned, gummy glaze on a small bowl (No. 23) is in remarkably good condition. This bowl is quite similar to some excavated vessels assigned to the Spring and Autumn period and to some others attributed to the Warring States era.

By the late Spring and Autumn period, production of high-fired, glazed near-stoneware and stoneware was very rare in the Yellow River valley. Manufacture was almost entirely concentrated in the area south of the Yangtze River, most notably in southern Jiangsu and northern Zhejiang provinces. This region was to hold a dominant position in the production of high-fired glazed ceramics for centuries to come.

Geometric-impressed pottery. Like their high-fired glazed counterparts—with which they have frequently been excavated—Spring and Autumn ceramics with impressed geometric designs developed from similar Western Zhou pottery. These hard-bodied wares are relatively uncommon in the Yellow River valley; they were produced for the most part in the middle and lower Yangtze River valley and along the Southeast China coast. They are illustrated here by the squat, dark gray jar with a deeply impressed zigzag design (No. 24).

Architectural pottery. Along with the kinds of material already mentioned, architectural pottery of the Spring and Autumn era included eave tiles and thin, rectangular or square building bricks.

The Warring States Era

Although a few types maintained their fundamentally ceramic nature during the Warring States segment of the Eastern Zhou period, much of the pottery manufactured during this era reflects the greater importance of bronzes and other materials in Zhou society.

Gray wares. Finer gray earthenwares are particularly likely to show bronze influences; indeed, there seem to be few shapes among these vessels for which counterpart shapes in bronze—or, to a lesser extent, lacquer—cannot be found.

In ornamenting these wares, too, the Warring States potters extended themselves to copy more precious objects. Probably inspired by the decoration of contemporary inlaid bronzes and painted lacquers, they often painted their gray earthenware vessels with polychrome pigments that were frequently applied over a coating of slip. Unlike most Neolithic painted pottery, which was decorated before the vessel was fired, these later Zhou wares were painted after a piece came from the kiln. The adhesive element used with the colors to fix them to the vessel was somewhat fugitive in nature; consequently, Zhou colors were not as permanent as most Neolithic ones, and today they are frequently badly damaged or have almost completely disappeared. A covered footed bowl, known as a *dou* (No. 25), is a fine example of these Zhou painted wares.

Burnished pottery. The shapes of burnished gray wares with blackish surfaces were often copied from those made of other materials. Designs, which are slightly glossy and a little darker than the matte ground, were derived from those on contemporary bronzes and lacquers. While this technique of burnishing decorative figures on pottery originated in the Spring and Autumn era, it became especially popular during the Warring States period, when some extraordinary examples (No. 26) were produced. Burnished designs could also be combined with patterns that were incised into the body before it was completely dry; and again, late Zhou gray wares might just be enriched with bronze-derived incised decoration.

Tinfoil decoration. Eastern Zhou potters—particularly those in the vicinity of the modern Changsha, Hunan Province, which was an important center in the state of Chu—also applied thin sheets of tinfoil to their wares (No. 27). This was a rather novel way to make humble gray pottery vessels approximate more valuable metal objects, presumably those made of silver. Painted designs were sometimes added to these pieces, perhaps to create the illusion of inlaid work. Unfortunately, in most cases the adhesive material used to attach the foil and fix the paints has disintegrated, and little original decoration remains on extant examples.

Lacquered pottery. The technique of lacquering pottery, which originated in the Shang period, was also followed to some extent in the Western and Eastern Zhou eras. While the method of application seems to have been fairly successful, and some known examples are in

28. JAR. Earthenware with ribbing and cord markings. Height: 8 5/8 in. (21.9 cm.). Eastern Zhou dynasty, probably Warring States period, 475–221 B.C. Gift of Dr. Benjamin Pasamanick and Dr. Hilda Knobloch, 1972. 1972.275.1.

reasonably good condition even today, lacquered pottery apparently was never as popular as the contemporary lacquered wood.

Glass paste decoration. There is a rare type of Warring States red-bodied earthenware that was coated with white slip and further decorated with pigments and applied glass paste. As with so many other Eastern Zhou ceramics, the shapes of these vessels, as well as their designs, reflect the inspiration of contemporary metal wares.

"Cord-marked" pottery. The serviceable, workaday "cord-marked" family of ceramics had done yeoman duty as what might be thought of as China's kitchenware since earliest times. It is still apt to be found in shapes more natural to clay and seldom shows evidence of the influence of bronzes. These "cord-marked" gray or red earthenwares, which, as always, have bodies that range from fine to coarse in texture, are represented here by two gray jars (Nos. 28 and 29) that are reported on good authority to have come from Shandong Province. They certainly are not grand pieces, but they have the honest design of a type of utensil that has served well for many centuries.

Mortuary ceramics. Many vessels that had been used in life were buried with the dead; however, pottery specifically manufactured for burial also played an important role in the Warring States period. (Objects expressly made for entombment with the dead are known as *mingqi* in China.) Generally these wares were totally unsuitable for daily use, as they were quite low fired and very soft; however, they were adequate substitutes in the tomb for the objects made of more precious material, such as bronze and lacquer, that they copied. The body of these mortuary ceramics was sometimes burnished so that the surface of the piece had a soft luster, or decoration might be added in the form of incised or painted designs.

In addition to a wide variety of vessels, among the more interesting examples of tomb furniture excavated from Warring States graves in recent years were some rather crudely fashioned pottery figurines.[4] These are early examples of the practice of burying ceramic facsimiles

31. BELL. Stoneware with impressed and relief decoration, remnants of glaze. Height: 14 in. (35.6 cm.). Eastern Zhou dynasty, ca. 7th–5th century B.C. Charlotte C. and John C. Weber Collection, Gift of Charlotte C. and John C. Weber through the Live Oak Foundation, 1988. 1988.20.8.

29. JAR. Earthenware with cord markings. Height: 10 1/8 in. (25.7 cm.). Eastern Zhou dynasty, probably Warring States period, 475–221 B.C. Gift of Dr. Benjamin Pasamanick and Dr. Hilda Knobloch, 1972. 1972.275.3.

of people to accompany the dead in the afterlife, a practice that was to become widespread in later dynasties.

Glazed stonewares. A number of high-fired glazed stonewares have recently been excavated from tombs and kiln sites in Jiangsu, Zhejiang, and Jiangxi provinces; these finds have been dated by investigators to the late Spring and Autumn and Warring States periods. The shapes of these wares show distinct regional characteristics. They are represented here by a plump-bodied jar with ring handles (No. 30), which unfortunately retains only remnants of its glaze. Some of these glazed stonewares have been fashioned in simple ceramic forms; others, such as the bell (No. 31), are close imitations of contemporary bronzes. They can be completely plain, or they might carry relief, incised, or impressed designs under a greenish to yellowish or brownish green glaze that is frequently mottled.

In the mid-fourth century B.C., after the state of Chu exterminated the state of Yue that had controlled much of this region, production of high-fired glazed ceramics virtually stopped in the area. Glazed stonewares probably began to be manufactured here again by the end of the Warring States period or the Qin/early Han

era; however, they were quite different from this Warring States type of pottery.[5]

Farther south, a variant type of glazed ceramic was being made during the Warring States period. Excavations in Guangdong, Guangxi, and southern Hunan provinces have yielded pottery with brownish or reddish bodies and brownish or greenish glazes. Apparently the ceramic traditions in this part of the country were not as severely interrupted during the late Warring States period as they were in the lower Yangtze River valley/Hangzhou Bay region.

Geometric-impressed pottery. The tradition of pottery with impressed geometric patterns persisted in southern China from a period contemporary with the Shang dynasty through the early Han dynasty. This tradition can be seen in numerous Warring States unglazed earthenwares and stonewares excavated from Jiangsu to Guangxi provinces. In the vicinity of Jiangsu and Zhejiang provinces, however, production of geometric-impressed material, like that of glazed stonewares, seems to have suffered considerably during the late Warring States period.

The stamped motifs on these wares are widely varied, ranging from designs that resemble fine woven textiles

(Nos. 32 and 33) to large checkers arranged in fairly regular rows. A thin brownish luster that resembles a glaze often covers the surface of these utilitarian vessels.

Architectural pottery. Architectural pottery also had its place in the list of wares produced during this period. Among the building materials excavated at the remains of Warring States palaces and other buildings were water pipes and bricks, as well as ornamental roof tiles, end tiles, and waterspouts.

1. E.g., 100 glazed vessels are reported to have been found in 1981 in and near the remains of a tomb in Yiwu xian, Zhejiang Province (*Kaogu*, 1985, no. 7, pp. 608–13, 622, and figs. 2:3,4,6–17, 3–5).

2. *Kaogu Xuebao*, 1959, no. 4, pp. 59–90, and color pl.; pls. 11–16, 17:1,2, 18:1,2; figs. 4–6.

3. *Kaogu Xuebao*, 1978, no. 3, pp. 317–36, and pl. 7; figs. 16, 17.

4. E.g., figures from Fenshuiling, outside Changzhi, Shanxi Province (*Kaogu Xuebao*, 1957, no. 1, pp. 103–18, and pl. 2:1,2). • From the suburbs of Luoyang, Henan Province (*Kaogu*, 1959, no. 12, pp. 653–57, and pl. 3:2,3). • From Langjiazhuang, Zibo, Shandong Province (*Kaogu Xuebao*, 1977, no. 1, pp. 73–104, and pl. 18).

5. Feng Xianming et al., eds., *Zhongguo taoci shi* (Beijing, 1982), pp. 102–3.

32. JAR. Stoneware with impressed decoration. Height: 2 3/8 in. (6 cm.). Eastern Zhou dynasty, Warring States period, ca. 5th–mid-4th century B.C. Anonymous loan. L.1972.77.1.

33. COVERED JAR. Stoneware with impressed and relief decoration. Diameter: 4 1/2 in. (11.4 cm.). Eastern Zhou dynasty, Warring States period, ca. 5th–mid-4th century B.C. Purchase, Gloria H. Spivak Gift, 1986. 1986.75.2.

CHAPTER FOUR

THE QIN AND HAN DYNASTIES

THE QIN DYNASTY

Constant interstate hostilities of the Warring States period came to an end in 221 B.C., when the state of Qin finally succeeded in conquering all other independent states. The country was then unified, and the first Chinese empire was founded. Adopting the title of "Qin Shihuangdi" ("First Emperor of Qin"), the king of Qin did much to consolidate the country. He provided a centralized administration, established standardized systems of weights and measures and coinage, and standardized the Chinese writing system. He also expanded the empire: Qin armies pushed the boundaries east to the sea, west to Gansu and Qinghai provinces, north to the loop of the Yellow River, and south to Guangdong and Guangxi provinces. Several existing defensive walls at the northern frontier were incorporated into one long barrier, fundamentally the same Great Wall that stretches across northern China today.

39. INCENSE BURNER. Earthenware with relief decoration, remains of pigments. Height: 8 3/4 in. (22.2 cm.). Eastern Han dynasty, A.D. 25–220. Gift of Miss Florance Waterbury, 1965. 65.74.2.

In 1974, an enormous subterranean chamber was discovered near the Qin Shihuangdi mausoleum in Lintong xian, Shaanxi Province; this was to be the first of four such finds that have been excavated to date. Three of these chambers contained a heretofore unimaginable imperial bodyguard of fully equipped, life-sized, painted earthenware figures, estimated to comprise more than ten thousand men, plus another five hundred ceramic horses, all in military formation. These large, explicitly detailed, pottery warriors and horses—which were made in molds and then individually sculpted—are the antithesis of the crude little ceramic mortuary figures of the late Zhou period. They offer awe-inspiring testimony to the grandiose concepts of the megalomaniacal First Emperor.

THE HAN DYNASTY

The Qin empire was short-lived: in 202 B.C., after a brief period of wide political disorder and warfare, Liu Bang, a commoner, won out over his rivals and declared himself emperor. He called his dynasty Han and established his capital at Changan, the modern Xian, in

Shaanxi Province. Traditionally, the Han dynasty is reckoned as beginning in the year 206 B.C., when Liu Bang was given the title of King of Han. The Han dynasty, which in essence lasted for about four centuries, was interrupted for a brief period in A.D. 8, when Wang Mang, a statesman, seized the throne. In A.D. 23, the reign of this interloper ended, and after two years of turmoil, a descendant of the Han rulers established a new Han dynasty with its capital at Luoyang in Henan Province. A distinction is generally made between the Former, or Western, Han—before the Wang Mang interregnum—and the Later, or Eastern, Han, when the dynasty was, in effect, restored.

The Han era was one of China's most glorious periods. A strong, unified country experienced a period of enormous power and prestige, with an unprecedented expansion in military, diplomatic, and cultural areas. The empire was extended farther south than ever before, east as far as Korea, and west well into Central Asia. Via the overland trade routes of Central Asia and the sea lanes leading to and from South China, China sent its precious silk to the Western world and received in return a wealth of ideas and products from lands as far away as the Roman Empire.

The commanding position of metal wares, particularly bronzes, which had made a very deep imprint on Chinese ceramics since Shang times, can still be observed in Han pottery. However, a new interest in naturalism that swept through all phases of art at this time also touched the potter's craft. As a result, ornamental styles of Han ceramics are not strictly limited to those derived from metal wares, but also include a refreshing new repertoire of naturalistic motifs that perhaps are best typified by the Han hunting scene motif.

Glazed stonewares. Several types of glazed stonewares were produced during the Han period. Among them is a homogeneous family of jars (Nos. 34 and 35) that are frequently decorated on the upper portion with freely moving, combed or incised designs and raised grooved

35. JAR. Stoneware with incised and relief decoration and olive green glaze. Height: 12 in. (30.5 cm.). Han dynasty, probably late Western Han period, ca. 1st century B.C. Rogers Fund, 1917. 17.154.

34. JAR. Stoneware with incised and relief decoration and olive green glaze. Height: 15 1/8 in. (38.4 cm.). Han dynasty, probably late Western Han period, ca. 1st century B.C. Purchase, Mrs. Richard E. Linburn Gift, 1984. 1984.15.

41

36. JAR. Stoneware with celadon glaze. Eastern Han dynasty, A.D. 25–220. Excavated at Zhongzhoulu, Luoyang, Henan Province. From *Luoyang Zhongzhoulu*, 1959.

bands. A pair of flattened-loop handles, copying those on Han bronzes, are on the shoulder.[1] The high-fired lime glaze, which usually is slightly mottled, is restricted to the upper areas; its greenish or brownish color is due to the presence of iron and titanium oxides. On the lower half of the vessel, the exposed body has turned a distinctive dark reddish brown.

Before the existence of earlier glazed ceramics was documented, this Han group was designated "proto-porcelain" to indicate that, in essence, it represented the beginnings of porcelain. Since the discovery of Shang-dynasty glazed wares, however, the term no longer applies to Han wares. Although examples of this type of jar have been found in locations as widely distant as Shaanxi and Zhejiang provinces, it would seem that many—if not all—of these wares were manufactured in the vicinity of northern Zhejiang and southern Jiangsu provinces.

By the Eastern Han period, high-fired glazed stoneware had been developed to the point that it meets the Chinese and Japanese criteria for porcelain: the body is compact, impermeable, and resonant when struck, and the relatively even green glaze adheres firmly to the body. In recent years, this kind of material has been excavated from tombs in many locations; some of these tombs carried precise Eastern Han dates. Fragments of green-glazed stonewares have also been found at several contemporary kiln sites, the most notable being those in Zhejiang Province.[2]

A rather distinctive type of squat, green-glazed, stoneware jar (No. 36) has been found in Eastern Han tombs in a number of provinces.[3] While there are some variations in their shapes, all of these jars have a short straight mouth, well-defined shoulder, and horizontal loop handles; the light-colored body may be impressed with a clothlike pattern under the glaze. At least some of these jars are known to be the product of kiln complexes in Shangyu xian, Zhejiang Province.[4]

Celadon glazes. High-fired green glazes, which take their color from small amounts of iron—and generally titanium—oxides and are fired in a reducing atmosphere,[5] are usually called celadon glazes in the West.[6] The term "celadon" is believed to stem from a seventeenth-century French play, *L'Astrée*, in which a character named Céladon was costumed in grayish green. Compared with those of later date, the Eastern Han celadons are somewhat immature in quality; however, they were the all-important parents of a tradition of celadon-glazed ceramics that would become one of China's proudest achievements.

Brown- and black-glazed stonewares. Stonewares with brown or black glazes have also been found in Eastern Han tombs in several provinces, and fragments with dark brown glazes were recently unearthed at kiln sites in Zhejiang Province.[7] The shapes and decoration of these dark-glazed ceramics were frequently quite similar to those of the green-glazed wares from the same area. According to Chinese authorities, the earliest dark glazes had a color that resembled soy sauce, and these brown glazes later developed into high-fired glazes of a blacker tone.[8]

Stonewares from southernmost China. It would appear that the ceramic traditions in the most southern parts of China were somewhat different from those in other regions during the Han dynasty. Glazed—and very similar unglazed—stoneware objects found in Western and Eastern Han tombs, especially in the neighborhood of Canton in Guangdong Province, frequently had their own special style. Wares in the same stylistic tradition have been found to a lesser extent in the environs of Changsha, Hunan Province, and in several other provinces as well. Their shapes are somewhat unusual and often show a close relationship to bronzes found in the same vicinity. The incised and impressed decoration is especially characteristic, displaying a fondness for multiple narrow rows of geometric designs or very stiff, angular patterns. Thin, primitive-looking glazes range in color from brown to yellowish or olive green, sometimes with streaks of blue, as in the bottle (No. 37). Because of the remarkably close similarities in shapes and decorative treatments displayed by many of the objects, it has been theorized that at least some of these wares were produced in the Canton area and exported to the other provinces.

Burnished pottery. Several other Zhou-dynasty ceramic traditions were also continued during the Han period. Among them was the ornamental technique of burnishing the surfaces of earthenwares to a lustrous black color. This burnished pottery is represented here by the dramatically shaped flask (No. 38), most popularly known as a *canjian hu* ("silkworm cocoon–shaped flask").

Lacquered pottery. A number of archaeological reports noting the excavation of Han-dynasty lacquered pottery have been published in recent years. The colors of these lacquer dressings included brown, red, and black; some lacquered vessels were additionally painted in red and white.[9]

Han white wares. Glazed white ware is reported to have been discovered in an Eastern Han tomb in Changsha, Hunan Province.[10] Evidence concerning Han

37. BOTTLE. Stoneware with incised designs under blue-splashed brown glaze. Height: 9 1/8 in. (23.2 cm.). Eastern Han dynasty, 1st century A.D. Type found in southernmost China. Harris Brisbane Dick Fund, 1950. 50.61.11.

43

38. FLASK. Burnished earthenware with incised decoration.
Height: 10 3/4 in. (27.3 cm.). Qin–Western Han dynasty,
ca. late 3rd–1st century B.C. Gift of Mrs. Richard E.
Linburn, 1981. 1981.466.

glazed white ware is extremely sketchy at this writing, and it is too soon to say if this finding signals the establishment of one of China's major ceramic traditions. Future excavations will no doubt provide further information on the subject.

Lead glazes. Until about the beginning of the Han era, Chinese potters could glaze their wares only by applying a suitable glaze to a body made of stoneware-type clay and then firing the object at a high temperature, in excess of about 1200° C. The glazed near-stonewares or stonewares that resulted were attractive and approximated the dense, hard-bodied, nonporous ware most desirable for everyday use; however, this high-fired pottery was relatively expensive to produce. By the early Western Han period, a technique had been developed by which low-fired, earthenware vessels could also be glazed. It was found that adding a certain amount of lead oxide to the glaze, which was predominantly composed of silica, would cause it to melt at the comparatively low temperature of about 700° C. These lead glazes—that is, glazes in which lead oxide is employed as the principal fluxing agent—were probably applied to unfired vessels that were then fired to earthenware hardness at temperatures much lower than those required for high-fired stonewares. While neither the glaze nor the body had the serviceable qualities of high-fired wares, low-fired, lead-glazed ceramics were quite ornamental and most acceptable for placement in tombs, where their use was merely symbolic.

Lead-glazed earthenwares can be documented as early as the late second–early first century B.C.[11] This introduction of lead glazes marked the beginning of a tradition of similar glazes that has continued, in several different forms, to the present day.

Mortuary pottery (mingqi). The practice of burying objects with the dead for use in the afterlife goes back to earliest times in China, and countless tombs throughout the country have served as a vast repository for all sorts of art that would otherwise have been lost over the centuries. Some objects found in tombs had been used by the deceased and were deposited with him when he died, and other material (*mingqi*) was expressly made for the grave; however, one cannot always differentiate between the two categories.

As we have seen, pottery objects had been specifically produced for burial before the Han dynasty; however, the quantities and types of *mingqi* were so greatly expanded during the Han that tomb furniture becomes a major element in our study of early Chinese ceramics.

There are fundamentally two types of Han ceramic funerary wares. The first consists of miniaturized earthenware replicas of almost everything known in life. In reduced scale, these *mingqi* models form a microcosm of people and possessions such as houses, farm buildings, wells, animals, and all manner of household effects; they were meant to provide company and comfort for the spirit of the dead. Taken from real life, they give us an invaluable insight into many facets of Han life, from modes of dress to methods of preparing food. A second type of funerary ware, life-sized earthenware vessels and utensils that were generally used for ritual offerings of food, also has frequently been found in Han tombs. Unlike the highly representational models of people and chattels, for the most part these large pieces still cling to the bronze tradition in form as well as in much of their ornamentation.

Unglazed mingqi. An abundance of burial material has been excavated from Han tombs throughout China. Some of the Han *mingqi* were made of grayish earthenware; they either were left undecorated or were painted with unfired colored pigments that, unfortunately, were usually quite impermanent. From the relatively few known specimens that have retained their original decoration, such as the ebulliently painted covered jar (Color No. 1), we can surmise that these wares must have been quite splendid when they were placed in a tomb. A certain amount of red and white paint still remains on a minutely detailed incense burner of exceptional quality (No. 39), but the figure of a beautiful Han lady (No. 40) has only a few touches of color left.

Glazed mingqi. Once lead-glazed earthenwares were established, they were often used as mortuary pottery, particularly in the metropolitan areas of northern China and in the vicinity of the modern Changsha, Hunan Province. By and large, glazed Han *mingqi* have brick red bodies. Generally the soft lead glazes have been colored with copper oxide and are dark green (No. 41), although on occasion they can be brown, a color derived from iron oxide; in either case, they were fired in an oxidizing atmosphere. Han green lead glazes were extremely vulnerable, and after long exposure to moisture in the tomb, most of them have decomposed to a certain extent, acquiring a silvery iridescence. While this iridescence may not have been intentional, it serves to soften the

rather strong color of the glaze, and the effect can be quite pleasing.

Other Han pottery. Apart from the wares described above, the collateral everyday pottery of the Han dynasty shows little change from that of the Zhou; it still comprises a broad range of sturdy, practical wares in the "cord-marked" and geometric-impressed pottery traditions. Han potters also crafted large quantities of architectural pottery, primarily roof tiles and antefixes, as well as the hollow ornamental tomb tiles used in underground burial chambers.

41. JAR. Earthenware with relief decoration under iridescent green glaze. Height: 14 1/2 in. (36.8 cm.). Late Western–Eastern Han dynasty, ca. 1st century B.C.–2nd century A.D. Gift of Mrs. Samuel T. Peters, 1926. 26.292.83.

1. Although some members of this family do not precisely qualify as stoneware, it is convenient here to include all examples under the same banner.

2. Penelope Hughes-Stanton and Rose Kerr, comps., *Kiln Sites of Ancient China: An Exhibition Lent by the People's Republic of China*, exhib. cat. (London and Oxford, 1980), nos. 1–10, from the Shangyu kilns; nos. 25, 26, from the Ningbo kilns.

3. E.g., from a tomb in Luoyang, Henan Province (Zhongguo kexueyuan kaogu yanjiusuo, comp., *Luoyang Zhongzhoulu* [Beijing, 1959], pl. 85:7). • From a tomb dated in accordance with A.D. 164, in the suburbs of Bo xian, Anhui Province (*Wenwu*, 1978, no. 8, pp. 32–45, and fig. 2). • From a tomb in Hanjiang xian, Jiangsu Province (*Wenwu*, 1981, no. 11, pp. 1–11, and figs. 4:10, 28).

4. Feng Xianming et al., eds., *Zhongguo taoci shi* (Beijing, 1982), p. 129, and color pl. 9:1.

5. Robert Tichane, *Those Celadon Blues* (Painted Post, N. Y., 1978).

6. There is some controversy concerning how early this term can be properly applied to Chinese green-glazed stonewares.

7. Hughes-Stanton and Kerr, *Kiln Sites*, nos. 11–13, from the Shangyu kilns; nos. 27–29, from the Ningbo kilns.

8. Zhu Boqian and Lin Shimin, *Kaogu*, 1983, no. 12, pp. 1130–36, 1129.

9. E.g., 21 pieces of reddish brown–lacquered pottery were found in 1973 in tomb no. 4 near Linyi xian, Shandong Province; this tomb has been attributed to the early Western Han period (*Kaogu*, 1975, no. 6, pp. 363–72, 351, and fig. 5:1,5; pls. 6, 8:1,3). • Several ceramics that have been covered with black lacquer and further painted in red and white were found in 1978 near Xiangyang, Hubei Province, in a tomb that has been attributed to the early Western Han period (*Kaogu*, 1982, no. 2, pp. 147–54, and fig. 10:1,2,5; pl. 6:1,2,5,6).

10. Feng et al., *Zhongguo taoci shi*, pp. 166–67. Huang Ti, ed., *Shanghai bowuguan cangci xuanji* (Beijing, 1979), p. 2, and fig. 4.

11. Li Zhiyan reports that lead-glazed wares have been found in the vicinity of Xian, Shaanxi Province, in a tomb that is datable to the Wu Di period, 141–87 B.C. (*Kaogu yu Wenwu*, 1984, no. 2, pp. 91–95).

40. FIGURE OF A LADY. Earthenware with traces of pigments. Height: 16 1/4 in. (41.3 cm.). Western Han dynasty, 206 B.C.–A.D. 8. Rogers Fund, 1920. 20.39.1.

51. ANIMAL TOMB GUARDIAN. Earthenware with
remains of pigment. Height: 12 1/4 in. (31.1 cm.). Six
Dynasties, Northern Wei dynasty, ca. first third 6th
century. Purchase, Ann Eden Woodward Foundation
Gift, 1979. 1979.438.

CHAPTER FIVE
THE SIX DYNASTIES

After the middle of the second century, the authority of the Eastern Han, or Later Han, dynasty declined rapidly; it ended in A.D. 220, when the throne was usurped by the son of a powerful general. The country then began an epoch of political disunity that lasted for over three and a half centuries. Historians refer to this period as the Six Dynasties, named after the six successive dynasties that had their capitals at the present-day Nanjing between 222 and 589. This Six Dynasties era is generally further subdivided into the major periods of the Three Kingdoms (220–80), Western Jin dynasty (265–317), and Northern (386–581) and Southern (317–589) Dynasties. During much of the Six Dynasties era, the whole of northern China was dominated by various invading barbarian tribal bands from the north; in regions to the south, a succession of states were standard bearers of the old Han traditions.

Despite the obvious political unrest, there was substantial technological and cultural growth. One of the most profound influences on the fabric of Chinese life was the spread of Buddhism, which had been introduced to China during the Han dynasty. Serving as an important link between China and South and Central Asia, Buddhism brought numerous foreign influences to China from other great cultures to the west. As it became widespread, it left its own distinctive imprint on the form and content of all facets of Chinese art.

In the field of Chinese ceramics, the Six Dynasties period was once considered a rather unimportant interval between the Han and Tang dynasties. However, recent archaeological activities have produced evidence that it actually was a time of impressive development and invention, when Chinese ceramics came into their own in many respects.

Before we discuss Six Dynasties pottery, a certain problem in terminology should be noted. Chinese ceramics, like most fields of study, has its own shorthand vocabulary, and groups of similar wares are often classified generically for easy reference. The names that past historians have assigned to many groups of ceramics— particularly those made before the fifteenth century— are geographic in nature and usually indicate the place— or what was once thought to be the place—in which a specific ware was manufactured. Although recent archaeological evidence has proven that production of a type of pottery was seldom, if ever, confined to a single kiln, it seems both convenient and practical to retain the familiar names sanctioned by common usage. Today, however, these traditional designations are used in the very broadest sense.

Yue wares. A case in point is the large body of celadon-glazed stonewares known as Yue ware. The name Yue has been associated with the modern Zhejiang Province since at least as early as the Warring States period, when the state of Yue was the major power in the area. During the Sui and Tang dynasties, the modern Shaoxing, which is in northern Zhejiang Province, was an administrative capital known as Yuezhou. "Yue ware" appears several times in Tang-dynasty literature, and it is quite possible that Yuezhou, the center of one of the areas where this pottery was made, gave its name to the Tang-dynasty wares. Today, although there is some disagreement as to how precisely it should be applied, many people use the all-encompassing name of Yue to describe a large body of stonewares produced from the Eastern Han period into the Song era in numerous kilns in northern Zhejiang and southern Jiangsu provinces.[1]

As recently as the 1940s, specialists in Chinese ceramics tended to assume that a particular family of early ceramics such as Yue ware emanated from only one group of kilns, and that a given kiln center manufactured only one type of pottery. Since 1949, however, archaeological research in China has shown that the exact opposite is true. Ceramics of a given type could have been produced in a primary kiln complex—which might have developed and possibly perfected the techniques—but these wares were then copied extensively at many kilns within a wide radius of the original kilns. Furthermore, rather than "one kiln–one ware," each kiln complex might produce many wares. In response to the basic economic rules of supply and demand, kilns met the needs of consumers in the area by manufacturing whatever was required.

A number of early Yue-ware kiln sites have been found in recent years. For the most part, production seems to have been concentrated in Shangyu xian, Yuyao xian, and Shaoxing xian, all in northern Zhejiang Province. The discovery of five Yue celadons in an Eastern Han tomb in northern Zhejiang Province[2] proves that this kind of material was being manufactured at least as early as the second half of the second century A.D.

Since 1949, an enormous amount of Yue ware has been excavated from tombs in Zhejiang and southern Jiangsu provinces—particularly in the vicinity of Nanjing—that can be dated from the mid-third century onward. Such finds have provided enough documentary material for scholars to develop a rough chronological classification based on the evolution of style, shapes, and designs, as well as the improvement in quality of potting and glazing. Typical Yue wares of the early Six Dynasties era are high-fired stonewares with hard, fairly fine-grained bodies. They are covered with thin, semitranslucent, and rather uneven glazes that range in tone from olive green to grayish green, sometimes even tending toward brownish yellow.[3] While they often show the influence of bronzes in their forms and impressed, incised, and low-relief decoration, many shapes and ornamental motifs are more ceramic in concept.

Aside from material found at kiln sites, the only Yue wares we know are those that have been found in tombs, and it is sometimes difficult to distinguish the objects made for daily use from those solely intended to be *mingqi*, or tomb pottery. These stonewares are represented here by four vessels (Color No. 2; Nos. 42, 43, and 44).

As the Six Dynasties progressed, Yue stonewares eventually broke free of the bronze orbit and came to exhibit a totally ceramic style of their own. Step by step, in the laboratory of their experience, Yue potters developed methods that would improve the quality of their wares. They gradually refined the grayish bodies and corrected the high-fired glazes until they were better controlled, greener in tone, and more uniform in color.

Spotted Yue. A number of Yue stonewares, most of which are datable to the fourth century, were decorated with deliberately placed daubs of iron oxide to produce dark brown spots against the green ground.

Brownish black Yue. In another Yue variant, the glaze is not green, but dull brownish black; this ceramic tradition of high-fired brownish black glazes originated during the Han dynasty. Black Yue wares have been excavated at the Yuhang and Deqing kiln complexes in Zhejiang Province.[4] (As has been noted, in most cases a number of kiln complexes manufactured a certain type of pottery at the same time. For convenience, however, in surveys of Chinese ceramics it has become a general practice to note only a few important kilns. They may be the most recent kilns to have been discovered, or those that seem to have produced the finest quality or the greatest quantity of a particular class of wares.)

42. HANDLED BOWL. Stoneware with celadon glaze. Diameter: 7 3/4 in. (19.7 cm.). Six Dynasties, Eastern Jin dynasty, 317–420. Yue ware. Gift of Dr. and Mrs. George Fan, 1978. 1978.395.

Other Six Dynasties celadons. In recent years, material has been excavated from Six Dynasties tombs and kiln sites in areas other than Zhejiang and southern Jiangsu provinces. Green-glazed stonewares have been found in tombs in at least half a dozen other provinces. It would appear that some of these finds were Yue wares that had been imported from the Zhejiang/Jiangsu region. Others, however, were local products with distinct regional characteristics, and sometimes they can be matched with ceramics discovered at neighborhood kiln complexes.[5]

Northern and southern Chinese ceramics. The two primary geographic areas of northern and southern China are marked by a natural boundary that falls between the Yellow and Yangtze rivers, running on a west-east axis approximately along the crest of the Qinling Mountains and, farther east, the Huai River. In addition to a considerable dissimilarity in the geologies of the two areas, there are numerous ecological differences between the grain-growing northern region and rice-cultivating southern region.

This geological diversity of the two regions manifests itself in the widely varied properties of local raw materials. Therefore, the composition of the high-fired ceramics manufactured in northern China is significantly different from that of wares produced in the south. This distinction between northern and southern Chinese high-fired pottery is quite evident in Six Dynasties celadon wares.

Celadons produced in the north. Ceramics discovered in tombs in the north, in Shanxi, Henan, Hebei, and Shandong provinces, indicate that the tradition of manufacturing celadon-glazed stonewares was probably established in the area during the sixth century. A number of celadons, including some jars with quite flamboyant decoration (No. 45), were found in 1955 in the Feng-family tomb complexes in Jing xian, Hebei Province.[6] Two of these flamboyant jars reportedly came from the tomb of a prominent family member who died in 565. Some celadons from these Feng-family burials have been analyzed; their composition is different from that of their southern counterparts, and they are indigenous to northern

43. VESSEL. Stoneware with celadon glaze. Length: 9 1/8 in.
(23.2 cm.). Six Dynasties, late Western/Eastern Jin
dynasty, ca. 4th century. Yue ware. Gift of Stanley
Herzman, 1985. 1985.207.

44. VESSEL. Stoneware with celadon glaze. Length: 6 5/8 in.
(16.8 cm.). Six Dynasties, Western Jin dynasty, 265–317.
Yue ware. Purchase, Mr. and Mrs. William P. Frankenhoff,
Ann Eden Woodward Foundation, Ashkenazie & Co., Earl
and Irene Morse, Betsy Erskine Gifts and Rogers Fund,
1985. 1985.66.

kilns. At the present time, only a few of the kilns that produced the celadons discovered in northern Six Dynasties tombs have been located. One of the most notable of these kilns is the Zhaili kiln complex near Zibo, Shandong Province,[7] which appears to have been the source of celadon wares found in nearby Six Dynasties tombs.

A beautifully modeled vessel (Color No. 3) has a very fine, white body. Analysis of this body by the Metropolitan Museum Research Laboratory has indicated that the composition is consistent with the bodies of some northern wares that have been tested; it therefore may be assigned to an as-yet-unknown northern kiln.

Brown- and black-glazed wares produced in the north. Although brown- and black-glazed stonewares had been manufactured farther south as early as the Eastern Han period, it would appear that this type of pottery was not produced in the north until the sixth century. Recent excavations of late Northern Dynasties tombs, particularly in Hebei Province, have unearthed a number of brown- and black-glazed vessels,[8] frequently along with celadon-glazed wares.

Lead glazes. The green or brown lead glazes on low-fired earthenware bodies, so popular during the Han dynasty, do not seem to have been used to any great extent during the early part of the Six Dynasties period. Lead glazes probably began to be used more widely in northern China in the fifth century, as evidenced, for

45. JAR. Stoneware with celadon glaze. Six Dynasties, Northern dynasties, ca. mid-6th century. From the Feng-family tombs. Excavated in Jing xian, Hebei Province. From *Hebei sheng chutu wenwu xuanji*, 1980.

46. JAR. Earthenware with yellow glaze. Six Dynasties, Northern Qi dynasty. From the tomb of Kudihuiluo (died 562). Excavated in Shouyang xian, Shanxi Province. From *Kaogu Xuebao*, 1979, no. 3.

47. JAR. Earthenware with applied relief decoration under green glaze. Height: 13 3/8 in. (34 cm.). Six Dynasties, late Northern Dynasties–Sui Dynasty, ca. late 6th century. Bequest of Ann Eden Woodward (Mrs. William Woodward, Jr.), 1975. 1978.264.2.

example, by a large number of lead-glazed *mingqi* found near Datong, Shanxi Province, in the Northern Wei tomb of Sima Jinlong, who died in 484.[9] Some figures from this tomb illustrate an interesting technique of enlivening these glazes: details, such as stripes in clothing, have been picked out in colored pigments applied over the monochrome glaze.

Lead-glazed figures and vessels of the later Northern Dynasties period can be documented by their recovery from tombs in Hebei, Henan, Shanxi, and Shandong provinces.[10] (Until recently, the Chinese usually did not specifically identify lead glazes as such in their archaeological reports, making it difficult at times to know the exact nature of the ceramics under discussion.) Bodies of these excavated wares generally were light in tone, and glaze colors included white, yellow, amber, brown, and green. Sometimes there were splashes of a contrasting color, and occasionally three colors had been

used at the same time. This early use of multicolor lead glazes was the precursor of a particularly brilliant phase in the decoration of Chinese mortuary pottery, the famous *sancai* ("three-color") palette of Tang-dynasty burial wares.

The elaborate ornamentation seen on some of these lead-glazed vessels often bears a strong stylistic resemblance to that on other late Six Dynasties ceramics.[11] For example, seven very unusual yellow-glazed jars were found in 1973 in Shouyang xian, Shanxi Province, in the Northern Qi tomb of Kudihuiluo, who died in 562; one of them is illustrated here (No. 46). The relief, segmentate lotus petals on this lead-glazed jar are quite similar to those at the shoulder of the contemporary northern, celadon-glazed jar from the Feng-family tombs (No. 45).

At this writing, the only kilns known to have produced this type of material during the Six Dynasties era are the Zhaili kiln complexes near Zibo, Shandong Province.[12] Until other kilns are discovered, one can only conjecture that lead-glazed pottery such as the seventy-six vessels recently removed from the Northern Qi tomb of Lou Rui, which is datable to 570, in the suburbs of Taiyuan, Shanxi Province,[13] was of local manufacture.

Two objects here represent the tradition of lead glazes in northern China at the end of the sixth century. A large jar with beaded medallions and Buddhist figures (No. 47) is one of a homogeneous group of vessels decorated in a relatively simple manner with applied-relief motifs under green lead glazes. The more flamboyantly ornamented lead-glazed earthenwares of the period are illustrated by a most unusual footed lamp with both green and brown glazes (No. 48). Several of its motifs, such as the segmentate lotus petals in relief that circle the bottom, relate this piece to the families of elaborately ornamented celadon- and lead-glazed vessels represented by two jars discussed above (Nos. 45 and 46).

White wares. While the Chinese were apparently capable of producing white wares as early as the Yangshao Neolithic culture—and did, indeed, capitalize on the potentials of white-burning clays in the Shang dynasty —for some as-yet-unexplained reason they did not then

48. LAMP. Earthenware with green and brown glazes. Height: 11 3/4 in. (29.8 cm.). Six Dynasties, late Northern Dynasties–Sui dynasty, ca. late 6th century. Fletcher Fund, 1927. 27.46.

49. BOTTLE. White ware with green splashes. Six Dynasties, Northern Qi dynasty. From the tomb of Fan Cui (died 575). Excavated near Anyang, Henan Province. From *Wenhua dageming qijian chutu wenwu*, 1972.

Dynasties white wares, in effect, were the roots of a tradition of white pottery—including earthenware, porcelaneous ware, and porcelain—that has remained paramount in the panorama of Chinese ceramics up to the present day.

Mingqi. In recent years, archaeological reports from The People's Republic of China have contained illustrations of a profusion of Six Dynasties ceramic tomb material that has included a wide variety of vessels, as well as representations of people, animals, and inanimate objects ranging from stoves to chicken coops. Differing in style according to the date and the region in which it was produced, this burial pottery was made of unglazed earthenware that was frequently slipped and painted, lead-glazed earthenware, or celadon-glazed stoneware. Two well-modeled, unglazed figures illustrated here reflect the differing stylistic conventions of the early and late Six Dynasties periods.[15] Despite its bantam size, the model of a tricorn (No. 50) conveys all the power of a full-sized beast. This kind of horned animal has frequently been found in company with a unicorn-type horse in early Six Dynasties tombs. The ferocious fantastic animal (No. 51) was placed at the entrance of the burial chamber, along with several other similar creatures, to serve as a tomb guardian.

pursue the development of white pottery. In fact, they all but dropped its manufacture for many centuries after the Shang period.

We have some indication that the possibilities of manufacturing white wares again aroused the interest of Chinese potters during the Han dynasty; however, there is little concrete information about the revival of white pottery until the late Six Dynasties period. White vessels of various sorts have been included in the inventory of effects from several late sixth-century burials. The Northern Qi tomb of Fan Cui, who died in 575, was unearthed near Anyang, Henan Province, in 1971; among the tomb furnishings were whitish-bodied cups, bottles (No. 49), and jars with translucent, white-toned glazes, some with decorative splashes of green.[14] This important find proves that fairly sophisticated white wares existed by the final quarter of the sixth century. These Six

1. These wares are also called "old Yue," "green-glazed wares," and "proto-Yue" (Margaret Medley, *The Chinese Potter: A Practical History of Chinese Ceramics* [New York, 1976], p. 60).
2. These ceramics were found in 1978 in a tomb in Fenghua xian. The tomb contained a land deed dated in accordance with A.D. 175 (Zhejiang sheng wenwu kaogusuo, comp., *Zhejiang sheng wenwu kaogusuo xuekan* [Beijing, 1981], pp. 208–11, and pl. 10:6,7; fig. 3).
3. These reduction-fired glazes probably have a composition somewhere between the lime and lime-alkali types (Nigel Wood, *Oriental Glazes: Their Chemistry, Origins and Re-creation* [London, 1978]).
4. Penelope Hughes-Stanton and Rose Kerr, comps., *Kiln Sites of Ancient China: An Exhibition Lent by the People's Republic of China*, exhib. cat. (London and Oxford, 1980), nos. 30, 31, 34–39, 41.
5. E.g., celadons found at the Yuezhou kilns in Xiangyin xian, Hunan Province, are compared with Six Dynasties tomb finds in Hunan (*Wenwu*, 1978, no. 1, pp. 69–81). • Celadons found in several tombs in Jiangxi Province are compared with wares from kilns at Luohu, Fengcheng xian, Jiangxi (*Kaogu*, 1984, no. 4, pp. 345–48).

50. MODEL OF A TRICORN. Earthenware.
Length: 17 1/4 in. (43.8 cm.). Six Dynasties, Western Jin dynasty, 265–317. Bequest of Florance Waterbury, in memory of her father, John I. Waterbury, 1968. 68.149.15.

6. Zhang Ji illustrates a flamboyant jar in his report (*Kaogu Tongxun*, 1957, no. 3, pp. 28–37, and pl. 9:1).

7. Feng Xianming et al., eds., *Zhongguo taoci shi* (Beijing, 1982), pp. 163–64. Wenwu bianji weiyuanhui [WBW], ed., *Zhongguo gudai yaozhi diaocha fajue baogaoji* (Beijing, 1984), pp. 352–59.

8. E.g., some yellowish brown or soy sauce–colored pieces found in 1973 near Jing xian, Hebei Province, in the Eastern Wei (537) tomb of Gao Ya and his family (*Wenwu*, 1979, no. 3, pp. 17–31, and figs. 6:2, 7:1, 20, 22, 49). • Seven pieces with soy sauce–brown glazes were found in 1974 near Ci xian, Hebei Province, in the Eastern Wei tomb of Yao Huren (née Zhao), who was buried in 547 (*Kaogu*, 1977, no. 6, pp. 391–400, 428, and pl. 10; fig. 9:2–8).

9. *Wenwu*, 1972, no. 3, pp. 20–33, and pl. 14:3; figs. 14, 16–20, 23, 24. Also illustrated in color, Zhongguo Shanghai renmin meishu chubanshe, ed., *Chūgoku tōji*

zenshū, vol. 28, Shanxi (Kyoto, 1984), pls. 4–19. (There seems to be some question as to whether any of these were two-color glazes.)

10. E.g., the Feng-family tombs and the tomb of Gao Run in Hebei Province; the Fan Cui and Li Yun tombs in Henan Province; those of Kudihuiluo, Han Yi, and Lou Rui in Shanxi Province; and the Fang Yue and Cui-family tombs in Shandong Province (Feng et al., *Zhongguo taoci shi*, pp. 171–73. Feng Xianming, *Wenwu*, 1983, no. 10, pp. 30–32).

11. Hin-cheung Lovell demonstrates that many of the motifs on these late Six Dynasties ceramics were drawn from contemporary Buddhist sculpture ("Some Northern Chinese Ceramic Wares of the Sixth and Seventh Centuries," *Oriental Art*, n.s. vol. 21 [Winter 1975], pp. 328–43).

12. WBW, *Zhongguo gudai yaozhi*, 1984, pp. 352–59.

13. *Wenwu*, 1983, no. 10, pp. 1–23, and pl. 7; figs. 25–33, 43. Ibid., pp. 24–39 (see especially Feng Xianming, pp. 30–32).

14. *Wenwu*, 1972, no. 1, pp. 47–57, and figs. 33–37.

15. See Annette L. Juliano, *Art of the Six Dynasties: Centuries of Change and Innovation*, exhib. cat. (New York, 1975).

CHAPTER SIX

THE SUI DYNASTY

Short-lived though it was, the Sui dynasty (581–618) was important; its founder, who had been a Northern Zhou–dynasty general, accomplished the estimable feat of reuniting China after more than three hundred and fifty years of political disunity. Under Sui rule, a strong centralized government was reestablished, capitals were rebuilt, the canal system—a means of transportation vital to China's economic prosperity—was improved, the Great Wall was reconstructed, and China's political and military influence was extended in many directions beyond its borders.

Sui ceramics continued the ceaseless evolution of Chinese pottery, building on the foundations of the late Six Dynasties and frequently showing many affinities to late Six Dynasties wares. At the same time, Sui ceramics heralded the coming of the Tang dynasty with the introduction of vessels related to those that were made in the early Tang years.

Porcelain. The use of the word "porcelain" in discussing Chinese ceramics presents a problem in semantics. In the West, porcelain, strictly defined, is a ware that is hard, white, translucent, impervious to liquid, and resonant when struck. "Porcelaneous ware" is a term sometimes used to denote wares that are superior to the average stonewares, yet not quite "true" porcelain in the Western sense. Dividing lines between these classifications are very subtle and in practice are not always possible to draw. Generally the Chinese and Japanese classify all ceramics that are resonant when struck, whether they are white bodied and translucent or not, under an all-inclusive umbrella term. They are called *ci* in China and *ji* in Japan, and the written character is the same in both languages. For *ci*, most Chinese–English dictionaries offer "porcelain," "crockery," and/or "chinaware" as translations. Vessels described as *ci* in China may be considered to be either stoneware, porcelaneous ware, or porcelain in Europe and America. These differences in terminology can make it rather difficult for Westerners to determine the character of the early white wares described in Chinese archaeological reports.

Sui white wares. Relatively few Sui-dynasty white wares have been excavated from tombs. Those examples that have been found, as represented by several vessels from the tomb of Li Jingxun, who died in 608, which

52. BOTTLE. Porcelaneous ware with clear glaze. Height: 8 3/4 in. (22.2 cm.). Probably Sui dynasty, 581–618. Rogers Fund, 1917. 17.130.

53, 54. PAIR OF FIGURES. White ware with dark brown accents. Sui dynasty. From the tomb of General Zhang Sheng (buried 595). Excavated in Anyang, Henan Province. From *Historical Relics Unearthed in New China*, 1972.

Western criteria for porcelain, and it might best be regarded as porcelaneous ware. It typifies the family of white wares produced by the late sixth century that represent a step toward the "true" porcelains that were to follow. This bottle is somewhat similar in shape to the green-splashed white bottle (No. 49) that was found in the Northern Qi tomb of Fan Cui, who died in 575.

Sui celadons. Celadon-glazed stonewares have been excavated from Sui-dynasty tombs in at least a dozen provinces and from contemporary kiln complexes in at least half a dozen provinces. In some instances, the tomb pottery can be identified as coming from kilns that have been discovered in the same area. These Sui celadons exhibit distinct regional characteristics in body, shape, glaze, and decoration.

The exceptional bottle with an impressed design of what presumably are dancers (Color No. 4) probably

55. JAR. Earthenware with brown glaze. Height: 7 7/8 in. (20 cm.). Sui dynasty, 581–618. Anonymous loan. L.1974.31.2.

was found in 1957 in the suburbs of Xian, Shaanxi Province,[1] show continued advances in potting techniques.

Few Sui-dynasty white-ware kilns have been located so far. In 1982, some bowls, cups, and dishes that have been attributed to the Sui period were discovered at the Chenliuzhuang kiln complexes in Lincheng xian, Hebei Province.[2] These vessels are described as high-fired white *ci*, with fine, grayish bodies, and white glazes over a layer of slip. (Chinese potters frequently used a coating of white slip to camouflage inferior bodies in the manufacture of many kinds of ceramics.)

A bottle (No. 52) has a whitish body showing a rather high degree of vitrification. While it is resonant when struck, it does not precisely conform to all of the belongs to the tradition of celadon wares made in the north. Placing this piece accurately is a little difficult. Its shape is somewhat similar to that of a few ceramic and metal bottles excavated from Six Dynasties tombs. While the same type of impressed leaf can be found on some late Six Dynasties celadons, these leaves, as well as groups of parallel lines, are more characteristic of Sui-dynasty decoration.

Mingqi. Sui-dynasty burial figures and other tomb furnishings generally have light-colored, earthenware bodies. Some of them are unglazed and have been detailed in colored pigments that were often applied over a layer of slip; a few of these painted figures show evidence of having had gilt added.[3] Other Sui *mingqi* have been covered in a thin, straw-colored lead glaze.

Four white-ware figures, represented here by two of them (Nos. 53 and 54), were excavated in 1959 from the tomb of Sui general Zhang Sheng, who was buried in 595, in Anyang, Henan Province.[4] These dignitaries and tomb guardians are remarkable not only for the fine quality of their modeling but also for the fact that various features have been picked out in dark brown glaze.

Other Sui lead-glazed wares. Although most Sui lead-glazed wares have light-colored bodies and pale glazes, a few red-bodied wares with deep yellow glazes have also been excavated from Sui tombs.[5] This leads to the assumption that some jars with fine-textured, soft, brick red bodies and brownish glazes (No. 55), which are quite close to many Sui celadons in shape, are also of the period.

1. Tang Jinyu, *Kaogu*, 1959, no. 9, pp. 471–72, and pl. 3:1,5,8.
2. Yang Wenshan, *Wenwu*, 1984, no. 12, pp. 51–57, and figs. 7, 9, 11, 13. Yang feels that these kilns were the forerunners of the Tang-dynasty Xing kiln system.
3. E.g., some figures from a tomb found in 1973 in the suburbs of Hefei, Anhui Province. This tomb is probably datable to 586 (*Kaogu*, 1976, no. 2, pp. 134–40, 77, and pls. 10:3,4, 11; figs. 3–6).

4. *Kaogu*, 1959, no. 10, pp. 541–45, and pl. 9:1–3,5,8. Reports differ as to the exact nature of the ceramics excavated from this tomb.
5. E.g., some vessels excavated in 1954 in the suburbs of Xian, Shaanxi Province, from the Sui-dynasty tomb of Liu Shigong. There was a tomb epitaph dated in accordance with 615 (Yu Weichao, *Kaogu Xuebao*, 1956, no. 3, pp. 33–75, and pl. 3:6; figs. 17, 18).

60. MODEL OF A HORSE. Earthenware with remains of pigments and gilt. Height: 29 3/4 in. (75.6 cm.). Tang dynasty, ca. late 7th–first half 8th century. Rogers Fund, 1925. 25.20.4.

CHAPTER SEVEN
THE TANG DYNASTY

Partly because of the overly ambitious projects of its second emperor, the Sui dynasty collapsed. This opened the way for Li Yuan, a prominent official of the Sui era, to capture the Sui capital of Daxingcheng—which would become the Tang capital of Changan—near the modern city of Xian, in Shaanxi Province, and to initiate one of the most brilliant periods in Chinese history, the Tang dynasty (618–906). The Tang empire was strong and prosperous, and as the country flourished, China's culture reached new heights. Tang China's influence was widespread, reaching the borders of Korea to the east and well into Central Asia to the west; it traded extensively with countries far beyond its own frontiers. China drew from all of the artistic influences with which it came into contact and assimilated and sinicized these exotic styles in its own unique manner.

The imprint of this internationalism can be seen in Tang ceramics. Native styles were combined with imported Western elements: shapes and decorative motifs from Persia, India, Greece, and Syria became part of the Tang ceramic repertoire. A climate of prosperity is also evident in Tang pottery, which is charged with vitality; its decoration is jubilant and its forms burst with enthusiasm.

Tang lead glazes. Relatively low-fired, light-bodied, earthenware vessels and tomb figures decorated with lead glazes were produced in considerable numbers during the Tang period. Here the potter exploited the wide color range of these low-fired glazes to the fullest. Using the clear glaze as a base, he added iron oxide to produce a tone that ranges from straw through amber yellow to dark brown; copper oxide gave rich, grassy greens; and cobalt oxide, dark, vibrant blues. A creamy white actually is the clear glaze washed over the whitish body or a coating of white slip. These colors provided the basic palette from which an impressive variety of effects was drawn. The colored glazes were applied to unadorned, impressed, or relief-decorated surfaces. Recent reports indicate that the unglazed earthenware bodies were given a preliminary firing, after which the objects were glazed and fired a second time. [1]

Most lead-glazed earthenwares manufactured from the later part of the sixth century onward are somewhat different from the low-fired wares of the Han dynasty.

56. BOTTLE. Earthenware with blue glaze. Height: 3 7/8 in. (9.8 cm.). Tang dynasty, ca. 8th century. Rogers Fund, 1923. 23.180.3.

Han reddish-earthenware bodies make the green or brown glazes look rather muddy and somber; however, the light-colored bodies characteristic of most later wares, which generally were further lightened with a layer of white slip, give the translucent glaze a much brighter, truer color.

Relatively few kilns that produced Tang lead-glazed wares have been located so far. The most fully published are those at Gong xian in Henan Province, where both monochrome and polychrome lead-glazed earthenware fragments have been excavated. Similar wares were recently discovered at the Yaozhou kilns at Huangbaozhen, in Tongchuan, Shaanxi Province.[2]

Monochrome- and "three-color"–glazed vessels. Lead-glazed earthenware vessels have been found in large quantities in Tang tombs; there is some uncertainty as to whether or not they were used in everyday life. There are stark monochrome glazes that emphasize the elegant lines of a vessel, such as the small, blue-glazed bottle (No. 56), exhibiting a perfect harmony between glaze and shape. Then again, there are opulent polychrome glazes— generally called *sancai* ("three-color") glazes, although the hues are not strictly limited to that number—in an extensive list of elaborate patterns. Frequently the designs were impressed into the clay while it was still damp, and these intaglio lines served to confine the colored glazes. This may be seen on the tripod plate with its popular motif of a goose flying in the center of a floral medallion (No. 57). These *sancai* glazes seem to have found their fullest expression when applied in either random mottles or specific arrangements, without the restraint of guidelines, and allowed to flow at will in the heat of the kiln, as in the amphora with dragon handles (No. 58). Despite their enormous variety, the uninhibited designs created with combinations of two or more colored glazes in Tang *sancai* were almost invariably governed by an innate good taste that kept the design appropriate to the object it adorned.

Tang tomb figures. Earthenware tomb figures made up a sizable segment of the ceramics manufactured during the Tang period. Literally hundreds of figures, including soldiers, servants, musicians, tomb guardians, horses, and camels—as well as models of articles used in everyday life—were placed in tombs to provide for the needs of the dead. Made in all sizes—some are miniatures only inches high, others reach several feet in stature—and in a wide range of qualities, these figures reflect the status of the deceased. By the beginning of the eighth century,

57. PLATE. Earthenware with impressed design under "three-color" glazes. Diameter: 11 3/8 in. (28.9 cm.). Tang dynasty, ca. 8th century. Rogers Fund, 1914. 14.66.

the sculptural quality of Chinese tomb figures had reached its zenith. They were modeled with unprecedented naturalism and animation. As never before, the potter imparted life and movement to his creations, capturing the essence of a gesture or a mood with superlative fidelity.

Unglazed tomb figures. A great many Tang tomb figures, with bodies ranging from red to dark gray to buff white in color, are unglazed. Colored pigments were frequently used to dress these figures after they were fired; they were applied directly to the body or over a coating of white slip, and gilt was sometimes added to enrich the decoration. Unfortunately, all of these embellishments

58. AMPHORA. Earthenware with "three-color" glazes. Height: 11 1/2 in. (29.2 cm.). Tang dynasty, ca. 8th century. Gift of Mrs. Stanley Herzman, 1984. 1984.483.3.

were somewhat impermanent in nature, and in most cases little of the original ornamentation remains. The figure of a rather corpulent court lady (No. 59) exemplifies the ideal female form during the second half of the Tang period. On a far grander scale is the piebald stallion (No. 60), on which a certain amount of pigment and gilt can still be seen. His size, the quality of modeling, and the elegance of his trappings suggest that, like so many particularly splendid funerary wares surviving today, he may have been part of the tomb furniture of a high official or member of the aristocracy.

Overglaze-painted tomb figures. Another method of decorating tomb figures during the Tang dynasty was to overpaint monochrome glazes with polychrome pigments and gilt. This practice of overglaze painting is now known to have been in use as early as the late fifth century. Its popularity in the Tang dynasty is shown, for example, by the discovery of 466 figures with this type of adornment in the tomb of Zheng Rentai, who died in 663, in Liquan xian, Shaanxi Province. [3]

"Three-color"–glazed tomb figures. The showy magnificence of light-bodied tomb figures with "three-color" glazes has made them one of the hallmarks of the Tang dynasty. While the horses, dogs, camels, and other animals—which were invariably modeled with the affection the Chinese have always lavished on their representations of animals—were completely covered in polychrome glazes, the faces and hands of supernatural figures and human attendants were usually left unglazed, often to be painted after firing. A commanding group (Color Nos. 5 and 6; Nos. 61 and 62), which is decorated in both "three-color" glazes and pigments, depicts foreigners of Western origin: one tomb official is identifiable as a Uighur Turk; the other three figures all have what has been characterized as a Khotanese physiognomy. This admixture of alien personages with such a characteristically native art form as burial furniture demonstrates the cosmopolitan attitude of China during the Tang period.

It would appear that the production of especially splendid *sancai*-glazed figures was, for the most part, confined to the period known as "high," or "florescent,"

59. FIGURE OF A LADY. Earthenware with white slip and remains of pigments. Height: 16 in. (40.6 cm.). Tang dynasty, ca. 8th century. Gift of Mr. and Mrs. Stanley Herzman, 1979. 1979.108.

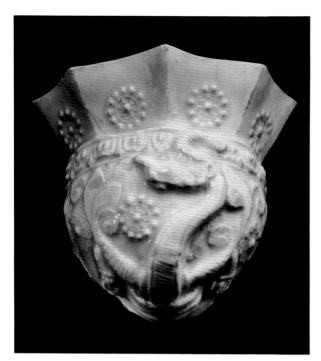

63. RHYTON-TYPE CUP. Porcelaneous ware with relief decoration under clear glaze. Height: 3 1/4 in. (8.3 cm.). Tang dynasty, 7th century or possibly earlier. Rogers Fund, 1924. 24.180.1.

63. RHYTON-TYPE CUP, reverse view.

Tang (about the late seventh–first half of the eighth century). After a rebellion launched by General An Lushan in 755, which was disastrous to the country's economy, especially in the north, the use of sumptuous polychrome-glazed wares declined sharply.

Marbled wares. An ingenious technical accomplishment is seen in another type of earthenware, marbled pottery; apparently it was introduced during the Tang dynasty. The fabric of marbled wares was formed in several ways. Sometimes thin layers of dark brown- and buff-colored clays were folded and twisted together to form bodies with elaborately veined patterns. In another method, these contrasting clays were worked into complex rolls and sliced, much like a jelly roll; several of the rosette-patterned cross sections were then set into the body of an object to form the final design. After the object was fashioned—probably by hand rather than on a wheel, so as not to smudge the clays—it was generally covered with a straw-colored, amber, or green glaze. A "false marble ware" was produced by painting a solid-color body with dark and light slips and then raking them to achieve the marbled effect.

The discovery of some fragments of marbled ware at the Gong xian kilns in Henan Province[4] established at least one place of manufacture for this type of pottery.

Tang high-fired wares. Paralleling the Tang lead-glazed earthenwares were high-fired glazed ceramics; these range from stoneware to porcelain, according to the body composition and the combination of firing time and temperature. Probably the most satisfying of these high-fired wares are the monochromes, which rely on strong forms to speak for themselves with a minimum of further elaboration.

61, 62. TOMB DIGNITARIES. Earthenware with "three-color" glazes and pigments. Height of each: 33 in. (83.8 cm.). Tang dynasty, late 7th–first half 8th century. Rogers Fund, 1911. 11.83.3 and .2.

65. GLOBULAR JAR. Porcelaneous ware with clear glaze.
Height: 7 in. (17.8 cm.). Tang dynasty, 9th century. Gift
of Mrs. Richard E. Linburn, 1977. 1977.388.

4. AMPHORA. Porcelaneous ware with clear glaze.
Height: 13 1/2 in. (34.3 cm.). Tang dynasty, 7th century.
Bequest of Mrs. H. O. Havemeyer, 1929, H. O. Havemeyer
Collection. 29.100.217.

71

White wares. There is a considerable variation in both the style and physical characteristics of the Tang white wares. Some vessels with rather elaborate, low-relief ornamentation show a strong influence of Western metalwork, which was the source of many forms and decorative motifs used by Tang artisans, particularly in the early part of the era. The Western influence seen in the shape of the rhyton-type cup (No. 63), as well as in its beaded medallions, a palmette, and semipalmettes, has been counterbalanced in typically Chinese fashion by a distinctly homegrown dragon. Other Tang white wares, such as the amphora (No. 64) and globular jar (No. 65), are severely plain, their appeal lying entirely in beautiful forms and the smooth flow of uncluttered surfaces. Tang white wares can be either thinly or thickly potted. The bodies have frequently been washed with white slip to provide a background for the clear glaze. This glaze generally is slightly bluish in tone, although sometimes it can look almost dead white; it has often run unevenly to form drops on the side of the vessel.

Two late Tang white bowls (Nos. 66 and 67) are shown with the bottom parts of three other bowls (Nos. 68, 69, and 70). These fragments, which are very similar in potting to the complete examples, were excavated at the late ninth/tenth–century sites of Samarra in present-day Iraq and Nishapur in present-day Iran. They show that the Chinese were manufacturing fine white wares in sufficient quantities to export them to distant lands even at this early date.

Tang porcelain. In all likelihood, porcelain, as it is known in the West, was developed during the Tang period. (There is some difference of opinion among ceramic specialists as to how scrupulously one should apply Western standards when assessing Tang porcelains; therefore, objects called porcelain by one authority are not necessarily considered so by another.) Porcelain bodies are fired at a temperature in excess of about 1250° C., which is sufficient to achieve vitrification: the hardening, tightening, and partial glassification of the clay body. With porcelains that are glazed before firing, there is a reaction in the kiln between the clay body and high-temperature glaze resulting in a bond so close that it is frequently difficult to see where the body stops and the glaze begins. An intimate relationship between the body and glaze occurs in many high-fired glazed stonewares as well, but it is not universal.

Until a short time ago, it was believed that all Chinese porcelains were produced by combining white-burning kaolin, or china clay, with suitable proportions of petuntse, or porcelain stone. Recently, however, laboratory analyses of several categories of Chinese porcelain have revealed that the raw materials used in the production of these porcelains varied considerably among different kiln centers. Furthermore, at certain kiln centers, the composition of porcelain bodies changed over the centuries.[5]

The progression from porcelaneous wares to "true" porcelain—essentially a matter of refinement—probably was a gradual one. Porcelains with hard, dense, impervious, resonant, white, translucent bodies and hard glazes that adhere firmly to the body became a reality when Chinese potters (1) arrived at the proper composition of the body and the glaze and (2) learned to fire their wares at the combination of temperature and time necessary to vitrify the body and fuse the glaze.

Tang white wares have been found at kiln sites in several northern Chinese provinces; the two most notable sites are in Hebei Province. Chinese authorities consider those found in 1980–81 at Qicun in Lincheng xian to be the earlier of the two. They identify products of these kilns as the famous Xing ware described in the *Chajing*, an essay on tea written in the eighth century.[6] White wares were found in a late Tang stratum at the Ding kiln complexes in Jiancicun, Quyang xian, in the early 1960s.[7] These were the forerunners of the classic Ding wares of the Song dynasty.

While white wares have been found in Tang tombs in a number of provinces south of the Yangtze River, identification of the kilns that produced these southern white wares is still in its early stages. Some wares with *rubai* ("milky white," or "cream color") glaze have been found at the Jizhou kilns in Jiangxi Province. According to the archaeological report, these white wares started to be made in the late Tang/Five Dynasties period.[8] White wares have also been excavated at the Tang kiln site at Tongguanzhen, near Changsha, Hunan Province.[9] It is quite possible that much of the Tang white ware found in southern tombs will eventually be matched to kilns in the immediate area.[10]

Yue wares. Relatively little datable material is available to establish firm guideposts for the attribution of Tang Yue celadons until the later part of the dynasty. During the Tang period, the center of production seems to have been a group of kilns in the vicinity of Shanglinhu in Yuyao xian, Zhejiang Province, where at least twenty separate kiln sites have been discovered. These kilns,

66. BOWL WITH CINQUEFOIL MOUTH RIM.
Porcelaneous ware with clear glaze. Diameter: 8 in.
(20.3 cm.). Tang dynasty, 9th century. Rogers Fund, 1917.
18.56.42.

67. BOWL WITH THICK MOUTH RIM. Porcelaneous ware
with clear glaze. Diameter: 4 1/4 in. (10.8 cm.). Tang
dynasty, 9th century. Gift of Mr. and Mrs. James Stein,
1980. 1980.365.

68. (LEFT) FRAGMENT: BOTTOM OF A BOWL WITH
FLARING FOOT. Porcelaneous ware with clear glaze.
Greatest width: 3 1/4 in. (8.3 cm.). Tang dynasty, 9th
century. Excavated at Village Tepe, Nishapur, Iran.
Rogers Fund, 1940. 40.170.456a.

69. (TOP) FRAGMENT: BOTTOM OF A BOWL WITH
WIDE FOOT. Porcelaneous ware with clear glaze.
Greatest width: 2 3/4 in. (7 cm.). Tang dynasty, 9th
century. Excavated at Tepe Madraseh, Nishapur, Iran.
Rogers Fund, 1940. 40.170.456e.

70. FRAGMENT: BOTTOM OF A BOWL WITH WIDE
FOOT. Porcelaneous ware with clear glaze. Greatest
width: 2 3/8 in. (6 cm.). Tang dynasty, 9th century.
Excavated at Samarra, Iraq. Rogers Fund, 1923. 23.75.19.

and those in the region following their lead, catered to a segment of Tang society that appreciated the subtle appeal of honest shapes, either unembellished or with very little decoration, clothed in smooth green glazes. The austere beauty of Yue celadons was evidently admired by the court in the Tang period: "tributes from Yuezhou" are mentioned in historical texts, and finds of Yue wares were made at the site of the Daming Gong, a Tang palace at the capital of Changan.

By and large, what little decoration there is on Tang Yue wares was discreetly executed under the monochrome glaze. On occasion, however, Yue celadons were embellished with bold designs painted in underglaze brown,[11] or they were inlaid with marbled patterns.[12]

Other Tang celadons. Fondness for celadon-glazed wares in the Tang dynasty is well documented: they have been found at kiln complexes outside the primary Yue complex in Zhejiang Province and in many other provinces as well. Regional variations, caused by such factors as the differences in raw materials and methods of production, are observable from area to area. For example, celadons manufactured in Guangdong Province were apparently fired at relatively low temperatures, and as a result their bodies are rather soft and their glazes flake off easily. Celadons excavated from Tang tombs can often be assigned to local kilns found in the same province.

Brown- and black-glazed wares. Among the most dramatic Tang monochrome-glazed stonewares are those with fairly thick, opaque, dark brown or black glazes that seem to add an extra quality of power to already energetic shapes. The tradition of black glazes can be established as early as the Eastern Han period in Zhejiang Province; however, it does not seem to have begun until somewhat later in the north. Tang-dynasty kilns that manufactured brown- or black-glazed wares have principally been excavated in Shaanxi, Henan, and Shandong provinces.

Suffused glazes. An interesting variant of the brown and black monochrome-glazed wares is seen in a group of buff-bodied stonewares with thick, high-fired glazes that are suffused with bold splashes of another glaze in a contrasting color. Generally the background glaze, which can be matte or rather glossy, ranges from brown to black; the varicolored mottles show different shades of cream, gray, blue, and lavender. Occasionally the format is reversed, and the ground is light, either blue or olive green, with suffusions of a darker color. The splashes usually appear to have been applied at random and allowed to run more or less at will over the underlying glaze; but

there are some examples with more-deliberate-looking patterns in which the splashes are well controlled. Tang suffused glazes are exemplified here by the stunning flask (Color No. 7); its unusual shape was based on a leather prototype. Kilns that produced these wares have mainly been excavated in Henan Province, the most notable being those at Huangdao in Jia xian and the Duandian kilns in Lushan xian. Ceramics with suffused glazes were recently found at the Yaozhou kilns at Huangbaozhen, Tongchuan, in Shaanxi Province, as well.

Yellow-glazed wares. For the most part, the tradition of yellow-glazed stonewares seems to have been confined to kilns in northern China during the Tang era: so far, they have been found almost exclusively at kiln sites north of the Yangtze River. The yellow glaze was frequently applied over a coating of white slip; this can be seen in the short-spouted ewer (No. 71). This white slip serves to give the translucent glaze a better final color than it would have if washed directly onto the body.

Other Tang decorations. Free and inventive decorations call attention to other Tang-dynasty stonewares. For example, white wares enlivened with green splashes have been discovered at some kiln sites in the general vicinity of northern Henan and southern Hebei provinces. (Several types of Tang pottery have been found at the same kiln centers in Henan and Hebei provinces that produced some of the large family collectively known as Cizhou ware during the Song dynasty. A few decorative techniques employed by the Song Cizhou potters can be found in this Tang material, and there is little doubt that these Tang wares may be considered direct ancestors of the Song Cizhou pottery.)

At Tang kiln complexes in other areas, such as the Yaozhou group at Huangbaozhen, in Tongchuan, Shaanxi Province, different types of decoration were used. In addition to a considerable number of other kinds of wares, ceramics painted in several different manners[13] have been excavated at these kilns. These Yaozhou kiln complexes are famous for their celadon-glazed wares in the Song period.

Tang blue-and-white wares. Evidence of Tang-dynasty ceramics being painted in cobalt oxide to produce blue designs came to light in 1975, when a fragment of a pillow with blue decoration was excavated at the remains of a Tang city at Yangzhou, Jiangsu Province.[14] In 1983, more blue-and-white fragments that have been attributed to the Tang period were found in the Yangzhou area.[15] A layer of slip was apparently used to coat the bodies of these wares before they were decorated; there is some disagreement as to whether they were painted before or after they were glazed.[16] Analysis of the 1975 fragment has identified the blue pigment as being made from cobalt ore with a low manganese content, indicating that it probably was not native Chinese ore. The body and glaze are similar in composition to wares of the Gong xian kilns in Henan Province,[17] and it is theorized that these early blue-and-white wares were produced in the Henan area.

Changsha pottery. Ceramics produced during the Tang period in the vicinity of modern Changsha, Hunan Province, are slightly different from the general run. These Changsha wares are best known from kiln complexes excavated at Wazhaping and Tongguanzhen.[18] Recent analyses have shown Tang Changsha wares to be made of rather low-grade clay that was not finely prepared; at times the somewhat inferior body was dressed with a layer of slip. Lime was the chief flux used in Changsha glazes, with decorative effects achieved by using either iron or copper oxide; the ceramics were fired at about 1170–1220° C. in a weak reducing atmosphere.[19]

Perhaps to compensate for a lack of quality in their wares as compared with other, more sophisticated, Tang-dynasty ceramics, Changsha potters were extraordinarily inventive in decorating their material. One particularly distinctive group of Tang Changsha glazes, all of which consistently show a tendency toward fine crazing (accidental cracks in the glaze), ranges in tone from almost buff to a yellowish shade to a rather pale yellowish green. While they can be found on otherwise-undecorated vessels, these pale glazes have frequently been applied over impressed or low-relief designs. Sometimes the glazes are splashed with patches of dark brown, a particularly effective technique when the brown has been washed over applied, low-relief medallions. Such a piece is the ewer (Color No. 10), which has three different medallions: a pair of birds in a dense leafy spray, a lion seated on a fringed mat, and a long-haired foreigner holding a stringed instrument. Again, dark brown and dark green splashes are combined. Changsha kilns also produced dark green-glazed and brown-glazed ceramics that sometimes carry relief ornamentation under the glaze. Some white Changsha wares are embellished with different kinds of bluish green (Color No. 9), green, or brown decoration.

Among the most striking Changsha ceramics are those painted with a wide variety of delightfully uninhibited designs in green, brown, and/or blue under a

71. EWER. Stoneware with rouletted decoration under yellow glaze. Height: 6 1/8 in. (15.6 cm.). Tang dynasty, ca. 9th century. Gift of Dr. Paul Singer, 1977. 1977.449.3.

pale glaze. They are represented here by the particularly charming, small quatrefoil dish with a bird perched on a flowering branch (Color No. 8).

Ceramics with splashed glazes or underglaze painting, which are similar to the Changsha wares, have also been found at kiln complexes in Qionglai xian, Sichuan Province.[20]

Exportation of Tang pottery. The size and the importance of Tang China's ceramic industry are suggested by the discovery of various types of Tang pottery at such distant, late ninth/tenth–century sites as Samarra and Ctesiphon in present-day Iraq and Nishapur in present-day Iran. Tang wares have also been excavated on the east coast of Africa as well as at early sites in Egypt and India. In the main, the ceramics found at these sites were Yue-type stonewares and several qualities of white ware. Changsha-type pottery with brown-splashed, appliqué designs and mottled earthenwares similar to the Tang *sancai* types were also exported to the West,[21] although apparently in much smaller quantities than celadons and white wares. Tang "three-color" wares were especially appreciated in Japan and have been excavated there, along with other types of Tang ceramics, in many contemporary sites. All of these finds not only suggest an output of sufficient quantity to supply a widespread export market, in addition to a sizable home market, but they also document the high regard with which Chinese pottery must have been held abroad at this time.

1. Li Zhiyan and Zhang Fukang, "A Discussion on the Technological Aspects of the Three Colored Tang Wares," in *Abstracts*, International Conference on Ancient Chinese Pottery and Porcelain (Shanghai, 1982), p. 18. • Evidence of *sancai* wares being given two firings was found at the Gong xian kilns in Henan Province (Penelope Hughes-Stanton and Rose Kerr, comps., *Kiln Sites of Ancient China: An Exhibition Lent by the People's Republic of China*, exhib. cat. [London and Oxford, 1980], p. 80).• Reports of the 1984–86 excavations at the Yaozhou kilns at Huangbaozhen, Tongchuan, Shaanxi Province, note that the Tang-dynasty *sancai* and low-fired monochrome-glazed wares found at that site had also been fired twice (*Kaogu yu Wenwu*, 1987, no. 1, pp. 15–25. Zuo Zhenxi, ibid., pp. 26–41, 25). These recent Yaozhou excavations are also reported in *Wenwu*, 1987, no. 3, pp. 23–31, 37.

2. For the Gong xian kilns, see Zhongguo Shanghai renmin meishu chubanshe [ZSRMC], ed., *Chūgoku tōji zenshū*, vol. 7, Tang "three-color" (Kyoto, 1983), pls. 140–58. Hughes-Stanton and Kerr, *Kiln Sites*, nos. 367, 368, 371, 372. • For the Yaozhou kilns, see note 1.

3. *Wenwu*, 1972, no. 7, pp. 33–44, and pls. 4:1,3, 10, 11, 12:1,2; figs. 6–8, 15:1,2,5,6, 16–23.

4. Liu Jianzhou, *Zhongyuan Wenwu*, 1981, no. 3, pp. 16–22, and pl. 4:3. Hughes-Stanton and Kerr, *Kiln Sites*, no. 370. • Marbled wares are also briefly mentioned in the report of the recent excavations at the Yaozhou kilns, but no particulars are given (Zuo Zhenxi, *Kaogu yu Wenwu*, 1987, no. 1, pp. 26–41, 25).

5. Nigel Wood, *Oriental Glazes: Their Chemistry, Origins and Re-creation* (London, 1978). Idem, "Chinese Porcelain," *Pottery Quarterly*, vol. 12 (1978), pp. 101–28. M. S. Tite, I. C. Freestone, and M. Bimson, "A Technological Study of Chinese Porcelain of the Yuan Dynasty," *Archaeometry*, vol. 26, pt. 2 (August 1984), pp. 139–54.

6. *Wenwu*, 1981, no. 9, pp. 37–43. Li Huibing, ibid., pp. 44–48. Ye Zhemin, ibid., pp. 49–52.

7. *Kaogu*, 1965, no. 8, pp. 394–412, and pls. 5:5,6, 6:1–5,7,8, 8:1–3,5–7,13, 9:2,5(right),6,8; figs. 6:1,2,5,6,8,9,15,22, 7:1–6,8,10, 8:1,2.

8. *Kaogu*, 1982, no. 5, pp. 481–89.

9. *Kaogu Xuebao*, 1980, no. 1, pp. 67–96.

10. E.g., white wares found in a number of Tang and Five Dynasties tombs in the vicinity of Changsha, Hunan Province, are thought to have been made in the area (Gao Zhixi, *Wenwu*, 1984, no. 1, pp. 84–93).

11. E.g., three objects found in 1980 near Linan xian, Zhejiang Province, in the tomb of Qian Kuan's wife (née Shuiqiu), who died in 901 (Zhejiang sheng wenwu kaogusuo, comp., *Zhejiang sheng wenwu kaogusuo xuekan* [Beijing, 1981], pp. 94–104, and pl. 8:4,5; fig. 2:1–3).

12. E.g., a Yue wrist pillow with a marbled pattern set into the top that was excavated in the 1970s at Ningbo, Zhejiang Province (*Wenwu*, 1976, no. 7, pp. 60–61, and pl. 6:4. This piece is illustrated in color, ZSRMC, *Chūgoku tōji zenshū*, vol. 4, Yue [Kyoto, 1981], pl. 138).

13. *Kaogu yu Wenwu*, 1980, no. 1, pp. 123–32, and pl. 10:3; fig. 2. Hughes-Stanton and Kerr, *Kiln Sites*, no. 438.• Tang-dynasty painted wares—as well as monochrome white, black, and celadon wares; ceramics with suffused glazes; and wares with low-fired "three-color" and monochrome glazes—were found in 1984–86 at these Yaozhou kilns (*Kaogu yu Wenwu*, 1987, no. 1, pp. 15–25. Zuo Zhenxi, ibid., pp. 26–41, 25).

14. *Wenwu*, 1977, no. 9, pp. 16–30, and pl. 2:1.

15. *Wenwu*, 1985, no. 10, pp. 67–71, and color pl.; figs. 1–4. Ibid., pp. 72–76, and fig. 5. Gu Feng and Xu Liangyu, ibid., pp. 77–80, and figs. 1–6.

16. While most archaeological reports describe these wares as being painted in underglaze blue, Gu Feng and Xu Liangyu suggest that the cobalt might have been applied on the glaze rather than under it (*Wenwu*, 1985, no. 10, pp. 77–80).

17. Luo Zongzhen et al., "The Great Significance of the Blue-and-White Porcelain Unearthed from the Ruins of an Ancient City of the Tang Dynasty (A.D. 618–907) in Yangzhou," in *Abstracts* (Shanghai, 1982), p. 32.

18. *Kaogu Xuebao*, 1980, no. 1, pp. 67–96. Hughes-Stanton and Kerr, *Kiln Sites*, nos. 285–301.

19. Zhang Fukang, "A Discussion on the Technological Aspects of Changsha Ware," in *Abstracts*, The Second International Conference on Ancient Chinese Pottery and Porcelain (Beijing, 1985), p. 31.

20. Hughes-Stanton and Kerr, *Kiln Sites*, nos. 302–5.

21. E.g., see Charles K. Wilkinson, *Nishapur: Pottery of the Early Islamic Period* (New York, 1973), pp. 254–58, and nos. 4, 13, 17. Of particular interest is the small, green-and-yellow–glazed medallion of a coiled dragon set into the bottom of a bowl, no. 13. This medallion is very similar to the one on the bottom of a bowl excavated in 1983 at Sanyuanlu, Yangzhou (*Wenwu*, 1985, no. 10, pp. 72–76, and figs. 3, 4).

CHAPTER EIGHT
THE FIVE DYNASTIES

Popular uprisings helped to dissipate the power of the Tang dynasty toward the end of the ninth century and led to the fractionalization of authority and struggles for control. The Tang fell in 907, and China was again plunged into a period of political chaos. From 907 to 960, there were five successive, short-lived dynasties in northern China, while in the south, ten independent kingdoms held sway for part or all of the period. For convenience, these turbulent years are usually referred to as the period of the Five Dynasties.

Despite this civil unrest, the ceramic industry apparently managed to keep some semblance of normalcy, and many fine examples of various wares can be dated to this period. In general, Five Dynasties ceramics might be viewed as bridging the gap between the tastes of the Tang and Song dynasties. They exhibit forms and many decorative elements that are related to those found in one period or the other. Because of the very close relationship of most Five Dynasties ceramics to pottery already discussed or to be discussed later, only two types of Five Dynasties wares will receive special comment.

Yue wares. At the many Yue kiln complexes of northern Zhejiang Province, especially those in the Shanglinhu area of Yuyao xian, the quality of potting peaked during this period; Yue potters produced some of the finest wares in the history of the region. An important part of their output, known as *bise yao* ("prohibited-color ware," or "private-color ware"), was reserved for the exclusive use of the Qian family, the ruling house of the Wu–Yue kingdom. This special *bise yao* is probably represented by one of the great treasures of the Metropolitan's collection, the bowl with a splendidly carved design of three high-spirited dragons under a lustrous, translucent, soft green glaze (Color No. 11 and No. 72). The elegantly shaped ewer (No. 72A) is another illustration of the remarkably fine craftsmanship frequently seen in Five Dynasties Yue ware.

72A. EWER. Stoneware with incised decoration under celadon glaze. Height: 6 1/4 in. (15.9 cm.). Five Dynasties, 10th century. Yue ware. Gift of Dr. and Mrs. Roger G. Gerry, 1979. 1979.502.

72. BOWL. Stoneware with carved and incised design under celadon glaze. Diameter: 10 5/8 in. (27 cm.). Five Dynasties, 10th century. Yue ware. Rogers Fund, 1917. 18.56.36 [also Color No. 11].

White wares. White wares described as belonging to the Five Dynasties period in archaeological reports from the Jiancicun kilns in Quyang xian, Hebei Province, stood midway between the Tang and Song ceramics found at the site. While the potting was a little more refined than that of the Tang wares, the glaze did not yet show the warm ivory tone that distinguishes the Song-dynasty Ding porcelains found at these kilns.

A small, white porcelain globular jar (No. 73) possesses both Tang and Song features and may be attributed to the Five Dynasties period. The inscription *Xin guan* ("new official") is incised on its unglazed base. This inscription, or *Guan* ("official"), has been found on the base of a number of widely varied white ceramics that have been excavated in several provinces. It is likely that a great deal of this *Xin guan*– and *Guan*-marked white pottery is Ding ware, manufactured at the Jiancicun kilns; these kilns are suggested as the provenance of the Metropolitan's globular jar.

Jingdezhen. A number of kilns in the vicinity of the modern city of Jingdezhen in Jiangxi Province were producing both celadons and white wares in the Five Dynasties period. [1] These Jingdezhen kiln complexes were to become the center of Chinese porcelain production during the Yuan dynasty.

73. JAR. Porcelain with incised design under white glaze. Height: 3 3/8 in. (8.6 cm.). Mark: *Xin guan*. Five Dynasties, 10th century. Probably Ding ware. Rogers Fund, 1919. 19.56.2.

1. E.g., the Yangmeiting kilns at Jingdezhen (Penelope Hughes-Stanton and Rose Kerr, comps., *Kiln Sites of Ancient China: An Exhibition Lent by the People's Republic of China*, exhib. cat. [London and Oxford, 1980], nos. 224–26). The Hutian kilns at Jingdezhen (Liu Xinyuan and Bai Kun, *Wenwu*, 1980, no. 11, pp. 39–49, and figs. 22, 23. Liu Xinyuan, ibid., pp. 50–60, and figs. 1, 13, 14).

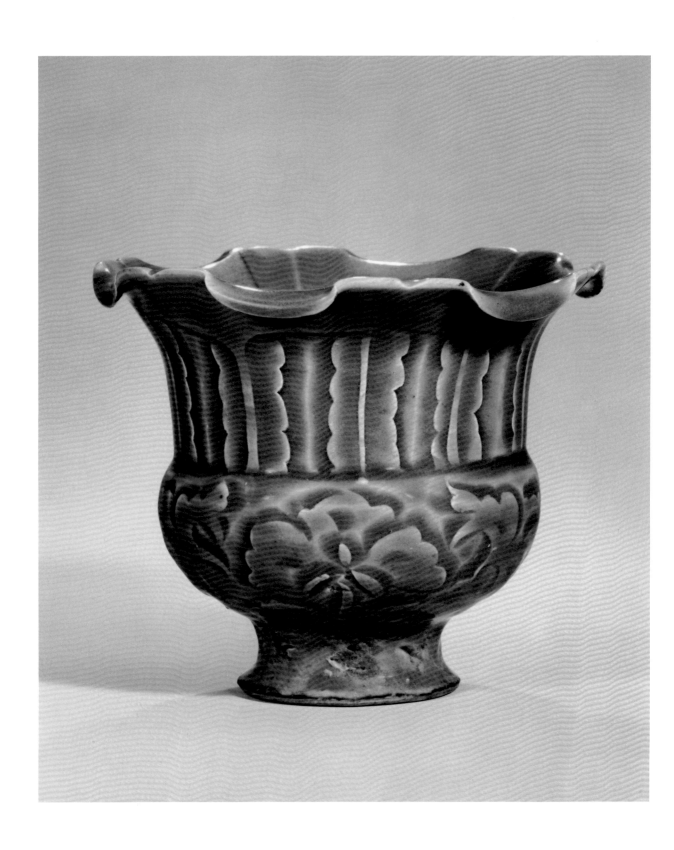

CHAPTER NINE

THE NORTHERN SONG, JIN, AND SOUTHERN SONG DYNASTIES

In 960, the throne of the Later Zhou dynasty in northern China was seized by Zhao Kuangyin, a general who succeeded in establishing a stable government in the north and then moved to conquer most of the south. When he died in 976, the major portion of China had been reunited. The Song dynasty (960–1279) that Zhao Kuangyin founded consisted of two phases. The first was the Northern Song era, from 960 to 1127, when the main provinces of China were united, with the capital at Bianjing, the modern Kaifeng, in Henan Province. During the second phase, the period after 1127, China was again divided. Jurchen Tartars, who had overrun the Liao empire that lay to the north of the Song, also defeated the Northern Song. Most of the northern Chinese provinces, as far south as the Huai River, were then ruled by the Jurchen, who called themselves the Jin dynasty. A son of a former Northern

Song emperor continued the dynasty in Central and South China, with the Southern Song capital firmly established at Linan, the modern Hangzhou, in Zhejiang Province, by 1135. Inevitably, these events influenced the character of ceramics produced throughout the country.

Unlike that of the Tang, which was marked by a considerable absorption of Western influences, the culture of the Song dynasty was essentially introverted. Menacing neighbors at most of China's borders kept the Song fairly well isolated from the West and the stimulus of cultural interchange. Within its borders, however, the country experienced a time of relative peace and tranquillity—purchased, it must be noted, at the cost of extremely heavy tributes. Looking inward for artistic inspiration, the Chinese found it, to a large extent, in a consuming interest in nature, which is mirrored in almost every facet of Song creative endeavor.

The highly aesthetic, placid, and introspective atmosphere of both the Northern and Southern Song periods is reflected in the quiet elegance of those ceramics that are in the classic court taste. Refined forms serve as suitable foils for sensuous glazes that bring to mind the muted tones of nature; designs, when used, seldom intrude

76. VASE. Stoneware with carved decoration under celadon glaze. Diameter: 5 1/4 in. (13.3 cm.). Northern Song dynasty, 11th–12th century. Northern celadon ware. Rogers Fund, 1913. 13.195.2.

74. MOLD (WITH IMPRESSION). Stoneware.
Diameter: 5 1/2 in. (14 cm.). Northern Song dynasty,
11th–12th century. For Northern celadon ware. Gift of
C. T. Loo, 1916. 16.149.1.

but may be investigated at the viewer's leisure. Departing from the polished court tastes, the more common Song wares show the preference of the popular market for stronger colors and bolder decoration, which was executed in a variety of ways.

SONG-DYNASTY KILNS IN NORTHERN CHINA

Northern celadon wares. Grayish-bodied stonewares that form a fairly homogeneous group known generically as Northern celadon wares are usually decorated with bold designs under thin, translucent, deep olive green glazes. Sometimes a layer of light-colored slip has been applied to the body to help enrich the color of the glaze.

Decoration can be incised, combed, carved, mold impressed, or in applied relief; several of these ornamental techniques are frequently combined on one piece. The glaze, which derived its color from iron and titanium oxides, has accumulated in the recessed areas, intensifying in tone and thereby emphasizing the pattern.

A mold for Northern celadon wares (No. 74), shown with an impression taken from it, illustrates a most efficient method of shaping and decorating pottery. Damp clay was pressed against the matrix, which was carved in reverse; the mold helped to shape the vessel and also left a positive imprint of the design in relief on the inside face. After the mold was removed, the design might be touched up by hand; the potter would use a pointed instrument to correct faults in the impression or to further accent various details.

Kiln complexes that produced this ware have been found in at least three northern provinces. The most important one seems to be the nucleus kiln complex at Huangbaozhen, Tongchuan, Shaanxi Province, which in Song times was under the administration of Yaozhou.[1] In quality of potting and decoration, these Yaozhou stonewares are usually superior to Northern celadons produced elsewhere. Although in most cases somewhat inferior to the splendid Yaozhou products, the output of a number of kiln complexes in Henan Province, most notably those in Linru xian, nevertheless was also important.

While a great many Northern celadons can be attributed to the Northern Song period, there are quite a few that differ in shape and design and most likely are products of kilns that continued to operate after the Jurchen established their Jin dynasty in the area. Certain characteristics seen in some other Northern celadon pieces suggest that they may have been manufactured even later, probably during the earlier years of the Mongol occupation of northern China.

Representing a deeply carved type of ware that has recently been found at the Yaozhou kilns, the small jar (No. 75) has a glaze that is much more matte than the usual Northern celadon glaze. A thoroughly enchanting ewer with its splendidly carved design of two phoenixes flying against a conventionalized floral-scroll ground (Color No. 12) epitomizes Northern celadon wares at their finest. The petal-rimmed vase (No. 76) could also have been produced at the Yaozhou kilns.

Jun wares. A point that cannot be stressed too strongly is that the various groups of Chinese ceramics are not bodies of wares in which each piece is a carbon copy of the next and all conform with mechanical precision to a given standard of potting, glaze, decoration, and so on. These ceramic categories are extensive families whose members adhere to a characteristic norm to a greater or lesser degree. It is sometimes found—particularly with certain Song pottery such as the Jun wares to be discussed below—that a pot conforms in most ways to the characteristics of one kind of ware, but has some affinities with a different family as well. Such variances are understandable if one remembers that the manufacture of early Chinese ceramics was not standardized. These wares are the products of an incalculable number of people, who worked at an enormous number of kilns scattered over a vast territory, over a very long period of time.

As noted, Chinese ceramic families are often classified according to what is, or was once thought to be, their place of origin. Thus several types of stonewares with thick, opalescent, light blue glazes, which were primarily made in Henan Province from the Northern Song period onward, are called Jun ware for kilns that were in an area once known as Junzhou. Jun wares vary

75. JAR. Stoneware with carved design under celadon glaze. Height: 4 in. (10.2 cm.). Northern Song dynasty, 11th–12th century. Northern celadon ware. Rogers Fund, 1917. 18.56.68.

widely in quality: there are many differences in the character of the potting, bodies, and glazes. These stonewares were produced at quite a few kiln complexes, the most important of which seem to have been in Linru xian and Yu xian, Henan Province.

The best examples of Jun wares, such as two small bowls (Nos. 77 and 78), have fine-grained, light gray bodies. Such choice Jun vessels illustrate a special serenity often found in Song pottery. Their graceful shapes are simple and well proportioned, and their delicate blue glazes, which are somewhat matte in texture, are as pleasing to the hand as to the eye. High-quality Jun wares like these are generally considered to have been manufactured during the Northern Song period. To date, however, no stonewares of this type from documented Northern Song tombs appear to have been published.[2]

77. BOWL. Stoneware with blue glaze. Diameter: 4 1/8 in. (10.5 cm.). Northern Song dynasty, 11th–12th century. Jun ware. Rogers Fund, 1920. 20.45.

78. BOWL. Stoneware with blue glaze. Diameter: 3 1/4 in. (8.3 cm.). Northern Song dynasty, 11th–12th century. Jun ware. Fletcher Fund, 1924. 24.170.8.

"Splashed Jun." While most earlier Jun wares rely
on chaste monochrome glazes as their sole decoration,
light crimson flushes may be found on a few objects of
late Northern Song date, for example, the lovely covered
jar (No. 79). These timid blushes of color became
increasingly bold during the Jin dynasty. Eventually they
evolved into prominent splashes of crimson or purple—
which were produced by deliberately adding copper to
the glaze—as can be seen on the delightful little "bubble
bowl" (No. 80). Although several kilns that manufactured
these "Splashed Jun" wares have recently been excavated,
most of them in Henan Province, there is little
information as to exactly when they started to be produced.
Of the relatively few excavated tombs containing Jun
ware to be published so far, that of Feng Daozhen, which
is datable to 1265, found in 1958 near Datong, Shanxi

79. COVERED JAR. Stoneware with blue glaze.
Height: 3 7/8 in. (9.8 cm.). Northern Song dynasty,
11th–12th century. Jun ware. Bequest of Mary Stillman
Harkness, 1950. 50.145.314.

80. SMALL BOWL. Stoneware with splashed blue glaze.
Diameter: 3 3/8 in. (8.6 cm.). Probably Jin dynasty,
12th–13th century. "Splashed Jun" ware. Bequest of
Mary Stillman Harkness, 1950. 50.145.316.

81. DISH. Porcelain with incised design under ivory white glaze. Diameter: 10 3/8 in. (26.4 cm.). Northern Song dynasty, 11th–12th century. Ding ware. Gift of Ernest Erickson Foundation, 1985. 1985.214.133.

Province, [3] is one of the most important. This tomb contained eleven pieces of Jun ware, a few of which showed copper splashes in the glaze. [4]

"Green Jun." "Green Jun" ware is a Jun variant. It exhibits the customary Jun body and shapes but is covered in an olive green glaze that is rather bubbly and inclined to craze. "Green Juns" show affinities to two Song ceramic families: Jun and Northern celadons. They have been found at several kiln complexes, most notably those in Linru xian, Henan Province.

Ru wares. According to old literary sources, the very special Ru wares were expressly manufactured for court use. They were made over a period of about twenty years, during the end of the eleventh and the beginning of the twelfth century, at kilns in Ruzhou, the modern Linru xian, Henan Province. Ceramics answering the traditional description of Ru ware are known, but they are exceedingly rare: there are less than forty examples in the West. While they are closely related to the Jun family, these wares have several characteristics that set them apart from other Song products. The potting is quite fine, and there often are three or more distinctive, small oval spur marks, which have been likened to sesame seeds, on the base. A beautiful smooth glaze is greenish blue in tone, and while it may be uncrazed, it usually shows faint crazing or a peculiarly "flaky" quality that resembles cracked ice.

Very recently, material of this type was collected from what the Chinese identify as the Ru-ware kiln site in Henan Province. [5] As yet, the site has not been systematically excavated, and further details of this find can only be awaited with eager anticipation.

Ding wares. The many high-fired white porcelains known as Ding ware are among the most refined of all Song ceramics. These beautifully potted vessels may be quite plain, but they frequently carry well-executed, freely flowing, incised, combed, or carved designs that reflect, or even epitomize, the Song penchant for unobtrusive decoration. Toward the end of the Northern Song period, mold-impressed designs were introduced; these were to become increasingly popular during the Jin era.

Ding wares were usually fired on their unglazed mouth rims, and the bare rims have often been capped with metal bands. They are thinly crafted porcelains with a fine, hard, and resonant white body that generally shows a distinctive orange translucency. The mellow, ivory white glaze has an extremely rich quality, and it characteristically

82. SMALL BOWL. Porcelain with incised design under ivory white glaze. Diameter: 3 1/2 in. (8.9 cm.). Late Northern Song–Jin dynasty, ca. 12th century. Ding ware. Gift of Dr. and Mrs. Roger G. Gerry, 1980. 1980.532.

83. VASE. Porcelaneous ware with reddish brown glaze.
Height: 7 1/4 in. (18.4 cm.). Northern Song dynasty,
11th–12th century. "Red" ("Brown") Ding ware. Fletcher
Fund, 1927. 27.119.16.

84. BOWL. Porcelaneous ware with reddish brown glaze.
Diameter: 4 1/2 in. (11.4 cm.). Northern Song dynasty,
11th–12th century. "Red" ("Brown") Ding ware. Rogers
Fund, 1917. 17.118.21.

85. VASE. Stoneware with sgraffito decoration.
Height: 18 1/2 in. (47 cm.). Northern Song dynasty,
ca. 11th century. Cizhou ware. Gift of Mrs. Samuel T.
Peters, 1926. 26.292.56.

86. PILLOW. Stoneware with sgraffito decoration.
Length: 12 7/8 in. (32.7 cm.). Northern Song dynasty,
ca. 11th century. Cizhou ware. Rogers Fund, 1916.
16.156.1.

87. VASE. Stoneware with sgraffito decoration. Height: 12 in. (30.5 cm.). Northern Song dynasty, 11th–early 12th century. Cizhou ware. Rogers Fund, 1923. 23.54.2.

exhibits small, light khaki-toned streaks that have been likened to tear marks. Recent laboratory analyses have shown that the Ding body seems to have been almost entirely composed of a kaolinitic clay without the addition of any porcelain stone, which is an important component of most true porcelains. Apparently the glaze, which was fired at a very high temperature, lies outside the traditional system of Chinese high-fired glazes.[6]

There is literary evidence that Ding wares were among those ceramics supplied to the Northern Song court. They certainly deserved imperial favor, as is eloquently illustrated here by three very fine porcelains (Color No. 13; Nos. 81 and 82).

Enormous quantities of fragments have been found at the primary Ding kiln complex at Jiancicun, Quyang xian, in Hebei Province. In Song times, this area was administered under Dingzhou, from which Ding porcelains take their name. As mentioned above, recent excavations at these kilns proved that the manufacture of white pottery had begun there by the late Tang dynasty; this was the foundation from which the classic Ding porcelains of the Northern Song and Jin periods eventually evolved.

Black, Brown, Green, and other Ding. In addition to the classic white-glazed Ding wares, among the Song finds at the Jiancicun kiln complexes were fragments of pottery with monochrome black, reddish brown, and green glazes. The vase and small bowl (Nos. 83 and 84), both of which have fine white bodies and russet glazes, are examples of the type alternately described as red, brown, soy sauce–colored, or persimmon red Ding ware. Fragments ornamented in the sgraffito technique—in which the decoration is made by cutting away parts of a surface layer to expose a different-colored ground—have also been discovered at the Ding kilns.[7]

Other northern white wares. A wide variety of other white wares was made in Hebei Province, as well as in a number of other northern Chinese provinces, during the Northern Song and Jin periods. Some are stylistically close to the classic Ding wares, emulating the Ding as nearly as possible within the limits set by local materials and the skills of local potters. For example, some monochrome white members of the Cizhou family, to be discussed shortly, are closely related to the Ding. Others, which vary considerably in quality, can claim kinship only by virtue of their white glazes.

Cizhou wares. The term "Cizhou" is rather loosely used as an all-encompassing name for the popular ceramics that were principally made in northern China during the

Northern Song period, the Jin era, and later. Almost synonymous with the name Cizhou is the robust ornamentation, which has been executed in one of several ways, found on many of these wares.

Painting is frequently seen as a Cizhou decoration; it has often been done with great flair and movement, generally in either brown or black on a white ground. The sgraffito technique has been used in different ways, usually with most arresting results.

Stonewares with high-fired monochrome glazes are also included under the broad Cizhou umbrella. Ceramics with green-splashed or brown-splashed white glazes are members of this group as well.

Monochrome low-fired lead glazes have been used over painted, incised, or sgraffito decoration. Again, two or more of these colored glazes have been applied to wares with incised, carved, impressed, and/or sgraffito designs; this technique was used for the most part on Cizhou ceramic pillows.

Archaeologists have located numerous kiln centers producing Cizhou-type wares, particularly in the vicinity of northern Henan and southern Hebei provinces. Among the latter were several very important kilns in Ci xian, which was known in the Northern Song and Jin periods as Cizhou, from which the entire family takes its name. While the Henan–Hebei kiln complexes might be considered the primary Cizhou kilns, production has also been documented in many other provinces, reaching from Shandong to Ningxia.[8]

Three of the Cizhou objects shown here have been decorated in the sgraffito technique by cutting designs through a layer of thick white slip to reveal the underlying body. On the large vase and pillow (Nos. 85 and 86), some of the incised designs are set against backgrounds of small stamped circles; on another vase (No. 87), the floral motif is set against a striated ground. This vase shows a type of staining that is characteristic of wares found at the site of Julu xian, Hebei Province, a city that was inundated about 1108. The next two vases have also been ornamented in the sgraffito manner, but here a dark-colored slip has been carved away to reveal an underlying white slip that in turn covers the body. A very fine khaki-and-white vase (Color No. 14) resembles a group of Ding wares with similarly colored decoration; unfortunately the neck has been restored on this piece, and its original profile is not known. Part of the glaze on the black-and-white vase (No. 88) is stained in the typical Julu xian manner. Somewhat later in date is the impressive

88. VASE. Stoneware with sgraffito decoration. Height: 12 1/2 in. (31.8 cm.). Northern Song dynasty, 11th–early 12th century. Cizhou ware. Rogers Fund, 1925. 25.65.

pillow with a design of waterfowl in marsh grasses painted in brownish black pigments on a background of heavy white slip (Color No. 15). The mark *Zhang jia zao* ("made by the Zhang family") is impressed on its base. Several groups of pillows with Zhang-family marks are known; the delightful little painted pillow (No. 89) bears the somewhat unusual mark *Zhang da jia zhen*, meaning "pillow [of the] great Zhang family."

Northern dark wares. A group of northern brown- or black-glazed stonewares sometimes classified as "Henan *temmoku*" are, to a large extent, the output of the same kilns that produced the various types of Cizhou wares. Very often these stonewares require no more than plain glazes, either matte reddish brown or fairly glossy black, to dramatize their strong yet simple shapes. Occasionally vertical ribs of applied clay show through the glaze, punctuating the contours of the body. Other decorative

89. PILLOW. Stoneware painted in black on white ground. Length: 11 1/4 in. (28.6 cm.). Mark: *Zhang da jia zhen.* Late Northern Song–Jin dynasty, 12th–13th century. Cizhou ware. Harris Brisbane Dick Fund, 1960. 60.73.2.

90. BOWL. Stoneware with splashed black glaze. Diameter: 7 3/4 in. (19.7 cm.). Northern Song–Jin dynasty, ca. 11th–12th century. Dodge Fund, 1960. 60.81.3.

effects include rust-colored spots or splashes, such as those on the fine bowl (No. 90), or bold, sweeping, rusty brown designs against a lustrous black ground. A somewhat rare type is the oil-spot glaze, illustrated by the winning little bowl (No. 91) that has a black glaze paved with small silvery "bursts."

Wares in a lead-glaze tradition. As has already been seen in one type of Cizhou pottery, the convention of using low-fired glazes with lead oxide as the principal fluxing agent, which reached such a glorious height in Tang polychrome wares, did not die out in subsequent dynasties. Recent discoveries have documented the use of this family of glazes on other types of wares, such as reliquaries and tomb furnishings, during the Song dynasty.[9]

91. SMALL BOWL. Stoneware with oil-spot glaze. Diameter: 3 in. (7.6 cm.). Northern Song dynasty, ca. 11th–12th century. Harris Brisbane Dick Fund, 1960. 60.81.5.

Liuli *glazes*. The Chinese sometimes use the special term *liuli*—most recently translated as "colored glaze"—for several types of low-fired lead glazes in the tradition of the Tang *sancai* ("three-color") glazes. This family of lead glazes ranges from those on the Song reliquaries and tomb furnishings mentioned above through those on the splendidly colored architectural pottery of the Yuan, Ming, and Qing eras. Actually, earlier lead glazes, from the relatively simple green or brown glazes on Han-dynasty tomb pottery through Tang "three-color" glazes, are all *liuli* glazes. In modern Chinese writings, however, the term is usually restricted to the family of multicolored lead glazes of the Song dynasty and later. Recent Chinese publications indicate that these *liuli* glazes were generally applied to prefired bodies and given their own separate firing.

"Northern Guan" ware. Much has been written about a special Guan ("official") ware of the Northern Song period, and there has been considerable speculation as to which of the known or unidentified types of Northern Song ceramics really is the legendary "Northern Guan" ware. Some modern Chinese scholars, quoting old literary sources, say that kilns near the capital of Bianjing, the modern Kaifeng, in Henan Province, manufactured pottery for the exclusive use of the Northern Song court. These scholars feel that inasmuch as these kilns are too deeply buried to be excavated, the character of this special Bianjing "Northern Guan" ware probably will never be known. They also point out that the Ding and Yaozhou kiln complexes, among others, in addition to producing their standard wares, manufactured choice ceramics to be sent to the court during the Northern Song period.[10]

JIN-DYNASTY KILNS IN NORTHERN CHINA

After the fall of the Northern Song dynasty in 1127, many kilns in those northern provinces of China within the domain of the new Jin dynasty (1115–1234) continued their production. To some extent, they maintained the style of the Northern Song; Jin taste, however, which took its inspiration from the Tang and Liao dynasties, may also be seen in these wares. As with the Northern celadons, there are numerous ceramics of northern Chinese provenance that differ from Northern Song

92. PLATE. Porcelain with mold-impressed designs under
     ivory white glaze. Diameter: 8 3/8 in. (21.3 cm.). Jin
     dynasty, 12th–13th century. Ding ware. Rogers Fund,
     1918. 18.69.1.

93. BOWL. Stoneware with crackled greenish blue glaze.
Diameter: 8 1/2 in. (21.6 cm.). Probably Jin dynasty,
12th–13th century. Jun-type ware. Purchase, Mary Griggs
Burke Gift, 1966. 66.89.

examples of the same kind of ware in style, shape, glaze,
decorative motifs, or manner of decoration. These may
be assigned with some confidence to the northern kilns
that were active during the Jin era. Many of these Jin-
dynasty wares display a certain diminution of quality
when compared with Northern Song specimens; this
may be the result of the less exacting standards set by
the Jin rulers.

Ding wares. Several dated molds give stylistic
evidence to support the attribution of a Ding plate
(No. 92) to the Jin portion of the twelfth and thirteenth
centuries. This piece has a mold-impressed design of
deer in pomegranate scrolls that is beautifully detailed
and exceptionally crisp.

Jun wares. A Jun-type bowl of admirable quality
(No. 93) has a crackled glaze that is somewhat greener
in tone than the usual Jun wares. Precise attribution of
this piece is rather difficult; however, it can probably be
dated to the Jin period. The large Jun bowl with a lustrous,
minutely streaked blue glaze (No. 94) and the Jun pillow
with the word *zhen* ("pillow") conspicuously splashed on
the top (No. 95) may be placed in the Jin or early Yuan
period, the late twelfth–thirteenth century.

Cizhou wares. Included in the Cizhou family of
ceramics are many objects with Jin rather than Northern
Song characteristics. For example, the pillow with sgraffito
and mold-impressed decoration under green and yellow
glazes (No. 96) has a floral diaper pattern on the sides,
and a peacock and rock on the back panel. These
decorative elements are similar to those found on stone
wall carvings in Jin-dynasty tombs.

Overglaze polychrome enamels. Near the end of the twelfth century, painting over the glaze in red, yellow, and green enamels was introduced into the Cizhou decorative repertoire. (Enamels basically are glasses that have been colored with metallic oxides; they are fired at low temperatures.) These simple enamel colors were applied to stonewares that had been coated with white slip, glazed, and fired at a temperature high enough to vitrify the body and mature the glaze. After a piece was painted, it was refired at the much lower temperature needed to fuse the enamels. The small bowl decorated with a beehive-shaped peony flower (No. 97) is a thirteenth-century example of this type of decoration. In essence, this new group of painted Cizhou stonewares laid the foundation for centuries of Chinese ceramics decorated in overglaze polychrome enamels. Kilns that produced these wares have been found in at least three provinces, but apparently they constituted a very small percentage of the total ceramic output.

SONG-DYNASTY KILNS IN SOUTHERN CHINA

All of the kilns of the Northern Song and Jin periods discussed so far functioned in the northern part of China. Let us now turn to the products of southern kilns that were active at the same time as these northern factories.

Yue wares. Sometime during the late eleventh or early twelfth century, the long and illustrious tradition of Yue celadon-glazed stonewares in northern Zhejiang Province came to an end. While there is literary evidence of tributes of Yue wares being paid to Northern Song emperors at least until the middle of the eleventh century, the popularity once enjoyed by this noble pottery faded, and wares from kilns in southern Zhejiang Province became more valued.

Zhejiang celadons. A varied family of green-glazed stonewares, represented here by a five-spouted jar that probably has its original cover (No. 98), seems to have been manufactured in Zhejiang Province during the early Northern Song period. Some similar five-spouted jars can be assigned to the Longquan kiln complexes that are discussed below, and others are described as Yue ware in various publications. The exact provenance of the Metropolitan's jar has not yet been established.

Longquan wares. An enormous body of celadon-glazed porcelaneous wares known as Longquan ware, after the district in southwestern Zhejiang Province that was the focus of its production, played an important role in China's ceramic history from as early as the beginning of the Northern Song period until well into the Ming era.[11] Investigations carried out in this part of Zhejiang Province have unveiled literally hundreds of kilns, situated in several different localities, that produced these celadon wares. The densest concentration was at the Dayao and Jincun kiln complexes in Longquan xian. Apparently these were the most productive kilns, and it also would seem that the quality of their output was consistently superior.

Northern Song Longquan. The Northern Song–period celadons excavated at the Longquan kiln complexes showed a marked influence of the popular Yue wares produced in northern Zhejiang Province.[12] These Northern Song Longquan wares were decorated with carved and combed decoration under a translucent green glaze. In all likelihood, the nucleus of activity was in Longquan xian itself, and production must have been considerable: it is reported that one kiln excavated at Jincun in that area could fire twenty to twenty-five thousand pieces at a time.

Southern Song Longquan. By the time the Song dynasty was established in the south in the twelfth century and its capital, Linan, the modern Hangzhou, had become the hub of China's cultural activities, there was a standing tradition of celadon wares at the Longquan kilns. This inheritance was carried to a superb realization under the Southern Song. It is quite probable that the court extended its patronage beyond the local kilns at Hangzhou to those in the Longquan area, and that with this new backing, Longquan potters rapidly developed and refined their wares. Few ceramics are likely to arouse as much admiration as the finest Longquan celadons: they have elegant, simple, and well-proportioned forms sheathed in a wide range of thick, smooth, lustrous green glazes that look and feel like polished jade.

Laboratory analyses conducted in recent years have shown that by the Southern Song period, many of the earlier, high-lime glazes had evolved through glazes with somewhat less lime into lime-alkali–type glazes.[13] This is true of the Longquan celadon glazes. Evidence has been found at some Longquan kilns that these glazes could be applied in a number of layers and fired several times to

94. BOWL. Stoneware with blue glaze. Diameter: 7 1/2 in. (19.1 cm.). Jin–Yuan dynasty, late 12th–13th century. Jun ware. Gift of Mrs. Samuel T. Peters, 1926. 26.292.26.

get the desired deep effect. The body of the highest-quality Longquan ware is fine grained, compact, and of a grayish white tone that shows through the glaze where it runs thin. Apparently these Longquan bodies were made of a pulverized local porcelain stone to which some iron-rich clay might be added.[14]

Decoration on Southern Song Longquan wares is always underplayed: perhaps a few lotus petals carved on the outside of a bowl or dish, or at most a plastic decorative element that is totally appropriate to the piece. This is exemplified here by the beautifully articulated dragon that winds around the shoulder of the jar (No. 99), and by handles in the form of two fish that appear on the superb vase (No. 100).

Kinuta *quality*. Longquan celadons have long been favored by the Japanese, who have named some of the different grades. Prime Southern Song pieces with an exquisite thick glaze that is equally blue and green in

95. PILLOW. Stoneware with blue glaze, showing the
character *zhen* ("pillow"). Length: 12 1/4 in. (31.1 cm.).
Jin–Yuan dynasty, late 12th–13th century. Jun ware.
Gift of Mrs. Samuel T. Peters, 1926. 26.292.40.

tone are called *kinuta* ("mallet") quality, supposedly
after a famous mallet-shaped vase that had this
matchless bluish green glaze color.

Longquan Guan-type wares. Stonewares with dark
bodies and crackled glazes, closely resembling a Guan
("official") ware made at the Jiaotan kilns in Hangzhou,
to be discussed presently, have also been discovered at
kilns in Longquan xian, notably at Dayao and Qikou.

Like the Hangzhou wares, these Longquan ceramics are
quite thinly potted; the bodies of smaller pieces reportedly
can be only one millimeter thick. The glaze, which is
often thicker than the body, was sometimes applied in
very perceptible layers, as it was done at Hangzhou.

Other Longquan wares. Reports of finds at the
Qikou Longquan kiln complex, for one, emphasized the
wide range in both the color and quality of the body, as
well as the broad spectrum of glaze colors, which included
celadon, straw, brown, and black. This again confirms

the assertion that virtually every early Chinese kiln almost always produced a variety of wares. In this context, it is interesting to study a famous kiln waster in the Metropolitan collection (No. 101), which consists of two small bowls that fused together during firing. The outer bowl with a handle is typical, whitish-bodied Longquan celadon ware with an uncracked glaze; the inner one with lobed sides has a dark brown body and a glaze that is liberally crackled in some areas. ("Crackle" is a deliberate effect in the glaze, as opposed to "crazing," which happens accidentally.)

Other celadon kilns. Celadon wares have been found at numerous kiln complexes in other districts of Zhejiang

96. PILLOW. Earthenware with sgraffito and mold-impressed decoration under colored glazes. Length: 14 in. (35.6 cm.). Jin dynasty, 12th–13th century. Cizhou ware. Gift of Mrs. Samuel T. Peters, 1926. 26.292.51.

Province; they have also been excavated, frequently along with black, white, or *qingbai* wares, at kiln sites in Fujian, Guangdong, Guangxi, Hunan, and Jiangxi provinces. A bowl with carved and stippled designs under a yellowish green glaze (No. 102) is very similar to celadon wares excavated in Fujian Province, such as those from the Tongan kiln complexes.

97. BOWL. Stoneware painted in overglaze enamels. Diameter: 7 1/8 in. (18.1 cm.). Jin dynasty, 13th century. Cizhou ware. Gift of Mrs. Samuel T. Peters, 1926. 26.292.64.

104

"Ge" wares. There is a legend concerning two brothers from the Zhang family who had potteries at Liutian, the present Dayao, in Zhejiang Province. The older brother is said to have made celadon wares with a crackled glaze. Some writers today use "Ge" ("elder brother") to refer to almost all Southern Song crackled celadon wares; however, inasmuch as these "Ge"-ware kilns have not yet been located, this generic usage is questionable.

Hangzhou Guan wares. Products of at least two different kilns make up the family of stonewares known as Hangzhou Guan ("official") wares. According to old Chinese texts, after remnants of the Northern Song court moved south and established the new Southern Song capital at Linan, the modern Hangzhou, in Zhejiang Province, wares for the exclusive use of the court were manufactured on orders of the Xiuneisi, the Palace Works Department, in the "back park" of the palace grounds, close to the Phoenix Hill. Ceramic remains have been found near the place where the kilns are said to have been located; however, identification of these fragments as *the* Xiuneisi Guan has been disputed.

A second group of kilns was most likely inaugurated at a somewhat later date at the Jiaotan ("Suburban Altar"), at the foot of Black Turtle Hill. The site of these Jiaotan kilns, which probably manufactured ceramics for the general public as well as the palace, has been found. Material excavated at this site provides a standard by which at least one type of Hangzhou Guan ware may be identified. It is generally assumed in the West that the Xiuneisi Guan wares resembled these Jiaotan wares, although the former may have been of somewhat better quality.

While there is considerable variety in Jiaotan pottery, several features are characteristic of the group as a whole. Most typically ranging from slate gray to almost black, the body is extremely thin; indeed, vessels have sometimes been potted so finely that the body is thinner than the glaze that envelops it. Glaze color seems to vary with every piece: now light buff or shades of pale brown, now soft blue or a light greenish hue, and now bluish or greenish gray. The thick glazes have been applied in

99. JAR AND COVER. Porcelaneous ware with carved and full-relief decoration under celadon glaze. Height with cover: 10 in. (25.4 cm.). Southern Song dynasty, 12th–13th century. Longquan ware. Jar, Rogers Fund, 1918. 18.139.1. Cover, Fletcher Fund, 1934. 34.113.4.

98. COVERED JAR. Stoneware with incised and carved decoration under celadon glaze. Height: 15 1/4 in. (38.7 cm.). Early Northern Song dynasty, 10th–11th century. Fletcher Fund, 1937. 37.124.

many coats; this is evident at the foot, where the effect of these layers has been likened to the lines left on the shore by a receding tide. Tests have shown that Hangzhou Guan glazes are an exceptional type of lime glaze,[15] and that the Jiaotan glazes were applied to prefired bodies.[16] Jiaotan Guan wares usually show a profuse crackle that generally is brownish or blackish in color. This type of Hangzhou Guan ware cannot be better represented than by the superb dish (No. 103), the essence of understatement, with a glaze resembling pale grayish blue polished marble, cobwebbed with broad, light brown crackle.

Similar Guan-type wares continued to be manufactured in the vicinity of Hangzhou after the fall of the Southern Song court. It is assumed that this output continued through the Yuan and into the Ming dynasty; however, the precise date at which production ended is uncertain.

Guan-type wares produced elsewhere. As has been seen, thinly potted, dark-bodied wares closely resembling the Jiaotan type have been found at kiln sites in other areas as well, most notably at the Dayao and Qikou kiln complexes in Longquan xian, Zhejiang Province, which

100. VASE. Porcelaneous ware with relief decoration under celadon glaze. Height: 6 3/4 in. (17.1 cm.). Southern Song dynasty, 12th–13th century. Longquan ware. Bequest of Mary Stillman Harkness, 1950. 50.145.301.

101. KILN WASTER. Porcelaneous ware and stoneware with celadon glazes. Diameter of bottom bowl: 4 1/2 in. (11.4 cm.). Southern Song dynasty, 12th–13th century. Longquan ware. Gift of Mrs. Samuel T. Peters, 1926. 26.292.80.

102. BOWL. Stoneware with carved and stippled decoration under celadon glaze. Diameter: 6 3/4 in. (17.1 cm.). Song dynasty, 960–1279. From Fujian Province. Bequest of Mrs. H. O. Havemeyer, 1929, H. O. Havemeyer Collection. 29.100.368.

were mentioned in connection with Southern Song Longquan celadons. A glaze that has been applied in layers, once thought to be unique to Hangzhou wares, also appears on these dark-bodied Longquan ceramics. These important finds again demonstrate the validity of the principle that each kiln complex manufactured more than one kind of pottery and, conversely, that virtually every kind of pottery was made in more than one kiln.

103. DISH. Stoneware with crackled blue glaze.
Diameter: 8 5/8 in. (21.9 cm.). Southern Song dynasty,
12th–13th century. Hangzhou Guan ware. Fletcher
Fund, 1924. 24.172.1.

Other Hangzhou wares. Excavations at Hangzhou have yielded stonewares that were as finely crafted as Jiaotan Guan ware, but with whitish bodies and bluish green glazes that were usually uncrackled. While some authorities insist that these are products of the Xiuneisi kilns, their exact provenance remains unsettled. If one accepts the thesis that "Guan" wares are many wares from many kilns in the north and the south that provided choice ceramics to the two courts, then one might agree that these particular ceramics found at Hangzhou could be one of the Southern Song Guan wares.

Qingbai wares. *Qingbai* ("bluish white," or "greenish white") is an apt term for a thin, clear glaze, generally of very faint bluish tone, which has a deeper color where it is thick in crevices or has collected in intaglio designs. There is an extensive group of Song-dynasty porcelains with *qingbai* glazes; these wares vary greatly in quality, from exquisite and delicate objects of remarkable thinness to much sturdier works of relatively little aesthetic merit. Bodies of the better *qingbai* porcelains are white and translucent; they generally are fine grained and frequently have a distinctive "sugary" texture. Designs, which may have been incised, combed, carved, or—toward the end of the Southern Song period—mold impressed, show an interesting relationship with those of Ding and Northern celadon wares. (A most engaging aspect of the study of Chinese ceramics is the interrelationship of decorative styles, motifs, and techniques found in different wares. The Song dynasty is especially fruitful in this area: a considerable mutual influence is noticeable in the ornamentation of several Song ceramic families.)

Qingbai-glazed wares were also decorated with iron oxide during the Song dynasty. Some round *qingbai* boxes with brown splashes have been excavated from tombs datable to the Northern Song period in Jiangxi Province.[17] A small head of a Bodhisattva, described as *qingbai* ware painted with black glaze, has been found in Jiangsu Province; it was in a tomb attributed to the early Northern Song era.[18] Fragments of porcelains with brown decoration have been found at some *qingbai* kilns, most notably those in Fujian Province.[19]

Although they are reported to have been found at kilns as far north as Henan Province, *qingbai* porcelains are basically indigenous to southern China. They have been found, frequently along with celadons, white-, and/or black-glazed wares, at kiln sites in almost every province south of the Yangtze River. Jiangxi Province was the major source, and it is probable that kilns in the

104. FIGURE. Porcelain with *qingbai* glaze. Southern Song dynasty. From the tomb of Shi Shengzu (died 1274). Excavated at Quzhou, Zhejiang Province. From *Kaogu*, 1983, no. 11.

105. CUP. Porcelain with bluish-toned glaze. Height: 3 1/8 in. (7.9 cm.). Northern Song dynasty, ca. second half 11th century. *Qingbai* ware. Gift of Mrs. Samuel T. Peters, 1926. 26.292.47.

vicinity of Jingdezhen were responsible for the greatest volume and the best quality.

Technical studies of the raw material used in Song *qingbai* wares manufactured at Jingdezhen have shown that in all probability these porcelains were entirely made of a pulverized, local kaolinized porcelain stone without the addition of china clay, or kaolin. As has been pointed out,[20] the Chinese porcelain industry is based on some "wonderful geological luck." The Chinese porcelain stone, known as petuntse, is volcanic in origin, and this has given it special properties that make it especially well suited to the manufacture of porcelain. (Chinese petuntse is very different from the porcelain stones used in the production of porcelain in the West.) There are some rather exceptional petuntses that are slightly kaolinized and actually contain enough true clay substance so that—after being suitably crushed and washed—they can be used alone to make satisfactory porcelain bodies. Limestone "glaze-ash" was added to this porcelain stone to make the *qingbai* glaze.

In 1974, a small porcelain figure of a seated Guanyin (No. 104) was found in a late Song tomb, which is datable to 1274, in Zhejiang Province.[21] Parts of the figure have been left unglazed, while other areas are covered with *qingbai* glaze. This small ceramic Buddhist sculpture wears applied-relief, beaded jewelry and has other embellishments that relate it, and some analogous Guanyins, to a group of much larger, similarly decorated Buddhist figures traditionally dated to the Yuan dynasty.

It would appear that the *qingbai* family of porcelains was quite long-lived; its manufacture began by the eleventh century and continued uninterruptedly to at least the middle of the fourteenth century.

By an interesting coincidence, two *qingbai* objects, a cup and a vase (Nos. 105 and 106), that came into the Metropolitan's collection together in 1926 have counterparts that were excavated together in 1963. The latter were found in Anhui Province in a Northern Song tomb that can be dated to 1087. Over forty *qingbai* porcelains were found in this tomb; they have been described as having glazes that were white, yellow, or rice

106. VASE. Porcelain with bluish-toned glaze. Height: 15 in. (38.1 cm.). Northern Song dynasty, ca. second half 11th–early 12th century. *Qingbai* ware. Gift of Mrs. Samuel T. Peters, 1926. 26.292.87.

107. PILLOW. Porcelain with incised, carved, and full-relief decoration under bluish-toned glaze. Length: 9 in. (22.9 cm.). Southern Song dynasty, 12th–13th century. *Qingbai* ware. Gift of Mrs. Samuel T. Peters, 1926. 26.292.82.

white, tinged with blue. Many early *qingbai* glazes can be characterized in this manner: at times the bluish tone is so faint that it can only be seen in daylight. In fact, this is true of the glazes on the Metropolitan's two pieces. In the archaeological report, it is suggested that some *qingbai* wares in the Anhui tomb were of local manufacture, and others were produced in the Jingdezhen area.

The pillow (No. 107), a virtuoso piece, was produced at a slightly later date. Its base is a beautifully modeled reclining lady whose elaborately coiffed head rests on her hand. On the surface of the oval pillow itself, there is an incised and combed design of two boys crawling among peonies, which is done in a style especially popular in the Southern Song era.

A kind of *qingbai* ware generally associated with kilns in Fujian Province is represented here by the covered jar with full-relief figures and painted decoration under a greenish-toned glaze (No. 108).

Southern white wares. White wares were manufactured in the southern portion of China as well as in the north during the Song dynasty. A number of these white wares, such as those found at the Jizhou kiln complexes in Jiangxi Province, show a considerable influence of material from northern kilns, particularly the classic Ding porcelains of Hebei Province.

108. COVERED JAR. Porcelain with full-relief decoration and brown painting under greenish-toned glaze. Height: 12 1/4 in. (31.1 cm.). Song dynasty, 960–1279. From Fujian Province. Purchase, Mr. and Mrs. Stanley Herzman Gift, 1985. 1985.218.

109. TEA BOWL. Stoneware with hare's-fur glaze.
Diameter: 5 in. (12.7 cm.). Song dynasty, 960–1279.
Jian ware. Edward C. Moore Collection, Bequest of
Edward C. Moore, 1891. 91.1.226.

Jian wares. Several types of dark-glazed stonewares
were produced in the southern part of China during the
Song dynasty. Perhaps the most striking are the Jian-
ware tea bowls that were made in Fujian Province, a
homogeneous group of vessels with coarse-grained, dark
stoneware bodies. These bowls have lustrous, brownish
black or bluish black glazes that are generally shot through
with brownish streaks, which have been likened to hare's
fur; more rarely, they are marked with mottles resembling
oil spots. One can see how the thick glaze on these bowls
flowed downward when they were in the kiln. It pulled

away from the mouth rim, resulting in a dry, rough edge,
which has usually been capped with a metal rim. On the
inside, the glaze thickened toward the bottom, where it
formed a puddle; outside, it ended above the foot in a
distinctive, heavy, uneven roll that often ran into several
large drops. Jian tea bowls are rather limited in shape;
they range in diameter from a little over three inches to
what has been reported to be almost one foot. The most
common bowl is deep with somewhat rounded sides and
a slight indentation below the mouth rim; a few bowls
with widely flared rims are also known.

Temmoku. A popular designation for these wares is
temmoku, the Japanese pronunciation of Tianmu, the
Chinese name of a mountain in northern Zhejiang
Province. According to tradition, this Tianmushan was

114

the site of a Buddhist temple visited by Japanese Buddhist monks, who obtained these tea bowls and took them back to Japan, where they have always been highly appreciated.

Primary kiln complexes for Jian tea bowls have been located in the vicinity of Shuijizhen in Jianyang xian, in northern Fujian Province. Several other kilns that produced Jian-type wares, sometimes along with celadon-glazed ceramics, have also been found in the same province. The dates of these Jian *temmoku* bowls are rather uncertain. Literary references to them seem to go back as far as the Northern Song period, and what little archaeological evidence there is tends to confirm a Song-dynasty attribution. How long production continued

beyond the Song era is not known. (Of all the old ceramics being copied in The People's Republic of China today, Jian tea bowls are among the most successful reproductions.[22])

A Jian tea bowl (No. 109) is covered inside and out with a thick, lustrous, black glaze patterned with fine, light brown lines; when it catches the light, it shows a beautiful, multicolor surface iridescence. Another tea bowl (No. 110) exhibits the less commonly encountered shape with a widely flaring rim.

Jizhou wares. Some other Song-dynasty dark-glazed stonewares made in the south were the products of the Jizhou kiln complexes at Yonghezhen, near Jian, in Jiangxi Province. These kilns were previously mentioned in connection with Song-dynasty southern white wares.

One of the main creations of the Jizhou kilns was a series of somewhat unrefined but nonetheless charming objects, predominantly tea bowls, that are lightly potted

110. TEA BOWL. Stoneware with hare's-fur glaze. Diameter: 4 5/8 in. (11.7 cm.). Song dynasty, 960–1279. Jian ware. Bequest of Mrs. H. O. Havemeyer, 1929, H. O. Havemeyer Collection. 29.100.226.

111. BOWL. Stoneware with dark reserve designs on lighter
variegated field, tortoise-shell glaze on reverse.
Diameter: 4 3/4 in. (12.1 cm.). Southern Song–Yuan
dynasty, ca. 13th–14th century. Jizhou ware. Bequest of
Mrs. H. O. Havemeyer, 1929, H. O. Havemeyer
Collection. 29.100.222.

112. BOWL. Stoneware with painted decoration on brownish
black glaze. Diameter: 4 3/4 in. (12.1 cm.). Southern
Song–Yuan dynasty, ca. 13th–14th century. Jizhou ware.
Rogers Fund, 1924. 24.100.1.

of rather coarse, buff or grayish buff stoneware. It would
appear that these Jizhou stoneware bodies were entirely
made of a pulverized, local low-grade porcelain stone.
Jizhou dark wares compensate for their lack of finesse
with ingenious decorative effects, all of which are
variations on a basic brown color scheme. The thin glaze,
which can be fairly matte, ranges in tone from brownish
black to deep chocolate brown to yellowish brown. One
of several interesting ornamental devices has been worked
against this background. Sometimes a leaf was used to
make a creamy buff or yellowish imprint against a brownish
black ground. It is probable that paper cutouts were
employed as a resist to produce different patterns in dark
brown that are reserved in a variegated field of lighter
tone (No. 111). Designs were painted in buff or yellowish
slip on a brownish black glaze. Some painted designs,

such as the plum branch and crescent moon on the bowl
(No. 112), could be quite freely executed and have a
marked calligraphic quality. Other motifs, such as one
based on a distinctive spiky scroll (No. 113), were drawn
with more precision.[23]

A frequently seen effect is the so-called tortoise-shell
marking, a dark brown glaze with irregular, yellowish or
somewhat creamy splashes. While it makes a recurrent
appearance on the outside of the types of bowls described
above, it can also be found as the sole ornamentation on
several kinds of vessels, primarily bowls (No. 114), and a
few vases and incense burners.

On other Jizhou wares, decoration has been painted
in brownish black against a cream-colored ground.
Elsewhere, unglazed bodies contrast with brownish black
or white glazes; this effect could have been produced in

116

113. BOWL. Stoneware with painted decoration on dark
brown glaze, tortoise-shell glaze on reverse.
Diameter: 4 3/4 in. (12.1 cm.). Southern Song–Yuan
dynasty, ca. 13th–14th century. Jizhou ware. Purchase,
The B. D. G. Leviton Foundation Gift, 1986. 1986.208.2.

114. BOWL. Stoneware with tortoise-shell glaze.
Diameter: 4 1/4 in. (10.8 cm.). Southern Song–Yuan
dynasty, ca. 13th–14th century. Jizhou ware. Rogers
Fund, 1923. 23.183.1.

several different ways. The strongly potted vase and more
delicate covered box (Nos. 115 and 116) are two especially
fine examples of this type of ornamentation. They display
a branch of flowering plum,[24] one of the most popular
Jizhou motifs.

According to recent archaeological reports, the Jizhou
kilns probably started to operate in the late Tang dynasty
or Five Dynasties period, when pottery with brown, white,
or celadon glazes was manufactured. Production seems to
have peaked during the Song dynasty, by which time a
considerable number of different types of ceramics were
being made, and it continued into the Yuan era.[25]

Other southern dark-glazed wares. Other southern
Chinese kiln complexes also manufactured dark-glazed
stonewares, often along with celadon-, white-, or *qingbai*-
glazed ceramics. One of the more interesting of these is

the Qilizhen kiln group near Ganzhou, Jiangxi Province.[26]
Among the different kinds of wares found at these
Ganzhou kilns were some distinctive jars with incised
lines on a biscuit body, brown glaze, and yellow bosses;
they were quite similar to the one illustrated (No. 117).
This type of jar, sometimes called a rice measure, has
also been found at the Jizhou kiln complexes.

Hunan painted wares. As has been seen, kiln
complexes in Hunan Province are notable for the
innovative decoration they used during the Tang dynasty.
This use of unusual ornamentation was apparently carried
into the Song period at the Hunan potteries. In 1982,
excavations of several kilns in the northeastern part of
the province unearthed ceramics decorated in a number
of different ways. Among them were some striking wares
showing broadly drawn floral designs that have been

115. VASE. Stoneware with reserved, carved, and painted decoration against a brownish black glaze. Height: 8 in. (20.3 cm.). Late Northern–Southern Song dynasty, 12th–13th century. Jizhou ware. Purchase, Lita Annenberg Hazen Charitable Trust Gift, in honor of Cynthia and Leon Polsky, 1985. 1985.87.

118

described as being painted with glaze over a layer of slip or painted with slip under the glaze.[27] While a precise date cannot be given, the archaeological reports ascribe these kilns to the Song and Yuan periods.

Song-dynasty tomb figures. In addition to the archaeological evidence that low-fired, *liuli*-glazed tomb furniture was manufactured during the Song period, there is other evidence to show that some high-fired ceramic tomb material was also produced at this time. For example, in the Jingdezhen area, excavations of several tombs that are datable to the Northern and Southern Song periods have produced a considerable quantity of porcelaneous or porcelain figures.[28] Some of these figures were unglazed and had originally been decorated with colored pigments that have mostly disappeared; others had *qingbai* glazes, and some had been painted with iron-brown under the glaze.

Song blue-and-white wares. Emergent evidence of the production of Song-dynasty blue-and-white wares[29] provides a link between blue-and-white pottery of the Tang dynasty, about which little is known, and the well-documented blue-and-white porcelains of the Yuan period. Fragments of porcelaneous ware decorated in underglaze blue were found in 1957 in the foundations of the Jinsha Pagoda near Longquan xian, Zhejiang Province. When they were pieced together, they formed parts of three different bowls. Analysis of a small particle of cobalt on one of these bowls indicated that a native pigment had been used. There is reason to believe that this find dates to the Northern Song period, probably 977. In 1970, a blue-and-white fragment was found in the foundation of the Huancui Pagoda in Shaoxing xian, also in Zhejiang Province. Inasmuch as the foundation of this pagoda was laid in 1265, the fragment has been attributed to the Southern Song era.

Parts of a small saucer and of a bowl, both painted in blue under a *qingbai*-type glaze, were discovered in 1975 at the Jizhou kiln complexes in Jiangxi Province. There is no precise dating for these fragments; however, they are thought to be native products that were manufactured during the Song dynasty.

116. COVERED BOX. Porcelaneous ware with cut-glaze decoration. Diameter: 3 1/4 in. (8.3 cm.). Southern Song–Yuan dynasty, 13th–14th century. Possibly Jizhou ware. Purchase, Gloria H. Spivak Gift, 1986. 1986.75.4.

2. A large cache of ceramics was excavated in 1976 in Fangcheng xian, Henan Province. Most of these pieces were monochrome glazed, and—judging by the illustrations in the archaeological report—their quality seems to have been very good (*Wenwu*, 1983, no. 3, pp. 92–94, and figs. 2–6). The ceramics have been described as Song-dynasty Jun ware in the report, but there was no firm evidence to support the dating. A flattened-rimmed plate with large areas of dark red splashes in the glaze that would appear to be a Jin-dynasty piece was included in the find (ibid., fig. 1). This plate suggests that the cache was buried during the Jin era rather than in the Northern Song period. • A monochrome-glazed bowl and two dishes excavated in Houma xian, Shanxi Province, and at Yanling, Henan Province, respectively, have been attributed to the Song period; however, no further information is given (Zhongguo Shanghai renmin meishu chubanshe [ZSRMC], ed., *Chūgoku tōji zenshū*, vol. 12, Jun [Kyoto, 1983], pls. 1, 3).

3. *Wenwu*, 1962, no. 10, pp. 34–42, and figs. 7–10.

4. Two of them are illustrated in color, ZSRMC, *Chūgoku tōji zenshū*, vol. 12, Jun, pls. 49, 56.

5. Fragments and kiln equipment were found near Dayingzhen, Baofeng xian, Henan Province. I am most grateful to Fan Dongqing, of the Shanghai Museum, for showing me slides of the material that she collected at the site in November 1986.

1. Penelope Hughes-Stanton and Rose Kerr, comps., *Kiln Sites of Ancient China: An Exhibition Lent by the People's Republic of China*, exhib. cat. (London and Oxford, 1980), nos. 439–45, from the Yaozhou kilns.

117. JAR. Stoneware with incised design on a biscuit body,
      brown glaze, and yellow bosses. Height: 4 in. (10.2 cm.).
      Southern Song–Yuan dynasty, 12th–14th century.
      Possibly Ganzhou ware. Purchase, Mr. and Mrs. Nathan
      L. Halpern Gift, 1986. 1986.208.3.

6. M. S. Tite and I. C. Freestone suggest that the Ding
    bodies were made from sedimentary kaolinitic clays to
    which some feldspar was probably added ("Raw Materials
    Used to Produce Chinese Greenwares and Porcelains," a
    paper read at The Second International Conference on
    Ancient Chinese Pottery and Porcelain, Beijing, 1985
    [forthcoming]). • Nigel Wood notes that Ding glazes are
    low in both calcia and alkalis and relatively rich in
    magnesium oxide ("Rapid Synthesis of Chinese Glazes
    Through Simple Systems," a paper read at the Beijing
    1985 Conference [forthcoming]).

7. E.g., Hughes-Stanton and Kerr, *Kiln Sites*, nos. 337, 339.

8. Among the more interesting kiln complexes that have
    been found in recent years are those that were excavated
    in 1976 at Cicun, in the vicinity of Zibo, Shandong
    Province, where a wide variety of pottery was manufactured
    from the Tang to the Yuan dynasties (*Wenwu*, 1978,
    no. 6, pp. 46–58. Hughes-Stanton and Kerr, *Kiln Sites*,
    nos. 429–37). The ceramics resemble wares produced
    farther to the west, and those manufactured during the
    Song, Jin, and Yuan periods show very close affinities with
    the Cizhou types. • Kilns at Podi, also in the vicinity of
    Zibo, produced similar material (Wenwu bianji weiyuanhui
    [WBW], ed., *Zhongguo gudai yaozhi diaocha fajue baogaoji*
    [Beijing, 1984], pp. 360–73). • In the Ningxia Hui
    Autonomous Region, excavations made in 1983–84
    uncovered kilns in Lingwu xian where Cizhou-type wares
    were manufactured. The kilns have been tentatively
    attributed to the Xi Xia period through the Qing dynasty,
    the most important production taking place during the
    Xi Xia period (*Kaogu*, 1986, no. 1, pp. 51–55).

9. E.g., several elaborate Buddhist reliquaries, some of them carrying inscriptions dated in accordance with 998 and 999, were found in 1966 in the foundations of a Northern Song pagoda in Mi xian, Henan Province. These reliquaries have been decorated in the traditional Tang-style "three-color" glazes (Jin Ge, *Wenwu*, 1972, no. 10, pp. 63–66, and pls. 2, 8). • A considerable number of ceramic figures, models of buildings, and vessels with monochrome or polychrome lead glazes were found in 1978 in the tomb of Li Bin and his wife—both died in 1091—in Liyang xian, Jiangsu Province (*Wenwu*, 1980, no. 5, pp. 34–44, and figs. 3–6, 9–27[left]).

10. Feng Xianming et al., eds., *Zhongguo taoci shi* (Beijing, 1982), pp. 289–91.

11. According to the older archaeological reports, these kilns began to operate during the Five Dynasties period.

12. E.g., Hughes-Stanton and Kerr, *Kiln Sites*, nos. 93, 95, 96.

13. Nigel Wood, *Oriental Glazes: Their Chemistry, Origins and Re-creation* (London, 1978). Li Jiazhi, "The Evolution of Chinese Pottery and Porcelain Technology," in *Ancient Technology to Modern Science*, Ceramics and Civilization, ed. W. D. Kingery, vol. 1 (Columbus, Ohio, 1984), pp. 135–62.
      Nigel Wood has summarized this evolution in Chinese high-fired lime glazes: "At the high-lime extreme the glazes are rich in colouring oxides (iron and titania) and the minor oxides (magnesia, phosphorous pentoxide and manganous oxide). They also tend to be low in silica and below average in alumina, potassa and soda. As the glazes develop towards the low-lime extreme they become richer in silica, alumina and alkalis, and the other oxides decline. The great mass of classic Chinese glazes are found midway in the 'system' and are of the lime-alkali type" ("Rapid Synthesis of Chinese Glazes").

14. Nigel Wood, "The Two International Conferences on Ancient Chinese Pottery and Porcelain," *Transactions of The Oriental Ceramic Society*, vol. 50 (London, 1985–86), pp. 37–57.

15. Wood, *Oriental Glazes*.

16. Chen Xianqiu et al., "A Fundamental Research on Ceramics of Southern Song Altar Guan Ware and Longquan Ge Ware," in *Abstracts*, International Conference on Ancient Chinese Pottery and Porcelain (Shanghai, 1982), p. 45.

17. E.g., a box from a tomb found in 1982 in Ruichang xian, Jiangxi Province; the tomb contained a land deed dated in accordance with 1025 (*Wenwu*, 1986, no. 1, pp. 70–72, and fig. 2). • Two boxes were found in 1966 in Dean xian, Jiangxi Province, in the 1037 tomb of Cai Qing (Peng Shifan and Tang Changpu, *Wenwu*, 1980, no. 5, pp. 28–33, and pl. 4:2).

18. This head was found in a tomb in Lianyungang, Jiangsu Province, in 1982. Inasmuch as the latest coins found in the tomb were dated to the time of the Tianxi emperor, 1017–21, it has been attributed to the early Northern Song period (*Kaogu*, 1987, no. 1, pp. 51–57, and fig. 7 [lower right]).

19. Hughes-Stanton and Kerr, *Kiln Sites*, nos. 118, 119, from the Anxi kilns; no. 163, from the Quanzhou kilns, both in Fujian Province.

20. Nigel Wood, "Chinese Porcelain," *Pottery Quarterly*, vol. 12 (1978), pp. 101–28.

21. This figure was found in the Southern Song tomb of Shi Shengzu, who died in 1274, and his wife (née Yang) at Quzhou, Zhejiang Province (*Kaogu*, 1983, no. 11, pp. 1004–11, 1018, and pl. 6:1). In the archaeological report, the figure has been related to a small, seated Guanyin that is in the Shanghai Museum; this figure is illustrated in color, ZSRMC, *Chūgoku tōji zenshū*, vol. 16, Song and Yuan *qingbai* (Kyoto, 1984), pl. 76. The Shanghai Museum's figure is mostly in the biscuit, with touches of *qingbai* glaze; the remains of red paint can also be seen. Wang Qingzheng, of the Shanghai Museum, reports (in personal correspondence) that there is an ink inscription on the bottom of the figure that dates it in accordance with 1251. • A third figure was excavated in the Beijing area; it has been attributed to the Song period (ibid., pl. 66). It also shows red paint in many of the biscuit areas.

22. E.g., a modern *temmoku* bowl much like the Song-dynasty example illustrated herein (No. 109) is shown, ZSRMC, *Chūgoku tōji zenshū*, vol. 27, Fujian (Kyoto, 1983), pl. 180.

23. The design of flowering plum with crescent moon and the spiky scroll motif are both quite familiar in Yuan-dynasty material; however, they were used at an earlier date as well. E.g., a silver dish and covered vase with these motifs, respectively, were found in the tomb of Zhang Tongzhi's wife (née Zhang), who died in 1199. The tomb was excavated in 1971 in Jiangpu xian, Jiangsu Province (*Wenwu*, 1973, no. 4, pp. 59–66, and figs. 17–19).

24. Mary Gardner Neill, "The Flowering Plum in the Decorative Arts," in Maggie Bickford et al., *Bones of Jade—Soul of Ice: The Flowering Plum in Chinese Art*, exhib. cat. (New Haven, 1985), pp. 193–244 (see especially pp. 198–204).

25. E.g., Hughes-Stanton and Kerr, *Kiln Sites*, nos. 253–79.

26. Xue Qiao and Tang Changpu in *Zhongguo gudai yaozhi*, ed. WBW, 1984, pp. 124–32. Hughes-Stanton and Kerr, *Kiln Sites*, nos. 251, 252.

27. Zhou Shirong et al., *Kaogu*, 1984, no. 10, pp. 915–26, 894, and (from the Yueyang area) figs. 2:1,5,7,10,13,15, 20,22,23,29, 3:2,3,9,10, 4:9,10,19,24,35,36, 5:2,12, 6:1,2. Similar finds have also been reported in *Kaogu*, 1985, no. 3, pp. 241–56; WBW, *Zhongguo gudai yaozhi*, 1984, pp. 251–65; ibid., pp. 266–69.

28. Liu Nianzi discusses some Southern Song figures (*Wenwu*, 1979, no. 4, pp. 23–25).

29. *Wenwu*, 1980, no. 4, pp. 1–3, and pl. 5:1–4. Tang Changpu, ibid., p. 4, and pl. 5:5,6. Feng Xianming, ibid., pp. 5–9.

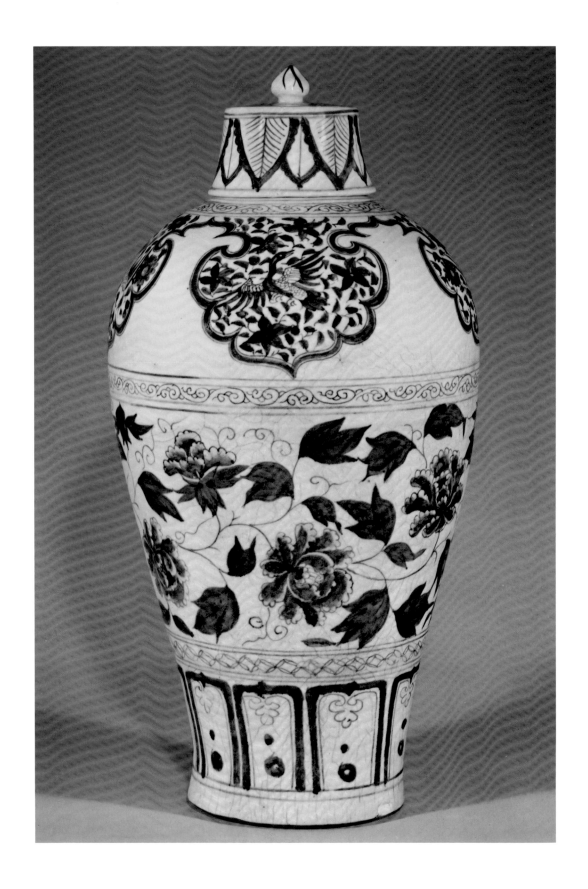

CHAPTER TEN
THE YUAN DYNASTY

I n the thirteenth century, the Mongols, a group of nomadic tribes who had been united into a cohesive entity by Genghis Khan, swept down from the north and, in a somewhat lengthy process, conquered China. They made their first aggressive move against the Jurchen Jin dynasty in 1211–15, but it was not until 1234 that they succeeded in completely overthrowing the Jin to become supreme in northern China. Genghis Khan's grandson, Khubilai Khan, who was proclaimed Great Khan in 1260, began to rule from his new capital at Khanbaligh, or Dadu, the modern Beijing, in 1270. In southern China, however, the Song dynasty resisted Mongolian attacks until 1279, and it is from that year that most Chinese chronicles date the beginning of the Mongol's Yuan dynasty (1279–1368). Under the new regime, China entered a period that was very different from the introverted Song era. It became part of a vast empire extending from Korea to southern Russia and Persia, and it had considerable commerce with distant nations. New ideas, innovations, and cultural influences again flowed into Chinese life.

Most likely, the subtle nuances of Song-style ceramics were completely lost on the Mongols, as well as on many of the foreign merchants whose patronage played a very important part in the manufacture of Yuan wares. Chinese potters under the administration of the "barbarians" began to produce material that would satisfy a new taste for more obvious ornamentation. Numerous elements of design found in Yuan wares can be traced to another dynasty of nomadic origin, the Jin—who, in turn, drew much of their style from the Tang. Near Eastern metalwork also served as a source of new decorative motifs and shapes, which the Yuan potters adopted as their own. Other forms and decorative elements reverted to Chinese archaic bronzes and jades, especially those of the Han era.[1]

Yuan ceramics offer a particularly favorable opportunity to observe the thread of tradition and innovation that runs through the entire fabric of Chinese ceramic history. Preservation of the old along with the constant exploration and testing that leads to the new are among the salient features of virtually all Chinese ceramic development through the ages.

One of the most momentous events affecting the study of Chinese pottery since the publication of the first edition of this book in 1975 was the discovery in

134. COVERED VASE. Porcelain painted in underglaze blue. Height with cover: 17 1/2 in. (44.5 cm.). Late Yuan dynasty, ca. third quarter 14th century. Rogers Fund, 1926. 26.271.1.

118. BOTTLE-SHAPED VASE. Porcelain with incised decoration under bluish-toned glaze. Height: 11 in. (27.9 cm.). Yuan dynasty, ca. late 13th–early 14th century. *Qingbai* ware. Fletcher Fund, 1925. 25.215.6.

1976 of the remains of an early fourteenth-century Chinese merchant ship that sank off the southwestern coast of Korea, near Sinan.[2] The excavation of this Sinan ship has produced one of the largest and most important assemblages of Chinese ceramics ever to be brought to light outside of mainland China. As of September 1982, a total of almost 18,000 articles had been salvaged from what was left of the wooden hull, and close to 16,800 of these objects were pottery. Packing slips found attached to bundles of coins and herbs indicate that a considerable portion of the cargo was destined for Japan. According to these slips, it is reasonably certain that the ill-fated vessel sailed from the modern port of Ningbo, in Zhejiang Province, not long after June 1323. With this established *terminus ad quem*, the relics from the Sinan ship are of paramount documentary importance, a fact reflected in much of the text that follows.

JINGDEZHEN WARES

The late Southern Song/early Yuan period (from about the second half of the thirteenth century through the early decades of the fourteenth century) was a fertile era for experiment and innovation at kilns in the vicinity of Jingdezhen, in the administrative area of Raozhou, in Jiangxi Province. (These Jingdezhen kiln complexes have been particularly well characterized by finds made at the Hutian group of kilns in recent years.[3]) During this time, potters not only added a spate of new kinds of decoration to their repertoire but also changed the raw materials they used to manufacture their porcelains.[4] While the wares produced during this period will be considered under the separate categories of *qingbai*, *shufu*, blue-and-white, red-and-white, and brown-and-white, it should be noted that these five types of porcelain are intimately related to one another. Many objects combine two or more distinguishing characteristics of several wares, and the repeated appearance of the same design components— usually treated in a uniform way—among the five groups of wares further illustrates the interrelationship. Although the Jingdezhen kilns may be considered the principal source of these porcelains, excavations have shown that some of these types were also produced at kiln complexes in other areas.

Qingbai wares. *Qingbai* porcelains of the early Yuan years were a continuation of the tradition of wares with bluish-toned clear glazes that were manufactured during the Southern Song dynasty; indeed, many Yuan *qingbai* pieces show definite affinities to the late Song style and may be considered transitional. As is true with the Song-dynasty wares, Yuan *qingbai* porcelains display a wide variety in the quality of material and potting; generally speaking, however, they are stronger and heavier than their Song forerunners. Studies have shown that *qingbai* porcelains manufactured in the Jingdezhen region were probably produced in two different ways during the Yuan era. The first method was the same as that used during the Song dynasty: both the body and glaze were made of a pulverized kaolinized porcelain stone, with limestone "glaze-ash" added to make the glaze. The second method appears to have involved the use of a somewhat different porcelain stone containing a negligible amount of kaolinite; kaolin (china clay) was added to make the body, and limestone "glaze-ash" was added to make the glaze.[5]

The varied and inventive methods of decoration found in *qingbai* wares of Yuan date testify to the ingenuity of the potters, who did not hesitate to elaborate on their theme by incorporating several enrichments on one object. Designs that have been freely incised, combed, and/or lightly carved are often seen on Yuan *qingbai*; this is illustrated here by the lovely bottle-shaped vase, known as a *yuhuchun ping* (No. 118), with a motif of lotus sprays. More vigorous carving is seen on a *meiping*-shaped vase (No. 119) with an overall design of elaborate spiral scrolls. Mold-impressed patterns are known, and elements such as birds and floral scrolls occasionally appear in applied relief.

Another, and more ornate, kind of garnish, consisting of applied strings of pearl beading or twisted cord, is sometimes found in conjunction with an element that resembles the embroiderer's French knot. Also associated with the beaded-string type of decoration are elaborate relief panels, generally of a floral nature, in applied openwork.

A group of large Buddhist ceramic sculptures is linked to the vessels with appliquéd fillets of beaded relief by the decorative elements, such as ropes of beaded jewelry, that adorn them. The Metropolitan's statue of a Bodhisattva (No. 120), wearing a particularly rich ornament of chains and pendants at its chest and skirt, is such a figure. As was mentioned before, similar but smaller Buddhist figures can now be documented as having been made late in the Southern Song period.

119. VASE. Porcelain with incised and carved design under bluish-toned glaze. Height: 12 3/8 in. (31.4 cm.). Late Southern Song–Yuan dynasty, 13th–first half 14th century. *Qingbai* ware. Rogers Fund, 1923. 23.182.1.

Fully modeled figures that are an integral part of a vessel, such as the lions sculpted in the round that crown the pair of incense burners (Nos. 121 and 122), are another feature of Yuan *qingbai* porcelains. These incense burners also display mold-impressed and carved decoration, and the lions' eyes are punctuated with iron-oxide brown, yet another mark of these wares. Three-dimensional *chi* ("hornless dragons," or "immature dragons") may be used as handles of ewers and cups; they are employed as purely decorative devices as well.[6]

An engaging group of small *qingbai* objects is decorated with iron-brown spots arranged in small groups or scattered individually over the surface (No. 123). The shapes of many of these brown-spotted vessels correspond to those of unspotted *qingbai*, blue-and-white, and red-and-white wares. For the most part, these wares have been excavated in Southeast Asia.

Although kilns in the Jingdezhen area probably were the primary source of Yuan *qingbai* porcelains, wares of a very similar nature were also produced elsewhere in southern China, most notably in Fujian and Guangdong provinces. One very distinctive type of *qingbai* porcelain, represented here by a round covered box (No. 124), has a scroll pattern molded in relief. Comparable material has been excavated at several kiln complexes in Fujian Province.

Shufu wares. Yuan-dynasty *shufu* porcelains—mostly bowls and small dishes—are usually more heavily potted than the *qingbai* wares. They are well made, with fine, hard, white bodies and have a thick, opaque, slightly blue green glaze that is frequently called *luanbai* ("egg white") by the Chinese. Analyses have shown that the *shufu* body was probably made by adding kaolin, or china clay, to a porcelain stone containing a negligible amount of kaolinite; the glaze was most likely made by adding limestone "glaze-ash" to the same porcelain stone.[7] These vessels carry various mold-impressed, low-relief designs on the inside and sometimes have combed or incised decoration on the reverse. Two relief characters are included in the interior composition; they often are *shu* and *fu*, which have been interpreted as "Privy Council." *Shufu* wares take their name from these characters. Combinations of other characters such as *fu* ("happiness"), *lu* ("emoluments"), and *shou* ("longevity") are also found.

Generally the use of the term *shufu* is extended to include a series of kindred wares. While these correspond to the first group in their mold-impressed interior designs and thick, opaque glazes that are faintly touched with blue green, they lack the distinctive relief characters as part of the decoration. The stemcup with a low-relief floral scroll in its cavetto (No. 125) is a fine example of this particular category.

There are a number of objects with glazes that are an intermediate between the translucent *qingbai* and the opaque *shufu*. *Shufu* ware should probably be considered an offshoot of *qingbai* rather than an immediate substitute for it. Both wares appear to have been manufactured simultaneously for a while—and both types of porcelain were found in the above-mentioned wreckage of an early fourteenth-century Chinese ship near Sinan, Korea. However, *shufu* porcelains seem to have survived *qingbai* wares.

Early blue-and-white porcelains. As has been seen, production of blue-and-white wares in China can now be traced as far back as the Tang dynasty, and sporadic evidence carries this tradition through both the Northern and Southern Song periods. In 1978, a *qingbai*-glazed porcelain statuette depicting a seated Guanyin flanked by two attendants was found in Hangzhou, Zhejiang Province, in a Yuan tomb that can probably be dated to 1276 (which was before the official beginning of the Yuan dynasty).[8] Many details on this triptych had been picked out in underglaze blue and underglaze brown. This discovery seems to document the continuation of decoration in both cobalt-blue and iron-brown into the opening years of the Yuan period.

However, it is likely that the significant manufacture of porcelains decorated in underglaze blue in a painterly style did not begin until a little later in the Yuan dynasty, although the actual date is the subject of some debate. Some scholars feel that the absence of any blue-and-white wares in the salvaged cargo of the Chinese ship that sank off the Korean coast in 1323 indicates that porcelains painted in underglaze blue were not yet being manufactured. Other scholars feel that the presence on the ship of analogous *qingbai* and *shufu* wares, as well as a few porcelains painted in either underglaze red or underglaze brown, indicates that there also were contemporary blue-and-white wares. Important evidence supporting the second argument is found in a jar that

120. SEATED BODHISATTVA. Porcelain with relief decoration under bluish-toned glaze. Height: 20 in. (50.8 cm.). Yuan dynasty, late 13th–early 14th century. *Qingbai* ware. Gift of Judge Edgar Bromberger, in memory of his mother, Augusta Bromberger, 1951. 51.166.

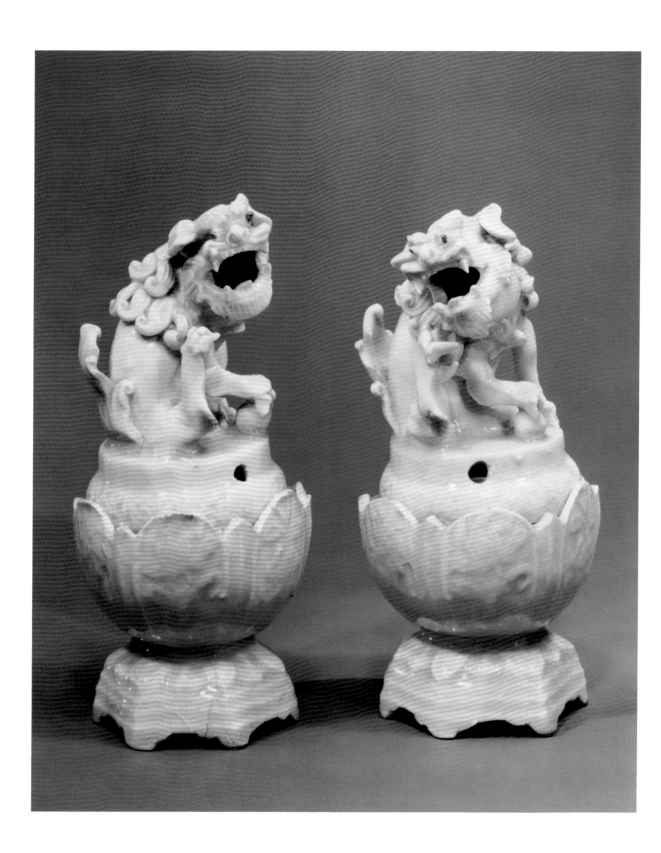

was excavated in 1975 near Jiujiang in Jiangxi Province, from a tomb that can be dated to 1319.[9] This jar (No. 126) has a lid in the shape of a pagoda, relief animal heads at the shoulder, and a freely drawn peony scroll supported by a band of petals painted in underglaze blue on the body.

Future archaeological discoveries will no doubt determine when the technique of painting porcelains in underglaze blue became a major addition to the index of decorative devices. Once they were established, blue-and-white porcelains would claim a position of paramount importance in Chinese ceramic history.

Blue-and-white wares were generally made by painting designs in cobalt oxide on the unbaked body of an object that was then covered with a clear glaze. Subsequently the piece was fired at a temperature in excess of about 1250° C., which was sufficient to vitrify the clay and fuse the glaze. According to analyses of Yuan-dynasty blue-and-white wares from the Jingdezhen kiln center, the bodies were probably fabricated by adding an impure kaolin to a kaolinite-free porcelain stone.[10] The properties of these raw materials made the porcelain bodies easier to throw or mold—as well as to finish and fire—than the earlier Jingdezhen wares. Glazes were most likely made by adding limestone "glaze-ash" to the same porcelain stone.

Several groups of blue-and-white wares may be early examples of the technique; apparently these blue-and-white porcelains are an offshoot of the *qingbai–shufu* tradition. It is difficult to determine the precise dating of these blue-and-white wares or the sequence of their development, either individually or in relation to the *qingbai* and *shufu* porcelains.

The first group, which shows a most obvious link with *shufu* wares, includes some rather good quality stemcups, bowls, and dishes that combine various *shufu*-type, mold-impressed interior designs with rather loosely painted blue motifs on the inside and/or exterior.

Some other blue-and-white wares lack the mold-impressed decoration of the first group, but they still show certain physical and stylistic affinities. The painting

123. COVERED EWER. Porcelain with brown-spotted bluish-toned glaze. Height: 4 1/2 in. (11.4 cm.). Yuan dynasty, ca. first half 14th century. *Qingbai* ware. Anonymous loan. L.1972.77.2.

121, 122. PAIR OF INCENSE BURNERS. Porcelain with brown, low-, and full-relief decoration under bluish-toned glaze. Height: 8 3/4 in. (22.2 cm.). Yuan dynasty, ca. early 14th century. *Qingbai* ware. Fletcher Fund, 1934. 34.113.2 and .3.

124. COVERED BOX. Porcelain with relief decoration under bluish-toned glaze. Diameter: 6 1/8 in. (15.6 cm.). Yuan dynasty, 1279–1368. *Qingbai* ware, from Fujian Province. Gift of Mrs. Stanley Herzman, 1984. 1984.483.2.

on these vessels has frequently been done a bit more carefully than on the others. While this group is generally attributed to the first half of the fourteenth century, it is not certain whether these porcelains were exactly contemporary with the first body of wares or an outgrowth of that type. The *yuhuchun ping* vase and the stemcup (Color Nos. 16 and 17) are two admirable examples of this class; the painting of a ribbon-tied bouquet of aquatic plants inside the stemcup (No. 127) is exceptionally fine.

Another blue-and-white family thought to date to about the first half of the fourteenth century has been found in sizable quantities throughout Southeast Asia. These wares are distinguished by a rather sketchy style of painting; they often show simple floral sprays that might end in a group of buds or berries, and they give the impression of having been decorated in a hurry. This "sketchy-flower" type of drawing can be found on vessels of many different shapes; most of them are rather small and were produced in molds (No. 128). While this blue-and-white group shows a distinct resemblance to *shufu* wares in several respects, many pieces have applied strings of fairly perfunctory pearl beading or small *chi* dragons in relief, two features that also relate the type to the *qingbai* family.

Early red-and-white wares. Underglaze red decoration was produced in the same manner as its counterpart, underglaze blue, with copper oxide being used instead of cobalt oxide. In shape, fabric, and style of decoration, a number of red-and-white porcelains show striking similarities to what is believed to be early blue-and-white wares, suggesting that the two decorative media could have begun about the same time at the Jingdezhen kilns. However, these red-and-white porcelains are by far the rarer of the two types—perhaps because the potters were discouraged by the difficulty in controlling the copper

125. STEMCUP. Porcelain with low-relief decoration under bluish white glaze. Diameter: 5 1/8 in. (13 cm.). Yuan dynasty, 14th century. *Shufu* ware. Fletcher Fund, 1925. 25.222.5.

pigment, which often yielded a rather muddy or gray shade. Indeed, it was not until about the middle of the seventeenth century that Chinese potters were totally successful in mastering the technique of producing underglaze red–painted wares of consistently good color.

An oval plate that is painted in underglaze red (No. 129) has been decorated with a couplet superimposed over two leaves. It was found in 1983 among the remains of the Chinese ship near Sinan, Korea.[11] This plate offers documentary evidence of the existence of red-and-white porcelains by 1323. Four quite extraordinary porcelains decorated in underglaze red or in underglaze red and blue—a pavilion-type storehouse (No. 130), a pagoda-style lidded jar, and two figures of officials—were recently excavated at Jingdezhen, Jiangxi Province.[12] The storehouse and covered jar, both of which carry inscriptions, have been further embellished with full-relief figures and strings of pearl beading. These porcelains were in the tomb of a lady from the Ling family, who died in 1338, and offer valuable information about the dating of Yuan-dynasty porcelains in general and underglaze red wares in particular.

Those more ordinary red-and-white porcelains that are usually attributed to the early decades of the fourteenth century show several kinds of decoration. Sometimes wide bands of red have been washed in to provide a background for reserved designs that can have incised

126. JAR. Porcelain painted in underglaze blue. Yuan dynasty. From a tomb datable to 1319. Excavated near Jiujiang, Jiangxi Province.

127. STEMCUP, INTERIOR VIEW. Porcelain painted in underglaze blue. Diameter: 3 5/8 in. (9.2 cm.). Yuan dynasty, ca. first half 14th century. Gift of Diane and Oscar Schafer, 1986. 1986.97.1 [also Color No. 17].

accents. Other red-and-white wares have been painted in a rather sketchy style (No. 131); they frequently carry the same swiftly drawn, simple floral sprays found in some blue-and-white wares.

Brown-and-white wares. As has been seen, iron oxide was used to decorate *qingbai* porcelains as early as the Northern Song period, and underglaze brown decoration has been found in conjunction with underglaze blue on a statuette that probably dates to the very early Yuan era. Ten dishes painted in iron oxide under the glaze were recovered in 1982 from the wreck of the Chinese ship at Sinan, Korea.[13] They were decorated with a variety of blackish brown floral sprays or animals that were depicted in a rather whimsical style. These porcelain dishes, which are believed to be from the Jingdezhen kiln complexes, demonstrate that iron oxide was being used in a painterly manner before 1323. Yuan-dynasty porcelains painted in underglaze brown are quite rare. A most unusual head with blackish brown decoration (No. 132) comes from a statue of a Buddhist deity; it probably is a late Yuan example of this type of material.

Mid-fourteenth–century blue-and-white wares. Each of a pair of temple vases in the Percival David Foundation of Chinese Art in London (No. 133) is dated in accordance with 1351. With this date, these vases aid us in defining the blue-and-white porcelains of the mid-fourteenth century as an extensive, yet homogeneous,

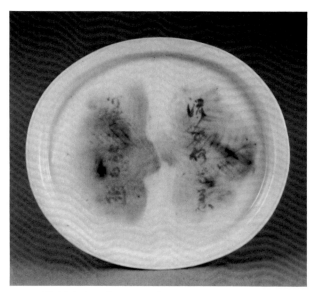

129. PLATE. Porcelain painted in underglaze red. Yuan dynasty. From the remains of a Chinese merchant ship that sank off the coast of Sinan, Korea, in 1323. Courtesy of The National Museum of Korea.

128. JARLET. Porcelain with relief decoration, painted in underglaze blue. Height: 2 3/8 in. (6 cm.). Yuan dynasty, ca. first half 14th century. Anonymous loan. L.1972.77.3.

130. STOREHOUSE. Porcelain painted in underglaze blue
and red. Yuan dynasty. From the tomb of Madam Ling
(died 1338). Excavated at Jingdezhen, Jiangxi Province.

family comprising some of the most dynamic wares in
Chinese ceramic history.[14] Examples in collections today
are mostly large and heavily potted—although a few
extant smaller and lighter pieces suggest that they were
also made but did not survive the rigors of use. The
enthusiastic ornamentation commands attention: the
drawing is sure and spontaneous, and the typically strong
blue color emphasizes a virtuosity of brushwork. The
blue often shows rather blackish flecks, an effect known
as "heaped and piled," which is probably due to the
presence of iron oxide in the cobalt pigment. Many
elements form the fundamental grammar; they are worked
into the overall composition in innumerable combinations
and are distributed within the decorative fields in a highly
individualistic manner. While patterns are customarily
painted in blue on a white ground, some pieces show an
arrangement of white designs reserved against a blue
ground, and in a few cases the white figures have been
executed in low relief against the blue field.

The Metropolitan's *meiping* vase (No. 134) belongs
to this mid-fourteenth–century blue-and-white family.
Its interesting cover, which in all probability is original,
actually is a double lid: inside, there is a hollow conical
projection that fits into the mouth of the vase. Another,
and more spectacular, example is the large plate (Color
No. 18).[15] Here, with unerring strokes of a cobalt-tipped
brush, the artist has managed to portray a mandarin fish
swimming with enormous exuberance among aquatic
plants. Painting of the lotus scroll in the cavetto is
particularly well done; some of the leaves on this scroll
are the very distinctive "spiky" variety that typifies this
group of porcelains.

Blue-glazed wares. Recent excavations in China
have unearthed Yuan porcelains covered in a monochrome
dark blue glaze—which derived its color from cobalt
oxide—and overpainted with gilt designs. There are a
few related porcelains of the same date with dark cobalt-
blue glazes against which white designs, usually in low
relief, stand out most effectively. Because these wares
show an obvious connection with those blue-painted
pieces that have some part of the design carried out in
white reserved against a blue ground, they are assumed
to be of the same period.

131. VASE. Porcelain painted in underglaze red.
Height: 9 1/2 in. (24.1 cm.). Yuan dynasty, ca. first
half 14th century. Seymour Fund, 1970. 1970.214.

Yunnan blue-and-white wares. In addition to the kiln complexes at Jingdezhen, a few kilns in other parts of China also produced blue-and-white wares during the Yuan period. For example, a vase decorated in underglaze blue that was excavated in 1973 from a Yuan-dynasty burial in Yunnan Province has been identified as coming from kilns in Yuxi xian in the same province.[16] This pottery is rather crude in comparison to the wares produced at Jingdezhen.

OTHER YUAN-DYNASTY WARES

Many of the kilns that had flourished during the Song period continued to manufacture pottery during the Yuan dynasty. Like the Jingdezhen kiln complex and its porcelain, these other kilns felt the impact of Mongol rule, a fact that is quite apparent in all of these Yuan ceramics.

Longquan wares. As of September 1982, over 9,600 celadons had been recovered from the hull of the Chinese merchant ship that sank in 1323 near Sinan, Korea. Large quantities of comparable celadons, as well as other types of wares, have been excavated from the remains of Yuan-dynasty docks at Ningbo, Zhejiang Province,[17] from which the ship probably sailed. Others have been found at the site of the Yuan capital of Dadu in Beijing and in several Yuan-dynasty tombs and hoards.[18] Inasmuch as virtually all of these excavated celadons have been assigned to the widespread Longquan kiln complexes in Zhejiang Province, we have a clear picture of the nature of Yuan-dynasty Longquan wares.

These celadons tend to be large and rather heavily potted, although smaller and lighter pieces were also made. The shapes often parallel those of blue-and-white porcelains from the Jingdezhen factories, and designs on the two wares can show considerable similarities as well. The glaze of Yuan Longquan pottery seldom has the blue green tone of the Song wares; rather, it is apt to shade toward olive green.

While the Yuan potters sometimes continued the Song tradition of forthright simplicity in their celadons, using pure glazes as the only adornment (No. 135), much more often they decorated these ceramics heavily to meet prevailing tastes for the elaborate. Old techniques such as incising and carving under the glaze were practiced extensively; underglaze relief decoration, used quite sparingly in the Song era, began to be employed in a lavish manner. A large, baluster-shaped vase (No. 136) is embellished with a low-relief floral scroll that is characteristic of the Yuan period: it is a very "stalky" sort of scroll, with few leaves filling out its undulating stem, and even fewer flowers.

Other types of ornamentation were added to the existing repertoire, and there was no reluctance to combine several decorative devices on one piece. Sets of large pendant rings, suspended from an assortment of small supports or full handles, became quite popular. Another new treatment was to leave relief motifs unglazed so that, sometimes with the aid of a dressing, the unprotected body would turn various shades of brown in the kiln. As can be seen in the early Ming-dynasty basin (Color No. 19), on which three fish swim among aquatic plants, this dry-looking brown biscuit provides an attractive counterpoint to the surrounding lustrous green glaze. Some Longquan celadons of Yuan date have deliberately placed brown splashes in the glaze. These spotted celadons, sometimes known by their Japanese name, *tobi-seiji*, have an obvious relationship to spotted *qingbai* porcelains, illustrating once again the exchange of ideas among various kilns.

Jizhou wares. According to current archaeological reports, production at the Jizhou kiln complexes at Yonghezhen, in Jiangxi Province, peaked during the Southern Song period; however, some ceramics were manufactured at these kilns when they were under Mongol rule. A small Jizhou-ware bottle found on the Sinan ship has been decorated in brown on a buff field; its knobby scroll pattern has been drawn in a particularly tight style.[19] This bottle represents a special variety of Yuan-dynasty Jizhou pottery with a limited list of motifs that are painted in a very compact manner.

"Jinhua Jun" wares. A group of coarse stonewares covered with somewhat crude, opaque, variegated blue glazes was found on the Sinan ship.[20] These wares have been given the name "False Jun" in many recent writings on this find. Consisting for the most part of deep flower pots or tripod bulb bowls that are decorated with a band

132.   HEAD. Porcelain painted in underglaze brown. Height: 7 in. (17.8 cm.). Late Yuan dynasty, 14th century. Gift of Robert E. Tod, 1938. 38.56.9.

133. TEMPLE VASE (ONE OF A PAIR). Porcelain painted in underglaze blue. Yuan dynasty. Dated in accordance with 1351. Courtesy of the Percival David Foundation of Chinese Art, London.

of studs below the mouth rim, these Jun-type stonewares do, indeed, bear a certain resemblance to the class of "Numbered Jun" ware to be discussed below. At the same time, the shapes of many of the blue-glazed vessels that were found on the ship corresponded to those of some Longquan celadons that came from the same wreck. Excavation reports of several kiln complexes that were reinvestigated in 1983 in the vicinity of Jinhua, Zhejiang Province, suggest these were the kiln groups that produced this family of Yuan-dynasty Jun-type stonewares.[21] Inasmuch as the name "False Jun" can be somewhat misleading, perhaps "Jinhua Jun" might be more appropriate for these ceramics.

Fujian lead-glazed wares. An exceptionally fine amber-glazed kendi that was excavated in the Philippines (No. 137) represents an assorted group of earthenware vessels with colored lead glazes that were exported— notably to the Philippines—during the Song and Yuan dynasties. Recent archaeological discoveries indicate that at least some of these ceramics were manufactured at kilns in the vicinity of Quanzhou in Fujian Province.

Yuan-dynasty northern wares. As we have seen, after more than one hundred years of domination by the Jin, the northern part of China came under Mongol control in 1234. Following the Mongol invasion, many kilns in that region appear to have reduced the quality and quantity of their output, while others were forced to cease production entirely. As might be expected, those northern Chinese ceramics that were manufactured in the Yuan era exhibit many decorative treatments taken directly from the earlier Jin wares. They are cast in the same hearty spirit found in the contemporary southern pottery.

Cizhou wares. Cizhou wares of Yuan date can be recommended for their particularly robust qualities. One group, represented here by a bottle (No. 138), is decorated with vigorously carved patterns that have been cut through the thick brownish or blackish glaze to a buff-colored body underneath. For the most part, this type of cut-glaze decoration is associated with kilns in Shanxi Province. While most Westerners date these stonewares to the Yuan period, many Chinese authorities attribute them to the Jin era.

135. VASE. Porcelaneous ware with celadon glaze. Height: 10 1/8 in. (25.7 cm.). Yuan dynasty, 14th century. Longquan ware. Bequest of Mary Stillman Harkness, 1950. 50.145.300.

There are several types of Yuan Cizhou painted wares. The commanding presence of many pots with designs painted in blackish brown on a whitish ground is the result of a free-moving and powerful brushwork that more than compensates for an obvious lack of finesse. This is illustrated here by a jar (No. 139) with sketches of a sage in a landscape, a crane standing on one leg, and a full-faced flower reserved against a striated ground. Painting in overglaze polychrome enamels was a continuation of the technique initiated under the Jin about the end of the twelfth century. The Metropolitan's very handsome jar (No. 140) is painted in both underglaze black and overglaze reddish brown and green enamels.

Turquoise-glazed wares. Some buff-bodied wares with black designs painted under a thin, translucent turquoise glaze began to appear at this time. This type of decoration was a favorite in Islamic ceramics, and it has been suggested that the technique was brought to China when, as parts of the Mongol empire, Persia and China engaged in trade. A reddish-bodied plate with an impressed floral design under the remains of a turquoise glaze was found in 1981 on the Sinan ship,[22] establishing the use of this glaze in China before 1323.

Jun wares. Jun-type stonewares were still fabricated in northern China under the Mongols; however, there was a considerable diminution of quality in comparison with the Jun of the Song and Jin dynasties. Generally speaking, Yuan Jun vessels are thicker and more heavily potted than their progenitors; the shapes can be rather ponderous; and the glazes are poor imitations of those found on the finest Song examples.

"Ma Jun." Several other distinctive types of stonewares in the tradition of the Song blue-glazed Jun seem to fit more comfortably into a later dating, but their precise attribution has yet to be established. One of these is called "Ma Jun," or "soft Jun," and it is easy to identify by the characteristically waxen appearance of its thick blue glaze, which usually is minutely crazed and often is splashed with areas of purple or crimson. Problems of assigning the "Ma Jun" are twofold. Its place of manufacture is unknown, although the Canton area is frequently suggested. Also, its exact dating has not been determined, and many scholars feel "Yuan or later" must suffice for the time being.

"Numbered Jun." There is a special class of Jun stonewares consisting of heavily potted bulb bowls (Nos. 141 and 142), flower pots (No. 143), flower pot stands, and refuse receptacles, all of which are covered with variegated glazes that move from blue through crimson to deep purple. A numeral, ranging from one to ten, is almost always incised on the base or inside the foot under a thin, olive-toned glaze. This number, which probably refers to size, has given these ceramics the designation "Numbered Jun." Some of these "Numbered Jun" wares have an engraved inscription on the base, which appears to have been cut in the eighteenth century; it indicates that the piece was used in an imperial palace.[23]

As of this writing, no examples of "Numbered Jun" ware seem to have been excavated from any tombs. Kiln complexes that produced these ceramics have been located at Juntai and Baguadong in Yu xian, Henan Province.[24] Certain finds at these kilns[25] have convinced Chinese authorities that the "Numbered Jun" wares were manufactured for the court during the late Northern Song period. Many Western scholars, however, prefer to wait until there is further evidence before giving them an attribution as early as Northern Song.

It was mentioned above that a number of coarse, blue-glazed "Jinhua Jun" stonewares were salvaged from the Chinese ship that sank off the coast of Korea in 1323. The shapes of both the "Jinhua Jun" stud-decorated tripod bulb bowls and the deep flower pots that were found closely resemble some "Numbered Jun" wares (Nos. 142 and 143). A "Jinhua Jun"–type deep flower pot that was excavated at the site of the Yuan capital of Dadu in Beijing[26] also looks something like "Numbered Jun" examples. These discoveries would seem to suggest an attribution at least as early as the Yuan dynasty for the "Numbered Jun" wares.

136. VASE. Porcelaneous ware with relief decoration under celadon glaze. Height (the mouth rim has been reduced): 19 1/2 in. (49.5 cm.). Yuan dynasty, 14th century. Longquan ware. Gift of Mrs. Samuel T. Peters, 1926. 26.292.77.

Ding wares. Excavation reports from the Jiancicun kilns in Hebei Province, the principal source of Northern Song and Jin Ding wares, mentioned that a few Yuan porcelains were also found. However, these late Ding wares are of relatively little aesthetic merit, and one must surmise that, for the most part, the Ding kilns were among the casualties of the Mongol invasion.

Northern celadons. Archaeological finds at the Yaozhou kilns of Shaanxi Province have shown that the manufacture of Northern celadon wares probably continued in this area for a little while under the Mongol occupation.

Liuli glazes. Production of colorful, lower-fired *liuli* glazes continued in the Yuan dynasty, as is shown, for example, by an ornate incense burner (No. 144) and several fine examples of architectural pottery that were excavated at the remains of the Mongol capital of Khanbaligh, or Dadu, in Beijing.[27] While *liuli*-glazed wares were manufactured in many areas, it would appear that the kilns in Shanxi Province in particular had a long history of making this pottery and may have been the source of some of the finest examples.

137.   KENDI. Earthenware with amber-colored glaze.
       Height: 7 in. (17.8 cm.). Song/Yuan dynasty,
       ca. 11th–13th century. Gift of Gary and Naomi Graffman,
       1986. 1986.344.

138.   BOTTLE. Stoneware with cut-glaze decoration.
       Height: 8 in. (20.3 cm.). Jin–Yuan dynasty, 13th–14th
       century. Cizhou ware. Rogers Fund, 1917. 18.56.32.

139. JAR. Stoneware painted in brown on a white ground.
      Height: 12 1/4 in. (31.1 cm.). Yuan dynasty,
      ca. 14th century. Cizhou ware. Robert Lehman
      Collection, 1975. 1975.1.1664.

140. JAR. Stoneware painted in underglaze black and
overglaze polychrome enamels. Height: 12 1/2 in.
(31.8 cm.). Yuan dynasty, ca. 14th century. Cizhou ware.
Gift of Mrs. Samuel T. Peters, 1926. 26.292.53.

142. BULB BOWL. Stoneware with blue glaze. Diameter: 9 in. (22.9 cm.). Yuan dynasty, 13th–14th century. "Numbered Jun" ware. Gift of Mrs. Samuel T. Peters, 1926. 26.292.4.

141. BULB BOWL. Stoneware with blue glaze. Diameter: 9 3/4 in. (24.8 cm.). Yuan dynasty, 13th–14th century. "Numbered Jun" ware. Gift of Mrs. Samuel T. Peters, 1926. 26.292.2.

1. Suzanne G. Valenstein, "Some Chinese Celadons Reclaimed from the Sea," *Oriental Art*, n.s. vol. 25 (Spring 1979), pp. 88–102.

2. National Museum of Korea, *Sinan haejŏ munmul* [Special Exhibition of Cultural Relics Found off Sinan Coast], exhib. cat. (Seoul, 1977). The Tokyo National Museum et al., *Sinan kaitei hikiage bunbutsu* [The Sunken Treasures off the Sinan Coast], exhib. cat. (Tokyo, 1983). Committee of International Sinan Symposium [CISS] et al., *Kokusai shinpojūmu Sinan kaitei hikiage bunbutsu* [International Symposium on Cultural Relics Found off Sinan Coast, September 1983] (Nagoya, 1984). Munhwajaekwanliguk, Munhwakongbobu [MM], *Sinan haejŏ yumul*, vols. 1–3 (Seoul, 1981–85).

3. Liu Xinyuan and Bai Kun, *Wenwu*, 1980, no. 11, pp. 39–49. Liu Xinyuan, ibid., pp. 50–60. Penelope Hughes-Stanton and Rose Kerr, comps., *Kiln Sites of Ancient China: An Exhibition Lent by the People's Republic of China*, exhib. cat. (London and Oxford, 1980), nos. 233–42, 244–50.

4. M. S. Tite, I. C. Freestone, and M. Bimson, "A Technological Study of Chinese Porcelain of the Yuan Dynasty," *Archaeometry*, vol. 26, pt. 2 (August 1984), pp. 139–54. M. S. Tite and I. C. Freestone, "Raw Materials Used to Produce Chinese Greenwares and Porcelains," a paper read at The Second International Conference on Ancient Chinese Pottery and Porcelain, Beijing, 1985 (forthcoming). John Carswell, Edward A. Maser, and Jean McClure Mudge, *Blue and White: Chinese Porcelain and Its Impact on the Western World*, exhib. cat. (Chicago, 1985), pp. 18–21.

5. Tite, Freestone, and Bimson, "Chinese Porcelain of the Yuan Dynasty."

6. These *chi* dragons can be found as embellishments on Western Han–dynasty jade ornaments, e.g., those found in 1977 in a tomb near Juye xian, Shandong Province (*Kaogu Xuebao*, 1983, no. 4, pp. 471–99, and fig. 12:4[top], 5[top],7,8).

7. Tite, Freestone, and Bimson, "Chinese Porcelain of the Yuan Dynasty."

8. According to Feng Xianming, the tomb can be dated to the 13th year of the first Yuan Zhiyuan reign, or 1276 (*Wenwu*, 1980, no. 4, pp. 5–9). This statuette is illustrated, *Sekai tōji zenshū* [Ceramic Art of the World], vol. 13, *Liao, Chin and Yüan Dynasties* (Tokyo, 1981), figs. 168, 169.

9. *Wenwu*, 1981, no. 1, p. 83, and pl. 9:1.

10. Tite, Freestone, and Bimson, "Chinese Porcelain of the Yuan Dynasty."

11. Mary Ann Rogers, "Cultural Relics Found off the Sinan Coast," *Orientations*, vol. 14 (December 1983), pp. 32–40. Feng Xianming, *Gugong Bowuyuan Yuankan*, 1985, no. 3, pp. 112–18, 121, and fig. 9. MM, *Sinan haejŏ yumul*, vol. 3, color pl. 73.

12. Feng Xianming, "Red-glazed and Underglaze-red Porcelain of the Yuan Dynasty," *Orientations*, vol. 16 (July 1985), pp. 44–48, and figs. 4–6. *Wenwu*, 1981, no. 11, pp. 72–74, and pl. 1; figs. 1–4.

143. FLOWER POT. Stoneware with blue glaze.
Diameter: 10 1/8 in. (25.7 cm.). Yuan dynasty,
13th–14th century. "Numbered Jun" ware. Rogers Fund,
1916. 16.14.1.

13. CISS et al., *International Symposium*, 1984, color pls. 1, 2. Feng Xianming, *Gugong Bowuyuan Yuankan*, 1985, no. 3, pp. 112–18, 121, and fig. 10. Nine of these dishes are illustrated, MM, *Sinan haejŏ yumul*, vol. 3, color pls. 80–85.

14. Further evidence for dating this group of wares comes from a large number of broken porcelains found in 1960 at the ruins of the Kotla Fīrūzshāh palace in Delhi, India, that was destroyed in 1398 (Ellen S. Smart, "Fourteenth Century Chinese Porcelain from a Tughlaq Palace in Delhi," *Transactions of The Oriental Ceramic Society*, vol. 41 [London, 1975–77], pp. 199–230).

15. The rim of this plate has been repaired. According to Richard Stone, of the Metropolitan Museum's Objects Conservation Department, the composition of the body in both the plate itself and the restored section, as well as the surface composition of the glaze on both parts, respectively, are essentially identical. This would suggest that the restoration is coeval with the original plate.

16. Hughes-Stanton and Kerr, *Kiln Sites*, no. 319; see also ibid., nos. 316–18, 320.

17. Zhejiang sheng wenwu kaogusuo, comp., *Zhejiang sheng wenwu kaogusuo xuekan* (Beijing, 1981), pp. 105–29, and pl. 12:2–9; figs. 13–15, 20–22.

18. See Li Dejin et al., *Kaogu Xuebao*, 1979, no. 2, pp. 245–54 for a comparison of ceramics from the Sinan ship with other excavated Yuan-dynasty material.

19. National Museum of Korea, *Cultural Relics Found off Sinan Coast*, no. 222.

20. Ibid., nos. 239–45, 347–51.

21. Gong Chang, *Wenwu*, 1984, no. 12, pp. 45–50.

22. MM, *Sinan haejŏ yumul*, vol. 3, color pl. 93(top).

23. E.g., see plate 79 of the first edition of this book.

24. *Wenwu*, 1975, no. 6, pp. 57–63.

25. A ceramic mold for making coins that is marked *Xuanhe yuan bao* (Xuanhe was the reign title of the emperor Huizong from 1119 through 1125) was excavated at the kiln site (Zhongguo Shanghai renmin meishu chubanshe, ed., *Chūgoku tōji zenshū*, vol. 12, Jun [Kyoto, 1983], pl. 152). A fragment with the inscription *Feng Hua*, the name of a Song-dynasty palace, was also found at the kilns (ibid., p. 149, n. 8).

26. CISS et al., *International Symposium*, 1984, p. 30, fig. 5.

27. Zhang Ning, *Kaogu*, 1972, no. 6, pp. 25–31, 58, and pls. 6:2, 10:1,3.

144. INCENSE BURNER. Earthenware with *liuli* glazes. Yuan dynasty, 1279–1368. Excavated from the remains of the Mongol capital in Beijing. From *Historical Relics Unearthed in New China*, 1972.

145. PLATE. Porcelain painted in underglaze blue.
Diameter: 14 7/8 in. (37.8 cm.). Ming dynasty, early
15th century. Gift of Mrs. Richard E. Linburn, 1978.
1978.149.

THE MING DYNASTY

Primarily due to fratricidal struggles within the Mongol clan, the Yuan dynasty deteriorated in the second quarter of the fourteenth century. After a period of widespread insurrection, the Mongols were overthrown by Zhu Yuanzhang, a Chinese rebel leader who seized Nanjing in 1356, took the Mongol capital of Khanbaligh, or Dadu, in 1368, and by 1382 had consolidated all of China proper. Keeping Nanjing as his capital, Zhu Yuanzhang established the native Ming dynasty in 1368, taking the reign title of "Hongwu." His son, whose reign title was "Yongle," started plans in 1406 for a new capital on the site of Khanbaligh, or Dadu, which was extensively rebuilt and became the Ming capital of Beijing in 1421. Much of the glorious city that the Yongle emperor erected still stands to be admired today.

The porcelains of the Ming dynasty (1368–1644) have attained such recognition in the West that the word "Ming" has almost become a generic term for anything ceramic fabricated in China before the twentieth century. Unhappily, much of the pottery called Ming has no possible claim to that much-misapplied attribution.

Porcelains that were produced in that period, however, are some of the most beautiful and exciting wares in all of China's ceramic history.

Kilns at Jingdezhen, in Jiangxi Province, and in the surrounding area, had formed a most important center of manufacture during the Yuan dynasty. This ceramic metropolis became paramount in the Ming era, overshadowing all other kiln complexes, as it has continued to do until the present day. Inasmuch as most Ming and Qing porcelains came from these kilns, it does not serve much purpose to classify porcelains of these periods by place of origin, as is done with earlier wares. Therefore, Ming and Qing porcelains, which are assumed to be from Jingdezhen unless otherwise noted, are usually categorized according to the reign of the emperor in which they were produced.

The theme of tradition and innovation in Chinese ceramics that had been sustained since primeval times is especially apparent in Ming wares. Porcelains painted in underglaze cobalt-blue, a legacy from the Yuan period, were developed and refined into the exquisite blue-and-white wares for which this period is so justly famous.

Ornamental techniques such as painting in overglaze enamels, seen earlier on other wares, were used in the Ming era on fine porcelain bodies; underglaze blue and overglaze polychrome enamels were combined to form a totally new school of decoration.

THE LATE FOURTEENTH CENTURY

Sharp lines marking political shifts in China's history are not reflected in patterns of change in its ceramics, where the evolution in both physical qualities and style almost always occurred by degrees. Therefore, it is understandable that two families of porcelains dating to the Ming portion of the late fourteenth century are similar in many ways to mid-fourteenth–century Yuan wares. However, both types of Ming wares are as strongly affiliated with early fifteenth-century porcelains as they are with mid-fourteenth–century wares, and can be regarded as intermediate between the two.

Red-and-white and blue-and-white wares. The first of these fourteenth-century Ming groups is fairly sizable, comprising a miscellany of vessels painted in underglaze copper-red or in underglaze cobalt-blue. Although these porcelains have retained most mid-fourteenth–century features in their potting, the style of decoration has undergone subtle changes that set them slightly apart from the somewhat earlier wares. The copper pigment that was used in the red-and-white wares was still difficult to control and tended to turn rather gray or brown in the kiln. Therefore, the exceptionally good color of a large bowl (Color No. 20) makes it a notably fine example of this group.

Dragon-and-cloud motif. A fugal theme of dragons with clouds runs through the entire span of Ming porcelains. It makes its debut in a group of fourteenth-century Ming wares that carry a design of three separate clouds or a cloud formation incised or painted in the center, surrounded by two low-relief five-claw dragons. This last feature connects these wares to some *shufu* and blue-and-white stemcups with low-relief dragons that were made during the Yuan portion of the fourteenth century. Some late fourteenth-century porcelains with the dragon-and-cloud motif are painted in underglaze blue, and at least one example with overglaze red enamel is known. The design can also be found on objects with high-fired monochrome glazes: there are white glazes

146. VASE. Porcelain with dark blue glaze. Height: 13 in. (33 cm.). Ming dynasty, early 15th century. Rogers Fund, 1925. 25.13.

(actually, a clear glaze that allows the color of the body to show through); old-rose glazes; dark blue glazes; and combinations of blue and dark brown, brown and white, or red and blue glazes. These glazes derived their color from metallic oxides: the red glaze from copper, blue from cobalt, and brown from iron. Fragments of porcelain with the dragon-and-cloud motif executed in several of these various techniques were found in 1964 in the vicinity of the Ming imperial palace at Nanjing; they have been attributed to the Hongwu period in the excavation reports. [1]

Overglaze enamels. On one of the porcelain fragments found at the Nanjing palace site, the dragon-

147. BRICK. Porcelain with white glaze. Length: 10 1/2 in. (26.7 cm.). Ming dynasty, ca. 1412–30. From the Porcelain Pagoda in Nanjing. Gift of E. J. Smithers, 1889. 89.7d.

148. ARCHITECTURAL TILE. Stoneware with white, yellow, brown, and green glazes. Length: 13 in. (33 cm.). Ming dynasty, ca. 1412–30. Probably from the Porcelain Pagoda in Nanjing. Purchase by subscription, 1879. 79.2.789.

150. BOWL. Porcelain painted in underglaze blue. Diameter: 11 1/4 in. (28.6 cm.). Ming dynasty, Xuande mark and period, 1426–35. Gift of Mrs. Richard E. Linburn, 1982. 1982.294.

and-cloud motif has been drawn in overglaze iron-red enamel.[2] As we have seen, overglaze enamel painting was used on ceramics with stoneware bodies at the Cizhou kilns by about the end of the twelfth century. These Cizhou enamels were painted over the glaze of a previously slipped, glazed, and fired vessel that was then refired at a lower temperature to fuse the enamels. The technique of painting porcelains with overglaze enamels seems to have begun to be used at the Jingdezhen kiln complexes during

the fourteenth century. Once this ornamental process was established at Jingdezhen, it became an all-important factor in the decorative repertoire, eventually overshadowing everything else that these kilns produced.

Perhaps it might be well to explain the technique of producing these overglaze enamel–decorated porcelains. As has already been noted, an enamel—in essence a glass colored with a metallic oxide—fuses at much lower temperatures than those required to develop high-fired glazed porcelain. Therefore, at least two firings were always required for porcelains decorated with overglaze enamels: the first at a temperature in excess of about

149. DISH. Porcelain painted in underglaze blue. Diameter: 8 1/8 in. (20.6 cm.). Ming dynasty, Xuande mark and period, 1426–35. Gift of Mrs. Richard E. Linburn, in memory of Richard E. Linburn, 1975. 1975.99.

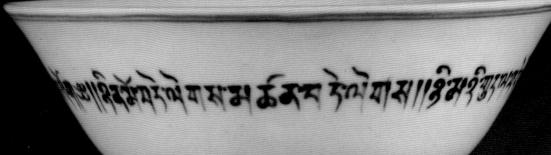

1250° C., which vitrified the body and fused the glaze, and the second at much lower heat to fuse the enamels.

THE EARLY FIFTEENTH CENTURY

There is an air of refinement about porcelains of the early fifteenth century—the era encompassing the reigns of the Yongle (1403–24), Hongxi (1425), and Xuande (1426–35) emperors—that distinguishes them from the somewhat heartier wares of the middle and late fourteenth century. Potting techniques had been further refined: the body is white, fine grained, and wonderfully smooth to the touch. Showing a characteristic surface unevenness that, appropriately, has been compared with the peel of an orange, the thick and brilliant glaze has an especially rich quality.

A general reduction of decorative elements and a corresponding emphasis on the large principal motif give blue-and-white wares a new sense of formality (No. 145). The blue is intense and resonant; however, although the cobalt was carefully prepared, it still shows occasional "heaped-and-piled" spots, which are probably due to the presence of iron oxide in the cobalt pigment. Although perhaps regarded as an imperfection by the potter, these spots, for us, add a fillip of interest to the piece.

Reign marks. Inscribing porcelains with the reign title of the incumbent emperor (the *nianhao*) does not seem to have been widely practiced in the Yongle period, for objects with a genuine Yongle mark are uncommon. Reign marks became more popular in the Xuande era and later, and such a mark can be helpful in dating the later porcelains—assuming, of course, that the mark is not apocryphal. In considering vessels manufactured during the reigns of consecutive Ming or Qing emperors, it can be difficult to assign a piece to one or the other specific regime without the documentation of this reign mark. Consequently, when the rule of a particular emperor is mentioned in conjunction with an unmarked porcelain here, this attribution can be considered somewhat conditional; precise reign designations are reserved for those objects carrying the proper indicia.

151. STEMBOWL. Porcelain painted in underglaze blue and with *anhua* decoration. Diameter: 6 5/8 in. (16.8 cm.). Ming dynasty, Xuande mark and period, 1426–35. Gift of Mrs. Stanley Herzman, 1984. 1984.483.1.

Late in 1982, what has been identified as part of an imperial kiln site was excavated in the city of Jingdezhen.[3] This extremely important discovery has provided a considerable amount of valuable new information about early fifteenth-century porcelains. Among the finds were broken porcelains with Yongle and Xuande reign marks, as well as unmarked material that has been attributed to these two periods.

Yongle blue-and-white wares. Very few Yongle-marked blue-and-white vessels have any serious claim to authenticity, and it is somewhat difficult to separate the blue-painted porcelains produced during this reign—which by and large do not have a *nianhao*—from those of the Xuande era that are not marked.

Yongle monochromes. Many monochrome white porcelains of the early fifteenth century repeat the shapes of contemporary blue-and-white vessels and copy the blue designs in incising or low relief. Frequently the design has been executed as *anhua* ("secret decoration," or "hidden decoration") that is almost invisible unless the object is held to the light. Most of the porcelains found at the imperial kiln site in Jingdezhen that were attributed to the Yongle period were white wares; many of these had what is called a *tianbai* ("sweet white") glaze.[4] Among them were some stembowls with a four-character Yongle reign mark in seal script incised or impressed on the bottom of the bowl.[5]

A very few porcelains with soy sauce–colored or light *qing* ("blue," or "green") glazes excavated at the Jingdezhen imperial kilns have also been attributed to the Yongle era. Some porcelains with monochrome copper-red or cobalt-blue glazes that most likely date to the Yongle period are known; these glazes were continued from the fourteenth century. The lovely *meiping* vase (No. 146), covered in dark cobalt-blue glaze, is related in shape to early fifteenth-century blue-and-white vases and can be assigned to that period.

The Porcelain Pagoda. One of the more spectacular examples of the use of architectural pottery during the Ming dynasty was the famous Baoensita, familiarly known to Westerners as the Porcelain Pagoda, built by the Yongle emperor outside Nanjing's Zhonghuamen. Accounts vary, but apparently construction started on this pagoda in 1412 and was completed in 1430; it was destroyed sometime between 1853 and 1864, at the time of the Taiping uprising. Part of the nine-storied building was made of *liuli*-glazed tiles that were manufactured at tileworks nearby. The tile showing a caparisoned elephant (No. 148), which

152. DISH. Porcelain painted in underglaze blue, with yellow overglaze enamel. Diameter: 10 1/4 in. (26 cm.). Ming dynasty, Hongzhi mark and period, 1488–1505. Rogers Fund, 1919. 19.28.10.

153. DISH. Porcelain with old-rose glaze. Diameter: 8 in.
     (20.3 cm.). Ming dynasty, Xuande mark and period,
     1426–35. Bequest of Mary Clark Thompson, 1924.
     24.80.198.

154. STEMBOWL. Porcelain painted in underglaze blue and overglaze red enamel. Diameter: 6 1/4 in. (15.9 cm.). Ming dynasty, late 15th century, Chenghua period. Gift of Alan and Simone Hartman, 1984. 1984.361.

is glazed in white, yellow, brown, and green, is quite like one found at kilns in Nanjing that made *liuli* wares. It shows evidence of having been affixed to a building and presumably was part of the Porcelain Pagoda.

Of equal interest is one of three L-shaped bricks in the Metropolitan's collection (No. 147). This brick is made of fine-grained porcelain—the unglazed body has turned an orange red on one side—and one surface is covered with a thick, high-fired white glaze. An inscription written in ink on an unglazed side reads, "Metropolitan Museum, New York. A porcelain brick from the Porcelain Tower at Nanking China, destroyed by Peking rebels. Found E. J. Smithers, Consul." Some white porcelain

155. DISH. Porcelain with biscuit and incised decoration.
Diameter: 6 3/8 in. (16.2 cm.). Ming dynasty, Hongzhi
mark and period, 1488–1505. Purchase, Mrs. Richard E.
Linburn Gift, 1987. 1987.86.

156. BOWL. Porcelain with incised and enameled
decoration. Diameter: 7 1/2 in. (19.1 cm.). Ming
dynasty, Zhengde mark and period, 1506–21. Anonymous
Gift, 1963. 63.175.2.

bricks discovered under a layer of Xuande material at the
imperial kiln site in Jingdezhen have been attributed to
the Yongle period in the excavation report.[6] These bricks
seem to confirm the general assumption that the
Metropolitan's three white porcelain bricks from the
Porcelain Pagoda, as well as similar bricks from the pagoda
in other museum collections, were made at kilns in
Jingdezhen.

   Xuande blue-and-white wares. Connoisseurs are
unanimous in their praise of Xuande blue-and-white

porcelains, which in many respects illustrate this decorative
technique at its apogee. They combine the freedom and
energy of a newly ripened art form with the sophistication
of concept and mastery of execution that come with
maturity. The very model of a bristling Xuande dragon
on the large *guan*-shaped jar (Color No. 21) in every
respect is representative of the highest traditions of early

157. COVERED JAR. Porcelaneous ware with carved, pierced,
and relief decoration; in the biscuit and under colored
glazes. Height with cover: 18 1/4 in. (46.4 cm.). Ming
dynasty, ca. first half 16th century. Bequest of John D.
Rockefeller, Jr., 1960. 61.200.15.

158. BOWL. Stoneware with cloisonné-style decoration.
Diameter: 7 1/4 in. (18.4 cm.). 16th century or later.
Mr. and Mrs. Isaac D. Fletcher Collection, Bequest of
Isaac D. Fletcher, 1917. 17.120.151.

159. VASE. Stoneware with cloisonné-style decoration.
Height: 7 3/4 in. (19.7 cm.). 16th century or later.
Edward C. Moore Collection, Bequest of Edward C.
Moore, 1891. 91.1.115.

160. BOWL. Porcelain painted in underglaze blue.
Diameter: 8 1/8 in. (20.6 cm.). Ming dynasty, Zhengde
mark and period, 1506–21. Harris Brisbane Dick Fund,
1963. 63.155.2.

fifteenth-century brushwork. His dorsal fins are like the teeth of a buzz saw; his claws have an underlying bone structure that is worthy of Michelangelo; he moves around the jar with total power, yet consummate grace.

Three very diverse Xuande blue-and-white porcelains, which the Metropolitan has acquired since publication of the first edition of this book, are also illustrated. Although the dragon on a dish (No. 149) is somewhat less formidable than the one on the large jar, it is still drawn with a fluency of statement that cannot be surpassed. Because they are so thickly potted, and because their undecorated interiors usually show considerable wear, the type of bowl (No. 150) is sometimes referred to as a dice bowl; however, many authorities prefer to call them fruit bowls. A continuous inscription in Tibetan characters painted in underglaze blue is on the exterior of the exquisitely potted stembowl (No. 151); this inscription is repeated in *anhua* technique on the inside. It has been translated as a prayer of blessings that may read, "May the days be auspicious; may the nights be auspicious. May the midday be filled with blessings. May days and nights be filled with blessings. May the blessings of the three jewels be realized." A four-character *anhua* Xuande reign mark is written in seal script on the bottom of the bowl.

For some years, considerable controversy has centered around whether or not the Xuande reign mark was used into the "Interregnum Period" that followed this reign.

161. DISH. Porcelain painted in underglaze blue.
      Diameter: 9 3/8 in. (23.8 cm.). Ming dynasty, Zhengde
      mark and period, 1506–21. Harris Brisbane Dick Fund,
      1963. 63.155.1.

162. BOWL. Porcelain painted in underglaze blue.
      Diameter: 6 1/8 in. (15.6 cm.). Ming dynasty, Zhengde
      mark and period, 1506–21. Fletcher Fund, 1925. 25.216.3.

While strong arguments have been put forward for each point of view, it seems probable that a number of unmarked vessels painted in the Xuande style continued to be made after 1435, and it is also possible that the Xuande reign mark was used for a while after the death of the Xuande emperor.

Red-and-white wares. There are a few reliably marked Xuande underglaze red–painted vessels, but many pieces once considered to be of the period are now recognized as later wares that carry the Xuande mark. The perverse nature of copper when used in underglaze painting has been mentioned, and—probably because of the difficulty in controlling this pigment—it was almost entirely supplanted by other, more tractable, decorative techniques in the fifteenth century.

Underglaze blue-and-red wares. There also are a few Xuande essays in underglaze blue combined with underglaze red; however, one or the other color usually did not mature well in firing, and this type of decoration was not pursued to any extent until the seventeenth century. Fragments of Xuande porcelains painted in underglaze blue, underglaze red, and a combination of the two colors have been found at the site of an imperial kiln in the city of Jingdezhen.[7]

Overglaze enamels. As we have seen, the technique of painting porcelains over the glaze with low-fired enamels was apparently introduced at Jingdezhen during the fourteenth century. At first, this decorative technique was used rather sparingly at these kilns; in fact, only two overglaze enamel colors are found on Xuande wares: iron-red and yellow.

Iron-red enamel. Iron-red occasionally constitutes the entire ornamentation, but more often it has been added to blue-and-white porcelains. (The iron-red enamel used on many Ming- and Qing-dynasty porcelains, frequently known as *rouge de fer*, is somewhat different from most other enamel colors. It is rather dull and matte and, unlike most other colors, does not lie on the glaze surface in any appreciable relief.) The results of using overglaze iron-red were much more satisfactory than those realized from underglaze copper-red, and the former became the principal type of red used throughout the Ming dynasty.

Yellow enamel. Yellow overglaze enamels are found on some Xuande porcelains, either functioning as a monochrome or silhouetting a blue-painted design to make a new blue-and-yellow style of decoration. Because the yellow enamel could have been applied at any time

and the vessel refired, some authorities question the probability that yellow was introduced at so early a date.

There are several Xuande-marked vessels with a full palette of polychrome enamels. These pieces might well be later than Xuande in date, and they may have been manufactured at kilns other than Jingdezhen.

A Ming design series. Several designs found on Xuande porcelains continued to be used well into the Ming dynasty, and porcelains with these designs offer an excellent opportunity to compare physical characteristics and painting mannerisms of different reigns. One of these design series consists of a sequence of rather heavily potted dishes that have one of two kinds of flowers as the principal motif. This series is found in several variations: designs are shown in blue against a white or a yellow background, the yellow being an overglaze enamel; in white reserved in a blue ground; or in underglaze brown against a white field. The dish (No. 152) with blue floral and fruit sprays silhouetted against a ground of yellow overglaze enamel is an example from the Hongzhi reign (1488–1505).

Xuande monochromes. The thoroughly arresting ornamentation of Xuande painted wares has been translated into a somewhat quieter eloquence in the monochrome porcelains of the time. Both very thin and more heavily potted white wares are known, and there are some particularly lovely copper-red–glazed porcelains attributable to this period, such as the dish (No. 153). In the illustration, one can see the typical form of a Ming reign mark: starting at top right, the characters read, *Da Ming Xuande nianzhi* ("made in the Xuande reign of the great Ming dynasty"). Some of these copper-red–glazed dishes are decorated with incised clouds and low-relief dragons on the inside. Other Xuande monochrome glazes include the high-fired dark blue that derived its color from cobalt oxide; some Xuande porcelains, such as a variant of the design series mentioned above, have patterns reserved in white against this blue ground. Fragments of Xuande porcelains with high-fired glazes, including an "imitation Longquan ware," were recently gathered in Jingdezhen at the site of an imperial kiln.[8]

Lower-fired glazes. In the manufacture of Chinese glazed ceramics, a great many variable factors influenced the final product. Among them were the composition of the body and of the glaze, the coloring material used in the glaze, the combination of firing time and firing temperature, and the kiln atmosphere. Without rather

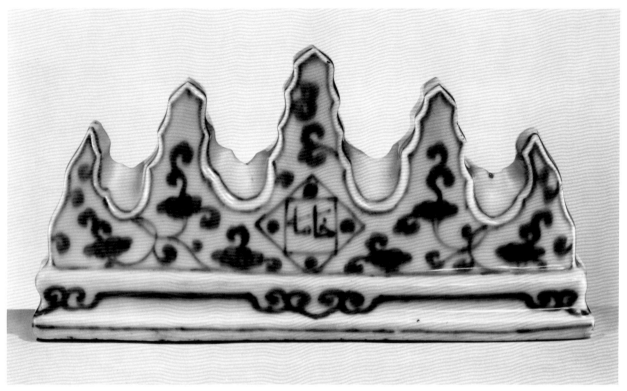

163. BRUSH REST. Porcelain painted in underglaze blue. Length: 8 3/4 in. (22.2 cm.). Ming dynasty, Zhengde mark and period, 1506–21. Rogers Fund, 1917. 18.56.14.

sophisticated laboratory analyses, it is not always possible to say exactly how some particular glaze effects were produced, or at what temperature the glaze was fired. The question of how certain Chinese glazes—such as the types about to be described—were made is rather complex and must be explored further.

As has been seen, Chinese low-fired lead glazes on earthenware bodies trace their ancestry at least as far back as the Han dynasty. However, similar low-temperature glazes do not seem to have been used on "true" porcelain bodies until the early fifteenth century.

At about the same time, medium-fired glazes also began to be used to decorate porcelains. This is the family of glazes the French have named glazes of the *demi-grand feu*, and the Chinese call *zhongwen you* ("middle-temperature glazes"). These medium-fired glazes mature at about 1000–1100° C.; they are fired in the remote chimney area of the kiln.[9]

Unlike the family of high-temperature lime glazes, which were generally fired at the same time as the porcelain bodies in the full heat of the kiln, most Chinese lower-temperature glazes were applied after the porcelain had received its initial firing in excess of about 1250° C., and they were given a separate firing to mature them. Among the fragments of Xuande porcelains found at the Jingdezhen imperial kiln site were some described as having *lu* ("green"), *salan* ("sprinkled blue"), and *kongquelu*, or turquoise, low-fired glazes. The turquoise glaze, at least, might be classified as one of the medium-temperature types.

Gilding. A few early fifteenth-century monochromes, primarily white wares, were enriched with overglaze gilding, a legacy from the Yuan period. While the fugitive gilt is likely to have worn off to a large extent over the years, it has almost invariably left its imprint in the "crust" of the glaze in the form of a matte shadow that is visible when light is raked across the otherwise shiny surface.

168

164. BOWL. Porcelain painted in overglaze polychrome
enamels. Diameter: 10 3/8 in. (26.4 cm.). Ming
dynasty, ca. first quarter 16th century. Rogers Fund, 1917.
17.146.2.

THE "CERAMIC INTERREGNUM" PERIOD

There is a paucity of evidence to document the nature of
high-quality ceramics manufactured in the Zhengtong
(1436–49), Jingtai (1450–57), and Tianshun (1457–64)
reigns, and authentically marked, fine porcelains from
this period—which is generally referred to as the "Ceramic
Interregnum"—are extremely rare. Because of this lack
of evidence, scholarly opinions vary as to what constitutes
the better "Interregnum" porcelains. As has been
mentioned, some authorities feel that the Xuande reign
mark, as well as the Xuande style, was continued into
the "Interregnum Period."

In recent years, a small number of lesser-grade
porcelains painted in underglaze blue or in underglaze
red have been excavated from tombs that are datable to
the "Interregnum" era.[10] These ceramics, which are
considered to be *minyao* ("people's ware," or "popular
ware") by the Chinese, have varied considerably in quality
and style of decoration. Evidence that they were
manufactured at several kilns in the Jingdezhen area has
been published.[11]

165. STEMBOWL. Porcelain painted in overglaze polychrome enamels. Diameter: 6 1/2 in. (16.5 cm.). Ming dynasty, early 16th century. Fletcher Fund, 1925. 25.222.6.

THE LATE FIFTEENTH CENTURY

During the final third of the fifteenth century—that is, in the reigns of the Chenghua (1465–87) and Hongzhi (1488–1505) emperors—Chinese porcelains touched greatness. In a constant search for improvement, potters at Jingdezhen perfected their wares to an unprecedented level of delicacy and refinement. The body shows even more careful preparation, and the potting exhibits even greater skill. Probably the most outstanding feature is the glaze, which is smooth, deep, and unctuous; the Chenghua glaze, in particular, has a mellow, creamy or slightly smoky tinge. However, these late fifteenth-century porcelains are never what Browning termed "faultless to a fault." They maintain a most rare and delicate balance between technical excellence and intrinsic artlessness that sets them apart from the almost perfect, but slightly mechanical, wares of the Qing dynasty. Indeed, some enthusiasts claim that the finest porcelains in China's long ceramic history were produced during the late fifteenth century.

166. VASE. Porcelain painted in underglaze blue. Height: 18 in. (45.7 cm.). Ming dynasty, Jiajing mark and period, 1522–66. Harris Brisbane Dick Fund and Anonymous Gift, 1965. 65.56.2.

167. COVERED BOX. Porcelain painted in underglaze blue. Diameter: 11 5/8 in. (29.5 cm.). Ming dynasty, Jiajing mark and period, 1522–66. Purchase, Anonymous Gift, 1965. 65.56.1.

168. COVERED BOX. Porcelain painted in underglaze blue.
Diameter: 15 1/2 in. (39.4 cm.). Ming dynasty, Jiajing
mark and period, 1522–66. Rogers Fund, 1925. 25.64.12.

Chenghua blue-and-white wares. Prime porcelains
of the Chenghua reign reflect the royal pleasures of the
emperor and his favorite, Wan Guifei, who is said to
have been particularly fond of ceramics. There is a special
grace to Chenghua blue-and-white wares. Sensitive
brushwork is favored over bold and spirited strokes; here
the tendency is to outline the designs before applying
slightly mottled washes of color. It is probable that the
cobalt pigment was more carefully prepared, for it rarely
shows the "heaped-and-piled" effect that characterizes
earlier blue-and-white wares. Although they do not carry
reign marks, the superb blue-and-white dish and leys jar

(Color Nos. 22 and 23) can be attributed to the Chenghua
period.

Underglaze blue with red enamel. In all likelihood,
another extremely fine, unmarked piece (No. 154) can
also be assigned to the Chenghua era. This stembowl
exemplifies the technique of decorating porcelains in
underglaze blue and overglaze iron-red enamel that had
been introduced earlier in the century.

Underglaze blue with turquoise glaze. A very few
Chenghua porcelains with blue designs painted under a
turquoise glaze are also known.[12]

Doucai. It is possible that the patronage of Wan
Guifei was responsible for the introduction, or the
promotion, of several decorative techniques at the

169. JAR. Porcelain painted in underglaze blue and overglaze polychrome enamels. Height: 9 1/8 in. (23.2 cm.). Ming dynasty, Jiajing mark and period, 1522–66. Rogers Fund, 1917. 17.127.2.

Jingdezhen kilns. Premier among these is the fabled Chenghua *doucai* ("contrasting colors," or "contending colors"), which is a combination of two previously known ornamental processes. In *doucai* decoration, designs were completely outlined in cobalt-blue on the unfired vessel, and a few areas of blue wash were painted in as well. After glazing and the usual high-temperature firing, outlines were filled in with overglaze red, green, yellow, and aubergine enamels that were then fired at low temperatures. Later in the dynasty, this combination of underglaze blue and overglaze polychrome enamels was to be even more important in a slightly different form. However, *doucai* is distinguished from other enameling styles in that its blue and its enamels are paler in tone, and the underglaze blue lines could constitute the entire design and stand alone if there were no enameling. *Doucai*-style enameling is usually confined to intimate little objects of exquisite refinement, and the rare examples of Chenghua date are some of the most highly treasured of all Ming-dynasty porcelains (Color No. 24).

Biscuit-and-white and green-and-white wares. The second innovation of the period was an amalgam of techniques that produced a group of bowls and dishes with buff-colored or green dragons on a white field. To decorate these wares, the potter would first incise dragons, clouds, and waves deeply into the unbaked body; then the dragons—except for their claws and streamers—and perhaps a few clouds would be coated with wax resist. Next the piece was glazed—avoiding the waxed areas—and fired. In the heat of the kiln, the wax vanished and the exposed body it had protected became a pinkish buff color. Occasionally, as in the Hongzhi example (No. 155), the piece was left as it was, with its lustrous glaze serving as an admirable foil for the buff-colored biscuit (the term for unglazed, fired porcelain). Most of the time, however, the dragons' biscuit bodies were painted with green enamel, their claws and streamers were painted over the

glaze in the same green, and the enamel was then fired at a low temperature. This biscuit-and-white/green-and-white series extended from the Chenghua reign into the Jiajing period; the green-and-white bowl (No. 156) dates to the Zhengde era (1506–21). Combining the techniques used to produce blue-and-white and green-and-white wares, a few Chenghua porcelains have been outlined in underglaze blue and painted in green enamel over the glaze.

Porcelains with colored glazes. As has been seen, Chinese potters used low- to medium-fired monochrome glazes on porcelains in the Xuande period. At what probably was a slightly later date, they began to apply these lower-temperature glazes in more than one color to prefired, or biscuit-fired, porcelain bodies. In brief, the decorative technique consisted of incising the design deeply into an unfired body; this part of the piece was left unglazed. Secondary areas were then covered with a clear, high-temperature glaze, and the vessel was fired at a temperature in excess of about 1250° C., which vitrified the body and fused the glaze. Colored, lower-temperature glazes were then applied to the unglazed biscuit areas—filling in the ground and the incised-outlined design with different colors—and the piece was refired at the lower heat necessary to fuse these glazes. The intaglio outlines served to check mixing of the colors, while the glazes that collected in incised details deepened in tone and accented these lines.

A few blue-and-turquoise–glazed porcelains of this type that may be of Chenghua date suggest that the technique could have started in that reign. Usually, however, the color combination is green and yellow, with occasional additions of aubergine; vessels with these colors are found from the Hongzhi period onward. The technique is exemplified here by a very fine leys jar (Color No. 25) with green designs against a yellow ground, dating to the Zhengde period.

Porcelaneous wares with colored glazes. An extension of the use of lower-temperature glazes is found in a large and widely varied class of sturdily potted porcelaneous wares. As with the previous family of porcelains with rather similar glazes over incised designs, the bodies of these wares were biscuit fired at a high temperature before the glazes were applied, and afterward the objects were refired at a lower heat. The diverse techniques that were used on these ceramics served to embellish and amplify what already was decorative and ornamental. There is a cloisonné style of decoration in

170. VASE. Porcelain painted in underglaze blue and overglaze yellow and red enamels. Height: 7 5/8 in. (19.4 cm.). Ming dynasty, Jiajing mark and period, 1522–66. Purchase by subscription, 1879. 79.2.866.

171. VASE. Porcelain painted in underglaze blue and overglaze yellow enamel. Height: 6 in. (15.2 cm.). Ming dynasty, Jiajing mark and period, 1522–66. Edward C. Moore Collection, Bequest of Edward C. Moore, 1891. 91.1.379.

which slender threads of clay were applied to define the outlines and some particulars of the motif, while less important details were picked out with incising. In a second, even more elaborate, process, the designs were both carved and pierced; again, the fine points were emphasized with incising. All of these devices would both indicate the design and control the colored glazes. For the most part, either deep blue or bright turquoise forms the background in this quite splendid group of ceramics, and other colors are played against them most handsomely. The exquisite vase and basin (Color Nos. 26

172. DOUBLE-BOTTOMED BOWL. Porcelain painted in overglaze polychrome enamels. Diameter: 5 in. (12.7 cm.). Ming dynasty, middle 16th century. Rogers Fund, 1918. 18.57.2.

173. SQUARE DISH. Porcelain painted in overglaze yellow and red enamels. Diameter: 7 1/2 in. (19.1 cm.). Ming dynasty, Jiajing mark and period, 1522–66. Gift of S. Chait, 1919. 19.137.

and 27) are paragons of this cloisonné type of decoration; a very fine covered jar (No. 157), on which some details have been left in the biscuit, has the pierced outer wall and solid inner wall typical of its class. This kind of ware is listed as *fahua* ware (which has no real translation) in modern Chinese journals.

Other wares with colored glazes. Earthenware and stoneware counterparts to the preceding group of porcelaneous wares were made for local consumption at different kilns throughout the country. There is a further, and usually slightly coarser, family of brownish-bodied stonewares with cloisonné-style decoration, in which the background and robust, relief-edged patterns have

174. BOWL WITH SILVER-GILT MOUNTS. Porcelain painted in underglaze blue, with blue glaze and gold decoration. Diameter: 4 3/4 in. (12.1 cm.). Mark: *Wan fu you tong*. Ming dynasty, middle 16th century, Jiajing period. (Mounts: German, ca. 1590–1610.) Purchase by subscription, 1879. 79.2.1122.

been washed with dominating turquoise and purple glazes. In some cases these glazes appear to be a bit softer than those on other cloisonné-type wares. This group of stonewares, illustrated here by a bowl and vase (Nos. 158 and 159), has traditionally been dated to the late fifteenth or sixteenth century; it is possible, however, that this attribution will eventually be brought forward a century or two.

Hongzhi porcelains. Hongzhi porcelains had the misfortune of following Chenghua wares, for they have been completely overshadowed by the earlier ceramics in the commentaries of both old and modern critics. Hongzhi porcelains often are of first quality; in fact, without a reign mark as a signpost, it can be difficult to distinguish the products of these two late fifteenth-century reigns. Nonetheless, as one recapitulates various Hongzhi types, it becomes quite obvious that, for the most part, these wares were continuations of earlier conventions and offer little that is untried or particularly imaginative.

Overglaze polychrome enamels. There is, however, one small group of seemingly valid, Hongzhi-marked dishes that display a fresh approach to polychrome decoration. This technique dispensed with the underglaze cobalt-blue that was used along with overglaze red, green, yellow, and aubergine enamels in *doucai* wares and replaced the underglaze pigment with a distinctive, turquoise blue

175. BOWL. Porcelain with yellow overglaze enamel. Diameter: 6 3/8 in. (16.2 cm.). Ming dynasty, Jiajing mark and period, 1522–66. Rogers Fund, 1919. 19.55.2.

177. BOWL. Porcelain painted in underglaze blue.
Diameter: 7 1/2 in. (19.1 cm.). Ming dynasty, Wanli
mark and period, 1573–1620. Gift of Marie-Louise
Garbáty, in memory of Eugene L. Garbáty, 1975.
1975.209.

176. VASE. Porcelain painted in underglaze blue.
Height: 25 1/8 in. (63.8 cm.). Ming dynasty, Wanli
mark and period, 1573–1620. Gift of Mrs. Eugene L.
Garbáty, in memory of Eugene L. Garbáty, 1979.
1979.109.

178. DISH. Porcelain painted in underglaze blue.
Diameter: 12 1/2 in. (31.8 cm.). Ming dynasty, Wanli
mark and period, 1573–1620. Rogers Fund, 1920.
20.41.12.

179. VASE. Porcelain painted in underglaze blue.
Height: 19 1/2 in. (49.5 cm.). Ming dynasty, Wanli
mark and period, 1573–1620. Rogers Fund, 1919. 19.160.

180. VASE WITH SILVER-GILT MOUNTS. Porcelain painted in underglaze blue. Height: 13 5/8 in. (34.6 cm.). Ming dynasty, before 1585. (Mounts: English, ca. 1585.) Rogers Fund, 1944. 44.14.2.

overglaze enamel. These wares seem to anticipate a characteristic style of painting solely in overglaze polychrome enamels—without the underlying cobalt-blue—that was to assume considerable prominence in the porcelains of Ming reigns that followed.

THE EARLY SIXTEENTH CENTURY

It was probably inevitable that after its steady ascent in the fifteenth century, the caliber of Ming porcelains should plateau, and this did occur in the early sixteenth century. Wares of the Zhengde era (1506–21) marked the end of a period of great development and high achievement, and, although on the whole their quality is very good, one can sense an impending downward trend. Zhengde porcelains can be said to represent a transition between the efflorescent ceramic period of the fifteenth century and the exuberant ceramic era of the mid-sixteenth century.

Zhengde blue-and-white wares. In Zhengde blue-and-white wares, the blue often has a distinctive grayish tone; the thick, glossy glaze commonly has a somewhat greenish tone, as opposed to the bluish cast of other Ming glazes. An especially fine bowl with aquatic plants (No. 160) illustrates a traditional direction followed in many Zhengde decorative motifs. This penchant for tradition is further illustrated by the popularity of a motif of dragons in a field of lotus scrolls that had been used during the early Ming. There is a large group of Zhengde vessels with this design, represented here by a dish and deep, cuplike bowl (Nos. 161 and 162).

"Mohammedan" wares. Another group of Zhengde blue-and-white porcelains, popularly called "Mohammedan" wares, represents a marked departure from tradition. These porcelains are distinguished by the Persian or Arabic inscriptions that are almost always included as part of the typical decoration of arabesques, conventionalized floral scrolls, and stiff, formal borders. This characteristic ornamentation is found on an

181. PLATE. Porcelain painted in underglaze blue. Diameter: 14 1/4 in. (36.2 cm.). Late Ming dynasty, late 16th–early 17th century. *Kraakporselein.* Rogers Fund, 1916. 16.93.

182. SHALLOW BOWL. Porcelain painted in underglaze blue. Diameter: 8 1/4 in. (21 cm.). Late Ming dynasty, late 16th–early 17th century. *Kraakporselein*. Rogers Fund, 1919. 19.136.13.

183. DEEP BOWL. Porcelain painted in underglaze blue. Diameter: 5 3/4 in. (14.6 cm.). Late Ming dynasty, late 16th–early 17th century. *Kraakporselein*. Rogers Fund, 1919. 19.136.17.

assortment of wares, including many objects in shapes that seem to be new at this time. Most "Mohammedan" wares are articles for the scholar's table, and it is assumed that the bulk of them were made for Muslim eunuchs, who exercised great power over the Zhengde emperor. The Metropolitan's brush rest (No. 163) has a Persian inscription on either side that, when put together, reads, *Khāmah dān* ("pen rest").

Iron-red enamel. Painting in the combination of underglaze blue and overglaze red enamel, a convention that originated in the Xuande reign, continued throughout the Ming dynasty, and there are a few Zhengde vessels decorated in this manner. Several others are embellished in overglaze iron-red alone; usually the reign mark is also written in red enamel, a practice that appears to have begun in the Zhengde period. Zhengde iron-red–painted porcelains include some interesting objects decorated with Persian verses in Arabic characters; the Zhengde reign mark on the base is transliterated into the Arabic alphabet.

The red-and-green family. The technique of painting exclusively in overglaze polychrome enamels gathered momentum in the early sixteenth century, and several distinctive groups of porcelains decorated in this manner can be ascribed to the Zhengde/Jiajing periods. Red and green generally are the dominant colors in a palette that may also include accents of yellow, turquoise, and aubergine; the designation "red-and-green family" is frequently given to wares in this color scheme. A large bowl (No. 164) shows several stylistic similarities to marked Zhengde wares. An inscription written in red enamel on its base states that the bowl was made by a member of the Chen family; there has been some disagreement about the reading of the given name. The dragons seen on the dish (Color No. 28) have carefully incised scales and twiglike claws. These same features can be observed in the rendering of dragons on a sizable group of red-and-green wares that vary considerably in quality. There are quite a few different inscriptions on these porcelains; most of them are written in overglaze red. It is somewhat difficult to give these wares a precise attribution.

Other overglaze polychrome enamels. Some early sixteenth-century polychrome-enameled stembowls, such as the one illustrated (No. 165), do not fit into the red-and-green category. Because of their extremely white body and glaze, it has been hypothesized that these stembowls may have been made at some as-yet-unidentified kiln in Fujian Province.

Porcelains with colored glazes. Among the wares with lower-fired colored glazes over incised designs, there are a few Zhengde vessels that have green, yellow, and aubergine patterns on a turquoise blue ground. These are in addition to porcelains decorated in the same technique with the usual combination of green and yellow glazes.

Architectural pottery. The tradition of *liuli*-glazed ornamental roof tiles, roof finials, and other architectural embellishments was maintained in the sixteenth century. Indeed, local tileworks throughout China have continued to manufacture colorfully glazed architectural pottery until the present day.

Other tilework products. Many of these various tileworks also produced other wares—including decorative figures and vessels for use at the altar—with the same green, yellow, aubergine, dark blue, and turquoise blue glazes that were used on the architectural pottery. Because they tend to be stereotyped rather than individualized, these figures and vessels, like their architectural counterparts, can be difficult to date.

An elaborate incense burner with high-relief dragons and flowers under green, yellow, and whitish glazes (Color No. 29) has the same incised inscription under each upstanding handle, *Zhengde qinian liuyue zao* ("made in the sixth month of the seventh year of the Zhengde reign"), corresponding in the Western calendar to July 1512. With its precise date, this vessel can serve as a yardstick for the dating of similar pieces.

THE MID-SIXTEENTH CENTURY

Porcelains of the reign of the Jiajing emperor (1522–66) steadily lessened in quality, and few ceramics approach the level of late fifteenth-century wares. Quantity now was the ultimate goal at the Jingdezhen kilns. There were enormous orders from the palace to be filled, amounting to thousands of objects annually; indeed, one year's requirements are reported to have exceeded one hundred thousand pieces. It is understandable that the potters, in their effort to meet production quotas, had little time for careful craftsmanship. Nonetheless, judging Jiajing wares by different values, one can perhaps appreciate the way their enthusiastic, somewhat insouciant style communicates a certain excitement of its own. This high-spirited quality has been more esteemed in Japan than in the West.

184. DISH. Porcelain painted in underglaze blue and
     overglaze red. Diameter: 6 5/8 in. (16.8 cm.). Ming
     dynasty, Wanli mark and period, 1573–1620. Bequest of
     Mary Clark Thompson, 1924. 24.80.185.

Jiajing blue-and-white wares. Blue-and-white
porcelains of the Jiajing period exhibit a measure of
renewed energy, particularly in those wares that depart
from the rather hackneyed traditional designs and venture
into new motifs. The finest Jiajing blue-and-white wares
are renowned for the rich purplish tone of the blue, as is
seen in both the vase and octagonal covered box (Nos. 166
and 167). As on this vase, many Jiajing porcelains are
decorated with Taoist symbols of longevity, reflecting the
emperor's strong Taoist beliefs. This is again seen in a

185. DISH. Porcelain painted in underglaze blue and overglaze polychrome enamels. Diameter: 14 3/4 in. (37.5 cm.). Ming dynasty, Wanli mark and period, 1573–1620. Rogers Fund, 1917. 17.118.17.

186. JAR. Porcelain with incised decoration under colored glazes. Height: 6 3/4 in. (17.1 cm.). Ming dynasty, Wanli mark and period, 1573–1620. Rogers Fund, 1923. 23.15.2.

blue-and-white covered box (No. 168) that is decorated with Shouxing (the Taoist God of Longevity), the Eight Taoist Immortals, and numerous Taoist symbols.

Other Jiajing blue-and-white porcelains vary greatly in type and quality. Of passing interest is a small group of blue-and-white bowls and bottle-vases with Portuguese inscriptions and the years 1541 and 1552, respectively, as part of the text. These are the earliest dated porcelains decorated to special European order that are known. Aside from these pieces—and a few undated objects with Portuguese armorial emblems that may have been made earlier—it appears that the Chinese did not decorate many blue-and-white porcelains to European specifications until the last two decades of the seventeenth and the early eighteenth century.

Jiajing polychromes. The ascendancy of polychrome enamel decoration over other ornamental techniques seen in porcelains of the Jiajing period could represent an attempt to compensate for the loss of quality in potting by making an ambitious display of color. Ceramic painters were adept and imaginative with their palette of enamels and sought to achieve a maximum number of effects. For purposes of simplification, it may be easiest to consider Jiajing polychromes under two major categories: those that employ underglaze cobalt-blue and those that do not.

Doucai. In the first category, the *doucai* style of outlining designs in underglaze cobalt-blue and filling them in with overglaze colored enamels, which was introduced during the Chenghua period, is found on a few Jiajing pieces.

Wucai. An important innovation of the Jiajing period, the so-called *wucai* ("five-color") decoration, was one of the last major additions to the lexicon of ornamental techniques that were developed during the Ming dynasty. Despite its name, the number of colors in *wucai* decoration is not strictly limited to five. *Wucai*, like *doucai*, is a combination of underglaze blue and overglaze polychrome enamels. However, where the soft underglaze blue of *doucai* was primarily used for dainty outlines that lay the groundwork for elegant little washes of pale enamel colors, the dark blue of *wucai* was applied in bold washes to complement vigorous splashes of strong overglaze colors, and outlining was mostly done in overglaze red, brown, or black.

The Ming enamels resemble—indeed, they are—bits of translucent colored glass that have been fused to the surface of the glaze. While some variety in tone

187. BOWL. Porcelain with low- and high-relief and pierced decoration; in the biscuit and under a clear glaze. Diameter: 3 5/8 in. (9.2 cm.). Ming dynasty, late 16th or 17th century. Bequest of Mary Stillman Harkness, 1950. 50.145.261.

could be achieved with them, gradations in color were quite limited, and any shading of individual colors was virtually impossible.

A jar in the Metropolitan's collection (No. 169) has a popular Jiajing *wucai* motif, fish in water weeds. The fish form a rebus: the Chinese word *yu* ("fish") is pronounced much like *yu* ("abundant"), and the pun symbolizes a wish for wealth.

Often, rather than using the white ground as part of the composition, porcelain painters covered the entire surface in combinations of underglaze blue and enamels, a style that was probably known as early as the Xuande reign. As can be seen in the vase (No. 171), blue designs can be silhouetted against a ground of yellow overglaze enamel. Less frequently, blue designs are set against a red enamel ground. Where the blue supports two overglaze colors, usually red with either green or yellow, one enamel forms the background and the other provides lively accents (No. 170).

The red-and-green family. The Jiajing family of red-and-green porcelains—without underglaze blue—takes pride of place in the judgment of Japanese connoisseurs. It is represented here by a double-bottomed bowl (No. 172) that is painted in overglaze red, green, and yellow enamels against a white ground. While it has no reign mark, this bowl can be assigned to the mid-sixteenth century on stylistic grounds.

Again, two colors taken from this red-and-green palette can envelop a piece with most effective results. For instance, there are handsome Jiajing vessels bedecked with green designs on red grounds, red patterns on green grounds, or yellow motifs on red fields (No. 173). Iron-red or green overglaze enamel can also be seen as a monochrome, sometimes on the reverse of bowls with underglaze blue decoration on the inside.

Gilding. Literally "gilding the lily," Jiajing potters further embellished many of their essays in the red-and-green theme with designs worked in thin sheets of applied gold leaf. In Japan, where they are called *kinrande* ("gold-brocaded") wares, these gilded red-and-green porcelains are highly treasured. Gilding is not restricted to the red-and-green family but can be found on several other types of Jiajing porcelains as well. Such a piece is the unusual bowl (No. 174) that has *kinrande* ornamentation over a high-fired blue glaze on the outside and underglaze blue decoration on the interior. This bowl is set in German silver-gilt mounts that date to the late sixteenth–early seventeenth century.

Monochromes. Monochrome-glazed wares continued to be manufactured along with their more ornate counterparts. In addition to the perennial high-fired white wares, there are some particularly fine lower-temperature dark blue glazes that have usually been applied over incised designs, and some monochrome turquoise glazes. Overglaze yellow enamel continued to be used as a monochrome (No. 175), along with the overglaze green and iron-red enamels previously mentioned.

THE LATE SIXTEENTH AND EARLY SEVENTEENTH CENTURIES

Deterioration in the quality of Ming porcelain, which started earlier in the century, quickened in the reigns of the Longqing (1567–72) and Wanli (1573–1620) emperors. Demands from the court continued to be enormous, and the export trade exacted its toll of manpower and raw materials. Inevitably, the majority of late sixteenth- and early seventeenth-century ceramics became quite pedestrian, and porcelains that reflect some degree of fine craftsmanship are comparatively rare.

There seems to have been little time or incentive for experimentation, and only one important addition was made to the numerous decorative innovations that had been an outstanding feature of the development of Ming porcelains. However, a large repertoire of ornamental techniques had been accumulated from the extremely prolific earlier years of the dynasty, and by using almost all of them, the late sixteenth- and early seventeenth-century artist-craftsmen could produce a wide and varied assortment of wares.

Longqing porcelains. By and large, Longqing porcelains continued the Jiajing style with little change,

188. FRAGMENT. Porcelain painted in underglaze blue. Length: about 1 3/4 in. (4.4 cm.). Transitional Period, ca. second quarter 17th century. "Transitional" ware. From the wreck of *Nuestra Señora de la Maravillas*, which sank in 1656 on the Little Bahamas Bank. Gift of John R. and Betty Menke, 1979. 1979.27.4.

189. VASE. Porcelain with incised decoration, painted in underglaze blue. Height: 18 1/4 in. (46.4 cm.). Transitional Period, ca. second quarter 17th century. "Transitional" ware. Rogers Fund, 1920. 20.41.4.

190. DISH. Porcelain painted in underglaze blue and
     overglaze polychrome enamels. Diameter: 6 1/2 in.
     (16.5 cm.). Ming dynasty, Tianqi mark and period,
     1621–27. Fletcher Fund, 1924. 24.170.6.

191. DISH. Porcelain painted in underglaze blue and
overglaze polychrome enamels. Diameter: 7 7/8 in.
(20 cm.). Apocryphal mark of Chenghua period,
1465–87, but Transitional Period, ca. second quarter
17th century. Purchase by subscription, 1879. 79.2.1085.

although a few Longqing vessels with some extraordinarily debonair dragons might deserve special mention.

Wanli blue-and-white wares. Five pieces that vary considerably in quality and decorative style represent the numerous types of Wanli blue-and-white wares here. The very large vase (No. 176) is quite similar to six vases—on which dragons replace the phoenix motif—that were found in the 1950s in the tomb of the Wanli emperor. A bowl shaped like an open lotus flower (No. 177) illustrates a group of bowls in this shape that have non-Chinese characters as part of the decoration. These bowls appear to have been made from the late Wanli period into the early Kangxi era, probably for use in Lamaistic temples.[13] A rare dish (No. 178) shows the white-on-blue type of ornamentation that frequently recurred after it first appeared in the Yuan period. Also executed in white on blue, the decoration of a vase (No. 179) repeats the enticing clutter of the fourteenth century; its shape makes reference to ancient Chinese bronzes.

The vase (No. 180) is as interesting for its splendid English silver-gilt mounts as for the pot itself. This is a typical example of the blue-and-white porcelains of fairly good quality being produced in the second half of the sixteenth century that were used at home and exported abroad. Its mounts, which are of unusually fine workmanship, were made by an unidentified London silversmith around 1585. These datable fittings can help us in our attribution of similar ceramics. They are typical of the fixtures that were attached to Chinese porcelains in Europe at this period, not only to embellish these treasures, but also to adapt the unfamiliar Chinese shapes to Western usage. Many of these porcelains were set into their elaborate metal fittings despite the fact that they were already broken, testifying to the high regard with which Chinese blue-and-white wares were held in sixteenth-century Europe. This particular vase is one of four mounted porcelains in the Metropolitan's collection that had been in the possession of William Cecil, Lord Burghley, who was Lord Treasurer under Queen Elizabeth I; they were part of the furnishings at Burghley House until they were sold in 1888.

192. PLATE. Porcelain painted in overglaze polychrome enamels. Diameter: 8 1/4 in. (21 cm.). Transitional Period, ca. second quarter 17th century. Purchase by subscription, 1879. 79.2.1244.

Kraakporselein. A particular type of blue-and-white porcelain that made its debut in the late sixteenth century appears to have been manufactured almost exclusively for export.[14] These wares are known as *kraakporselein*, supposedly after the Dutch name for the Portuguese carracks, or merchant ships, that originally brought them to Europe. They are reported to have caused quite a sensation when the booty from two Portuguese carracks, the *San Jago* and the *Santa Catarina*, was sold in Amsterdam in 1602 and 1604, respectively. *Kraakporselein* has a rather metallic feeling to it; examples are often slightly molded, as if in imitation of repoussé metalwork. It has a thin, resonant, and somewhat brittle body, and pieces are frequently chipped at the mouth rim. Even more distinctive is its style of decoration, which presents standard late sixteenth-century motifs in a very different fashion. One of the most characteristic features of *kraakporselein* decoration is the division of the border designs into radial segments. The copious painting on the important surface of a *kraak* piece is not matched on the reverse, where the treatment is generally quite superficial (Nos. 181, 182, and 183).

Kraakporselein was extremely popular in western Europe in the early seventeenth century; it repeatedly appears in Dutch and Flemish seventeenth-century still-life paintings and was copied by the Dutch in their Delft wares. (Nos. 182 and 183 were purchased in Holland.) In 1976, a considerable amount of *kraakporselein*—as well as lesser quantities of other wares—was salvaged from the wreck of the *Witte Leeuw*, a Dutch East Indiaman that sank near St. Helena on its homeward voyage in 1613.[15] This find has provided valuable evidence of the nature of several types of Chinese porcelains that were exported during the early seventeenth century.

Underglaze blue with red enamel. A nicely made, small Wanli dish with dragons chasing pearls over waves (No. 184) represents a continuation of the convention of porcelains decorated in underglaze blue and overglaze iron-red enamel. As we shall see, this Ming-dynasty convention was to continue well into the following Qing dynasty.

Wanli polychrome wares. Among the Wanli polychrome wares, the so-called *wucai* porcelains painted in underglaze blue and overglaze colored enamels are outstanding. The range of types and qualities is considerable; it extends from dishes with simple designs, such as a basket of fruit and flowers on a table or birds in a landscape, to profusely decorated objects with dragons,

193. BOTTLE. Porcelain painted in underglaze blue.
Height: 8 3/8 in. (21.3 cm.). Transitional Period,
probably Chongzhen reign, 1628–44. *Shonsui* ware. Gift of
Charles Stewart Smith, 1893. 93.3.46.

or dragons and phoenixes (No. 185), as the motif. One
occasionally finds *doucai*-decorated porcelains from this
period, and the red-and-green family of overglaze enamels
also maintained some of its former popularity.

Porcelains with colored glazes. A small jar with
yellow designs on a green ground (No. 186) illustrates
the continuation of an ornamental technique that made
its appearance in the fifteenth century. It is interesting
to compare the quality of this jar with that of the leys jar
(Color No. 25) that dates to the earlier Zhengde era.

Enamels on the biscuit. During the Wanli period,
polychrome enamels were painted on prefired, unglazed
(or biscuited) bodies, as well as over the glaze. The
technique of enameling on the biscuit is similar to
enameling on the glaze. A porcelain vessel was first fired
at a temperature in excess of about 1250° C. to vitrify
the clay body. Colored enamels, generally outlined in
brownish black, were then painted directly onto the rather
dry-looking biscuit body, and finally the vessel was refired
just to the low temperature required to fuse the enamels.
These Wanli porcelains were the forerunners of a most
important family of wares that flowered during the end
of the seventeenth century and later: porcelains painted
with *famille verte* enamels on the biscuit.

White slip designs. Monochrome wares continued
into the Wanli reign. There also is a group of high-fired
brown-, blue-, or celadon-glazed vessels with contrasting
designs painted in white slip, which survived well into
the seventeenth century.

Pierced and relief work. Neither relief nor pierced
decoration was a novelty to Chinese potters of the late
Ming era, and some especially fine porcelains employing
several variants of these ornamental techniques can be
ascribed to this period. Among these variants are low-
relief designs painted in unglazed white slip; there also
are applied, molded high-relief elements—generally
figures—that either have been left in the biscuit or have
been gilded and/or painted with colored pigments. Again,
the walls of the vessel might have been pierced in intricate
diaper patterns when the unfired porcelain was in the
leather-hard state. This *linglong* ("ingeniously and
delicately wrought") porcelain is especially fragile, and
one can understand why the arduous technique has been
called *guifu shengong* ("supernatural workmanship"),
denoting a skill that seems to be beyond human
capabilities. In a somewhat simpler type of ornamentation,
fretwork patterns have been partially cut into the body
but have not penetrated all the way through the wall.

Frequently, several of these relief and pierced decorative devices are found on the same piece, such as the small bowl (No. 187), a *chef d'oeuvre* of the potter's dexterity, which shows Shouxing and the Eight Taoist Immortals in pairs. The work on this piece is so meticulous that the basket carried by one Immortal, probably Lan Caihe, is loose and movable. Relief and openwork decoration of this type can also be found supplemented by underglaze blue painting. Although some members of this broad family carry Wanli marks, this kind of ware continued to be manufactured into the Qing dynasty.

THE TRANSITIONAL PERIOD

For the sake of providing a working date, the Transitional Period in Chinese ceramics is considered to have started with the death of the Wanli emperor in 1620. It spanned the changeover from the Ming to Qing dynasty in 1644 and extended to the arrival of Zang Yingxuan as director of the imperial factories at Jingdezhen in 1683. This stormy era in China's history produced a fascinating conglomeration of porcelains.

Traditional wares. Some rather routine wares that continued earlier decorative formulas were manufactured. In these tired echoes of earlier achievements one can follow the progressive change from Ming- to Qing-dynasty styles.

Nontraditional wares. Many of the porcelains dating to the Ming portion of the Transitional Period are quite different from the conventional Chinese ceramics that had been manufactured up to this point. Some of these wares were specifically made to European or Japanese order. In many of these wares for the foreign markets, the concepts of shape and/or decoration in Chinese ceramics have been perceptibly changed: they have been determined by foreign taste as never before. Other porcelains, while not expressly made to foreign order, took the fancy of overseas buyers and found their way to Europe and Japan.

"Transitional" wares. Although it actually was only one of many very different types of porcelain made in the Transitional Period, one distinctive type of porcelain is generally catalogued as "Transitional" ware. These ceramics are traditionally associated with the European—primarily Dutch—markets. It must be remembered, however, that some of the finest "Transitional" wares,

194. BOTTLE. Porcelain painted in underglaze blue. Height: 7 in. (17.8 cm.). Transitional Period, probably Chongzhen reign, 1628–44. *Shonsui* ware. Purchase by subscription, 1879. 79.2.1080.

such as the superb brush holder (Color No. 30), were obviously made for domestic use.

"Transitional" blue-and-white porcelains are skillfully potted and decorated in a lovely shade of deep blue that inspired the simile, "like violets in milk." The painting has been done with a talented hand. Many of the finest objects are embellished with groups of figures in distinctive landscapes that have steep walls of rocks improbably interrupted by clouds, isolated cone-shaped mountains, an ever-present moon, and characteristic V-shaped hooks in the drawing. Notable too is the use of stiff, acanthuslike leaves, as well as a tulip-shaped ornament, which was probably derived from a European source. Unlike the Ko-sometsuke and Shonsui wares discussed below, the decoration of "Transitional" wares is almost completely in Chinese taste, and there is very little foreign flavor to it. However, the forms of many pieces were adapted to Western demands: the Dutch were supplying Chinese merchants with wooden models of the shapes they wanted copied as early as 1635.

A few examples of "Transitional" wares have inscriptions that include the reign title of a Ming-dynasty emperor along with a cyclical date.[16] From these dated pieces, as well as other documentary evidence, we can attribute "Transitional" wares to as early as 1625. Although the majority of these ceramics were probably made in the Chongzhen period (1628–44), the type continued in a somewhat modified form into the early Qing dynasty.

In 1972, some fragments of typical "Transitional" wares were found on the Little Bahamas Bank by Willard Bascom, an oceanographer. He has identified these fragments, and other material found with them, as coming from the wreck of *Nuestra Señora de la Maravillas*. This was the second-in-command ship, or *almiranta*, of a Spanish royal armada of treasure galleons out of Havana, Cuba; it sank on 4 January 1656.[17] The banana leaves on one of the fragments found by Dr. Bascom (No. 188) are quite close to those on the "Transitional"-ware vase in the Metropolitan's collection (No. 189).

Enameled wares associated with the Japanese market. Three porcelains decorated in very different manners illustrate several kinds of end-of-Ming-dynasty ceramics with overglaze polychrome enamels. Although there seems to be no proof that these porcelains were especially manufactured for export, their style is so much to Japanese taste that it is generally assumed they were produced for the Japanese market. The dish (No. 190) represents a group of dishes painted in a combination of underglaze blue and overglaze enamels that frequently carry the Tianqi (1621–27) reign mark. These wares show little refinement in their potting and minimal detail in their decoration. A brown-rimmed dish (No. 191) has an apocryphal Chenghua reign mark. Its scene, which is painted in underglaze blue and overglaze enamels, is typical of the seventeenth-century style. The decor of the brown-rimmed plate (No. 192) is quite different from those of the two dishes. Here the designs, which have been painted in overglaze enamels alone, have been carefully drawn, and there is considerable attention to detail.

In the early years of the seventeenth century, the Japanese tea ceremony was enjoying a new vogue, and porcelains like these fitted into the ritual admirably. Japanese patrons often bought these wares in sets of five, and some of these sets can still be found intact today.

Ko-sometsuke *wares.* Quantities of rather coarsely potted blue-and-white porcelains were ordered by Japanese tea masters for specific use in the tea ceremony. These wares are entirely in Japanese taste: they often have delightfully eccentric, un-Chinese shapes, and their nonchalant decorative style, as well as many of their motifs, also are Japanese. It would seem that the bulk of these Ko-sometsuke ("old blue-and-white") wares was produced during the Tianqi period.

Shonsui *wares.* Shonsui wares are another group of blue-and-white porcelains that have Japanese shapes and Japanese patterns. They were made at the Jingdezhen kilns to the special order of Japanese tea masters. Unlike the coarse Ko-sometsuke wares, however, Shonsui vessels are beautifully potted and well painted in a good violet blue; in fact, in quality they compare quite favorably with "Transitional" wares. In the Shonsui style of decoration, the pendulum of taste has completely swung away from the Ko-sometsuke casualness, and the effect is now quite studied; the many decorative elements have been drawn with great attention to detail. Shonsui wares are rare in the West, and the Metropolitan is fortunate to have three examples, including two lobed bottles of the so-called double-gourd shape (Nos. 193 and 194). There is some disagreement regarding the origin of the name Shonsui. There also is some disagreement about dating these porcelains; however, many authorities feel that they were all manufactured during the reign of the Chongzhen emperor (1628–44).

Southern Ming wares. An interesting blue-and-white vase (No. 195) has the mark *Xuande zhizao* ("made in the Xuande reign") written in very large seal characters

195. VASE. Porcelain painted in underglaze blue.
Height: 7 1/2 in. (19.1 cm.). Apocryphal mark of Xuande
period, 1426–35, but Southern Ming dynasty, before
1645. Bequest of Robert West, 1950. 50.221.47.

on the base; this mark is obviously apocryphal. Two published blue-and-white porcelains that are decorated in the same manner are marked *Fu fan zhizao* ("made for the prince of Fu").[18] This prince of Fu probably was the Wanli emperor's grandson who, under the reign title of Hongguang, set up a Southern Ming court at Nanjing in 1644; his reign was very brief. Based on these analogous porcelains, we can assign the Metropolitan's vase to the very end of the Ming dynasty.

OTHER MING-DYNASTY WARES

While the Jingdezhen kiln complexes overshadowed all others in the Ming dynasty, the eclipse was not total; there were several kiln centers that played a smaller, but still important, part during this era. Cizhou-type wares, for example, continued to be manufactured throughout the period, as attested to by a number of vessels carrying Ming-dynasty reign marks. This widely varied family of ceramics enjoyed lasting popularity, and wares in the Cizhou tradition have been continuously potted up to modern times. Jun-type ceramics were also made, to some extent, in the Ming dynasty, but most of them are quite ordinary and far from the exquisite pieces that were produced under the Song.

Longquan wares. Among the various Ming factories that survived from the Song and Yuan periods, many of the kilns that produced the famous Longquan celadons in Zhejiang Province remained active for a while. However, with the rising popularity of the Jingdezhen painted porcelains, it was inevitable that demand for the less ornamental Longquan monochromes should start to decline in the early Ming dynasty. Although some extremely good Longquan wares were still produced in the late fourteenth and early fifteenth centuries (No. 196), they seldom attain the superb quality of these ceramics in their heyday. Quite frequently, these early Ming celadons parallel the shapes of contemporary blue-and-white porcelains. In an apparent effort to cater to the prevailing taste for the more decorative painted wares,

Longquan potters often transcribed the underglaze blue designs into incised and carved equivalents.

As the Ming era progressed, blue-and-white and polychrome porcelains gained favor to the detriment of the Longquan celadons. The quality of Longquan wares began to deteriorate markedly, and by the end of the era they were coarse and badly potted. During the Qing dynasty, those kilns that had not completely shut down were reduced to producing routine, everyday pottery for local consumption.

Dehua wares: blanc de chine. Kiln complexes in the vicinity of the town of Dehua in Dehua xian, Fujian Province, are the source of a special type of porcelain known in the West as *blanc de chine*. These wares have a fine-grained, vitreous, white body that seems to have been entirely made from a pulverized local porcelain stone; it is embraced by a thick, satiny glaze that ranges in tone from milky white through warm ivory to a faint rosy hue. There is a large variety of *blanc de chine* vessels, including numerous objects for the writing table, but the many porcelain figures that often represent Buddhist or Taoist deities are the most glamorous of these wares. Dehua ceramic sculptures vary considerably in quality; at best they exhibit a virtuosity of modeling that raises them to the rank of true masterpieces. No better illustration can be found than the superb figure of Bodhidharma (No. 197), whose serene expression and fluid robes celebrate the skill of a master craftsman.

In addition to splendid white porcelains, the Dehua kilns manufactured a certain amount of blue-and-white wares and some porcelains with monochrome glazes, notably brownish red and purplish blue. Some Dehua porcelains have been embellished with overglaze enamel decoration; however, where this enameling was done has not been established.

Kilns in Dehua xian date back at least to the Song dynasty. Apparently the distinctive *blanc de chine* porcelains were initiated toward the end of the Ming dynasty, and production considerably increased during the seventeenth and eighteenth centuries. Because these wares followed a traditional style over a long period of time, it is rather difficult to date them precisely.

"Swatow" wares. A large and diversified family of provincial ceramics that were made in southern China in the sixteenth and seventeenth centuries is loosely identified as "Swatow" ware, although the precise place or places of origin are not known. This rather crude "Swatow" pottery often has a distinctive slanting foot

196. PLATE. Porcelaneous ware with incised decoration under celadon glaze. Diameter: 20 in. (50.8 cm.). Early Ming dynasty, late 14th–early 15th century. Longquan ware. Gift of Dr. Vallo Benjamin, 1984. 1984.358.

and large amounts of coarse sand adhering to the base and foot. "Swatow" wares have been decorated in a number of ways. Some, such as the dish (No. 198), which was purchased in the former port of Shantou, or Swatow, in the 1930s, are painted in underglaze blue; others have incised designs under whitish, blue, or celadon glazes. In one variety, painted slip designs have been used against pale grayish blue (No. 199), light celadon (No. 200), or brown grounds. Sometimes "Swatow" wares have been freely and vigorously painted in a combination of underglaze blue and overglaze enamels, or in various combinations of overglaze red, green, turquoise, black, and sepia enamels (Color No. 31). "Swatow" wares were exported in large quantities to Europe, the Near East, and Southeast Asia; they were among the ceramics that were found in the cargo of the *Witte Leeuw*, a Dutch ship that sank in 1613 near St. Helena.[19]

"Martaban" wares. Among the many kinds of Chinese ceramics that were exported is a variety of unrefined, stoneware storage jars. These ovoid jars are sometimes called "Martaban" wares after the transit port of Martaban in Burma, a common stop in the trade route traveled by the ships carrying this pottery. These robust jars have bold, incised or relief decoration under different kinds of glazes, principally olive green, golden brown, brown, or almost black. Loop handles or pierced masks, through which a rope could be passed to secure a cover, are generally placed around the shoulder. "Martaban" jars can be quite large, sometimes reaching up to three feet in height.

This enigmatic group cannot be given a single place of origin. In general, it is agreed that these jars came from various kilns in southern China, and one source has been located at Qishicun, near Foshan, in Guangdong Province.[20] It is most difficult to date them: some authorities believe that "Martaban" wares originated as early as the Tang dynasty; other experts think that they started to be made during the Song period. At least two of the fragments that were found at the Qishicun kilns carried the reign marks of Northern Song–dynasty emperors.[21] "Martaban" jars have been mentioned by travelers as early as the fourteenth century. Many of

them can probably be dated to the Ming era—they were found in the load of the *Witte Leeuw*[22]—and they have continued to be manufactured until recent times. Natives of the Philippines have treasured these wares; and in Borneo, the Dyaks and other peoples have sometimes given jars names and even credited them with powers of speech and movement. (It should be noted that in the Near East the term "Martaban" is applied to large Yuan and Ming celadon jars and dishes rather than to the kinds of storage jars discussed here.)

Yixing wares. Potteries in Yixing xian, which lies west of Taihu (Lake Tai) in Jiangsu Province, were operative as early as the Han dynasty, when they produced gray- and red-bodied earthenwares as well as green-glazed stonewares.[23] The ceramics for which kilns in this vicinity are most famous, however, are of a much later date and of a very different nature. The variety of clays available to these kilns fire to many different colors, ranging from buff to reddish brown to dark chocolate brown; they also lend themselves to the creation of interesting textures as well as unusual and fanciful shapes. Yixing kilns are famous for their unglazed reddish and brownish stoneware teapots, which are often embellished with incised, stamped, or relief decoration. These Yixing teapots were extensively copied in Holland, England, and Germany in the late seventeenth and the eighteenth centuries.

Based on recent kiln-site discoveries, the distinctive type of Yixing stoneware, which is called *zisha* ("purple clay") ware in China, is thought to have developed during the Northern Song period.[24] A few excavated teapots document its manufacture during the sixteenth and seventeenth centuries,[25] and production has continued to the present day. Many Ming and Qing Yixing wares have been signed by potters whose dates are known, and a number of these pieces are accepted as genuine. However, with typical Chinese reluctance to part with the past, Yixing craftsmen have sustained old styles over long periods of time, making it difficult to give an exact date to the majority of these wares. Indeed, it is hard to distinguish some modern Yixing teapots from examples that were produced during the Ming and Qing periods.

197. FIGURE OF BODHIDHARMA. Porcelain. Height: 11 3/4 in. (29.8 cm.). Late Ming dynasty, 17th century. Dehua ware, Fujian Province. Gift of Mrs. Winthrop W. Aldrich, Mrs. Arnold Whitridge, and Mrs. Sheldon Whitehouse, 1963. 63.176.

198. DISH. Porcelaneous ware painted in underglaze blue.
Diameter: 10 1/2 in. (26.7 cm.). Late Ming dynasty,
late 16th–early 17th century. "Swatow" ware. Gift of
Mr. and Mrs. Stanley Herzman, 1980. 1980.471.5.

1. *Wenwu*, 1976, no. 8, pp. 71–77, and color pl. 1; pl. 5:5;
   fig. 7. *Sekai tōji zenshū* [Ceramic Art of the World], vol. 14,
   Ming Dynasty (Tokyo, 1976), pls. 173–75(bottom).

2. *Wenwu*, 1976, no. 8, color pl. 1.

3. Bai Kun et al., *Zhongguo Taoci*, 1982, no. 7, pp. 171–82.

4. Ibid., pl. 20:2,4,5,7; figs. 3, 4.

5. Ibid., p. 173, and fig. 3.

6. Ibid., pp. 173–75.

7. Underglaze blue–painted wares: ibid., pls. 19, 20:8, 21:14,
   22:19–21, 23, 24, 25:31–34; fig. 8(center). Underglaze
   red–painted wares: ibid., pls. 21:13,16, 26:39,40.
   Underglaze red-and-blue: ibid., p. 176.

8. White-glazed porcelains: ibid., pl. 21:17; fig. 10. Red-glazed
   porcelains: ibid., pl. 26:41,42; fig. 8(left). White design
   on blue ground: ibid., pl. 22:22. Imitation Longquan:
   ibid., pl. 26:36–38; fig. 8(right).

199. PLATE. Stoneware with white slip decoration on light
     blue glaze. Diameter: 15 in. (38.1 cm.). Late Ming
     dynasty, late 16th–early 17th century. "Swatow" ware.
     Rogers Fund, 1917. 17.35.1.

9. Zhang Fukang, in conversation with the author, 1987. Zhang Fukang, "The Origin and Development of Traditional Chinese Glazes and Decorative Ceramic Colors," in *Ancient Technology to Modern Science*, Ceramics and Civilization, ed. W. D. Kingery, vol. 1 (Columbus, Ohio, 1984), pp. 163–80. According to Zhang, most of these medium-fired glazes belong to the potassia system of glazes.

10. E.g., five blue-and-white covered jars excavated in 1958 in Xinjian xian, Jiangxi Province, from a tomb that can probably be dated to 1437 (J. M. Addis, *Chinese Ceramics from Datable Tombs and Some Other Dated Material: A Handbook* [London and New York, 1978], pls. 42:a,b). • Blue-and-white and red-and-white wares found in 1974 in the suburbs of Jingdezhen, in two tombs datable to 1453 and 1456, respectively (Ouyang Shibin and Huang Yunpeng, *Wenwu*, 1981, no. 2, pp. 46–50, and pls. 5:1,2,4–7, 6:1–3,5; fig. 1). • Many of these documentary blue-and-white wares—as well as some other porcelains of the same general quality—are illustrated in color, Zhongguo Shanghai renmin meishu chubanshe [ZSRMC], ed., *Chūgoku tōji zenshū*, vol. 19, Jingdezhen blue-and-white people's ware (Kyoto, 1983), pls. 12–48, where they have been attributed to the "Interregnum Period."

11. E.g., Liu Xinyuan and Bai Kun, *Wenwu*, 1980, no. 11, pp. 39–49, and pl. 5; fig. 13. Ouyang and Huang, *Wenwu*, 1981, no. 2, pls. 5:3, 6:4; figs. 2, 3.

12. E.g., *Wenwu*, 1978, no. 7, p. 83, and color pl. 1.

13. This group of bowls is discussed by Jan Wirgin, who feels that the characters on them were inspired by Indian script and could be described as a kind of ornamental *lan-tsha*, closest to what in China and Japan is usually known as *siddham* ("K'ang-hsi Porcelain: Selected Objects from Swedish Collections," *The Museum of Far Eastern Antiquities* [Stockholm] *Bulletin*, vol. 46 [1974], pp. 74–76). He notes that they were written by someone unfamiliar with the language and seem to have been adapted to resemble Chinese seal characters.

14. There is at least one notable exception to this statement. In 1979–80, in Nancheng xian, Jiangxi Province, a fairly large *kraakporselein* dish was found in the coffin of Zhu Yiyin, who died in 1603 (*Wenwu*, 1982, no. 8, pp. 16–28, and pl. 5:4,7). The rim of this dish had been broken, and the piece had been repaired, reglazed, and refired. Until this excavation, finding a piece of *kraak* ware in a Chinese tomb was virtually unknown.

15. C. L. van der Pijl-Ketel, ed., *The Ceramic Load of the 'Witte Leeuw' (1613)* [Amsterdam, 1982], pp. 46–142.

16. E.g., three censers with the reign title of the Tianqi emperor. Two are dated in accordance with 1625. One is in the British Museum (Duncan Macintosh, *Chinese Blue-and-White Porcelain* [Rutland, Vermont, 1977], pl. 44). One is in a private collection (Stephen Little, *Chinese Ceramics of the Transitional Period: 1620–1683*, exhib. cat. [New York, 1983], fig. 3). The third is dated in accordance with 1626 (Richard S. Kilburn, *Transitional Wares and Their Forerunners*, exhib. cat. [Hong Kong, 1981], no. 56). • A bowl that has the Chongzhen reign title and is dated in accordance with 1639 is in the Museum of Chinese History in Beijing (Regina Krahl, "A Dated Chinese Porcelain Bowl of the Transitional Period," *Oriental Art*, n.s. vol. 32 [Spring 1986], pp. 51–53, and figs. 1, 2. Idem, *Chinese Ceramics in the Topkapi Saray Museum, Istanbul*, ed. John Ayers, vol. 2, *Yuan and Ming Dynasty Porcelains* [London, 1986], pp. 602–3).

17. Private communication with the author. Willard Bascom, *The Crest of the Wave: Adventures in Oceanography* (forthcoming). I am grateful to Dr. Bascom for allowing me to read an advance copy of his chapter "Finding a Treasure Galleon."

18. An incense burner in the Palace Museum, Beijing. The mark on this piece has been written in exactly the same style as the mark on the Metropolitan Museum's vase (Geng Baochang, *Ming, Qing ciqi jianding* [Hong Kong, 1984], pp. 156–57, and fig. 163[two views]). A vase in the British Museum that is extremely close to the Metropolitan's (Soame Jenyns, *Ming Pottery and Porcelain* [London, 1953], pl. 110:B).

19. Van der Pijl-Ketel, *Ceramic Load of the 'Witte Leeuw,'* pp. 195–219.

20. *Kaogu*, 1978, no. 3, pp. 195–99, and fig. 5:4.

21. Ibid., p. 197, and fig. 4.

22. Van der Pijl-Ketel, *Ceramic Load of the 'Witte Leeuw,'* pp. 220–45.

23. Wenwu bianji weiyuanhui, ed., *Zhongguo gudai yaozhi diaocha fajue baogaoji* (Beijing, 1984), pp. 39–44.

24. Song Boyin, "Tea Drinking, Tea Ware and Purple Clay Ware," in *K. S. Lo Collection in the Flagstaff House Museum* [Hong Kong] *of Tea Ware*, pt. 2, exhib. cat. (Hong Kong, 1984), pp. 14–24.

25. E.g., a *zisha* teapot found in 1966 outside Nanjing's Zhonghuamen in the tomb of the eunuch Wu Jing; this tomb is datable to 1533 (Feng Xianming et al., eds., *Zhongguo taoci shi* [Beijing, 1982], p. 394, and pl. 31:1). • Another was excavated in 1968 at Jiangdu, Yangzhou, Jiangsu Province; it was found in a tomb along with a land deed dated in accordance with 1616 (*Wenwu*, 1982, no. 6, p. 91, and fig. 2). This hexagonal teapot carries the mark *Dabin*, presumably referring to Shi Dabin, one of three famous Yixing potters of the Wanli period. This vessel is illustrated in color, ZSRMC, *Chūgoku tōji zenshū*, vol. 23, Yixing (Kyoto, 1982), pl. 1.

200. PLATE. Stoneware with white slip decoration on pale celadon glaze. Diameter: 16 1/2 in. (41.9 cm.). Late Ming dynasty, late 16th–early 17th century. "Swatow" ware. Rogers Fund, 1917. 17.146.1.

209

CHAPTER TWELVE
THE QING DYNASTY

As the Ming dynasty's power weakened in its later years, certain Jurchen tribes were gaining strength in southern Manchuria. United under vigorous leadership, the Jurchens, who had earlier adopted the name Manchu, proclaimed their Qing dynasty at Mukden in 1636. These Jurchens, or Manchus, made repeated forays into China, and in 1644, primarily owing to internal rebellions, they were able to overcome Beijing and bring their Qing rule (1644–1912) to China.

201. VASE. Porcelain painted in underglaze blue and red. Height: 8 1/4 in. (21 cm.). Later Transitional Period, ca. 1662–83. Purchase by subscription, 1879. 79.2.453.

202. STEMCUP. Porcelain painted in underglaze blue. Height: 4 1/4 in. (10.8 cm.). Apocryphal mark of Chenghua period, 1465–87, but later Transitional Period, ca. 1662–83. Gift of Mr. and Mrs. Raymond J. Horowitz, 1977. 1977.183.2.

203. VASE. Porcelain painted in underglaze blue. Height: 8 in. (20.3 cm.). Later Transitional Period, ca. 1662–83. Rogers Fund, 1918. 17.200.

THE LATER TRANSITIONAL PERIOD

Porcelains made during the reign of the first Qing-dynasty emperor, the Shunzhi emperor (1644–61), and in the early decades of the Kangxi emperor's reign (that is, from 1662 to 1683), offer little originality in the development of Chinese ceramics. Made during the later part of the Transitional Period that bridged the late Ming and early Qing dynasties, they exhibit, not surprisingly, some characteristics held over from the late Ming period and some that foresee the more established styles of the Kangxi era.

Underglaze-painted wares. Several kinds of porcelain in the Metropolitan's collection can be attributed to this period. A blue-and-white stemcup and vase (Nos. 202 and 203) are decorated in the so-called Master-of-the-Rocks style that is characterized by a distinctive penciled type of drawing. The vase (No. 201) is painted in underglaze blue and red in a closely related manner.

Enameled wares. In two particularly fine, later Transitional Period porcelains, which are painted in overglaze polychrome enamels (Color No. 32 and No. 204), certain elements in the design are completely out of scale. This stylistic convention was to become

quite popular later in the Kangxi reign. A square vase painted in underglaze blue and overglaze polychrome enamels (No. 205) represents a group of wares that provide a link between the so-called *wucai*-type decoration of the late Ming period and some *famille verte* enamels of a slightly later date.

Enamels on the biscuit. The covered ewer (No. 206) is painted with enamels on the biscuit. Its design, a *haima* ("sea horse") with blossoms and auspicious symbols on spiral waves,[1] can be found on a number of early Qing-dynasty porcelains ornamented in the same technique. This piece has a somewhat unusual shape; the nearest documentary comparison seems to be an underglaze-painted, lidded ewer at Burghley House, Stamford, England, that was included in a 1690 inventory known as the "Devonshire Schedule."[2]

Porcelains with colored glazes. A peach-shaped wine pot (No. 207) represents a group of similarly shaped vessels that were produced from the very late Ming period onward.[3] These wine pots have been decorated in two different types of lower-temperature glazes. One type of glaze can be seen on the Metropolitan's pot, which has a green body, brownish aubergine handle and spout, and yellow leaves. Other peach-shaped vessels have deep purple, turquoise blue, and white glazes, which have been used singly or in various combinations. In this rather large family of peach-shaped wine pots, the leaves can be carefully formed, as they are on this example, or they can be quite perfunctory. It is possible that this lesser quality of modeling is related to the date of manufacture.

QING PORCELAINS

Porcelains of the Qing dynasty provide a dazzling grand finale to the cavalcade of Chinese ceramics that began well over eight thousand years before. Fostered in the earlier years of the dynasty by the patronage of the Manchu regime—which had been quick to appreciate and adopt all Chinese arts—the ceramic industry reached new

205. VASE. Porcelain painted in underglaze blue and overglaze polychrome enamels. Height: 14 in. (35.6 cm.). Later Transitional Period, ca. 1644–83. Purchase by subscription, 1879. 79.2.8.

204. VASE. Porcelain painted in overglaze polychrome enamels. Height: 11 3/4 in. (29.8 cm.). Later Transitional Period, ca. 1662–83. Bequest of Mary Clark Thompson, 1924. 24.80.164.

206. COVERED EWER. Porcelain painted in enamels on the biscuit. Height: 6 3/4 in. (17.1 cm.). Later Transitional Period, ca. 1644–83. Robert Lehman Collection, 1975. 1975.1.1693.

heights and created some of the most splendid pottery ever crafted. An enormous variety of porcelains was produced, ranging from brilliantly decorated objects that were exported in vast quantities to eager buyers outside of China, to quite different porcelains produced mainly for imperial use and little known in the West until relatively recent times. In contrast to the usual wares that were exported, this "court-taste" porcelain, also called "Chinese-taste" porcelain, exhibits a restrained, sensitive style that often is a masterpiece of understatement.

The majority of the finest Qing-dynasty wares were produced during a comparatively short period, from 1683 until about 1756, when the imperial factories at Jingdezhen were under the direction of several capable supervisors; the most famous were Zang Yingxuan, Nian Xiyao, and Tang Ying. During their incumbencies, the potting methods that were built on the accumulated experience of the past were developed and refined to produce porcelain that is the apogee of perfection. Old decorative techniques were enlarged and improved upon, and new ones were added to the traditional vocabulary. Frequently, several of these ornamental devices were combined on one piece, thus producing a kaleidoscope of monochromatic and polychromatic effects.

Enumerating all the types of porcelains produced in the Qing period is a formidable task, and, while most of them are discussed here, not every one can be mentioned.

Western influences. European contacts had an increasingly important effect on many facets of Qing culture, and porcelains of the period often display a definite Western influence. During the eighteenth century, in particular, there was a considerable cross-pollination of ideas. A craze for "things Chinese" swept Europe, and a corresponding Chinese fondness for foreign novelties resulted in the adoption of European methods of decoration and elements of design in Chinese ceramics. Indeed, there is a contemporary record of porcelains "decorated with colored pictures painted in the European style" that were being made in the imperial porcelain manufactory specifically for the Yongzheng emperor.

Copies of earlier wares. Qing potters drew inspiration from former times as well as from distant lands, and there was a notable effort, especially in the eighteenth century, to copy earlier pottery. Many of these later wares were merely inspired by past ceramics, most often Song- and Ming-dynasty classics, and could not be confused with their prototypes. Other deliberate imitations are

such faithful and skillful reproductions, however, that they present some of the most difficult problems of attribution in Chinese ceramic scholarship.

Tang Ying's list. Limitations of space prohibit an enumeration of all the later editions of past wares that were produced during the reigns of the individual emperors. However, a good illustration is found in a list of fifty-seven types of wares that were being made in the imperial factory at Jingdezhen, which was compiled by Tang Ying, one of its most able supervisors.[4] This list cites a number of wares emulating antique ceramics—some of which had been sent from the imperial palace to the kilns in Jingdezhen to serve as models—and it indicates the great interest in copying old ceramics at this time. A few of the types that are mentioned as having been copied are difficult to identify today, but among the recognizable categories are the so-called Ge, the Ru, Ding, Jun, and Longquan of the Song dynasty. Porcelains of most major Ming periods were also copied; these included monochromes, blue-and-white wares, and ceramics with polychrome decoration.

Père d'Entrecolles. The study of early Qing porcelain has been aided by a Westerner's eyewitness account of activities at the Jingdezhen kilns. It comes from Père d'Entrecolles, a Jesuit missionary who numbered artisans and workmen from the kilns among his converts. His account is contained in two letters that were written in 1712 and 1722.[5] These communications give such information as a detailed description of how the Chinese used kaolin (china clay) and petuntse (porcelain stone) to make porcelain. The way in which various objects were fashioned, the essentials of decoration, and the firing processes are all explained at some length.

Jingdezhen porcelain. Recent technical studies have shown that Chinese porcelain was not always made of kaolin and petuntse as described by Père d'Entrecolles. In particular, the composition of Jingdezhen porcelain changed radically from its early years of production to the eighteenth century. As we have already seen, in all probability the Song-dynasty *qingbai* wares manufactured at these kiln complexes were entirely made of a pulverized local kaolinized porcelain stone, without the addition of china clay. During the Yuan era, *qingbai* bodies appear to have been made either of a pulverized kaolinized porcelain stone, or of a somewhat different porcelain stone containing a negligible amount of kaolinite that was combined with a measure of china clay. According to recent reports, there was another change in raw materials,

217

218

apparently in the second half of the fifteenth century, when the Jingdezhen bodies became slightly more plastic versions of the Song bodies. Starting in the late Ming period, there was a gradual change to a high-kaolin porcelain body; and by the Kangxi era, nearly all Jingdezhen wares were made of this high-kaolin material. Finally, the composition of the body was changed again in the nineteenth/twentieth century.[6]

KANGXI PORCELAINS

The long reign of the Kangxi emperor (1662–1722) saw the beginning of what might be considered the golden age of Qing porcelains. With the arrival of Zang Yingxuan as director of the imperial factory at Jingdezhen in 1683, a brilliant new chapter in the history of the potter's art was under way. Inasmuch as they were produced over a period of sixty years, Kangxi porcelains understandably exhibit several changes in style. Generally speaking, they move from the somewhat robust character of the later Transitional Period–Kangxi wares that were made before 1683, to the elegant opulence of the middle Kangxi period, and then to the more refined and quieter taste of those later porcelains that foreshadow the delicate treatment of the Yongzheng era.

Blue-and-white wares. Blue-and-white porcelains of the Kangxi period continued a centuries-old decorative tradition, but far from appearing a jaded ornamental medium, cobalt-blue in the hands of the Kangxi painter presents a radiant new face. Kangxi blue has often been described as having a sapphire hue, and in its finest examples—set off by an almost faultless white background—this pure, deep, luminous blue does have that precious stone's quality. The lovely little vase with a landscape design (No. 208), painted in graded washes of pellucid blue over finely penciled lines, is a splendid illustration of Kangxi blue at its best. These porcelains vary enormously in quality, ranging from superb pieces that in all likelihood were intended for the court, to wares that were no better than they needed to be for the export trade.

210. VASE. Porcelain with slight relief decoration, painted in underglaze blue. Height: 17 3/8 in. (44.1 cm.). Mark: a double circle. Qing dynasty, late 17th–early 18th century, Kangxi period. Bequest of Mrs. H. O. Havemeyer, 1929, H. O. Havemeyer Collection. 29.100.308.

209. COVERED JAR. Porcelain painted in underglaze blue. Height with cover: 10 1/4 in. (26 cm.). Qing dynasty, late 17th–early 18th century, Kangxi period. Bequest of Benjamin Altman, 1913. 14.40.313.

211. VASE. Porcelain with low-relief decoration, painted in underglaze red. Height: 8 in. (20.3 cm.). Qing dynasty, Kangxi mark, probably late in the period, ca. 1700–22. Bequest of Mary Clark Thompson, 1924. 24.80.258.

The decorative motifs and their permutations that are found on these porcelains are virtually incalculable, and only two particularly famous patterns will be mentioned here. Slender and graceful Chinese ladies who were called *Lange Lijsen* by the old Dutch collectors—a name later corrupted to "Long Elizas" by the English—adorn innumerable blue-and-white vessels of the period. Branches of blossoming prunus reserved on a field of cracking ice, signifying the end of winter and coming of spring, is a design often found on the so-called ginger jars, or hawthorn jars (No. 209), used to carry gifts of tea and preserved fruits at the New Year.

Kangxi potters sometimes emphasized elements of the design, such as blossoms of flowers, by showing them in slight relief and silhouetting them against a wash of blue, as on the vase (No. 210).

Red-and-white wares. Painting porcelain in underglaze copper-red had been introduced during the Yuan dynasty and was used with mixed results into the early Ming. This technique was rarely used after the early fifteenth century; it appears to have been reintroduced into the decorative grammar in the seventeenth century. A special little vase (No. 211), showing two underglaze red, three-clawed dragons leaping from a field of waves, probably dates to the end of the Kangxi era, as do the red-and-white bottle (No. 212) and its blue-and-white counterpart (No. 213).

Blue-and-red decoration. The technique of combining underglaze cobalt-blue and copper-red, the bête noire of Ming potters, was finally mastered during the seventeenth century. Good examples of these two colors used in tandem can be dated to the part of the Kangxi reign that is included in the later Transitional Period. A dish with birds and a flowering branch painted in underglaze blue and red (No. 214) illustrates outstanding control of the copper pigment: the birds' bodies are reddish brown, a shade that is deliberately different from the more crimson red in the rest of the design.

Blue, red, and celadon. This kind of decoration was taken one step further. As in the vase (No. 215), areas of celadon have sometimes been added to designs that are painted in underglaze blue and red, creating a most harmonious polychromatic effect. As another variant in the seemingly endless exercise of mixing and matching decorative processes, a celadon-glazed vessel can serve as a setting for designs in underglaze blue and red on a backing of white.

212. BOTTLE. Porcelain painted in underglaze red. Height: 8 7/8 in. (22.5 cm.). Qing dynasty, Kangxi mark, probably late in the period, ca. 1700–22. Mr. and Mrs. Isaac D. Fletcher Collection, Bequest of Isaac D. Fletcher, 1917. 17.120.167.

213. BOTTLE. Porcelain painted in underglaze blue. Height: 9 3/8 in. (23.8 cm.). Qing dynasty, Kangxi mark, probably late in the period, ca. 1700–22. Gift of Edwin C. Vogel, 1966. 66.206.2.

214. DISH. Porcelain painted in underglaze blue and red.
Diameter: 10 1/2 in. (26.7 cm.). Apocryphal mark of
Xuande period, 1426–35, but Qing dynasty, late 17th–
early 18th century, Kangxi period. Rogers Fund, 1917.
18.56.59.

215. VASE. Porcelain with slight relief, incised decoration,
painted in underglaze blue and red, with a wash of
celadon. Height: 17 1/8 in. (43.5 cm.). Mark:
a fungus. Qing dynasty, late 17th–early 18th century,
Kangxi period. Bequest of Mary Clark Thompson, 1924.
24.80.165.

219. VASE. Porcelain painted in enamels on the biscuit (*famille noire*). Height: 16 3/4 in. (42.5 cm.). Qing dynasty, late 17th–early 18th century, Kangxi period. Gift of Edwin C. Vogel, 1964. 64.279.14.

217. HOOKAH BASE. Porcelain painted in underglaze blue, with brown glaze. Height: 10 1/2 in. (26.7 cm.). Mark: a leaf. Qing dynasty, late 17th–early 18th century, Kangxi period. Purchase by subscription, 1879. 79.2.359.

216. VASE. Porcelain painted in underglaze blue, with crackled and brown glazes. Height: 9 5/8 in. (24.4 cm.). Qing dynasty, late 17th–early 18th century, Kangxi period. Purchase by subscription, 1879. 79.2.263.

218. VASE. Porcelain with incised and slight relief decoration, painted in underglaze blue and red, with blue and brown glazes. Height: 8 7/8 in. (22.5 cm.). Mark: a double circle. Qing dynasty, late 17th–early 18th century, Kangxi period. Purchase by subscription, 1879. 79.2.255.

Underglaze-painted decoration with colored glazes.
Underglaze blue painting can also be complemented in
other ways. For example, bands of dark brown punctuate
the upper section of a hookah base (No. 217) that was
made for the Indian market.[7] Again, as seen in the vase
(No. 216), underglaze blue designs can be separated from
a brown glaze by a band of crackled glaze. On another
vase (No. 218), underglaze blue-and-red painting is
combined with a dark blue glaze, highlighted by a band
of brown.

Famille verte *enamels.* The possibilities of painting
porcelains with colored enamels, which were so
successfully developed during the Ming dynasty, were
exploited to the fullest in the Qing period. Essentially
the same low-fired enamels were now used with such
authority that Qing polychrome-decorated porcelains
outshine all others. The stellar polychrome decoration
of the Kangxi period, the *famille verte* palette of enamels,
takes its name from the several distinctive shades of green
that are almost invariably present in the color scheme.
Famille verte enamels are brightly colored and translucent;
they have been applied rather thickly over the darker
outlines and details. In addition to the various greens,
the *famille verte* colors include yellow; aubergine; coral-
toned iron-red (rather flat and almost opaque); white
(achieved by allowing the pure body to show through a
clear enamel); and black (a composite color made of
matte, brownish black pigment covered with green,
aubergine, or clear enamel). The blue enamel in this
assortment of colors is different from the Ming-dynasty
turquoise-tinted blue enamel; it is more violet or royal
blue in tone. Like their Ming antecedents, these
translucent *famille verte* enamels—appropriately named
yingcai ("hard colors") by the Chinese—did not permit
much gradation in color, and the effects of shading had
to be relegated to finely penciled lines in the preliminary
drawing.

Famille verte enamels were painted directly onto
unglazed, prefired bodies, known as enameling on the
biscuit, or they were painted over high-fired clear glazes.
In both instances, the decorated porcelains, which had
already been high fired to maturity, were given a second

221. VASE. Porcelain painted in *famille verte* enamels on the
biscuit. Height: 29 5/8 in. (75.2 cm.). Qing dynasty,
late 17th–early 18th century, Kangxi period. Bequest of
Benjamin Altman, 1913. 14.40.401.

220. VASE. Porcelain painted in enamels on the biscuit
(*famille jaune*). Height: 21 1/8 in. (53.7 cm.). Qing
dynasty, late 17th–early 18th century, Kangxi period.
Bequest of Benjamin Altman, 1913. 14.40.397.

223. PLATE. Porcelain painted in overglaze *famille verte* enamels. Diameter: 6 3/4 in. (17.1 cm.). Apocryphal mark of Chenghua period, 1465–87, but Qing dynasty, ca. 1700–22, Kangxi period. Gift of Edwin C. Vogel, 1963. 63.213.14.

222. FIGURE, POSSIBLY THE GOD OF WEALTH IN HIS MILITARY ASPECT. Porcelain painted in *famille verte* enamels on the biscuit. Height: 22 3/4 in. (57.8 cm.). Qing dynasty, late 17th–early 18th century, Kangxi period. Bequest of John D. Rockefeller, Jr., 1960. 61.200.12.

224. VASE. Porcelain painted in overglaze *famille verte* enamels and gilt. Height: 19 in. (48.3 cm.). Mark: a double circle. Qing dynasty, late 17th–early 18th century, Kangxi period. Bequest of John D. Rockefeller, Jr., 1960. 61.200.33.

firing. This firing was only to the low temperatures of an enameling kiln, known in the West as a muffle kiln, to fuse the enamels.

Famille verte *enamels painted on the biscuit.* The decoration of porcelains painted with *famille verte* enamels on the biscuit is often set against a dominant, solid-color ground of black, yellow, green, or, occasionally, aubergine; the first two groups are frequently placed in the subcategories of *famille noire* and *famille jaune*. At their peak these vessels are truly gorgeous, combining eloquent brushwork with well-mated colors and designs that are invariably right for the shape they grace. Three vases, representing the *famille noire* group (No. 219), the *famille jaune* class (No. 220), and the rare family with green grounds (No. 221), are excellent examples of their respective types. They are the sort of porcelains that were greatly treasured by past generations in both this country and Europe.

Enamel painting on the biscuit was particularly well suited to the decoration of porcelain figures because a thick, preliminary glaze under the enamels would tend to fill in and blunt the sharp modeling of the features and the garments. Two superb figures (Color No. 33 and No. 222) are masterful examples of modeling and decoration; they are at the summit of Kangxi porcelain figures. The iron-red on one of these figures (Color No. 33) has been painted on a pad of clear glaze that was applied just in that area to support the red, a technique generally employed in on-the-biscuit enameling to ensure a richer red color.

A certain amount of the openwork that was popular in the late Ming period is found again in *famille verte* on-the-biscuit wares, particularly in such objects as writing cases, brush holders, and lanterns.

Famille verte *enamels painted over the glaze.* When used over the glaze, the *famille verte* enamels present a somewhat different appearance. Supported by the lustrous glaze, they stand radiant and clear against the white ground that forms an integral part of the total composition. In addition to being used with the usual overglaze blue enamel of the palette, overglaze *famille verte* enamels are sometimes found in conjunction with underglaze cobalt-blue painting, and occasionally both underglaze and overglaze blue can be seen on the same object. Touches of gilt were often added to this group, providing an especially lively accent.

The designer's imagination has seldom been more fruitful or wider in scope than on these sumptuous

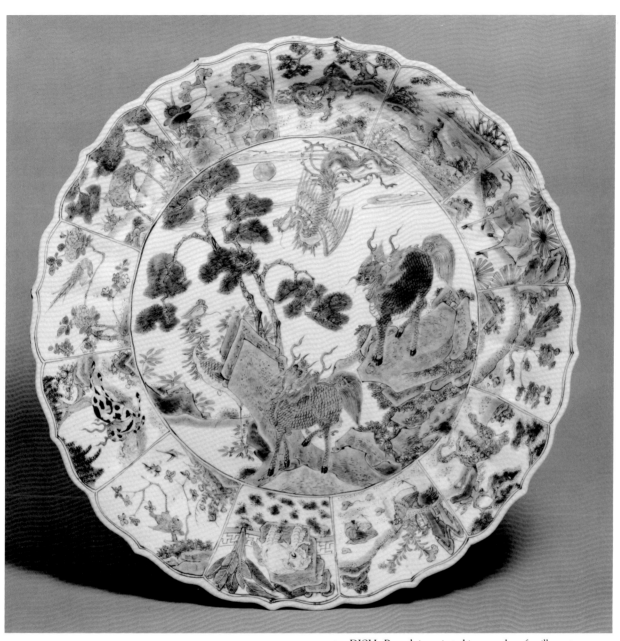

225. DISH. Porcelain painted in overglaze *famille verte* enamels. Diameter: 11 in. (27.9 cm.). Qing dynasty, Kangxi mark and period, 1662–1722. Rogers Fund, 1925. 25.64.9.

226. DISH. Porcelain painted in overglaze *famille verte*
enamels, green glaze on the reverse. Diameter: 6 7/8 in.
(17.5 cm.). Qing dynasty, Kangxi mark and period,
1662–1722. Bequest of Edmund Cogswell Converse,
1921. 21.175.39.

porcelains; they offer a galaxy of motifs handled in an
almost infinite variety of ways. Their decoration ranges
from relatively few figures discreetly placed on broad
expanses of white, in a style most likely to have appealed
to the court (No. 223), to extremely complex designs
featuring reserve panels of small scenes set against the
richly brocaded grounds that virtually cover the vessel's
surface (No. 224). The profusion of elements garnishing
some of the latter types may be overwhelming at times;
however, while not to every taste, these wares command
respect as decorative tours de force.

Among other noteworthy examples in the
Metropolitan's collection is the beaker-shaped vase (Color
No. 34), painted in a lively spirit with birds, rocks, and

227. DISH. Porcelain painted in underglaze blue, overglaze polychrome enamels, and gilt. Diameter: 10 5/8 in. (27 cm.). Qing dynasty, early 18th century, Kangxi period. "Chinese Imari" ware. Purchase by subscription, 1879. 79.2.521.

229. VESSEL IN THE FORM OF A DEER. Porcelain with colored glazes in the "egg-and-spinach" pattern. Height: 8 in. (20.3 cm.). Qing dynasty, late 17th–early 18th century, Kangxi period. Bequest of Mary Clark Thompson, 1924. 24.80.257.

230. BOWL. Porcelain with colored glazes in the "egg-and-spinach" pattern. Diameter: 8 3/4 in. (22.2 cm.). Qing dynasty, late 17th–early 18th century, Kangxi period. Purchase by subscription, 1879. 79.2.128.

flowers. A foliated dish with exceptionally fine drawing (No. 225) features fantastic creatures in a landscape. Three figures on the dish (No. 226) represent characters from *Shuihu zhuan* ("The Water Margin"), a popular novel based on the exploits of a minor bandit who lived during the Song period. The green glaze on the reverse of this dish is somewhat unusual.

Iron-red enamel. The thin, matte, coral-toned iron-red of the *famille verte* palette is sometimes seen as a ground color on Kangxi porcelains; it can be relieved by reserve white scrollwork or serve as a setting for decoration in underglaze blue or overglaze enamels. On occasion it can appear rather dramatically as the sole color in Kangxi overglaze-painted decoration.

"Famille verte *black.*" The composite black from the *famille verte* palette of enamels has occasionally been used to produce bright green designs that are dramatized by a greenish black background. In this type of decoration, the design was reserved in the black pigment ground under an overall wash of translucent green enamel.

"Chinese Imari" wares. "Chinese Imari" wares are interesting cousins of the *famille verte* family. These wares, which started to be made about the beginning of the eighteenth century, represent a turnabout of the age-old Japanese practice of copying Chinese porcelain. The so-called Old Imari wares that were made at the Arita kilns in Japan were decorated in dark underglaze blue, enlivened with overglaze iron-red enamel and gold. These Arita porcelains, which were exported in large quantities to Europe and the Middle East in the late seventeenth/early eighteenth century, were very ornamental and understandably popular in the Western markets. Not to be outdone in supplying salable merchandise for export, the Chinese copied these Japanese wares, and at first glance it is often difficult to distinguish between the Chinese and Japanese products. "Chinese Imari" wares were frequently manufactured to the tastes of buyers in Europe, the Middle East, and other parts of Asia.[8] The dish (No. 227) is a variant of the "Chinese Imari" type, in which a few overglaze colored enamels have been added to the basic blue, red, and gold color scheme.

Famille verte *colors used as glazes.* The green, yellow, aubergine, and white of the *famille verte* palette of enamels are the basic colors of a large family of Kangxi porcelains decorated with lower-fired glazes on the biscuit. (Because of their similarity to the *famille verte* enamels that were used in a more painterly style, some authorities classify them as enamel glazes.) Sometimes these glazes have been combined to color the individual parts of vessels and figures with complementing hues, as in the delightful little European on a lion (No. 228). The man's coat was painted with vermilion on the biscuit after the second firing, and because it was not fixed in the kiln, it has flaked off in several places. In other instances, these glazes have been washed over engraved designs of flowers or dragons on grounds of contrasting colors. Again, they can be daubed in variegated patterns, including the motley of colors given fanciful names such as "tiger-skin," "leopard-skin," and "egg-and-spinach" (Nos. 229 and 230).

After the Kangxi period, the *famille verte* palette of enamels lost much of its popularity; however, it did continue in minor use during subsequent reigns.

Monochrome glazes. Qing-dynasty monochrome porcelains are a fitting counterpart to the effulgent splendor

EIGHT OBJECTS FOR THE WRITING TABLE. Porcelain with peachbloom glazes. Qing dynasty, Kangxi marks, late in the period, ca. 1700–22.

231. Vase. Height: 8 in. (20.3 cm.). Bequest of Mary Stillman Harkness, 1950. 50.145.286 [also Color No. 37].

232. Vase. Height: 8 in. (20.3 cm.). Bequest of Benjamin Altman, 1913. 14.40.362.

233. Vase. Height: 8 1/4 in. (21 cm.). Gift of Edwin C. Vogel, 1965. 65.225.5.

234. Water coupe. Height: 3 1/2 in. (8.9 cm.). Gift of Edwin C. Vogel, 1965. 65.225.3.

235. Vase. Height: 6 1/8 in. (15.6 cm.). Bequest of Benjamin Altman, 1913. 14.40.381.

236. Brush washer. Diameter: 4 1/2 in. (11.4 cm.). Bequest of Mrs. H. O. Havemeyer, 1929, H. O. Havemeyer Collection. 29.100.352.

237. Seal color box. Diameter: 2 7/8 in. (7.3 cm.). Bequest of Benjamin Altman, 1913. 14.40.369.

238. Water coupe. Diameter: 3 7/8 in. (9.8 cm.). Bequest of Mrs. H. O. Havemeyer, 1929, H. O. Havemeyer Collection. 29.100.331.

239. VASE. Porcelain with relief decoration under clear glaze. Height: 8 in. (20.3 cm.). Qing dynasty, Kangxi mark, late in the period, ca. 1700–22. Bequest of Mary Stillman Harkness, 1950. 50.145.295.

of Qing polychrome wares, substituting for the latter's more obvious charms the aesthetic pleasures of elegant shapes and exquisite glazes, in which one appreciates a fundamental sense of the material itself.

Many Qing monochrome porcelains are completely plain. The decoration on the others generally is minimal and unobtrusive, consisting of underglaze intaglio or relief designs, including *anhua* ("secret decoration," or "hidden decoration"), which must be searched out before it can be enjoyed. Surprisingly few coloring materials were used in the Qing monochrome glazes: essentially, they were iron, copper, cobalt, and manganese oxides. With them, the Chinese potters managed to achieve what amounts to ceramic wizardry in turning out an extensive list of hues that span the color scale.

Among the Qing-dynasty single-color wares, as with virtually all of China's ceramic output, there are no sharp lines of demarcation that coincide with historical events such as changes in the reigns of individual emperors. Therefore, without the aid of an acceptable reign mark, arbitrary dating to a general span of time must often suffice.

High-fired glazes. Qing monochrome porcelains that were fired in the most intense heat of the furnace are the ultimate achievement of an age-old tradition. Many of these colored glazes had been known in earlier times; through the talents of the Qing potters, their development was consummated, and they reached a quality that is unsurpassed and unsurpassable.

Copper-red glazes. The Kangxi high-fired red glazes were produced by firing a glaze that contained copper oxide in a reducing atmosphere and perhaps finishing it in an oxidizing atmosphere. They include two that rank among the most popular of all Qing-dynasty single-color wares.

Sang de boeuf *glazes.* The first is the intense, brilliant, red glaze known as *langyao*, *sang de boeuf*, or "ox blood." In its finer examples, this spectacular glaze gives the impression that one is gazing through a limpid surface layer, which is slightly crazed and strewn with countless fine bubbles, to the color that lies underneath. *Sang de boeuf* color generally starts in a greenish gray tone at the top of the vessel; as it descends, it quickly turns red in changing shades that range from light red with tints of green to deep crimson, with an occasional overtone of dark reddish brown. A remarkable control of the thick glaze, which is checked in an even line where it stops above the foot, is considered to be a hallmark of genuine

THREE OBJECTS FOR THE WRITING TABLE.
Porcelain with *clair de lune* glazes. Qing dynasty, Kangxi
marks, late in the period, ca. 1700–22.

Kangxi *sang de boeuf* porcelains. The small vase (Color
No. 35) is an especially fine example of this type.

    Peachbloom glazes. In the second copper-red glaze,
the famous Kangxi peachbloom glaze, the effect is quite
subdued. This soft, velvety glaze varies in color from
piece to piece, but it essentially is pale pinkish red, often
shading to darker values. It sometimes is plain, frequently
is mottled, and in a particularly appealing version, it
shows tender flushes of moss green. The finest peachbloom
wares constitute an elite series—in all likelihood consisting
of no more than eight specific shapes—of small and
elegant vessels that were intended to be used at the
scholar's writing table. The refinement in the potting,
shapes, and glaze in this group indicates that it probably
dates to the final portion of the Kangxi reign. Not many

240. Water coupe. Diameter: 4 1/8 in. (10.5 cm.). Gift of
Edwin C. Vogel, 1966. 66.206.4.

241. Vase. Height: 6 1/4 in. (15.9 cm.). Bequest of Mary
Stillman Harkness, 1950. 50.145.294.

242. Brush washer. Diameter: 4 5/8 in. (11.7 cm.). Gift of
Edwin C. Vogel, 1964. 64.279.1.

collections can boast of having more than a few classic peachbloom examples, and the Metropolitan is fortunate to own seven of the eight basic forms and what most likely is a variation of the eighth (Color No. 37, also shown as No. 231, and Nos. 232 to 238).

White porcelains. High-fired white porcelains produced at the Jingdezhen kilns in the Kangxi period are beautifully represented here by the rare vase (No. 239) in a shape more closely associated with Kangxi peachbloom-glazed vessels. Because of its outstanding quality, one may assume that it was produced toward the end of the Kangxi reign.

Clair de lune *glazes*. The Kangxi period yielded a broad spectrum of high-fired blue glazes, which derived their color from cobalt oxide. They range from a fairly purplish midnight color through many lovely intermediate shades to the fragile tint known as *clair de lune*. *Clair de lune*–glazed porcelains frequently have the same shapes as the classic peachbloom vessels and, like the latter, show the daintiness and fineness of potting that is associated with the end of the Kangxi period. Three objects for the writing table—a water coupe (No. 240), vase (No. 241), and brush washer (No. 242)—are sheathed with a gentle, even glaze that shows just a breath of color. They illustrate why *clair de lune* is among the most treasured of the Qing-dynasty glazes.

"Powder-blue" glazes. "Powder-blue" glazes are somewhat different from other Qing blue glazes in that the cobalt coloring matter was not mixed with the glaze. Instead, it was blown dry onto the raw body of the vessel by using a piece of gauze stretched over the end of a bamboo tube. This was then covered with a clear glaze and fired. The result is a somewhat frothy effect, at its best a rich lapis lazuli tone, which might be further embellished with etched designs or, more often, gilding. Such gilding is seen on the imposing vase (No. 243), where the gilt is unusually well preserved. One of the poems on this vase is dated, "On a spring day of the year *jichou*" (1709). "Powder-blue" has frequently been used as a ground against which reserve white panels of various shapes, which contain sundry underglaze blue or overglaze polychrome enamel designs, are set.

244. VASE. Porcelain with relief decoration under celadon glaze. Height: 8 1/4 in. (21 cm.). Qing dynasty, Kangxi mark, late in the period, ca. 1700–22. Bequest of Benjamin Altman, 1913. 14.40.366.

243. VASE. Porcelain with "powder-blue" glaze, painted in gilt. Height: 17 1/2 in. (44.5 cm.). Qing dynasty, early 18th century (poem dated in accordance with 1709). Purchase by subscription, 1879. 79.2.153.

Celadons. The celadon glazes of the period—which were produced by firing a glaze that contained a small amount of iron oxide and perhaps other minerals in a reducing atmosphere—had deep roots in the history of Chinese ceramics. Eighteenth-century celadon wares often exhibit exceptional delicacy and finesse, with thin, pale glazes complemented by the fine white porcelain bodies of the Jingdezhen kilns. Some of these celadons are crackled, but the loveliest examples, such as the rare vase (No. 244) with a profile similar to one known in Kangxi peachblooms and the water pot (No. 245), are plain, with immaculate glazes that give full scope to the sophisticated forms and subtle underglaze ornamentation.

Brown glazes. Many ceramics with single-color, high-fired gray, beige, and brown glazes, the majority of which are crackled, were produced throughout the Qing dynasty. There is a group of wares with lustrous monochrome glazes that range from an "old-gold" tint to a dark bronze hue and include the popular shades of chocolate, "dead leaf," and café au lait. These golden brown glazes have also been used as a ground for reserve ornamental compartments that are decorated in underglaze blue or overglaze polychrome enamels; porcelains decorated in this manner have been given the trade name of "Batavian" ware. Sometimes the brown glaze has been used in conjunction with underglaze blue painting, and bands of crackled, buff-colored glaze can be added (No. 216); again, the glaze can be overlaid with white slip.

Mirror-black glazes. Among the high-fired black monochromes of the period, the most famous is a lustrous, dense black glaze that was derived from iron, cobalt, and manganese oxides. It is called *wujin* ("black bronze") by the Chinese and is commonly known in the West as mirror-black. These brilliant mirror-black wares have frequently been penciled over in gilt. Because of the extremely fugitive nature of such gilt decoration, it has often disappeared, leaving only the ghost of a pattern that can be seen when a light is raked over the glaze.

Apple-green glazes. The well-known apple-green glaze is composite in nature, consisting of a high-fired, stone-colored crackled glaze that has been given a coating of translucent emerald green and refired at a lower temperature. Some authorities feel that this group of monochromes was introduced during the Kangxi reign; however, most of these wares seem to date to somewhat later than the Kangxi period.

"Soft-paste" porcelain. In addition to their various innovations and improvements in the decorative

techniques, the Qing potters also experimented with the fabric of their wares. A new material called *huashi* ("slippery stone"), which was sometimes used to replace kaolin in the manufacture of porcelain, was mentioned by Père d'Entrecolles in his letters. These probably are the wares now known in the West—somewhat inaccurately—as "soft-paste" porcelain. They vary considerably in character but generally are thinly potted—and therefore light in weight—with a hard, fine-grained, opaque or semiopaque body that produces a rather distinctive "thunk" sound when struck. They have a creamy white, undulating glaze that has a tendency to craze. A modern practicing potter has suggested that the opacity and low resonance of the body, as well as the creamy tone and crazing of the glaze, are the result of firing "soft-paste" porcelain at a lower temperature than ordinary porcelain, perhaps to prevent warping in the kiln. *Huashi* material, which was extremely expensive, was also used more sparingly as a coating for ordinary porcelain vessels and for painting designs over the glaze in slip.

It appears that, along with using "soft-paste" material to fashion a number of objects in contemporary style, the Qing potters used something quite similar to imitate Song-dynasty Ding wares. Such a piece is the bottle (No. 246), which has dark brown dressing on its rim emulating the fitted metal bands found on the originals.

Blue-and-white "soft-paste" porcelain. The "soft-paste" bodies presented a particularly receptive surface for underglaze cobalt-blue painting (No. 247). When compared with ordinary porcelain as a vehicle for brushwork, they were likened by Père d'Entrecolles to vellum as opposed to paper. While the letters of Père d'Entrecolles document the manufacture of "soft-paste" porcelain during the Kangxi period, most of these wares were produced after the Kangxi reign.

THE REIGN OF THE YONGZHENG EMPEROR

In many respects, the porcelains of the brief Yongzheng reign (1723–35) represent the pinnacle of Qing ceramics: they often reach a point of exquisite refinement, but rarely go beyond that point, where there is the distinct danger of becoming mechanical or contrived. Nian Xiyao was put in charge of the imperial factory at Jingdezhen in

1726; however, the celebrated Tang Ying, who was appointed resident assistant in 1728,[9] was probably responsible for most ceramic triumphs after that date.

Many types of porcelain that had been produced in the preceding Kangxi reign continued to be made, at least to some extent, in this period; we shall touch on them only briefly.

Blue-and-white wares. Blue-and-white wares, apart from copies of earlier pieces, were going out of vogue; they lack the sparkling quality of the best Kangxi porcelains and frequently have a mannered air. A particularly handsome dish (No. 248), which has relief-punctuated white designs reserved against a "powder-blue" ground, has drawn on both Yuan-dynasty and Kangxi porcelains for its decorative techniques.

Red-and-white wares. Yongzheng porcelains painted in underglaze red can be extraordinarily fine, as can be seen in the select vase (Color No. 36) with a dragon floating through a cloud-filled sky.

"Soft-paste" porcelain. "Soft-paste" porcelains, whether with white-on-white designs or decorated in underglaze cobalt-blue, seem to have been quite popular during the Yongzheng emperor's reign.

Famille verte. Multicolor ornamental techniques from the past were also used. The *famille verte* palette of translucent enamels can be found on an occasional Yongzheng piece. These porcelains are relatively scarce: fashion is capricious and the *famille verte* had been virtually swept aside in favor of a new mode of decoration, the *famille rose* enamels.

Doucai. Ming *doucai*-decorated porcelains were copied with great proficiency in both the Kangxi and Yongzheng reigns (for example, see No. 297 in Chapter 13). This technique of using underglaze blue and overglaze enamels has also been employed on some first-class porcelains that are unmistakably Yongzheng in feeling, such as the two dishes that are decorated with a mixture of Taoist and Buddhist emblems (Nos. 249 and 250) and an exquisite piece with ducks in water weeds (No. 251).

Underglaze red with celadon glaze. A combination of two old decorative skills is mentioned in Tang Ying's list as being an innovation of the time: copper-red was now painted under a "Longquan" (i.e., celadon) glaze, and four different motifs are noted in this new style.

Overglaze silver, black, and red. From Tang Ying's valuable list we also learn of several current overglaze decorative techniques. There were two new techniques: vessels were being decorated in silver or ink, the latter

245. WATER POT. Porcelain with relief decoration under celadon glaze. Height: 3 in. (7.6 cm.). Qing dynasty, Kangxi mark, late in the period, ca. 1700–22. Gift of Edwin C. Vogel, 1967. 67.245.4.

246. BOTTLE. "Soft-paste" porcelain with incised
decoration under ivory white glaze. Height: 12 5/8 in.
(32.1 cm.). Qing dynasty, ca. first half 18th century.
Bequest of Benjamin Altman, 1913. 14.40.140.

presumably alluding to designs that were penciled in dry
black or sepia. Other vessels decorated in red, imitating
the old, are also mentioned.

Famille rose. The signal accomplishment of the
Yongzheng period was porcelain decorated in the *famille
rose* palette of enamels. These opaque and semiopaque
enamels differ from the earlier overglaze polychrome
enamels in two respects. First is the addition of a rose
pink, from which this type of enameling takes its name.
This pink, which was derived from colloidal gold, was
used in a wide spectrum of tones from the palest blush of
pink to deep ruby. Second—and perhaps even more
important—a lead-arsenic,[10] opaque white pigment was
mixed with the colors to modify them, enabling the
painter to achieve a range of color values for the first
time. These new graduated tones allowed the artist to
reproduce subtleties of shades and to model his drawing
as the artist who paints with oils does. In addition, a
variety of mixed tints was produced by combining colors,
usually with the addition of the opaque white. Iron-red
was occasionally added to the gentle hues of the *famille
rose* palette, and this combination of harsh and soft colors
can be surprisingly effective. The Chinese call the low-
fired *famille rose* palette *fencai* ("pale colors"), *ruancai*
("soft colors"), *yangcai* ("foreign colors"), or *falangcai*
("enamel colors").

Apparently the technique of painting porcelain in
these *famille rose* enamels was known in Europe before it
was known in China. For example, some Viennese
porcelains of the Du Paquier period that might be dated
to about 1725 illustrate a rather skillful use of shaded
overglaze enamels on porcelain bodies.[11]

In China, the *famille rose* palette could have been
adopted from the European painted enamels on gold and
copper that were introduced to China by Jesuit
missionaries; however, it could also have been adopted
from the decoration on South German tin-glazed
earthenwares brought by the Dutch.

There is some difference of opinion as to precisely
when the Chinese were able to perfect the use of these
enamels on porcelain. Although rudimentary *famille rose*
enamels can be found on some armorial porcelains dating
to the early 1720s, most likely the technique was not
fully developed much before 1730. Once established,

247. VASE. "Soft-paste" porcelain painted in underglaze
blue. Height: 16 3/4 in. (42.5 cm.). Qing dynasty, 18th
century. Gift of Mrs. Lewis G. Morris, 1968. 68.25.6.

245

248. DISH. Porcelain with reserve decoration and slight
relief on "powder-blue" ground. Diameter: 13 in.
(33 cm.). Qing dynasty, Yongzheng mark and period,
1723–35. Purchase by subscription, 1879. 79.2.129.

249, 250. TWO DISHES. Porcelain painted in underglaze blue and overglaze enamels. Diameter: 6 1/8 in. (15.6 cm.). Qing dynasty, 18th century, Yongzheng period. Rogers Fund, 1925. 25.35.3 and .4.

however, the *famille rose* style of painting became the dominant factor in the Chinese decorative vocabulary.

The finest *famille rose* porcelains of the Yongzheng period, which were probably made in imperial kilns at Jingdezhen for the exclusive use of the emperor and his court, are the epitome of delicacy and restraint in painting. The enameling on these "court-taste," or "Chinese-taste," wares is exquisite; the designs generally are sparse, allowing the beautiful white body to play an important part in the composition. A particular whimsy sometimes found on this type of porcelain may be seen on the impeccable bowl (Color No. 39): starting on the outside, the picture continues over the rim and is completed on the interior surface.

Ruby-back, or eggshell, porcelains. A widely varied class of porcelains, consisting mostly of dishes and cups, is often potted to a so-called eggshell thinness. The undersides can be plain, or they can be decorated with

251. DISH. Porcelain painted in underglaze blue and
overglaze enamels. Diameter: 7 in. (17.8 cm.). Qing
dynasty, Yongzheng mark and period, 1723–35. Rogers
Fund, 1925. 25.35.5.

252. DISH. Porcelain painted in overglaze *famille rose*
enamels, crimson pink glaze on the reverse.
Diameter: 8 in. (20.3 cm.). Qing dynasty, ca. 1730–50.
Purchase by subscription, 1879. 79.2.689.

254. PLATE. Porcelain painted in overglaze *famille rose* enamels and gilt, crimson pink glaze on the reverse. Diameter: 8 1/4 in. (21 cm.). Qing dynasty, ca. 1730–50. Bequest of Benjamin Altman, 1913. 14.40.252.

253. DISH. Porcelain painted in overglaze *famille rose* enamels and gilt. Diameter: 7 7/8 in. (20 cm.). Qing dynasty, ca. 1730–50. Purchase by subscription, 1879. 79.2.590.

251

255. CUP. Porcelain with crimson pink glaze.
Diameter: 3 7/8 in. (9.8 cm.). Qing dynasty, Yongzheng
mark and period, 1723–35. Bequest of Mary Clark
Thompson, 1924. 24.80.548.

256. DISH. Porcelain with crimson pink glaze.
Diameter: 5 1/4 in. (13.3 cm.). Qing dynasty, Yongzheng
mark and period, 1723–35. Bequest of Mary Clark
Thompson, 1924. 24.80.286.

257. BOWL. Porcelain with turquoise glaze.
Diameter: 3 5/8 in. (9.2 cm.). Qing dynasty, Yongzheng
mark and period, 1723–35. Rogers Fund, 1909. 09.194.23.

flowers or a diaper design; alternately, many of these vessels are covered on the reverse with a monochrome glaze that ranges from pink to ruby in tone. Sometimes the name "ruby-back," or the name "eggshell," is given to this group of porcelains. The pieces can be painted on the inside in a single color, perhaps sepia or blue, or in combinations of black, red, and gold; but most frequently they show the full spectrum of the *famille rose* palette.

These wares cover a broad range of tastes. Some are extremely modest in their statement, for example, the charming dish (Color No. 38) with a bird perched on a magnolia branch and another (No. 252) with a spray of flowers. Elsewhere the decoration can be quite elaborate, with a variety of central motifs that are sometimes surrounded by as many as seven intricate concentric diaper and foliate borders. In two especially fine examples of this type, one (No. 253), which is undecorated on the reverse, has an unusual design of a fan-shaped reserve containing a bird perched on a branch; the other (No. 254) carries the popular family scene motif surrounded by multiple ornate borders. While these ruby-back, or eggshell, wares presumably originated in the Yongzheng period, they doubtless continued to be made into the earlier years of the Qianlong reign. Although some pieces were probably painted at Jingdezhen, there is reason to believe that others were taken "in the white" to ateliers in Canton, where the enamel decoration was added.

In the 1822 auction catalogue of the effects of Fonthill Abbey, in Wiltshire, England, lot 63 of the first day's sale reads, "Four fine EGG-SHELL PLATES, red underneath with flowers and butterflies." During this sale, and a subsequent sale in 1823, no less than 168 ruby-back/eggshell porcelains were sold.[12] While it is not known when these ceramics entered the Fonthill Abbey collection, the quantity reflects the popularity of these wares in England before the early 1820s. However, there is some debate as to whether these porcelains should be classified as export wares or as fine ceramics that happened to be sold abroad.

Yongzheng monochromes. The *famille rose* palette forms the first category of Yongzheng monochromes mentioned here. These colors can be seen individually as rather opaque, low-temperature glazes; they were fired in an enameling, or muffle, kiln. Several of these *xiyang* ("Western," or "foreign") colors figure in Tang Ying's list. This series of glazes includes the distinctive *famille rose* crimson pink, seen here in a cup and dish (Nos. 255

and 256), as well as a lighter pink that was obtained by adding some opaque, lead-arsenic white to the crimson pink. Both of these hues can also be found on the reverse of the so-called ruby-back dishes discussed above. Other colors include a soft turquoise, seen here on the small bowl (No. 257), and several shades of yellow and green. Coral-toned iron-red, which is part of the *famille verte* palette and is also seen to some extent with *famille rose* painted enamels, is particularly striking as one of these low-fired monochrome glazes.

Other Yongzheng monochrome glazes. Green, yellow, aubergine, and turquoise single-color glazes, some of them used over engraved designs, are recorded in Tang Ying's list. A number of Yongzheng porcelains with these lower-temperature glazes are of exceptionally fine quality.

Polychrome glazes. In their endless quest for things original and different, the Yongzheng potters supplemented their inventory with several new polychrome glazes.

The application of a layer of one colored glaze over a glaze of another color can be traced as far back as the Tang-dynasty suffused glazes. This production of special effects by combining two different glazes on one piece became especially popular during the Yongzheng and subsequent Qianlong eras.

"Peacock feather" glazes. "Peacock feather" decoration is an example of this glaze-on-glaze technique: the effect of a peacock's plumage was achieved by applying areas of turquoise and dark, rusty red to a light blue ground. The rare bowl (Color No. 40) carries the Yongzheng reign mark: it is incised in four semiseal characters on the base under a "peacock feather" pattern that is somewhat different from the one used outside. This bowl has a light blue glaze on the inside.

Robin's-egg glazes. Another composite multicolor glaze of the Yongzheng and Qianlong periods, the so-called robin's-egg glaze, is a mottle of turquoise and blue that somewhat resembles the markings on a robin's egg.

Crimson-flushed blue glazes. The possibilities of playing crimson splashes against a blue ground had been fully exploited in the "Splashed Jun" wares of the Jin dynasty and later periods. It may well be that the type of lovely, high-fired, crimson-flushed blue glaze seen on a very large vase (No. 258) was inspired by these earlier wares.

Flambé glazes. Some glaze effects of the time were based on earlier kiln accidents. In his letter of 1722, Père d'Entrecolles mentioned kiln failures that had been experienced while producing Kangxi red-glazed wares,

saying that they were called *yaobian* ("furnace transmutations"). Apparently such kiln transmutations were soon being produced by design in the familiar glazes with flamelike streaks of varying color that the French aptly call *flambé*. These high-fired variegated glazes, in which the deep red is at times dominated by streaks and mottles in shades of blue, gray, crimson, or even brown and green, were especially popular in the succeeding Qianlong reign.

Tea-dust glazes. A precipitation of yellow crystals that stand out against a dark green field produced the *chayemo* ("tea-dust") glaze effect. This crystalline glaze was one of the new high-fired glazes of the period. The vase (No. 259) is an example of this particularly attractive stippled tea-dust glaze; it was made during the Qianlong era.

Iron-rust glazes. Another new high-temperature crystalline glaze is known as iron-rust. The metallic-looking markings in this dark reddish brown glaze were produced by supersaturating the glaze with iron pigment.

THE REIGN OF THE QIANLONG EMPEROR

Without a reign mark to serve as guide, porcelains of the early years of the lengthy Qianlong reign (1736–95) are difficult to separate from those of the Yongzheng era. This is not surprising; one must remember that the artist-craftsmen who did the potting and decoration during the brief Yongzheng period were apt to be alive and working after the accession of the new emperor. In addition, the genius of Tang Ying made itself felt, first as resident assistant and later as supervisor of the imperial kilns, during both of these periods. Conversely, the later Qianlong porcelains do not relate to those of the beginning of the reign as much as they herald the style of the succeeding Jiaqing period, and late Qianlong and Jiaqing wares can sometimes be confused without the aid of a reign mark.

It is likely that termination of Tang Ying's supervision of the imperial factory in 1756 was the milestone that

marked the beginning of the decline of Qing porcelains. By and large, wares produced after that time seldom match the marvelous quality of earlier ceramics. Qianlong pottery has two observable features. First, an archaistic style is frequently evident; for example, the shapes and decorative motifs of old bronzes served as models for many Qianlong ceramic forms and designs. This archaizing tendency can be explained by the fact that the emperor took an enormous interest in antiques of all sorts, and his interests duly influenced the cultural climate of the time. Second, there is a tendency toward more elaborate decoration. This seems to have increased as the period progressed, so that porcelains produced by the end of the reign are often extremely ornate, with the rather overripe air of a beauty past her prime.

Rather than presenting an encyclopedic listing of the many porcelains that were continued from the previous era, we shall simply note that the vast majority of the wares potted in the Yongzheng emperor's reign were also fabricated in the Qianlong period. (The notable exception is the family of *famille verte*–decorated porcelains; this palette of enamels, as such, had almost entirely fallen from grace.) Some objects decorated in these enduring techniques are of particular interest and are illustrated here. Almost all of them show stylistic elements derived from earlier material.

Although the blue-and-white vase (No. 260) does not have the handle and spout found on its prototype, its decoration has been taken almost line for line from an early fifteenth-century porcelain ewer. A small, covered ewer (No. 261), which repeats a "monk's-cap–jug" shape known in porcelains of the first half of the fifteenth century, shows that Qianlong potters were capable of remarkable control of underglaze copper-red. Equal success with underglaze blue and red is seen in a splendid vase (No. 262) with the perennially popular theme of dragons above rocks and waves. Three high-fired, dark blue–glazed sacrificial vessels (Nos. 263, 264, and 265) have been modeled after Zhou-dynasty bronzes. They are documented in part of an illustrated manuscript of the Qianlong period, now in the Victoria and Albert Museum, as having been made for ritual use in the Temple of Heaven in Beijing.[13] Continuing the celadon tradition that reaches back through the millennia, a vase (Color No. 41) is boldly carved with two confronting dragons in clouds. Representing another long-standing ornamental technique is a lobed vase with incised designs under lower-fired colored glazes (No. 266). A tall, turquoise-glazed vase,

258. VASE. Porcelain with crimson-flushed blue glaze. Height: 14 1/2 in. (36.8 cm.). Qing dynasty, Yongzheng mark and period, 1723–35. Bequest of Benjamin Altman, 1913. 14.40.200.

which is shaped like an ancient Chinese bronze vessel known as a *gu* (No. 267), is yet another illustration of the archaizing tendency of the period. Also taking its inspiration from archaic bronzes is a white, "soft-paste" porcelain vase (No. 268).

***Qianlong* famille rose.** The *famille rose* palette of enamels enjoyed wide currency during the Qianlong period. Early Qianlong *famille rose* porcelains in "court taste" are, for the most part, a continuation of the imperial wares of the Yongzheng period, exhibiting the same unforced elegance seen in previous examples. On an enchanting little dish with a goggle-eyed dragonfly hovering over peony flowers (No. 269), the plant is rooted on the reverse side and grows over the rim, ending in a flourish inside. The nine large peaches on the flowering peach tree that decorates a large vase (Color No. 42) are an emblem of marriage as well as a symbol of longevity.

An interesting feature sometimes seen in Qianlong *famille rose* porcelains is a new three-dimensional effect that has been achieved in the painting of figures and objects. The Chinese had learned the Western principles of perspective and of shading in drawing from European missionary artists. One of them was Brother Castiglione, known in China as Lang Shining, whose influence Nian Xiyao acknowledged in one of his books. These Westerners introduced their "exotic" style of painting to the Manchu court, and the techniques were eventually incorporated into the porcelain painter's repertoire. This new kind of painting is noticeable in the well-modeled faces of two men portrayed on a plate (No. 270).

There is a group of porcelains with a special style of meticulous enamel painting that is usually executed in *famille rose* colors. The drawing is the ultimate in delicacy and precision, and a strong European influence is frequently apparent in the treatment of the figures and landscapes. A poetic inscription that is written in black enamel, with attached red enamel seals, is almost invariably included as part of the design; the reign mark is generally written in very thick blue enamel on the base. While this family of porcelains probably originated in the Yongzheng reign, most examples belong to the Qianlong era. In the past, the name "Guyuexuan," the meaning of which is controversial, was given to ceramics decorated in this manner; however, many people now feel that the name should be discarded.

***Other* famille rose *wares*.** A great many thinly potted porcelains of the so-called ruby-back, or eggshell, type were apparently produced at this time. As we have seen,

259. VASE. Porcelain with tea-dust glaze. Height: 14 in. (35.6 cm.). Qing dynasty, Qianlong mark and period, 1736–95. Bequest of Mrs. H. O. Havemeyer, 1929, H. O. Havemeyer Collection. 29.100.284.

they formed part of China's vast export to Europe, as did quantities of more heavily potted ceramics decorated in the *famille rose* palette. In the latter wares, *famille rose* enamels have often been used in small panels that are reserved in ruby pink grounds or in high-fired blue or coffee brown glazes; they have also been used quite effectively in large, single motifs against white grounds. Some of the most grandiose examples of the period are the so-called *garnitures de cheminée*. These vases and covered jars were made by the thousands in China and were then sent as three- or five-piece "sets" to the West to become the pride of eighteenth-century European homes. Such a "set" is exemplified here by the handsome grouping of large vessels (Nos. 271 to 275).

Late *Qianlong* famille rose. Toward the later part of the eighteenth century, *famille rose* porcelains took on a different character: what had been a free and fresh style of decoration became, for the most part, labored and pedantic. Increasingly the tendency was to overdecorate and to smother the porcelain with enamels, filling in more and more background and leaving little white breathing space for the principal design. An impressive vase with *mille fleurs* ground (No. 276) is a fine example of late eighteenth-century porcelain in this new style of rather excessive ornamentation. The vase decorated on either side with a poem composed by the Qianlong emperor (No. 277) illustrates another popular convention of the period, in which *famille rose* enamels were used as strong background colors. It also shows the use of enamels painted over enamels, a technique that seems to have been new at this time.

As if to emphasize the *horror vacui* that dominated the decoration of late Qianlong *famille rose* wares, another new technique came into vogue: engraving opaque, colored-enamel backgrounds with overall feathery scrolls, as on the vase (No. 278). Also noticeable on many of these late Qianlong porcelains is an opaque bluish green that covers the interiors and bases of objects; it is quite similar to the opaque pale turquoise that is occasionally seen as a monochrome on Yongzheng porcelains.

Ceramic imitations of other materials. With the next group of additions to the repertoire of Qianlong wares, it appears that the potters had exhausted the natural potentials of their medium. Still required to appease the demands of jaded tastes for the novel, they turned to producing wares that were no longer ceramic in concept. Now the clay and glazes imitated other materials, and a spate of objects of simulated wood, bronze, cloisonné

260. VASE. Porcelain painted in underglaze blue. Height: 14 7/8 in. (37.8 cm.). Qing dynasty, Qianlong mark and period, 1736–95. Purchase by subscription, 1879. 79.2.469.

enamel, jade, bamboo, rhinoceros horn, lacquer, and so forth, began to be manufactured. Sometimes the deceit is most skillful, and one must handle these objects before one can tell if they are really made of clay. The flask (No. 279) is a good example of porcelain used in this new manner: it imitates the carved glass that was popular during the Qianlong reign.

Lac burgauté. In a type of lacquer decoration known in the West as *lac burgauté*, which was adopted for use on porcelain, an object was coated with black lacquer into which elaborate designs were inlaid in mother-of-pearl. At one time, this kind of decoration was thought to have originated as early as the Kangxi period, but many authorities now attribute examples to the Qianlong era and later. Six *lac burgauté*–decorated cups—presumably Chinese—are listed in Horace Walpole's 1784 inventory of his residence, Strawberry Hill, near Twickenham.[14] Unfortunately, it is not known when these porcelains entered the Walpole collection, or how old they were at that time.

"Famille verte black." The decorative style employing the so-called *famille verte* black, which originated in the Kangxi period, has a design in bright green against a greenish black ground. It can be most attractive when used alone. However, it becomes rather meretricious when combined with *famille rose* enamels on the same piece, as illustrated by a large covered jar (No. 280).

Bowls with reserve medallions. Other types of Qianlong porcelains most likely date to the later part of the period. Among them is a series of bowls that were introduced at this time and were especially popular in succeeding reigns. These bowls, which are sometimes called "Beijing medallion bowls," are heavily ornamented in opaque enamels on the outside. Crimson, pink, lavender, lemon yellow, or blue grounds frequently have overall, wispy scrollwork either painted over or incised into the enamel. Stiff, symmetrical floral sprays and other motifs are set against these colored grounds. They alternate with reserve roundels that contain well-drawn cameos of such subjects as flowers, figures, landscapes, or the *bogu*, or "Hundred Antiques."

Lacework. Some types of decoration emphasize the potter's marvelous technical skill and manual dexterity in handling the clay. Delicate lacelike tracery was incised deeply into the body to create the lacework effect. The glaze filled the deep intaglio designs and intensified in tone, producing a soft translucency that contrasts with the body when the object is held to the light.

Rice-grain. In the rice-grain technique, the translucent design—generally a diaper or starlike pattern—was produced by cutting series of perforations about the size and shape of rice grains through the wall while the clay was still fairly soft. The design was subsequently filled in with a clear glaze that coated the vessel. Rice-grain ornamentation has often been combined with underglaze blue painting or, more rarely, overglaze polychrome enamels.

Openwork. Great technical virtuosity is also seen in the wide variety of complicated openwork panels set into a great many objects such as lanterns, vases, and teapots that are opulently painted in the *famille rose* palette of enamels.

Applied molded decoration. A quantity of applied molded decoration appeared at this time as well. It ranges from low reliefs of simulated bronze that are set against crackled monochrome glazes to sundry figures, animals, and flowers that project from the background in full, undercut relief. This kind of ornamentation frequently has a pretentious quality, and it mirrors the generally overblown character of the late eighteenth-century porcelains. Applied decoration of this type has been used to blatant excess in some late eighteenth- and nineteenth-century export wares.

THE REIGNS OF THE JIAQING AND DAOGUANG EMPERORS

Porcelains made during the reign of the Jiaqing emperor (1796–1820) have little to offer in the way of originality. The tube of creativity had been squeezed to its limit, and what we find are basically extensions of late Qianlong wares. In the wares produced toward the end of the Jiaqing era, the decline in quality that can be detected in its

261.   COVERED EWER. Porcelain painted in underglaze red. Height with cover: 5 3/4 in. (14.6 cm.). Qing dynasty, Qianlong mark and period, 1736–95. Bequest of Mrs. H. O. Havemeyer, 1929, H. O. Havemeyer Collection. 29.100.314.

263, 264, and 265. THREE SACRIFICIAL VESSELS.
    Porcelain with low-relief decoration under dark blue
    glaze. Height of *dou* stemmed bowls: 10 3/4 in.
    (27.3 cm.). Height of *gui* vessel: 7 3/4 in. (19.7 cm.).
    Qing dynasty, Qianlong mark and period, 1736–95.
    Fletcher Fund, 1925. 25.143.1–.3.

262. VASE. Porcelain painted in underglaze blue and red.
    Height: 14 in. (35.6 cm.). Qing dynasty, Qianlong
    mark and period, 1736–95. Gift of Mrs. Eugene L.
    Garbáty, in memory of Eugene L. Garbáty, 1978.
    1978.529.

early stage in late Qianlong porcelains becomes more apparent. In the majority of pieces, the caliber of the body, potting, glaze, and decoration all begin to fail.

This worsening of quality becomes even more evident in wares of the Daoguang period (1821–50). There is an obvious deterioration in the fabric of the porcelain and a totally lackluster approach to the decoration. While a few finer types were still produced, they are the exception rather than the rule. Bowls with reserve medallions, which now often have underglaze blue designs inside, can be quite praiseworthy. They are illustrated here by a very good bowl (No. 281) with various articles from the group of *bogu*, or "Hundred Antiques," in the medallions. A bowl with white floral designs reserved in an iron-red field (No. 282) is also superior to the general wares of the time.

THE LATE QING DYNASTY

Domestic and foreign strife of one kind or another dominated the reigns of the Xianfeng (1851–61), Tongzhi (1862–74), Guangxu (1875–1908), and Xuantong (1909–12) emperors. These disturbances had a direct effect on the production of Chinese ceramics, which suffered considerably. Ceramic activity at the imperial kilns halted in 1855, when the town of Jingdezhen was taken by Taiping rebels, who burned the imperial factories to the ground. It is not certain if or when these imperial potteries were rebuilt. Some authorities maintain that porcelains such as those listed in an 1864 inventory of articles requisitioned for the use of the emperor were produced at the larger commercial kilns.[15] The tendency, therefore, is to dismiss wares of the remainder of the Qing dynasty as "crockery," and in the majority of cases, this judgment is quite accurate.

There was, however, a thin strain of much better porcelains that ran through this period. An occasional marked or unmarked example that is honestly nineteenth century in style, and of a quality not to be despised, proves that some rather good pieces were being produced. Superior workmanship can be found, for example, in late nineteenth-century porcelains carrying the hallmark of a pavilion where Cixi, the Empress Dowager, once resided. These porcelains were crafted at Jingdezhen especially for the Western Buddha, or Old Buddha, as she was called. Such a piece is the lovely little bowl

266. VASE. Porcelain with incised decoration under colored glazes. Height: 10 1/8 in. (25.7 cm.). Qing dynasty, 18th century, Qianlong period. Purchase by subscription, 1879. 79.2.1029.

(No. 283) that is painted in overglaze enamels and gilt against a yellow ground. It has several inscriptions: *Dayazhai* ("studio of great refinement"); *Tiandi yijia chun* ("springtime throughout heaven and earth"); and *Yongqing changchun* ("eternal prosperity and enduring spring").[16]

Reproductions of eighteenth-century wares. Numerous very competent reproductions of eighteenth-century pottery, many carrying eighteenth-century reign marks, were also made in the nineteenth century.

Reattributing some Qing wares. Certain types of porcelain that until recently were considered to have been manufactured in the eighteenth century may, in fact, be nineteenth-century products. For example, some very large and splendid porcelains with *famille noire* enamels on the biscuit that had been dated to the Kangxi period have been placed under suspicion.[17] While the argument against the eighteenth-century attribution of these porcelains was entirely based on negative evidence, nothing to contradict it has as yet come to light. Until there is further evidence, one should not overlook the possibility that some of these, as well as other porcelains heretofore regarded as above reproach, eventually may have to be reattributed to the late Qing period.

OTHER QING-DYNASTY WARES

In addition to the porcelains from Jingdezhen, which accounted for the major portion of the fine ceramics that were produced during the Qing dynasty, some extremely creditable pottery was manufactured in certain provincial kilns, where activities were frequently continued from the Ming period.

Dehua wares. Among these, the Dehua kilns of Fujian Province were the source of the large quantities of beautiful *blanc de chine* vessels and figures that were exported to Europe and elsewhere in the Qing period. It often was the fate of Dehua white figures to be covered with paint or gilt at this time, although there is some uncertainty as to where the work was done. Dehua wares were closely imitated by European factories in the early part of the eighteenth century.

As was noted when Ming-dynasty Dehua ceramics were discussed, precise dating of *blanc de chine* porcelain is rather difficult, particularly because production continued in much the same vein until modern times.

267. VASE. Porcelain with incised decoration under turquoise glaze. Height: 11 1/4 in. (28.6 cm.). Qing dynasty, Qianlong mark and period, 1736–95. Purchase by subscription, 1879. 79.2.94.

268. VASE. "Soft-paste" porcelain with relief decoration
under creamy white glaze. Height: 8 in. (20.3 cm.).
Qing dynasty, Qianlong mark and period, 1736–95.
Bequest of Benjamin Altman, 1913. 14.40.141.

270. PLATE. Porcelain painted in overglaze *famille rose* enamels, crimson pink glaze on the reverse. Diameter: 8 1/4 in. (21 cm.). Qing dynasty, 18th century, early Qianlong period. Purchase by subscription, 1879. 79.2.571.

269. DISH. Porcelain painted in overglaze *famille rose* enamels. Diameter: 5 1/2 in. (14 cm.). Qing dynasty, Qianlong mark, early in the period, 1736–95. Alfred W. Hoyt Collection, Bequest of Rosina H. Hoppin, 1965. 65.86.21.

271 to 275. *GARNITURE DE CHEMINÉE*. Porcelain painted
in overglaze *famille rose* enamels. Height of covered
jars: 24 in. (61.2 cm.). Height of vases: 18 3/4 in.
(47.6 cm.). Qing dynasty, 18th century, Qianlong
period. Bequest of Benjamin Altman,
1913. 14.40.189, .190, .195, .197, .198.

276.   VASE. Porcelain painted in overglaze *famille rose*
enamels. Height: 31 in. (78.7 cm.). Qing dynasty,
18th century, Qianlong period. Bequest of Benjamin
Altman, 1913. 14.40.229.

277. COVERED VASE. Porcelain painted in overglaze enamels, enamel on enamel, and gilt. Height with cover: 9 in. (22.9 cm.). Qing dynasty, Qianlong mark and period, 1736–95. Purchase by subscription, 1879. 79.2.612.

Therefore, it is helpful to find documentary evidence such as comparable material in a dated inventory. This is the case with the cheerful figure of Budai Heshang, "the monk with the sack" (No. 284), which has a fairly close counterpart at Burghley House, Stamford, England, that is listed in the Burghley House Inventory of 1688. (A four-character impressed inscription on the Metropolitan's figure is too faint to be read with any certainty.)

Yixing wares. In Jiangsu Province, the Yixing kilns were also extremely productive during the Qing dynasty, manufacturing miscellaneous articles for daily use. The famous Yixing stoneware teapots are illustrated here by a particularly fine example (No. 285) with what is described as a "pear-skin" surface. This teapot carries the two inscriptions *Yuzhaoge* and *Dabin*. Apparently the former is a hallmark; the latter has been associated with Shi Dabin, one of three famous Yixing potters of the Wanli period. Precise attribution of this beautifully made pot is somewhat uncertain.

Yixing vessels can be made in very imaginative shapes; they are frequently found in the form of familiar objects such as bamboo or sections of tree trunks with applied foliage. There also are representations of nuts and fruits, including the peach and Buddha's-hand citron. Some of the most remarkable Yixing stonewares are those that meticulously copy archaic Chinese bronzes, illustrated here by the magnificent *gu*-shaped vase (No. 286). This vase has a potter's seal mark *Chen Jinhou zhi* ("made by Chen Jinhou") stamped on the foot.

There also are glazed Yixing wares, some of which are accomplished copies of Song-dynasty Jun stonewares. In turn, these "Yixing Jun" are reported to have been copied at the Jingdezhen kilns in the eighteenth century. Yixing objects are occasionally decorated in overglaze enamels, including soft blue and the colors of the *famille rose* palette.

"Canton stonewares." Several kiln complexes were operating in Guangdong Province during the Qing dynasty. Among them were potteries in the general vicinity of Guangzhou (Canton) such as those at Shiwan and Foshan, as well as others in Yangjiang xian.[18] Recent excavations at some of these kilns have shown that they started

278. VASE. Porcelain painted in overglaze enamels and gilt, with engraved decoration. Height: 29 in. (73.7 cm.). Qing dynasty, Qianlong mark and period, 1736–95. Bequest of Benjamin Altman, 1913. 14.40.406.

279. FLASK. Porcelain painted in overglaze enamels.
Height: 9 1/2 in. (24.1 cm.). Qing dynasty, 18th
century, Qianlong period. Purchase by subscription,
1879. 79.2.437.

280. COVERED JAR. Porcelain painted in overglaze
enamels. Height: 24 in. (61.2 cm.). Qing dynasty,
18th century, Qianlong period. Bequest of Benjamin
Altman, 1913. 14.40.191.

281. BOWL. Porcelain painted in underglaze blue and overglaze enamels, with engraved decoration. Diameter: 5 7/8 in. (14.9 cm.). Qing dynasty, Daoguang mark and period, 1821–50. Purchase by subscription, 1879. 79.2.659.

282. BOWL. Porcelain painted in overglaze red enamel. Diameter: 5 in. (12.7 cm.). Qing dynasty, Daoguang mark and period, 1821–50. Purchase by subscription, 1879. 79.2.774.

production as early as the Tang dynasty. These and other kiln complexes in Guangdong Province are credited with a large group of "Canton stonewares." This is a family of vessels and figures with stoneware bodies that range from grayish buff to reddish or dark brown; they have a wide variety of thick, mottled or streaked glazes (No. 287). Some of these glazed "Canton stonewares" are rather similar to glazed Yixing wares, and on occasion each can be mistaken for the other. Like the Yixing kilns, the Canton factories imitated the Song-dynasty blue Jun glazes as closely as native raw materials would permit. While some "Canton stonewares" are given a Ming attribution, the majority of them should be dated to the Qing period; indeed, manufacture is flourishing even today.

Longquan wares. A few Longquan celadons with Qing-dynasty inscriptions prove that this type of material continued to be produced.[19] However, these pots are mere echoes of what had been a glorious tradition in the history of Chinese ceramics.

283. BOWL. Porcelain painted in overglaze enamels and gilt.
Diameter: 4 1/8 in. (10.5 cm.). Qing dynasty, Guangxu
period, 1875–1908. Gift of Mrs. Harry L. Toplitt, Jr., in
memory of Harry L. Toplitt, Jr., 1984. 1984.286.

283. BOWL, reverse view.

274

284. FIGURE OF BUDAI HESHANG. Porcelain.
Height: 6 7/8 in. (17.5 cm.). Early Qing dynasty, 17th
century. Dehua ware, Fujian Province. The Friedsam
Collection, Bequest of Michael Friedsam, 1931.
32.100.422.

285. TEAPOT. Stoneware. Height: 3 3/4 in. (9.5 cm.).
Marks: *Yuzhaoge, Dabin*. Probably Qing dynasty,
1644–1912. Yixing ware, Jiangsu Province. Purchase,
Ann Eden Woodward Foundation Gift, 1982. 1982.362.

286. VASE. Stoneware with relief decoration.
Height: 10 1/8 in. (25.7 cm.). Mark: *Chen Jinhou zhi*.
Qing dynasty, 18th century. Yixing ware, Jiangsu
Province. Gift of Michael Abraham, 1984. 1984.472.

287. VASE. Stoneware with blue glaze. Height: 5 1/4 in. (13.3 cm.). Qing dynasty, before ca. 1860. "Canton stoneware." Purchase by subscription, 1879. 79.2.79.

1. The motif of *haima* soaring above a field of blossom-strewn waves was popular in the seventeenth century. It is seen, for example, on six blue-and-white saucers found among the remains of an Asian vessel that sank in the South China Sea not long after the mid-1640s (Christie's Amsterdam B. V., *Sale of Fine and Important Late Ming and Transitional Porcelain, Recently Recovered from an Asian Vessel in the South China Sea: The Property of Captain Michael Hatcher,* auction cat. [14 March 1984], lot 342).

2. Gordon Lang, *The Wrestling Boys: An Exhibition of Chinese and Japanese Ceramics from the 16th to the 18th Century in the Collection at Burghley House,* exhib. cat. (Stamford, England, 1983), no. 169.

3. Peach-shaped wine pots decorated in underglaze blue were found in the cargo of the Asian vessel that sank in the South China Sea not long after the mid-1640s mentioned above (e.g., Christie's Amsterdam, *Sale of Fine and Important Late Ming and Transitional Porcelain* [14 March 1984], lots 417–22).

4. There are different versions of the date and authorship of this list. Most Westerners have relied on the full list published by S. W. Bushell as the work of Xie Min, who was governor of Jiangxi Province from 1729 to 1732. Bushell's source was the 1732 edition of the *Jiangxi tongzhi* (Bushell, *Oriental Ceramic Art: Collection of W. T. Walters* [New York, 1899], pp. 367–90). • Writing in 1937, Sir Percival David contended that the list was compiled in 1729 by Tang Ying, again citing the 1732 edition of the *Jiangxi tongzhi* ("A Commentary on Ju Ware," *Transactions of The Oriental Ceramic Society,* vol. 14 [London, 1936–37], pp. 34–35). • More recently, Fu Zhenlun and Zhen Li, in a special issue commemorating the 300th anniversary of Tang Ying's birth—under the heading of Tang Ying's activities in 1735—have published the list as it appears in Tang Ying's *Taocheng jishi bei* (*Jingdezhen Taoci,* 1982, no. 2, n.p.). • However, Wang Qingzheng says the *Taocheng jishi bei* was written by Tang Ying in 1736 (*Jingdezhen Taoci,* 1982, no. 2, p. 4). • The list published by Fu and Zhen, which is quite similar to the one translated and published by Bushell, is the one that has been consulted here.

5. Recently, these letters have been freshly translated by Robert Tichane (*Ching-te-chen: Views of a Porcelain City* [Painted Post, N. Y., 1983], pp. 51–128).

6. Mary Tregear et al., "Ceramic Changes at Jingdezhen in the Seventeenth Century," a paper read at The Second International Conference on Ancient Chinese Pottery and Porcelain, Beijing, 1985 (forthcoming).

7. Peter Hardie, "China's Ceramic Trade with India," *Transactions of The Oriental Ceramic Society,* vol. 48 (London, 1983–84), pp. 15–31, and pls. 8–10.

8. A considerable amount of "Chinese Imari"–style porcelain is in Istanbul (Regina Krahl with John Ayers, *Chinese Ceramics in the Topkapi Saray Museum, Istanbul,* vol. 3, *Qing Dynasty Porcelains* [London, 1986], notes by John Ayers, pp. 1197–98, and pls. 2941–3211).

9. For a brief summary of Tang Ying's career, see Rose Kerr, *Chinese Ceramics: Porcelain of the Qing Dynasty 1644–1911* (London, 1986), p. 19.

10. W. D. Kingery and P. B. Vandiver, "The Eighteenth-Century Change in Technology and Style from the Famille-Verte Palette to the Famille-Rose Palette," in *Technology and Style*, Ceramics and Civilization, ed. W. D. Kingery, vol. 2 (Columbus, Ohio, 1986), pp. 363–81.

11. The purple enamel, in particular, has been very carefully shaded on four Du Paquier dishes, one of which carries a mark that may be read as "Viennae 1725" (Clare Le Corbeiller, "Viennese Porcelain of the Du Paquier Period," in *Liechtenstein: The Princely Collections*, exhib. cat. [New York, 1985], pp. 171–77, and no. 114).

12. *Magnificent Effects at Fonthill Abbey, Wilts.: To be Sold by Auction, by Mr. Christie*, auction cat. (1 October 1822). *The Valuable Library of Books, in Fonthill Abbey . . . Which will be Sold by Auction, by Mr. Phillips*, auction cat. (9 September 1823).

13. Margaret Medley, "The 'Illustrated Regulations for Ceremonial Paraphernalia of the Ch'ing Dynasty' in the Victoria and Albert Museum," *Transactions of The Oriental Ceramic Society*, vol. 31 (London, 1957–59), pp. 95–105, and pls. 39:c,d, 40:b.

14. This 1784 inventory has been reproduced in the posthumous *The Works of Horatio Walpole, Earl of Orford*, vol. 2 (London, 1798). One entry reads, "Six fine old cups, white within; without, japanned black and mother of pearl: very rare" (p. 409). These cups have been described a little more fully in the 1842 sale catalogue of the contents of Strawberry Hill (although Horace Walpole died in 1797, the contents of his house were kept intact until this sale): "Six fine old black China cups, inlaid with mother-o'-pearl, representing Chinese Figures, &c., extremely rare" (. . . *The Valuable Contents of Strawberry Hill* . . . , auction cat. [25 April 1842], twelfth day's sale, lot 52). A vase might have entered the Walpole collection after the 1784 inventory: "A very rare and curious vase, of Oriental porcelaine, japanned black ground, on which is represented in mother-o'-pearl, Figures and Landscapes. A present from Mr. Barrett, of Lee" (ibid., lot 133). • Also of interest is lot 194 in the Dubois sale of 1782 in Paris, "Deux Vases de Porcelaine de la Chine, recouverts de vernis, de laque, & incrusté en burgos. Ils offrent des paysages ornés de magots. Espece rare" (*Catalogue d'une Très-belle Collection . . . Par J. B. P. Lebrun, Peintre*, auction cat. [12 March 1782]). Unfortunately, one has no way of knowing when the vases entered the Dubois collection.

15. Kerr, *Porcelain of the Qing Dynasty*, pp. 123–24.

16. Some doubts about the nineteenth-century date of any of the so-called *Dayazhai* group of porcelains have recently been voiced. While many examples of this type of ware undoubtedly are of twentieth-century date, proof that at least some of these porcelains were produced during the nineteenth century has been furnished by S. W. Bushell. Writing during the "present reign of Kuang-hsü," Bushell described a pair of bowls then in the possession of Sir Nicholas O'Conor, K.C.B., "her Britannic Majesty's late envoy plenipotentiary at Peking." These bowls have the same three inscriptions as on the Metropolitan's piece (Bushell, *Oriental Ceramic Art: Collection of W. T. Walters* [New York, 1899], pp. 81–82).

17. John A. Pope, "Oriental Porcelains," in *Porcelains: Oriental and French*, The Frick Collection: An Illustrated Catalogue, vol. 7 (New York, 1974), pp. 87–91.

18. For a particularly good account of these wares, see Fung Ping Shan Museum, *Exhibition of Shiwan Wares*, exhib. cat. (Hong Kong, 1979).

19. Ye Peilan, *Gugong Bowuyuan Yuankan*, 1982, no. 2, pp. 59–61.

CHAPTER THIRTEEN

THE TWENTIETH CENTURY, DESIGN CONTINUATIONS, AND COPIES

THE TWENTIETH CENTURY

Early in the twentieth century, under the auspices of Yuan Shikai, some ceramics of surprisingly fine quality were produced at Jingdezhen. Yuan had been named president of the Chinese Republic in 1912, and his ambitions to become emperor were realized in December 1915, when he "accepted" the throne. His reign was short-lived, however, as he died in June 1916. The pair of vases (Nos. 288 and 289) have mirror-image designs that have been painted in sepia and black with minute attention to detail. They are marked with Yuan Shikai's reign title,

Hongxian. These vases stand as proof of a degree of excellence in ceramic manufacture that is generally unexpected in wares of this period.

The turmoil of the ensuing years generated little, if anything, in the way of originality or ceramics of great merit. Nevertheless, good reproductions of earlier wares were certainly produced. A vase made at Jingdezhen in the 1930s, faithfully copying a Qianlong piece that had been published just a few years before, sits with the original in the Percival David Foundation of Chinese Art in London.

Under The People's Republic of China, which was established in 1949, the kilns at Jingdezhen have been making impressive copies of earlier porcelains along with ceramics of utilitarian caliber. There have been occasional reports of very fine wares being made, and perhaps we can hope for yet another splendid era of Chinese ceramics in the future.

290. DISH. Porcelain painted in underglaze blue, with yellow overglaze enamel. Diameter: 10 in. (25.4 cm.). Ming dynasty, Zhengde mark and period, 1506–21. Rogers Fund, 1919. 19.28.9.

288, 289. PAIR OF VASES. Porcelain painted in overglaze
sepia and black. Height: 6 3/8 in. (16.2 cm.).
Hongxian mark and period, 1915–16. Gift of Mr.
and Mrs. Harleigh G. Wathen, 1968. 68.4.1 and .2.

DESIGN CONTINUATIONS

Many Chinese ceramic designs from earlier periods were
used in later times and interpreted in the style of the day.
Frequently, the porcelains decorated in this manner have
been correctly marked and, unlike many copies, were
not meant to deceive. A comparison of two ceramics
decorated in the same fashion, but made at different
times, can be most rewarding.

The dish (No. 290) that dates to the Zhengde period,
for instance, is part of a Ming-dynasty design series that
started during the Xuande period. Comparison of this
dish with the Hongzhi example (No. 152) shows that
changes can occur from one reign to the next. Aside
from certain differences in potting, the most obvious
dissimilarity is in the treatment of the central motif:
while the Hongzhi branch is taut and lively, the later
one is loose and lacks some of its antecedent's vigor.
Sprays in the two cavettos differ as well: those on the
Zhengde dish seem somewhat flaccid when contrasted
with those on the earlier piece.

A Qing-dynasty dish from the Qianlong period
(No. 291) is decorated with the unflaggingly popular

291. DISH. Porcelain painted in underglaze blue and
overglaze red. Diameter: 7 in. (17.8 cm.). Qing dynasty,
Qianlong mark and period, 1736–95. Gift of Mr. and
Mrs. William Spielman, 1976. 1976.403.1.

293. COVERED BOX. Porcelain with relief decoration under bluish white glaze. Diameter: 6 3/4 in. (17.1 cm.). Ca. 1984. Made at kilns near Bangkok, Thailand. Purchase, Mr. and Mrs. Jerome A. Straka Gift, 1985. 1985.334.3.

292. VASE. Stoneware with sgraffito decoration. Height: 12 3/4 in. (32.4 cm.). Modern. Made at Cizhou kilns, The People's Republic of China. As sold by The Metropolitan Museum of Art through its Catalogue and Retail Shops.

motif of a dragon against waves painted in a combination of underglaze blue and overglaze red. If one compares this dish with a Ming-dynasty piece of the Wanli period (No. 184), a number of differences become apparent. In general, the Qianlong dish is more refined, and its haughty dragon lacks the Wanli monster's great enthusiasm. Many physical characteristics also differ. Iron-red enamel like that on the Ming dish has been described as deep tomato red, while the red on the Qing dish is a bit paler and a little more orange. The bottom of the Ming dish was fashioned by hand: its foot rim shows traces of tooling, and, as on most Ming dishes, the base is slightly convex. The bottom of the Qing dish was formed with a template: it is more mechanically perfect, its foot rim has been very carefully rounded, and the base is quite flat.

COPIES

Throughout the ages, Chinese ceramics have probably been counterfeited more than any other material. References have been made in earlier chapters to reproductions of Chinese pottery that were produced at various times, and a few specific examples will now be cited.

294. MODEL OF A MIRROR. Earthenware with painted decoration. Diameter: 4 3/8 in. (11.1 cm.). Modern. So-called Hui xian ware. Gift of Ernest Erickson Foundation, 1985. 1985.214.136.

295. MODEL OF A BELTHOOK. Earthenware with painted decoration. Length: 3 7/8 in. (9.8 cm.). Modern. So-called Hui xian ware. Gift of Ernest Erickson Foundation, 1985. 1985.214.137.

Copies of Chinese ceramics can be said to fall into two main categories. First there are those pots that were made in the style of a given object but cannot be confused with the original. A reproduction made at some Cizhou kilns in China rather recently (No. 292) is a very pleasant copy of a type of Song-dynasty Cizhou vase (No. 88). Although it imitates the Song stoneware, it was not meant to, and could not, deceive.

Then there are the deliberate fakes, and some of them can be quite good. A covered box (No. 293) that was made about 1984 in kilns near Bangkok, Thailand, emulates porcelains like the Yuan-dynasty *qingbai* example (No. 124) with jarring fidelity. Side-by-side comparison of the two boxes, however, does show certain differences. For example, the low-relief scrollwork has been applied on the box from Thailand, but it has been molded on the original.

It is not often that the exact provenance of a copy is known, as is the case with the two preceding pieces. Fortunately, modern scientific technology can be of considerable aid in ferreting out some skillful reproductions. Three earthenwares in the Metropolitan's collection discussed below are cases in point.

In 1942, a group of miniature black pottery objects that were said to be from Zhou-dynasty tombs in the Hui xian area of Henan Province came on the Beijing market. Among them were red-painted replicas of Zhou-dynasty bronzes like the models of a mirror (No. 294) and a belthook (No. 295); these have what appear to be the remains of cinnabar from the tomb as well as some "tomb dirt" on their surfaces. Many museums and collectors bought these miniatures as genuine Zhou tomb material, and sometimes they fetched prices that were equal to those of full-sized Zhou-dynasty bronzes. In the early

1950s, however, articles began to be published showing that at least some of the "Hui xian" ceramics are fake. Scientists at the Research Laboratory for Archaeology and the History of Art at Oxford University, England, tested a group of these "Hui xian" miniatures by the thermoluminescence method and published the results in 1972.[1] These tests proved that all of the miniatures are of modern origin. Recently, the Metropolitan's Objects Conservation Department had the "Hui xian" belthook (No. 295) tested by the same method; the findings were the same.

For many years, a marbled-ware vase (No. 296) had been catalogued as Tang dynasty, and few people questioned its authenticity. It is fairly easy to make stylistic comparisons between this vase and some Tang-dynasty earthenwares with "three-color" glazes; furthermore, marbled wares have been excavated from Tang-dynasty tombs and kiln sites. In 1973, however, a sample from the base of this vase was sent to the Research Laboratory for Archaeology in Oxford. The report on the thermoluminescent tests stated that the vase had been manufactured less than 120 years earlier.

Certainly, not all copies of Chinese ceramics were made in modern times. As was noted in Chapter 12, for example, Tang Ying's famous eighteenth-century list cites a number of wares emulating antique ceramics, some of which had been sent from the imperial palace to serve as models for the kilns in Jingdezhen. A lovely little Chenghua-marked cup with *doucai*-type decoration (No. 297) could very well be such a reverential replica. One of the reproductions Tang Ying mentioned is Chenghua "five-color" ware, and this might have referred to *doucai* decoration. The Metropolitan's cup is exquisitely potted and beautifully painted, and only after some consideration does one come to the conclusion that it was made in the eighteenth century and not during the Chenghua era. There is a fifteenth-century prototype of this cup in the National Palace Museum, Taibei, Taiwan.[2] This is a vivid illustration of the sometimes-forgotten fact that copies of Chinese ceramics can be very fine, valuable works of art in their own right.

Perhaps something should be said about the widespread use of apocryphal reign marks on Chinese ceramics. For example, several seventeenth- and eighteenth-century porcelains with false fifteenth-century reign marks are illustrated in this book. Sometimes, as in the case of the cup just discussed, these apocryphal reign marks might have been meant to deceive; but they were

296. VASE. Marbled earthenware with amber glaze. Height: 8 5/8 in. (21.9 cm.). Late 19th–early 20th century. Rogers Fund, 1930. 30.85.1.

297. CUP. Porcelain painted in underglaze blue and overglaze
enamels. Diameter: 3 1/4 in. (8.3 cm.). Apocryphal
mark of Chenghua period, 1465–87, but Qing dynasty,
18th century, Yongzheng period. Gift of Dr. and Mrs.
George Fan, 1984. 1984.362.

Seto kilns during the second quarter of the fourteenth
century. These same kinds of Chinese ceramics have
been excavated in Japan, and they have also been found
among the remains of the Chinese merchant ship that
sank in 1323 off the southwestern coast of Korea.[3]

The splendid blue-and-white porcelains that were
produced at Jingdezhen in the mid-fourteenth century
must have had an enormous impact on China's neighbors;
they undoubtedly would have wanted to emulate these
wares as closely as possible. Sometimes the copy was
made years later, as can be seen in the Annamese fifteenth-
century blue-and-white plate (No. 298). If one compares
this plate with the Chinese fourteenth-century example
(Color No. 18), one can see how the Annamese painter
managed to capture something of the spirit of the fish
swimming among eelgrass and other aquatic plants. It
would seem, however, that the lotus scroll with its
distinctive "spiky" leaves proved to be too difficult to
copy successfully. The Annamese craftsman also added
his own special signature in the form of a band of typically
Annamese scalloped waves around the main design.

often used as a kind of "salute" to ceramics of an earlier
time.

Producing imitations of Chinese pottery has been a
long-lived tradition in many other countries as well as in
China itself. For example, mention has already been
made of Yixing teapots being extensively copied in
Holland, England, and Germany in the late seventeenth
and the eighteenth centuries, as well as copies of Dehua
porcelains being manufactured in European factories in
the early eighteenth century. To cite just two further
examples: several types of thirteenth- and early fourteenth-
century Chinese ceramics were copied in the Japanese

1. S. J. Fleming and E. H. Sampson, "The Authenticity of
   Figurines, Animals and Pottery Facsimiles of Bronzes in
   the Hui Hsien Style," *Archaeometry*, vol. 14, pt. 2 (1972),
   pp. 237–44.

2. Teresa Tsao, *Ming Chenghua ciqi tezhan*, exhib. cat. (Taibei,
   Taiwan, 1977), color pl. 7.

3. Shoichi Narasaki, "Ceramic Wares of the Song and Yuan
   Dynasties Excavated in Japan and Japanese Ceramic
   Wares," in *Kokusai shinpojūmu Sinan kaitei hikiage bunbutsu*
   [International Symposium on Cultural Relics Found off
   Sinan Coast, September 1983], Committee of International
   Sinan Symposium et al. (Nagoya, 1984), pp. viii (English
   summary), 37–58.

298. PLATE. Porcelaneous ware painted in underglaze blue.
Diameter: 13 3/8 in. (34 cm.). Annamese, 15th
century. Lent by Mr. and Mrs. Leandro V. Locsin.
L.1984.49.15.

APPENDIX I:
SELECTED ARCHAEOLOGICAL
AND OTHER DOCUMENTARY
COMPARISONS

In the past, there was little other than old literary sources on which to base the study of Chinese ceramics, and objects in well-known museum or private collections were cited as the criteria against which other pieces were judged. Recently, however, excavations in The People's Republic of China—as well as important investigations elsewhere—have brought forth an enormous amount of pottery. These wares, which date from the Neolithic period into the Ming dynasty, are objective evidence of the when and where of Chinese ceramics. They have dictated that we change our standard of reference: today, in assessing the earlier Chinese pottery, the emphasis has shifted to comparisons with this documented excavated material.

There are relatively few archaeological comparisons that can be cited for ceramics manufactured during the Ming and Qing dynasties; therefore, we must frequently use a different strategy in attributing these wares. Among the kinds of evidence that can be useful are: the presence of an analogous piece either in datable shipwrecks or in a collection that can be documented as having been formed before a certain date; the illustration of a similar object in a datable painting; or the existence of a metal mount that carries an owner's emblem or a manufacturer's mark.

Space does not permit an exhaustive listing of all of the analogous material or every significant reference to each object cited in this section. The following are only representative archaeological or other documentary comparisons to some objects in the Metropolitan Museum that are illustrated in this book. (The sizes of the comparative ceramics are not necessarily the same as those shown here.) Frequently cited sources are abbreviated as follows:

Hughes-Stanton and Kerr, *Kiln Sites*.
> Penelope Hughes-Stanton and Rose Kerr, comps., *Kiln Sites of Ancient China: An Exhibition Lent by the People's Republic of China*, exhib. cat. (London and Oxford, 1980).

National Museum of Korea, *Cultural Relics Found off Sinan Coast*.
> National Museum of Korea, *Sinan haejŏ munmul* [Special Exhibition of Cultural Relics Found off Sinan Coast], exhib. cat. (Seoul, 1977).

WBW, *Zhongguo gudai yaozhi*, 1984.
> Wenwu bianji weiyuanhui, ed., *Zhongguo gudai yaozhi diaocha fajue baogaoji* (Beijing, 1984).

ZSRMC, *Chūgoku tōji zenshū*.
> Zhongguo Shanghai renmin meishu chubanshe, ed., *Chūgoku tōji zenshū*. 34 vols. (Kyoto, 1981—).

Chapter One: The Early Periods

No. 4. *Basin with painted decoration*, Majiayao Yangshao culture, Majiayao phase, ca. 3200–2700 B.C. (L.1986.82). Two similar Majiayao-type painted basins excavated in 1978 in Minhe xian, Qinghai Province, are ill., Qinghai sheng wenwu kaogudui, ed., *Qinghai caitao* (Beijing, 1980), pls. 14, 15.

No. 5. *Jar with painted decoration*, Majiayao Yangshao culture, Banshan phase, ca. 2600–2300 B.C. (1980.413). A similar painted jar from a Banshan-type cemetery that was excavated in 1973 in Guanghe xian, Gansu Province, is ill., *Kaogu Xuebao*, 1978, no. 2, pp. 193–210, and pl. 10:5.

No. 6. *Jar with painted decoration*, Majiayao Yangshao culture, Machang phase, ca. 2300–2000 B.C. (L.1986.22.1). Four comparable Machang-type painted jars from the Liuwan cemetery in Ledu xian, Qinghai Province, are ill., Qinghai sheng wenwu guanlichu kaogudui [QSWGK] and Zhongguo shehui kexueyuan kaogu yanjiusuo [ZSKKY], *Qinghai Liuwan: Ledu Liuwan yuanshi shehui mudi* (Beijing, 1983), vol. 2, pl. 133. This site was excavated from 1974 to 1978.

No. 7. *Jar with painted decoration*, Majiayao Yangshao culture, Machang phase, ca. 2300–2000 B.C. (50.61.4). Similar small, Machang-type painted jars from the Liuwan cemetery are ill., QSWGK and ZSKKY, *Qinghai Liuwan*, vol. 2, pls. 78–80, 81:1–4.

No. 8. *Jar with painted decoration*, Majiayao Yangshao culture, Machang phase, ca. 2300–2000 B.C. (1986.75.1). A jar with the same design, which resembles cowrie shells, is shown, QSWGK and ZSKKY, *Qinghai Liuwan*, vol. 2, pl. 78:6.

No. 9. *Jar with painted decoration*, Xindian culture, ca. 1000 B.C. (L.1986.23.2). An analogous Xindian-type painted jar excavated in 1977 in Dongxiang xian, Gansu Province, is ill., *Wenwu*, 1981, no. 4, pp. 16–20, and pl. 3:3; fig. 6:3.

No. 10. *Jar with painted and impressed decoration*, Xindian culture, ca. 1000 B.C. (50.61.3). An almost identical excavated piece is in the Gansu Provincial Museum, where it has been attributed to the Xindian culture.

Chapter Two: The Xia and Shang Dynasties

No. 18. *Tripod with cord markings*, late Shang dynasty, ca. 13th–11th century B.C. (1972.275.5). A similar tripod from Shandong Province is illustrated in F. S. Drake, "Ancient Pottery from Shantung," *Monumenta Serica* 4 (1939–40), pp. 383–405, and figs. 30:k (litho. 5), 12 (pl. 23). Drake is reported to have collected this and the following example in Shandong Province. • A sand-tempered gray pottery *li*-tripod from a Shang site in the suburbs of Jinan, Shandong Province, is ill., *Kaogu*, 1973, no. 5, pp. 272–75, and fig. 1:6.

No. 19. *Tripod with cord markings*, late Shang dynasty, ca. 13th–11th century B.C. (1972.275.4). A similar short-legged *li*-tripod from Shandong Province is in Drake, "Ancient Pottery," figs. 30:h (litho. 4), 9 (pl. 24). • Compare also a tripod collected in 1982 from a Shang site in the suburbs of Jinan, Shandong Province, ill., *Kaogu*, 1985, no. 8, pp. 753–55, and fig. 2:2.

No. 20. *Vessel with incised and relief decoration*, late Shang dynasty, ca. 13th–11th century B.C. (50.61.5). A parallel vessel, known as a *zun*, excavated in 1953–54 from a tomb at the late Shang Dasikongcun site near Anyang, Henan Province, is ill., *Kaogu Xuebao* 9 (1955), pp. 25–90, and pl. 3:2; fig. 13.

No. 21. *Covered jar with carved and relief decoration*, late Shang dynasty, ca. 13th–11th century B.C. or later (50.61.7). This could be a transitional piece. Similar examples have been attributed to the late Shang period. One was from the same tomb near Anyang as the *zun* in No. 20, above; it is ill., *Kaogu Xuebao* 9 (1955), pp. 25–90, and pl. 3:1; fig. 14. • See also *Kaogu Xuebao*, 1979, no. 1, pp. 27–146, and pl. 8:3; fig. 53:12,13, jars from tombs excavated from 1969 to 1977 at the Yinxu site, Anyang, Henan Province.

Comparable examples have also been attributed to the Western Zhou period. One was found inside a chariot in a chariot burial that was excavated in 1980–81 near the Western Zhou capital of Hao, in the modern Changan xian, Shaanxi Province; it is ill., *Wenwu*, 1986, no. 1, pp. 1–31, and pl. 5:4;

fig. 52:8. • See also *Kaogu Xuebao*, 1980, no. 4, pp. 457–502, and pl. 9:7; fig. 18:9, a parallel from a tomb cleared in 1967 in Changan xian, Shaanxi. • See also *Wenwu*, 1979, no. 10, pp. 50–59, and fig. 18, a jar from Hejiacun, Shaanxi.

Chapter Three: The Zhou Dynasty

No. 22. *Bowl with carved decoration*, Western Zhou dynasty, ca. 11th–10th century B.C. (50.61.6). A similar bowl excavated in 1958 at Dasikongcun, Anyang, Henan Province, from a group of tombs considered to date to the end of Yin/early Zhou period is ill., *Kaogu Tongxun*, 1958, no. 10, pp. 51–62, and pl. 4:8. • Two bowls were excavated in the 1970s from sites in the suburbs of Luoyang, Henan Province, that have been attributed to the Western Zhou period. They are ill., *Kaogu*, 1983, no. 5, pp. 430–41, 388, and pl. 6:6; fig. 9:9. *Wenwu*, 1981, no. 7, pp. 52–64, and fig. 8:6.

No. 23. *Bowl with olive brown glaze*, Eastern Zhou dynasty, ca. 7th–5th century B.C. (1977.449.5). A similar small, glazed bowl from a tomb that was found in 1976 in Deqing xian, Zhejiang Province, is ill., *Wenwu*, 1982, no. 4, pp. 53–57, and pl. 5:6(bottom). Another was discovered in 1975 in Anji xian, Zhejiang Province; it is ill., *Kaogu*, 1979, no. 2, pp. 186–87, and fig. 3:2. Both of these finds have been attributed to the Spring and Autumn period. • See also Feng Xianming et al., eds., *Zhongguo taoci shi* (Beijing, 1982), pl. 11:3, an example from Shanghai that has been attributed to the Spring and Autumn period. • The finds shown in *Kaogu*, 1979, no. 3, pp. 231–34, and figs. 4:2, 5(left) are from a kiln site attributed to the Warring States era near Shaoxing xian, Zhejiang Province.

No. 24. *Jar with impressed decoration*, middle Western–Eastern Zhou dynasty, Spring and Autumn era, ca. 9th–6th century B.C. (1986.97.2). Comparable jars, described as "*bu*-type Ia," excavated in the 1970s in the "first period" group of earth-mound tombs in Jurong xian, Jiangsu Province, are ill., *Wenwu Ziliao Congkan* 6 (1982), pp. 37–57, and figs. 10:25, 28:10. This group of tombs is considered in the report to be not earlier than middle Western Zhou and not later than the late Spring and Autumn period.

No. 25. *Covered footed bowl*, Eastern Zhou dynasty, 770–256 B.C. (50.61.9). A vessel of matching shape, known as a *dou*, excavated in 1953 in the suburbs of Luoyang, Henan Province, from a tomb attributed to the Warring States period is ill., *Kaogu Xuebao* 8 (1954), pp. 127–62, and pl. 5:2.

No. 28. *Jar with ribbing and cord markings*, Eastern Zhou dynasty, probably Warring States period, 475–221 B.C. (1972.275.1). A jar of this type is illustrated in F. S. Drake, "Ancient Pottery from Shantung," *Monumenta Serica* 4 (1939–40), pp. 383–405, and figs. 32:i (litho. 16), 27 (pl. 25). Drake is reported to have collected this and the following example in Shandong Province.

No. 29. *Jar with cord markings*, Eastern Zhou dynasty, probably Warring States period, 475–221 B.C. (1972.275.3). Drake, "Ancient Pottery," figs. 32:a,b (litho. 12), 24, 25 (pl. 25), showed somewhat similar high-necked, gray pottery jars.

No. 30. *Jar with remnants of glaze*, Eastern Zhou dynasty, Warring States period, ca. 5th–mid-4th century B.C. (50.61.10). An analogous jar is ill., *Kaogu Xuebao*, 1957, no. 1, pp. 133–40, and pl. 3:1. It came from the first type of tombs cleared in 1955 in Shaoxing xian, Zhejiang Province; these tombs have been attributed to the Warring States period. • Another is ill., *Wenwu*, 1980, no. 11, pp. 1–25, and figs. 13:19, 14:25; it came from cliff tombs found in 1978 in Guixi xian, Jiangxi Province. These tombs have been dated from one carbon-14 sample to the late Spring and Autumn/early Warring States periods.

No. 31. *Bell with remnants of glaze*, Eastern Zhou dynasty, ca. 7th–5th century B.C. (L.1985.133.2). A very similar bell excavated in 1955 in Zhenhai xian, Zhejiang Province, is ill., ZSRMC, *Chūgoku tōji zenshū*, vol. 4, Yue (1981), pl. 1, where it has been attributed to the Spring and Autumn period. • Thirteen similar bells in graduated sizes—thought to be from an original set of fifteen—were excavated in 1983 in Haiyan xian, Zhejiang Province. They are discussed in a Spring and Autumn/Warring States context, *Wenwu*, 1985, no. 8, pp. 66–72, and pl. 5:1; figs. 2, 4, 14, 16.

No. 32. *Jar with impressed decoration*, Eastern Zhou dynasty, Warring States period, ca. 5th–mid-4th century B.C. (L.1972.77.1). An analogous jar—which had three small feet—was collected during excavations in 1963–64 in Jinshan xian, Shanghai, ill., *Kaogu*, 1973, no. 1, pp. 16–24, 29, and pl. 1:3; fig. 9:3. It is thought to belong to the same period as the lower level of the excavations; this level has been attributed to the Spring and Autumn–Warring States era. • While this type of impressed pottery has generally been associated with the Jiangsu/Zhejiang area, similar ceramics have been found elsewhere as well. For example, a very similar jar that was one of thirteen small *guan*-type jars from four tombs cleared in 1974–75 in Qingjiang xian, Jiangxi Province, is ill., *Kaogu*, 1977, no. 5, pp. 310–12, and fig. 3:1. These tombs have been attributed to the early Warring States era.

No. 33. *Covered jar with impressed decoration*, Eastern Zhou dynasty, Warring States period, ca. 5th–mid-4th century B.C. (1986.75.2). A comparable jar—but without a lid—was found in one of the four tombs cleared in Qingjiang xian, Jiangxi Province (see No. 32, above), ill., *Kaogu*, 1977, no. 5, fig. 3:3. This type of impressed pottery, like the preceding jar, has generally been more associated with the Jiangsu/Zhejiang area.

The lid on the Metropolitan's jar is probably original. Similar pottery lids with bird-shaped finials are known, e.g., on one of four *yu*-cups found in 1975 inside a *gui*-vessel that was excavated in Wu xian, Jiangsu Province, ill., *Wenwu*, 1977, no. 7, p. 80, and fig. 1. • See also *Kaogu*, 1978, no. 3, pp. 151–54, and figs. 5:5, 6:7,11, examples from a group of

tombs excavated in 1975 in Jintan xian, Jiangsu Province. On the basis of carbon-14 dating, these tombs have been attributed to the middle to late Western Zhou period.

Chapter Four: The Qin and Han Dynasties

Nos. 34 and 35. *Two jars with olive green glazes*, Han dynasty, probably late Western Han period, ca. 1st century B.C. (1984.15 and 17.154). Parallel jars—with lids—from the tomb of Zhu Lechang that was found in 1958 in the suburbs of Hangzhou, Zhejiang Province, are ill., *Kaogu*, 1959, no. 3, pp. 150–52, and pl. 5:4,3. The tomb is considered to date to the middle Han period.

No. 37. *Bottle with blue-splashed brown glaze*, Eastern Han dynasty, 1st century A.D. (50.61.11). An analogous bottle from an Eastern Han tomb that was excavated in 1956 in the Canton area is ill., *Wenwu*, 1959, no. 11, pp. 14–18, and fig. 2. From an inscription on a tomb brick, this tomb can probably be dated to A.D. 76.

No. 38. *Flask with burnished surface*, Qin–Western Han dynasty, ca. late 3rd–1st century B.C. (1981.466). One of twelve cocoon-shaped, lidded flasks that came from a tomb cleared in 1973 in Tongshan xian, Jiangsu Province, is ill., *Wenwu Ziliao Congkan* 1 (1977), pp. 105–10, and fig. 6. The tomb has been attributed to the early part of the Western Han dynasty.

While this type of vessel has been found in tombs attributed to as early as the Warring States era, those flasks excavated from tombs assigned to the Qin or Western Han periods exhibit shapes that correspond more closely to the Metropolitan's example, particularly in the well-defined foot and beautifully turned neck and mouth.

Color No. 1. *Covered jar with painted decoration*, Western Han dynasty, ca. 1st century B.C. (1986.170). Two similarly painted jars—one with a cover—excavated in 1954 at Luoyang, Henan Province, are ill., The People's Art Publishing House, ed., *Ancient Relics of China* (Beijing, 1962), pls. 152, 153, where they have been attributed to the Western Han dynasty.

No. 39. *Incense burner with relief decoration*, Eastern Han dynasty, A.D. 25–220 (65.74.2). While no direct counterpart to the Metropolitan's censer comes to hand, a few excavated lids offer some help in its attribution. Comparable earthenware lids from a tomb attributed to the middle or late Eastern Han period that was found in 1963 in the vicinity of Nanyang, Henan Province, are ill., *Kaogu*, 1966, no. 2, pp. 108–10, and fig. 2:1,5. • Two glazed earthenware lids from a tomb found in 1962 near Nanyang xian, Henan Province, are ill., *Kaogu Xuebao*, 1963, no. 1, pp. 111–39, and pl. 2:4; fig. 17:1. The tomb has been attributed to the early or middle Eastern Han.

The Metropolitan's incense burner was based on a metal prototype, the most famous of which is the one made of bronze inlaid with gold that was found in 1968 in the tomb of Prince Liu Sheng (died 113 B.C.) near Mancheng, Hebei Province, ill., *Kaogu*, 1972, no. 1, pp. 8–18, 28, and pl. 4.

No. 40. *Figure of a lady*, Western Han dynasty, 206 B.C.–A.D. 8 (20.39.1). A similar figure is ill., *Kaogu*, 1959, no. 12, pp. 662–67, and pl. 5:1–3. It came from a group of tombs that were excavated in 1955 in Changan xian, Shaanxi Province; they have been attributed to the middle Western Han to late Western or early Eastern Han era. • Figures that are as well modeled as the Metropolitan's lady were excavated in 1966 from a group of burial pits in the vicinity of a Han mausoleum at Xian, Shaanxi Province, ill., *Kaogu*, 1976, no. 2, pp. 129–33, 75, and pls. 7:2, 8, 9.

No. 41. *Jar with iridescent green glaze*, late Western–Eastern Han dynasty, ca. 1st century B.C.–2nd century A.D. (26.292.83). A comparable jar was found in the 1980–82 excavations at the site of a Qin-dynasty capital, Xianyang, near Xian, Shaanxi Province; it is ill., *Kaogu yu Wenwu*, 1986, no. 6, pp. 28–41, and fig. 8:2. This jar was removed from one of sixteen Han-dynasty tombs that were cleared. The tomb is considered to be fairly contemporary with another nearby; that tomb was dated in accordance with A.D. 70. • Another analogous jar was found in the 1956 excavations near Shaan xian, Henan Province; it is ill., *Kaogu Xuebao*, 1965, no. 1, pp. 107–68, and fig. 11:3; pl. 10:1. This jar was found in tomb no. 91, which has been attributed to the early Eastern Han period.

Chapter Five: The Six Dynasties

No. 42. *Handled bowl, Yue ware*, Six Dynasties, Eastern Jin dynasty, 317–420 (1978.395). A similar bowl excavated in 1955 in Nanjing from what is described as an Eastern Jin tomb is ill., Nanjing bowuyuan, ed., *Jiangsu liuchao qingci* (Beijing, 1980), pl. 104. • Another handled bowl was excavated in Yuyao xian; it is ill., ZSRMC, *Chūgoku tōji zenshū*, vol. 4, Yue (1981), pl. 95, where it has been attributed to the Eastern Jin period.

Color No. 2. *Ewer, Yue ware*, Six Dynasties, Eastern Jin dynasty, ca. second half 4th century (1979.353). A green-glazed, brown-spotted ewer that is close in shape to the Metropolitan's piece was excavated—along with a brown-glazed example—in 1957 from Eastern Jin tomb no. M160 in Ruian xian, Zhejiang Province. They were found along with a tomb brick that was dated in accordance with 368, see *Kaogu*, 1960, no. 10, pp. 30–36, 46, and pl. 4:2.

No. 43. *Vessel, Yue ware*, Six Dynasties, late Western/Eastern Jin dynasty, ca. 4th century (1985.207). A similar vessel, known as a *huzi*, was found in 1965 near Nanjing. It was in a Western Jin tomb that had a tomb brick dated in accordance with 308, ill., *Kaogu*, 1966, no. 4, pp. 224–27, and fig. 7:2. • Another, found in 1956 in Eastern Jin tomb no. 20 in Huangyan xian, Zhejiang Province, is ill., *Kaogu Xuebao*, 1958, no. 1, pp. 111–31, and pl. 5:1. This tomb had a tomb brick dated in accordance with 327.

No. 44. *Vessel, Yue ware*, Six Dynasties, Western Jin dynasty, 265–317 (1985.66). A comparable vessel, called a *shi*, found in 1964 near Nanjing in a Western Jin tomb that is probably datable to 302, is ill., *Wenwu*, 1965, no. 6, pp. 37–44, and pl. 4:2.

Color No. 3. *Vessel with celadon glaze, northern ware*, Six Dynasties, late Northern Dynasties, ca. second half 6th century (60.75.2). A similarly modeled, stone crouching animal from the Northern Qi tomb of Lou Rui is ill., *Wenwu*, 1983, no. 10, pp. 1–23, and pl. 6:2. This tomb is datable to 570; it was excavated from 1979 to 1981 in the suburbs of Taiyuan, Shanxi Province.

No. 47. *Jar with green glaze*, Six Dynasties, late Northern Dynasties–Sui dynasty, ca. late 6th century (1978.264.2). One of six large earthenware jars of close shape from the Northern Qi (570) tomb of Lou Rui [see Color No. 3, above] is ill., *Wenwu*, 1983, no. 10, pp. 1–23, and fig. 41. • Green-glazed jars of this type have been attributed to the late Six Dynasties period in some publications and to the Sui dynasty elsewhere.

No. 48. *Lamp with green and brown glazes*, Six Dynasties, late Northern Dynasties–Sui dynasty, ca. late 6th century (27.46). In addition to the comparisons already mentioned in the main text, see three of eleven flamboyantly ornamented, lead-glazed earthenwares from the Lou Rui (570) tomb, ill., *Wenwu*, 1983, no. 10, pp. 1–23, and pl. 7; figs. 25–27. The band of segmentate lotus petals at the bottom of the tall-stemmed lamp from the tomb are somewhat similar to the band of petals on the Metropolitan's lamp. Note, too, the generous use of high-relief animal heads on the Lou Rui covered jar.

No. 50. *Model of a tricorn*, Six Dynasties, Western Jin dynasty, 265–317 (68.149.15). A comparable figure—but with two horns—from one of fifty-four tombs attributed to the Jin dynasty that were found in the 1953–55 excavations in Luoyang, Henan Province, is ill., *Kaogu Xuebao*, 1957, no. 1, pp. 169–85, and pl. 3:8(right). The somewhat similar figure in the same illustration (left) was from tomb no. 1; this tomb had a tomb epitaph dated in accordance with 287. • Another close figure is ill., *Kaogu Tongxun*, 1957, no. 1, pp. 37–41, and pl. 14:4(right). It came from a tomb that has been attributed to the Jin dynasty; this tomb was found in 1955 near Zhengzhou, Henan Province.

No. 51. *Animal tomb guardian*, Six Dynasties, Northern Wei dynasty, ca. first third 6th century (1979.438). Compare one of a pair of animal tomb guardians found in 1964 in the Northern Wei tomb of the wife (née Gao) of Han Hui, an official, ill., *Kaogu*, 1972, no. 5, pp. 33–35, and pl. 11:2. This lady was buried in 524 in Quyang xian, Hebei Province. • Another analogous animal tomb guardian, also one of a pair, excavated in 1965 from the Northern Wei tomb of Yuan Shao (died 528) near Luoyang, Henan Province, is ill., *Kaogu*, 1973, no. 4, pp. 218–24, 243, and pl. 12:2.

Chapter Six: The Sui Dynasty

No. 52. *Bottle, white ware*, probably Sui dynasty, 581–618 (17.130). One of two similarly shaped, gray-bodied bottles that are described as having been fired in the biscuit is ill., *Wenwu*, 1981, no. 4, pp. 44–45, and fig. 7. These bottles were found with other ceramics in the suburbs of Jinan, Shandong Province. This material has been attributed to the Sui dynasty; apparently it came from tombs that had already been destroyed.

Color No. 4. *Bottle with celadon glaze*, probably Sui dynasty, 581–618 (1985.214.130). A somewhat similar ceramic bottle from one of two Southern Dynasties tombs that were excavated in 1956 in the suburbs of Changsha, Hunan Province, is ill., *Wenwu Cankao Ziliao*, 1957, no. 12, pp. 45–46, 51, and pl. on p. 44(lower right). From the inscriptions on some bricks, these tombs can be dated to 499—the Southern Qi dynasty. • Two bronze bottles of similar shape were excavated in 1964 from the Northern Wei tomb of Han Hui's wife (née Gao), who was buried in 524 in Quyang xian, Hebei Province. One of them is ill., *Kaogu*, 1972, no. 5, pp. 33–35, and pl. 8:1. • A gilt-bronze bottle of comparable shape that was excavated in 1973 from the Northern Qi tomb of Kudihuiluo (died 562) in Shouyang xian, Shanxi Province, is ill., *Kaogu Xuebao*, 1979, no. 3, pp. 377–402, and pl. 5:3; fig. 7:1. • Similar impressed leaves can be seen on one of five lotus petal–decorated vessels that were excavated from Southern Dynasties tombs in the Wuhan area of Hubei Province. This vessel is ill., *Xin Zhongguo chutu wenwu* [Historical Relics Unearthed in New China] (Beijing, 1972), pl. 128; also *Kaogu*, 1959, no. 11, pp. 622–24, and pl. 6:2. • Similar leaves and/or groups of parallel lines seen in a number of Sui-dynasty ceramic designs are ill., Feng Xianming et al., eds., *Zhongguo taoci shi* (Beijing, 1982), pp. 190–91, and figs. 51, 52. • A bottle that has been attributed to the Sui period was excavated in Qufu xian, Shandong Province; it is ill., *Dai-koga bunmei no nagare: Santō-shō bunbutsu-ten*, exhib. cat. (Tokyo, 1986), color pl. 92. The glaze and body of this piece appear to be similar to the glaze and body of the Metropolitan's bottle, suggesting the possibility of a Shandong provenance for the latter.

No. 55. *Jar with brown glaze*, Sui dynasty, 581–618 (L.1974.31.2). Two comparable jars described as having fine red bodies and deep yellow glazes were excavated in 1954 from the Sui-dynasty tomb of Liu Shigong in the suburbs of Xian, Shaanxi Province. One of them is ill., *Kaogu Xuebao*, 1956, no. 3, pp. 33–75, and fig. 17:2. This tomb had an epitaph dated in accordance with 615.

Chapter Seven: The Tang Dynasty

No. 56. *Bottle with blue glaze*, Tang dynasty, ca. 8th century (23.180.3). Blue-glazed fragments from the Gong xian kilns, Henan Province, are ill., ZSRMC, *Chūgoku tōji zenshū*, vol. 7, Tang "three-color" (1983), pls. 151(top left and bottom center), 156. • A similarly shaped bottle with a white glaze, called a *tuoyu*,

was excavated in 1981 in the suburbs of Luoyang, Henan Province, from the Tang-dynasty (709) tomb of An Pu and his wife. It is ill., *Zhongyuan Wenwu*, 1982, no. 3, pp. 21–26, 14, and pl. 6:1.

No. 57. *Plate with "three-color" glazes*, Tang dynasty, ca. 8th century (14.66). Fragments with impressed designs under "three-color" glazes from the Gong xian kilns, Henan Province, are ill., ZSRMC, *Chūgoku tōji zenshū*, vol. 7, Tang "three-color," pl. 150(left and top). • A plate with the same impressed design—but in a different palette—was excavated in 1975 from a tomb in Luoyang, Henan Province. It is ill., Luoyang shi bowuguan, comp., *Luoyang Tang sancai* (Beijing, 1980), pl. 105, where it has been attributed to the high Tang period.

No. 58. *Amphora with "three-color" glazes*, Tang dynasty, ca. 8th century (1984.483.3). Fragments with "three-color" and monochrome lead glazes from the Gong xian kilns, Henan Province, are ill., ZSRMC, *Chūgoku tōji zenshū*, vol. 7, Tang "three-color," pls. 140–56. • A comparable amphora with dragon handles, one of two amphorae found in 1984 near Yichuan xian, Henan Province, in a tomb attributed to the high Tang period, is ill., *Kaogu*, 1985, no. 5, p. 459, and pl. 6:1(right).

No. 59. *Figure of a lady*, Tang dynasty, ca. 8th century (1979.108). A comparable figure found in 1954 in the suburbs of Xian, Shaanxi Province, in the Tang-dynasty (744) tomb of Shi Sili is ill., Shaanxi sheng wenwu guanli weiyuanhui, ed., *Shaanxi sheng chutu Tang yong xuanji* (Beijing, 1958), pl. 70.

No. 60. *Model of a horse*, Tang dynasty, ca. late 7th–first half 8th century (25.20.4). A somewhat larger, unglazed and painted horse that was excavated in Luoyang, Henan Province, is ill., *Kōga bunmei tenran*, exhib. cat. (Tokyo, 1986), pl. 118, where it has been attributed to the Tang period. There are many similarities in the modeling of this horse and the modeling of the Metropolitan's figure.

Color Nos. 5 and 6; Nos. 61 and 62. *Four tomb figures with "three-color" glazes*, Tang dynasty, late 7th–first half 8th century (11.83.1–.4). A group of analogous figures found in the 1958 excavation of the Tang-dynasty tomb of Dugu Sizhen, who died in 696, in the suburbs of Xian, Shaanxi Province, is ill., Zhongguo shehui kexueyuan kaogu yanjiusuo, comp., *Tang Changan chengjiao Sui Tang mu* (Beijing, 1980), pp. 29–43, and pls. 37, 39:1, 40:2, 41:1, 42–44.

No. 63. *Rhyton-type cup, white ware*, Tang dynasty, 7th century or possibly earlier (24.180.1). No exact documentary comparison to this cup comes to hand. However, see *Chūgoku no hakubutsukan*, vol. 1, *Shaanxi sheng bowuguan*, ed. Shaanxi sheng bowuguan (Tokyo and Beijing, 1981), pl. 87, a *sancai*-glazed, elephant-headed, rhyton-type cup that was excavated in 1957 in the suburbs of Xian, Shaanxi Province, from a tomb attributed to the Tang dynasty. See also *Wenwu*, 1987, no. 8, pp. 30–42, 51, and pl. 4:2,4; fig. 2:8,13, two *sancai*-glazed, dragon-headed, rhyton-type cups found in 1985 in Yun xian, Hubei Province, in the Tang-dynasty tomb of Li Hui (died 683). Although there is no similarity between these *sancai*-

glazed vessels and the Metropolitan's cup per se, the *sancai* pieces establish the rhyton shape in Chinese ceramics in the early Tang period.

No. 64. *Amphora, white ware,* Tang dynasty, 7th century (29.100.217). Compare one of two white amphorae from the Tang-dynasty tomb of Li Feng (buried 675) and his wife, ill., *Kaogu,* 1977, no. 5, pp. 313–26, and pl. 9:1. This tomb was cleared in 1973 in Fuping xian, Shaanxi Province.

No. 65. *Globular jar, white ware,* Tang dynasty, 9th century (1977.388). Compare one of three covered white jars from the Tang-dynasty tomb of Li Cun (died 845) near Yanshi xian, Henan Province, ill., *Kaogu,* 1984, no. 10, pp. 904–14, and figs. 4:2, 5:3. This tomb was cleared in 1984.

No. 66. *Bowl, white ware,* Tang dynasty, 9th century (18.56.42). A smaller white bowl of the same shape was excavated in 1956 in the suburbs of Hefei, Anhui Province, from a Five Dynasties tomb that was dated in accordance with 946. It is ill., *Wenwu Cankao Ziliao,* 1958, no. 3, pp. 65–68, and fig. 1. This bowl was not necessarily new when it was buried. • One of four similarly shaped white bowls found in 1985 in the suburbs of Xian, Shaanxi Province, in a cache attributed to the late Tang era is ill., *Kaogu yu Wenwu,* 1986, no. 4, pp. 20–21, and pl. 1:1.

No. 67. *Bowl, white ware,* Tang dynasty, 9th century (1980.365). Similarly potted white bowls with thick mouth rims and wide feet, excavated in the early 1960s from what is considered to be the late Tang stratum at the Ding kilns in Jiancicun, Quyang xian, Hebei Province, are ill., *Kaogu,* 1965, no. 8, pp. 394–412, and pls. 6:2,3, 8:1,5; fig. 7:5.

No. 68. *Fragment of a bowl, white ware,* Tang dynasty, 9th century (40.170.456a). This fragment was excavated at Village Tepe, Nishapur. It was published by Charles K. Wilkinson, *Nishapur: Pottery of the Early Islamic Period* (New York, 1973), pp. 254–58, and no. 10.

No. 69. *Fragment of a bowl, white ware,* Tang dynasty, 9th century (40.170.456e). This fragment was excavated at Tepe Madraseh, Nishapur. It was published by Wilkinson, ibid., no. 16, where he dated the fragment from its location at the site to the 9th century.

No. 70. *Fragment of a bowl, white ware,* Tang dynasty, 9th century (23.75.19). This fragment was excavated at Samarra; it was purchased from the British Museum in 1923. It is now recognized that Samarra was not totally abandoned in the late 9th century, but that it was occupied until at least the middle of the 10th century.

Color No. 7. *Flask with suffused glaze,* Tang dynasty, ca. 9th century (1972.274). Two vessels with suffused glazes are ill., *Chūgoku nisennen no bi* [China's Beauty of 2,000 Years], exhib. cat. (Tokyo, 1965), nos. 62, 63, where they are described as Tang-dynasty Huangdao yao, Jia xian, Henan Province. • Fragments of similar ware from the Lushan kilns, Henan Province, are ill., Hughes-Stanton and Kerr, *Kiln Sites,* nos. 403, 404, where they have been attributed to the Tang dynasty.

No. 71. *Ewer with yellow glaze,* Tang dynasty, ca. 9th century (1977.449.3). Ewers of this type were probably made in northern China. For example, see the description in Feng Xianming et al., eds., *Zhongguo taoci shi* (Beijing, 1982), p. 210, of some two-eared, short-spouted ewers with matlike designs under yellow glazes that were found in 1964 at kilns in Jia xian, Henan Province. These kilns have been attributed to the Tang dynasty. • See *Wenwu,* 1965, no. 9, pp. 26–56, and fig. 1:5, for a fragment from these kilns that has been attributed to the Tang period.

Color No. 8. *Dish, Changsha ware,* Tang dynasty, 9th century (1986.97.3). A foliated dish with a painted bird design that was excavated from the Tongguan kilns, Changsha, Hunan Province, is ill., *Kaogu Xuebao,* 1980, no. 1, pp. 67–96, and pl. 5:11. This dish also appears in the chronological chart, ibid., p. 90, under the late Tang period.

Color No. 9. *Waterpot, Changsha ware,* Tang dynasty, ca. 9th century (1986.75.3). The same type of water coupe from tombs in the vicinity of Changsha, Hunan Province, that have been attributed to the Tang dynasty is ill., *Kaogu Xuebao,* 1982, no. 4, pp. 509–23, and pl. 20:2. • The same type of coupe from the Tongguan, Changsha, kilns that have been attributed to the Tang era is ill., *Kaogu Xuebao,* 1980, no. 1, pp. 67–96, and pl. 9:12.

Color No. 10. *Ewer, Changsha ware,* Tang dynasty, ca. 9th century (1986.113). Compare one of two ewers with brown-splashed glazes excavated in 1973 at Hengyang, Hunan Province, from a well attributed to the Tang period, ill., *Kaogu,* 1980, no. 1, pp. 66–70, and fig. 1. • An ewer of the same shape that was decorated with three figures, but did not have brown splashes, was found in 1954 in a tomb in the suburbs of Shijiazhuang, Hebei Province. There was a tomb epitaph dated in accordance with 812, see *Kaogu,* 1984, no. 3, p. 283, and fig. 1. • One of a number of similar ewers from the Tongguan kilns at Changsha, Hunan Province, that have been attributed to the Tang dynasty is ill., *Kaogu Xuebao,* 1980, no. 1, pp. 67–96, and pl. 1:7.

Chapter Eight: The Five Dynasties

Color No. 11 and No. 72. *Bowl, Yue ware,* Five Dynasties, 10th century (18.56.36). Similar brilliantly carved dragons are on a Yue jar that was removed in 1965 from the Five Dynasties tomb of Qian Yuanguan of Wu–Yue (died 941) in the suburbs of Hangzhou, Zhejiang Province, ill., *Kaogu,* 1975, no. 3, pp. 186–94, and pl. 9:4; fig. 10. This jar is illustrated in color, ZSRMC, *Chūgoku tōji zenshū,* vol. 4, Yue (1981), pl. 170. • A similar dragon was on the lid of a silver-gilt box found in 1979 near Suzhou, Jiangsu Province, in a tomb attributed to the Five Dynasties period, ill., *Wenwu,* 1981, no. 2, pp. 37–45, and fig. 4:2.

No. 72A. *Ewer, Yue ware*, Five Dynasties, 10th century (1979.502). A Yue-ware ewer of very close shape—with a lid—is ill., *Kaogu Xuebao*, 1984, no. 3, pp. 361–81, and pl. 18:1; fig. 5. It was found in 1981 in Beijing, in the Liao-dynasty tomb of Han Yi (died 995) and his wife. • Note also the design of two parrots inside a basin found in the tomb, ibid., fig. 6:6, and on some fragments from the Yue kilns, ibid., fig. 13:3,4,6.

No. 73. *Jar with white glaze* (mark: *Xin guan* ["new official"]), Five Dynasties, 10th century (19.56.2). A number of porcelains with *Guan* or *Xin guan* marks on the base have been excavated recently; many of them are considered to have been produced in the Ding kilns, see WBW, *Zhongguo gudai yaozhi*, 1984, pp. 393–407. *Wenwu*, 1984, no. 12, pp. 58–63, 90.

Chapter Nine: The Northern Song, Jin, and Southern Song Dynasties

No. 74. *Mold with impression, for Northern celadon ware*, Northern Song dynasty, 11th–12th century (16.149.1). This design was found on bowls that were excavated from a stratum attributed to the middle Song period at the Huangbaozhen kilns; a drawing of it is shown, Shaanxi sheng kaogu yanjiusuo [SSKY], *Shaanxi Tongchuan Yaozhou yao* (Beijing, 1965), fig. 17:3. • A bowl with this motif from kilns in Xinan xian, Henan Province, is ill., WBW, *Zhongguo gudai yaozhi*, 1984, pp. 339–51, and pl. 13:2. • Jan Wirgin identifies this design as a "conventionalized flower and sickle-leaf scroll," see "Sung Ceramic Designs," in *The Museum of Far Eastern Antiquities* [Stockholm] *Bulletin*, vol. 42 (1970), pp. 24–27. The design was quite popular in the Song dynasty and was used as far south as the Xicun kilns near Canton, Guangdong Province, see Peter Y. K. Lam, "Northern Song Guangdong Wares," in *A Ceramic Legacy of Asia's Maritime Trade*, ed. Southeast Asian Ceramic Society, exhib. cat. (Kuala Lumpur, 1985), pp. 1–29, and figs. 25, 26, 28.

No. 75. *Jar, Northern celadon ware*, Northern Song dynasty, 11th–12th century (18.56.68). Similar deeply carved decoration can be seen on a celadon vessel from the Yaozhou kilns, Shaanxi Province, ill., *Kaogu yu Wenwu*, 1980, no. 1, pp. 123–32, and pl. 11:3; it has been attributed to the Northern Song period.

Color No. 12. *Ewer, Northern celadon ware*, Northern Song dynasty, 11th–12th century (26.292.73). Another extraordinary globular ewer—which also had an animal-head spout—was found in 1968 in the city wall at Bin xian, Shaanxi Province. It is ill., *Kaogu yu Wenwu*, 1983, no. 5, p. 106, and pl. 8:1, where it has been attributed to the Song dynasty, possibly Yaozhou ware. • Somewhat similar animal-head legs can be seen on a censer that was found in a stratum attributed to the middle Song period at the Huangbaozhen kilns, ill., SSKY, *Shaanxi Tongchuan Yaozhou yao*, pl. 12:2. • See Wirgin, "Sung Ceramic Designs," pp. 24–27, for his discussion of the "conventionalized flower and sickle-leaf scroll."

No. 76. *Vase, Northern celadon ware*, Northern Song dynasty, 11th–12th century (13.195.2). A comparable vase excavated in 1954 at Xian, Shaanxi Province, is ill., ZSRMC, *Chūgoku tōji zenshū*, vol. 10, Yaozhou (1985), pl. 12. Another, in the Yaozhou Museum, Tongchuan, Shaanxi, is shown, ibid., pl. 16. Both vases have been attributed to the Song dynasty. • A fragment with similar decoration that was from a stratum attributed to the late Song period at the Huangbaozhen kilns is ill., SSKY, *Shaanxi Tongchuan Yaozhou yao*, pl. 19:3.

No. 77. *Bowl, Jun ware*, Northern Song dynasty, 11th–12th century (20.45). One of two bowls from a cache found in 1976 in Fangcheng xian, Henan Province, is ill., *Wenwu*, 1983, no. 3, pp. 92–94, and fig. 6(right). The ceramics have been called Song-dynasty Jun ware in the report; however, the presence of a flattened-rim plate with large splashes of red in the glaze (ibid., fig. 1) suggests a Jin-dynasty rather than a Northern Song date for the cache itself. • A bowl of this shape from the Juntai kilns, Yu xian, Henan Province, is ill., *Jingdezhen taoci*, 1984, no. 2, pp. 169–76, and fig. 3:1(right); it has been attributed to the middle Northern Song period.

No. 78. *Bowl, Jun ware*, Northern Song dynasty, 11th–12th century (24.170.8). This small, "bubble bowl" shape has been found at Jun kilns such as those in Linru xian, Henan Province, ill., *Wenwu*, 1964, no. 8, pp. 15–26, and fig. 10:1.

No. 79. *Covered jar, Jun ware*, Northern Song dynasty, 11th–12th century (50.145.314). An uncovered jar of this shape excavated at kilns in the vicinity of Yanhedian, Linru xian, Henan Province, is ill., *Wenwu Cankao Ziliao*, 1958, no. 10, pp. 32–35, and fig. 6(right). These kilns have been attributed to the Song period.

No. 80. *Small bowl, "Splashed Jun" ware*, probably Jin dynasty, 12th–13th century (50.145.316). A small, "Splashed Jun" bowl found in 1977 in the early Yuan-dynasty tomb of Li Boyou (buried 1294) in Jianchang xian, Liaoning Province, is ill., *Wenwu*, 1983, no. 9, pp. 66–72, and fig. 21. This piece was not necessarily new when it was buried.

No. 81. *Dish, Ding ware*, Northern Song dynasty, 11th–12th century (1985.214.133). A fragment with a similar dragon from the Jiancicun Ding kilns, Quyang xian, Hebei Province, is ill., Hughes-Stanton and Kerr, *Kiln Sites*, no. 330, where it has been attributed to the Song dynasty. • See also *Wenwu*, 1984, no. 5, pp. 86–88, for a cache of porcelains found in 1981 in Quyang xian, Hebei Province. Most of these objects have been described as Northern Song Ding ware; many of them had carved or impressed dragon designs.

Color No. 13. *Head of a lion, Ding ware*, Northern Song dynasty, 11th–12th century (1985.214.131). A comparable stone head found in 1971 in the Northern Song tomb of Mr. Fan in Fangcheng xian, Henan Province, is ill., *Wenwu*, 1983, no. 8, pp. 40–43, and pl. 7:7. The tomb was dated in accordance with 1094.

No. 82. *Bowl, Ding ware*, late Northern Song–Jin dynasty, ca. 12th century (1980.532). A similar bowl excavated in 1958 from tomb no. 1 at Lindongzhen, Balin Left Banner, in the Inner Mongolian Autonomous Region, is ill., *Wenwu*, 1959, no. 7, pp. 63–64, and fig. 3:2. The tomb has been attributed to the Jin dynasty.

No. 83. *Vase, "Red" ("Brown") Ding ware*, Northern Song dynasty, 11th–12th century (27.119.16). Two kindred vases from the Northern Song tomb of Zhang Min (died 1071) that was found in 1974 in the suburbs of Zhenjiang, Jiangsu Province, are ill., *Wenwu*, 1977, no. 3, pp. 55–58, and pl. 4:3. One of these vases is illustrated in color, ZSRMC, *Chūgoku tōji zenshū*, vol. 9, Ding (1981), pl. 58.

No. 84. *Bowl, "Red" ("Brown") Ding ware*, Northern Song dynasty, 11th–12th century (17.118.21). A fragment of a bowl with a reddish brown glaze from the Ding kilns, Hebei Province, is ill., Hughes-Stanton and Kerr, *Kiln Sites*, no. 326, where it has been attributed to the Song dynasty.

No. 85. *Vase, Cizhou ware*, Northern Song dynasty, ca. 11th century (26.292.56). Stonewares decorated with incised designs set against backgrounds of small stamped circles have been found in a number of kiln complexes, e.g., Hughes-Stanton and Kerr, *Kiln Sites*, no. 358, from the Cizhou kilns, Hebei Province; nos. 375, 377, 381, from Mi xian, Henan Province; 384–86, from Dengfeng, Henan Province; 406, 407, from Lushan, Henan Province. (The fragment, no. 358, is also ill., *Wenwu*, 1964, no. 8, pp. 37–48, 56, and pl. 6:2[center], from the Guantai kilns.)

No. 86. *Pillow, Cizhou ware*, Northern Song dynasty, ca. 11th century (16.156.1). A similar floral motif against a background of small circles was on the side of a pillow that was found at kilns excavated in Xinan xian, Henan Province, ill., WBW, *Zhongguo gudai yaozhi*, 1984, pp. 339–51, and fig. 5:12.

No. 87. *Vase, Cizhou ware*, Northern Song dynasty, 11th–early 12th century (23.54.2). A fragment with a leaf motif set against a striated ground came from the Hebei Cizhou kilns; it is ill., Hughes-Stanton and Kerr, *Kiln Sites*, no. 353, where it has been attributed to the Song dynasty. (This fragment is also ill., *Wenwu*, 1964, no. 8, pp. 37–48, 56, and fig. 7[bottom left], from the Guantai kilns.)

Color No. 14. *Vase, Cizhou ware*, Northern Song dynasty, 11th–12th century (26.292.61). A fragment with a similar design from the Guantai kilns, Hebei Province, is ill., *Wenwu*, 1964, no. 8, pp. 37–48, 56, and fig. 11(upper left). This fragment could be an example of what is described in the text as eight fragments—mostly from *meiping* vases—showing painted and carved decoration of winding peony branches above lotus-petal panels in soy sauce brown on a white ground.

No. 88. *Vase, Cizhou ware*, Northern Song dynasty, 11th–early 12th century (25.65). Fragments with similar decoration from the Hebei Cizhou kilns are ill., Hughes-Stanton and Kerr, *Kiln*

Sites, nos. 347–51, where they have been attributed to the Song dynasty. (These fragments are also ill., *Wenwu*, 1964, no. 8, pp. 37–48, 56, and pl. 6:1, from the Guantai kilns.)

Color No. 15. *Pillow, Cizhou ware* (mark: *Zhang jia zao* ["made by the Zhang family"]), late Northern Song–Jin dynasty, 12th–13th century (1985.214.132). Fragments of pillows with comparable painted decoration from the Dongaikoucun kilns, Hebei Province, are ill., *Wenwu*, 1964, no. 8, pp. 37–48, 56, and pl. 6:4; figs. 18(top center), 19, 20. Fragments of pillows with the mark *Zhang jia zao* have been found at these kilns (ibid., fig. 24). • A pillow with a cloud-shaped top and a very similar scene of birds and water weeds was excavated in 1983 in Neihuang xian, Henan Province. It is ill., *Kaogu*, 1986, no. 3, pp. 284–85, and fig. 1:2, where it has been attributed to the Northern Song period. This pillow carries the mark *Zhang jia zao* (ibid., fig. 3[right]). • Another pillow, with a cloud-shaped top and a scene of a dragonfly skimming over marsh grasses, is ill., Hebei sheng bowuguan [HSB] and Wenwu guanlichu [WG], eds., *Hebei sheng chutu wenwu xuanji* (Beijing, 1980), p. 65 and pl. 378(left). This pillow has the two marks *Zhang jia zao* and *Zhang da jia zhen* (ibid., pl. 378[right]). It was found in 1954 in a tomb in Xingtai, Hebei Province. On the basis of coins found in the tomb, it has been attributed to the late Northern Song or early Jin period.

No. 89. *Pillow, Cizhou ware* (mark: *Zhang da jia zhen*, meaning "pillow [of the] great Zhang family"), late Northern Song–Jin dynasty, 12th–13th century (60.73.2). A pillow of this shape showing a little boy fishing was excavated at Baoding, Hebei Province. It is ill., *Wenwu*, 1965, no. 2, pp. 36–42, and pl. 4:2; fig. 4, where it has been described as Song-dynasty Cizhou ware. This pillow is marked *Zhang jia zhen*. (In some journals, such as HSB and WG, *Hebei sheng chutu wenwu xuanji*, pl. 376, it is reported that this pillow was excavated in 1954 near Xingtai.) • Similar decoration on fragments of pillows found at the Dongaikoucun kilns, Hebei Province, are ill., *Wenwu*, 1964, no. 8, pp. 37–48, 56, and fig. 19.

No. 90. *Bowl*, Northern Song–Jin dynasty, ca. 11th–12th century (60.81.3).
No. 91. *Small bowl*, Northern Song dynasty, ca. 11th–12th century (60.81.5).
Fragments with brown-splashed black glazes and oil-spot glazes from several kiln sites in Shanxi Province are ill., ZSRMC, *Chūgoku tōji zenshū*, vol. 28, Shanxi (1984), pl. 47, where they have been attributed to the Song period.

No. 92. *Plate, Ding ware*, Jin dynasty, 12th–13th century (18.69.1). A mold for a flattened-rim plate with a very similar design in the cavetto was found at the Ding kiln complex at Jiancicun, Quyang xian, Hebei Province; it is ill., *Kaogu*, 1965, no. 8, pp. 394–412, and pl. 10:11.

No. 95. *Pillow, Jun ware*, Jin–Yuan dynasty, late 12th–13th century (26.292.40). As with so much Jun ware, it is difficult to find archaeological comparisons for this pillow. However, a number of pillows with cloud-shaped tops are known in other types of ceramics, most of them attributable to the Northern Song and Jin periods. For excavated painted Cizhou-ware examples, see notes under Color No. 15, above.

No. 96. *Pillow, Cizhou ware*, Jin dynasty, 12th–13th century (26.292.51). Two carved wall panels—each showing a peacock and rock in a garden similar to the motif on the back panel of this pillow—were found in 1959 near Houmazhen, Shanxi Province, ill., *Wenwu*, 1959, no. 6, pp. 50–55, and figs. 5, 18. They were in two Jin-dynasty Dong-family tombs that are datable to 1210. • The fondness during the Jin dynasty for compact diaper patterns, such as the one on side panels of this pillow, is evident in a number of different compact diaper patterns in these tomb wall carvings.

No. 97. *Bowl, Cizhou ware*, Jin dynasty, 13th century (26.292.64). A bowl painted in overglaze red, yellow, and green enamels that was found between 1959 and 1961 in tomb no. 29 in the suburbs of Houma, Shanxi Province, is ill., *Kaogu*, 1961, no. 12, pp. 681–83, and fig. 1:3. The tomb was similar to another excavated nearby that was dated in accordance with 1212; it has been attributed to the Jin period in the excavation report. • A bowl painted in overglaze red and green enamels from kilns in Xinan xian, Henan Province, is ill., WBW, *Zhongguo gudai yaozhi*, 1984, pp. 339–51, and pl. 13:6.

No. 98. *Covered five-spouted jar with celadon glaze*, early Northern Song dynasty, 10th–11th century (37.124). A five-spouted jar that has been described as Northern Song Longquan ware from Zhejiang Province is ill., *Chūgoku nisennen no bi* [China's Beauty of 2,000 Years], exhib. cat. (Tokyo, 1965), no. 18. • Another five-spouted jar is ill., *Wenwu*, 1963, no. 1, pp. 27–39, and inside front cover, fig. 5; it has been called Five Dynasties Longquan ware. • Yet another spouted jar was excavated in 1976 in Longquan xian, Zhejiang Province; it is ill., *Wenwu*, 1979, no. 11, p. 95, and pl. 8:2, where it has been described as early Northern Song Longquan ware.

No. 99. *Jar, Longquan ware*, Southern Song dynasty, 12th–13th century (18.139.1). A comparable jar with a relief dragon was unearthed in 1956 at Longquan, Zhejiang Province; it is ill., *Zhonghua renmin gongheguo chutu wenwu xuan* [A Selection of Archaeological Finds of the People's Republic of China], exhib. cat. (Beijing, 1976), no. 95. This exhibition was in the Philippines; much the same material was exhibited in Tokyo in 1978.

No. 100. *Vase, Longquan ware*, Southern Song dynasty, 12th–13th century (50.145.301). A similar vase—but with phoenix-shaped handles—from the Dayao Longquan kilns is ill., *Wenwu*, 1963, no. 1, pp. 27–39, and figs. 8:4, 16, where it has been attributed to the Southern Song period. • A piece of a celadon vase with a fish-shaped handle was found during the 1978–79 excavations of the remains of ancient docks at Ningbo, Zhejiang Province; it is ill., Zhejiang sheng wenwu kaogusuo, comp., *Zhejiang sheng wenwu kaogusuo xuekan* (Beijing, 1981),

pp. 105–29, and pl. 11:8. This fragment was found in a stratum that has been attributed to the Song/Yuan period.

No. 101. *Kiln waster, Longquan ware*, Southern Song dynasty, 12th–13th century (26.292.80). A similar handled cup from the Dayao Longquan kilns is ill., *Wenwu*, 1963, no. 1, pp. 27–39, and figs. 8:8, 9, where it has been attributed to the Southern Song period. • Another similar handled cup, described as Guan ware, was excavated in 1972 from the tomb of a lady in Wuxing xian, Zhejiang Province; it is ill., *Wenwu Ziliao Congkan* 2 (1978), pp. 118–22, and figs. 4:1, 12. Inasmuch as the latest coins found in the tomb were of the Xuanhe period, 1119–25, the tomb has been attributed to the end of the Northern Song or early Southern Song period..

No. 102. *Bowl with celadon glaze, from Fujian Province*, Song dynasty, 960–1279 (29.100.368). The bottom of a celadon-glazed bowl that has been decorated in the same manner came from the Tongan kilns, Fujian Province. It is ill., Hughes-Stanton and Kerr, *Kiln Sites*, no. 130, where it has been attributed to the Song dynasty. • A similar bowl found in 1975 in a tomb in Shunchang xian, Fujian Province, is ill., *Wenwu*, 1983, no. 8, pp. 35–39, and pl. 6:5; fig. 5:8, where it has been described as Tongan-type ware. On the basis of some coins found in the tomb, it has been suggested in the report that the tomb dates to the Northern Song era, the Yuanfeng period, 1078–85.

No. 103. *Dish, Hangzhou Guan ware*, Southern Song dynasty, 12th–13th century (24.172.1). A fragment of similar ware from the Jiaotan kilns in Hangzhou is ill., *Sekai tōji zenshū* [Ceramic Art of the World], vol. 12, *Sung Dynasty* (Tokyo, 1977), color pl. 222(bottom).

No. 105. *Cup*, qingbai *ware*, Northern Song dynasty, ca. second half 11th century (26.292.47). One of two very similar *qingbai* cups found in 1963 in Susong xian, Anhui Province, in the Northern Song tomb of Wu Zhengchen and his wife is ill., *Jingdezhen Taoci*, 1984, no. 2, pp. 60–63, and fig. 1:6. See also *Wenwu*, 1965, no. 3, pp. 53–54. The tomb epitaph was dated in accordance with 1087.

No. 106. *Vase*, qingbai *ware*, Northern Song dynasty, ca. second half 11th–early 12th century (26.292.87). One of three analogous *qingbai* vases from the same tomb as above is ill., *Jingdezhen Taoci*, 1984, no. 2, fig. 2:1. • Several other similar vases have been discovered. Some of these vases have been described as having a white glaze or have been called Ding ware (as was mentioned in the main text here, the bluish tone of the glaze on the Metropolitan's vase is so faint that it can be seen only in daylight). For example, see one from the Northern Song tomb of Yan Liangzuo (buried 1113) and his wife, ill., *Kaogu*, 1965, no. 1, pp. 21–24, and pl. 4:4. This tomb was excavated in 1964 in Macheng xian, Hubei Province.

No. 107. *Pillow*, qingbai *ware*, Southern Song dynasty, 12th–13th century (26.292.82). The bottom of a very similar pillow that was excavated in 1977 from a tomb attributed to the Song period in Zhenjiang, Jiangsu Province, is ill., *Wenwu*, 1978, no. 11, pp. 92–93, and pl. 8:1. • Another pillow of this type, but of lesser quality, was found in the wreck of a Chinese merchant ship that sank off the coast of Korea not long after June 1323; it is ill., National Museum of Korea, *Cultural Relics Found off Sinan Coast*, pl. 148.

No. 108. *Covered jar with brown painting under greenish-toned glaze, from Fujian Province*, Song dynasty, 960–1279 (1985.218). One of a pair of comparable jars excavated from a tomb in Pucheng xian, Fujian Province, is ill., *Wenwu*, 1959, no. 3, inside back cover. The tomb has been attributed in the report to the Song dynasty. • Fragments of similar ware from the Anxi kilns in Fujian Province are ill., Hughes-Stanton and Kerr, *Kiln Sites*, nos. 118, 119, where they have been attributed to the Song dynasty.

No. 109. *Tea bowl, Jian ware*, Song dynasty, 960–1279 (91.1.226). A bowl that was excavated in 1972 from the tomb of a lady in Wuxing xian, Zhejiang Province, is ill., *Wenwu Ziliao Congkan* 2 (1978), pp. 118–22, and figs. 4:4, 10, where it has been described as Jian yao. Inasmuch as the latest coins found in the tomb were of the Xuanhe period, 1119–25, the tomb has been attributed to the end of the Northern Song or early Southern Song era. • James Marshall Plumer, *Temmoku: A Study of the Ware of Chien* (Tokyo, 1972), pl. 28, showed similarly shaped bowls from the kiln site.

No. 110. *Tea bowl, Jian ware*, Song dynasty, 960–1279 (29.100.226). A similar bowl with flaring sides was found in 1975 in a tomb in Shunchang xian, Fujian Province; it is considered to be Jian ware, ill., *Wenwu*, 1983, no. 8, pp. 35–39, and pl. 6:7; fig. 5:9. On the basis of some coins found in the tomb, it has been suggested in the report that the tomb dates to the Northern Song era, the Yuanfeng period, 1078–85. • Plumer, *Temmoku*, pl. 27, showed two wasters of analogous shape from the Jian kiln site.

No. 111. *Bowl, Jizhou ware*, Southern Song–Yuan dynasty, ca. 13th–14th century (29.100.222). A bowl with comparable reserve decoration on a variegated field was found in the 1980–81 excavations at the Jizhou kilns, Jiangxi Province; it is ill., *Kaogu*, 1982, no. 5, pp. 481–89, and pl. 8:3(right), where it has been attributed to the Southern Song period. • Another bowl was excavated in 1958 at Nanchang, Jiangxi Province; it is ill., *Wenwu*, 1975, no. 3, pp. 49–50, and pl. 5:4. The report mentions that this type of bowl has frequently been excavated from Song tombs in Jiangxi Province.

No. 112. *Bowl, Jizhou ware*, Southern Song–Yuan dynasty, ca. 13th–14th century (24.100.1). A fragment of a bowl with similar painted decoration from the Jizhou kilns, Jiangxi Province, is ill., Hughes-Stanton and Kerr, *Kiln Sites*, no. 278, where it has been attributed to the Southern Song dynasty.

No. 113. *Bowl, Jizhou ware*, Southern Song–Yuan dynasty, ca. 13th–14th century (1986.208.2). Part of a bowl with

painted spiky scrollwork was excavated at the Jizhou kiln complexes. It is ill., ZSRMC, *Chūgoku tōji zenshū*, vol. 15, Jizhou (1986), pl. 82, where it has been attributed to the Song dynasty.

No. 114. *Bowl, Jizhou ware*, Southern Song–Yuan dynasty, ca. 13th–14th century (23.183.1). Ibid., pl. 31, a bowl with splashed glaze, also from the Jizhou kilns, attributed to the Song period.

No. 115. *Vase, Jizhou ware*, late Northern–Southern Song dynasty, 12th–13th century (1985.87). A bottle-shaped vase with reserved flowering prunus on a black ground came from a tomb excavated in 1982 in the suburbs of Yichun, Jiangxi Province. It is ill., *Kaogu*, 1985, no. 5, p. 480, and fig. 1(left). The latest coins found in the tomb were those of the Daguan reign, 1107–10, and the tomb has been attributed to the late Northern Song period. • A *meiping* vase with a similar design was excavated in Nanchang xian, Jiangxi Province. It is ill., Wenwu bianji weiyuanhui, ed., *Wenwu kaogu gongzuo sanshinian* (Beijing, 1979), pp. 240–51, and pl. 21:3, where it has been described as Song-dynasty Jizhou ware. • Another *meiping* was found in 1956 at the Jizhou kiln site; it is ill., *Wenwu*, 1975, no. 3, pp. 49–50, and pl. 4:4.

No. 116. *Covered box, possibly Jizhou ware*, Southern Song–Yuan dynasty, 13th–14th century (1986.75.4). A similar box that was found in 1957 in a tomb in the suburbs of Nanjing is ill., *Kaogu Tongxun*, 1958, no. 12, pp. 35–38, and fig. 1:1. Some coins found in the tomb show that it was not built earlier than 1195–1200, and it has been attributed in the report to the middle Southern Song period.

This kind of ware has traditionally been attributed to the Jizhou kilns, e.g., ZSRMC, *Chūgoku tōji zenshū*, vol. 15, Jizhou (1986), pl. 78; however, there is little in the way of supporting kiln-site evidence. *Qingbai*-glazed wares with a carved decoration of plum blossom and crescent moon have been found at kiln complexes near Nanfeng, Jiangxi Province, e.g., Hughes-Stanton and Kerr, *Kiln Sites*, no. 222, a part of a bowl that has been attributed to the Song dynasty.

No. 117. *Jar, possibly Ganzhou ware*, Southern Song–Yuan dynasty, 12th–14th century (1986.208.3). A parallel jar was found in 1976 in Qingjiang xian, Jiangxi Province, in the Song-dynasty tomb of Liu Chun's wife (née Yang), who was reburied in 1173; it is ill., *Wenwu*, 1983, no. 8, p. 60, and fig. 1. The jar is considered to be Ganzhou ware. • Similar jars that were found in the wreck of a Chinese merchant ship that sank off the coast of Korea not long after June 1323 are ill., National Museum of Korea, *Cultural Relics Found off Sinan Coast*, pls. 236–38. • A jar and a fragment from the Ganzhou kiln complexes, Jiangxi Province, are ill., Hughes-Stanton and Kerr, *Kiln Sites*, nos. 251, 252, where they have been attributed to the Yuan dynasty. • Jars of this type have been found at the Jizhou kiln complexes as well.

Chapter Ten: The Yuan Dynasty

No. 118. *Vase*, qingbai *ware*, Yuan dynasty, ca. late 13th–early 14th century (25.215.6). A comparable *yuhuchun ping*–shape vase found in Jiangxi Province is ill., *Wenwu*, 1980, no. 2, pp. 73–74, and pl. 8:3, where it has been attributed to the Yuan Dynasty. • Three other similar vases found in the remains of a Chinese merchant ship that sank off the coast of Korea in 1323 are ill., National Museum of Korea, *Cultural Relics Found off Sinan Coast*, pls. 158–60.

No. 119. *Vase*, qingbai *ware*, late Southern Song–Yuan dynasty, 13th–first half 14th century (23.182.1). One of a pair of *qingbai meiping*-shape vases found in a cache in Lüeyang xian, Shaanxi Province, is ill., *Wenwu*, 1976, no. 11, pp. 84–85, and pl. 5:1. The porcelains found in the cache have been attributed to the Song period, but there is no proof of this date. • A covered silver *meiping* that has a cup-shaped mouth and is decorated in overall scrollwork is ill., *Wenwu*, 1973, no. 4, pp. 59–66, and figs. 17, 18. This piece came from the Southern Song tomb of Zhang Tongzhi's wife (née Zhang), who died in 1199. The tomb was excavated in 1971 in Jiangpu xian, Jiangsu Province.

No. 120. *Bodhisattva*, qingbai *ware*, Yuan dynasty, late 13th–early 14th century (51.166). A large *qingbai* image of Guanyin was excavated in 1955 in the western sector of Beijing, an area that had been the Yuan capital of Dadu; it is ill., *Kaogu*, 1972, no. 6, pp. 25–31, 58, and pl. 7.

Nos. 121 and 122. *Pair of incense burners*, qingbai *ware*, Yuan dynasty, ca. early 14th century (34.113.2 and .3). A *qingbai* figure of a crouching lion that is somewhat similar to the ones on the tops of these censers was found in the vicinity of the Yuan-dynasty city of Jininglu, in the Inner Mongolian Autonomous Region; it is ill., *Wenwu*, 1979, no. 8, pp. 32–36, and pl. 6:5.

No. 123. *Covered ewer*, qingbai *ware*, Yuan dynasty, ca. first half 14th century (L.1972.77.2). Kindred spotted *qingbai* ewers found in the remains of a Chinese merchant ship that sank off the coast of Korea in 1323 are ill., National Museum of Korea, *Cultural Relics Found off Sinan Coast*, pls. 198, 336.

No. 124. *Covered box*, qingbai *ware, from Fujian Province*, Yuan dynasty, 1279–1368 (1984.483.2). Fragments of similar ware from the Anxi kiln complexes, Fujian Province, are ill., Hughes-Stanton and Kerr, *Kiln Sites*, nos. 125–29, where they have been attributed to the Yuan dynasty.

No. 125. *Stemcup*, shufu *ware*, Yuan dynasty, 14th century (25.222.5). *Shufu* porcelains from the Yuan-dynasty Ren-family tombs in Qingpu xian, Shanghai, are ill., *Wenwu*, 1982, no. 7, pp. 54–60, and pl. 4:3,7; figs. 1–6. The earliest of these tombs was the tomb of Ren Renfa, who died in 1328 (ibid., p. 53); the latest is datable to 1353. • A *shufu*-marked dish from the Hutian kilns near Jingdezhen is ill., *Wenwu*, 1980, no. 11, pp. 39–49, and fig. 10:6.

Color No. 16. *Vase painted in underglaze blue*, Yuan dynasty, ca. first half 14th century (1984.297). Two silver vases of this *yuhuchun ping* shape were found in 1960 in the Yuan-dynasty tomb of Qian Yu, who died in 1320, near Wuxi, Jiangsu Province. One of them is ill., *Wenwu*, 1964, no. 12, pp. 52–60, and pl. 6:3. • An octagonal, blue-and-white *yuhuchun ping* with a similar disposition of decorative motifs was found in 1964 in a hoard attributed to the Yuan dynasty at Baoding, Hebei Province; it is ill., *Wenwu*, 1965, no. 2, pp. 17–18, 22, and pl. 3:1. • Similar aquatic plants on a part of a blue-and-white plate from the Hutian Jingdezhen kilns are ill., *Wenwu*, 1980, no. 11, pp. 39–49, and pl. 4:4.

Color No. 17 and No. 127. *Stemcup painted in underglaze blue*, Yuan dynasty, ca. first half 14th century (1986.97.1). Part of a group of nine blue-and-white stemcups that were found in 1980 in a large cache in Gaoan xian, Jiangxi Province, is ill., *Wenwu*, 1982, no. 4, pp. 58–69, and pl. 7:3–5 (note the design of a ribbon-tied bouquet of aquatic plants, pl. 7:4 [center]). The cache has been attributed in the report to the late Yuan period. • A ribbon-tied bouquet of aquatic plants on a piece of a blue-and-white bowl that was found at the Hutian Jingdezhen kilns is ill., *Wenwu*, 1980, no. 11, pp. 39–49, and pl. 4:3.

No. 128. *Jarlet painted in underglaze blue*, Yuan dynasty, ca. first half 14th century (L.1972.77.3). A comparable blue-and-white jarlet excavated at the Santa Ana site in Manila is ill., Leandro and Cecilia Locsin, *Oriental Ceramics Discovered in the Philippines* (Rutland and Tokyo, 1967), pl. 86.

No. 131. *Vase painted in underglaze red*, Yuan dynasty, ca. first half 14th century (1970.214). An underglaze red–painted *yuhuchun ping* vase unearthed in 1965 at Fengtai, Beijing, is ill., *Zhonghua renmin gongheguo chutu wenwu xuan* [A Selection of Archaeological Finds of the People's Republic of China], exhib. cat. (Beijing, 1976), no. 97, where it has been attributed to the Yuan period. (This exhibition was in the Philippines; much the same material was exhibited in Tokyo in 1978.) This vase is illustrated in color, Hua Shi, ed., *Zhongguo taoci* (Beijing, 1985), pl. 285.

No. 132. *Head painted in underglaze brown*, late Yuan dynasty, 14th century (38.56.9). Ten dishes painted in underglaze brown were found in 1982 during the eighth expedition among the remains of a Chinese ship that sank off the coast of Korea near Sinan in 1323. Three of them are ill., *Gugong Bowuyuan Yuankan*, 1985, no. 3, pp. 112–18, 121, and fig. 10. Nine of these dishes are illustrated in color, Munhwajaekwanliguk, Munhwakongbobu [MM], *Sinan haejŏ yumul*, vol. 3 (Seoul, 1985), pls. 80–85. This find documents the use of underglaze iron decoration in Yuan-dynasty porcelains.

No. 134. *Covered vase painted in underglaze blue*, late Yuan dynasty, ca. third quarter 14th century (26.271.1). Two of six lidded, blue-and-white *meiping*-shape vases found in 1980 in a large cache attributed to the late Yuan period in Gaoan xian, Jiangxi Province, are ill., *Wenwu*, 1982, no. 4, pp. 58–69, and pl. 6:4,5; fig. 2. Four of the lids, as diagramed in fig. 2, were double lids like the one on the Metropolitan's *meiping*. • A fragment of a blue-and-white vase with similar decoration from the Jingdezhen Hutian kilns is ill., *Wenwu*, 1980, no. 11, pp. 39–49, and pl. 3:10, where it has been attributed to the Yuan period.

Color No. 18. *Plate painted in underglaze blue*, late Yuan dynasty, ca. mid-14th century (1987.10). Two plates with the same motifs were found in 1960 among a large number of broken porcelains at the ruins of the Kotla Fīrūzshāh palace in Delhi, India; this palace was destroyed in 1398. They are ill., Ellen S. Smart, "Fourteenth Century Chinese Porcelain from a Tughlaq Palace in Delhi," *Transactions of The Oriental Ceramic Society*, vol. 41 (London, 1975–77), pp. 199–230, and pls. 80:a, 81:a. • Another plate with the same motifs is ill., John Alexander Pope, *Chinese Porcelains from the Ardebil Shrine* (Washington, D. C., 1956), no. 29.42, pl. 9. In September 1611, Shāh 'Abbās the Great of Iran made a gift of his collection of 1,162 Chinese ceramics to the shrine of his ancestor, Sheikh Safī, in Ardebil. This noble gift was placed in an especially prepared "China House" at the shrine. With its authenticated terminal date, the Ardebil collection is most valuable in documenting late Yuan- and Ming-dynasty ceramics. • Blue-and-white fragments with "spiky" leaves and with lotus blossoms that are similar to those on the outside of this plate are ill., Hughes-Stanton and Kerr, *Kiln Sites*, nos. 244, 246, 247. They came from the Jingdezhen Hutian kilns and have been attributed to the Yuan dynasty.

No. 135. *Vase, Longquan ware*, Yuan dynasty, 14th century (50.145.300). More-elaborate Longquan celadon vases with ring handles were found in the remains of a Chinese merchant ship that sank off the coast of Korea in 1323; they are ill., National Museum of Korea, *Cultural Relics Found off Sinan Coast*, pls. 49–51, 311.

No. 136. *Vase, Longquan ware*, Yuan dynasty, 14th century (26.292.77). A comparable large Longquan vase found in 1970 in a cache in the suburbs of Huhehot, Inner Mongolia, is ill., *Wenwu*, 1977, no. 5, pp. 75–77, and fig. 3. A Jun-ware incense burner in the same cache is inscribed with a date that is considered in the report to be in accordance with 1309, and the cache has been attributed to the Yuan dynasty. • Longquan celadons with "stalky" floral scrolls and large Longquan baluster-shaped vases were found in the remains of a Chinese merchant ship that sank off the coast of Korea in 1323. They are ill., National Museum of Korea, *Cultural Relics Found off Sinan Coast*, pls. 23, 49–51, 79, 88, 311, and pls. 46–48, 312, respectively. • Another vase, which was found in the 1983 explorations of this wreck, is ill., MM, *Sinan haejŏ yumul*, vol. 3, pl. 13; this vase had the same decoration as the Metropolitan's, but it was smaller.

Color No. 19. *Basin, Longquan ware*, early Ming dynasty, late 14th–early 15th century (1987.157). Biscuit-relief decoration on Longquan ware appeared by the first quarter of the fourteenth

century; this has been documented by the discovery of several celadons with this type of ornamentation in the cargo of the Chinese ship referred to above, ill., MM, *Sinan haejŏ yumul*, vol. 3, pls. 19, 27, 28. • A celadon dish with a similar incised floral scroll in the cavetto was found in early 1960 in a tomb outside the Zhonghuamen, Nanjing; it is ill., J. M. Addis, *Chinese Ceramics from Datable Tombs and Some Other Dated Material: A Handbook* (London and New York, 1978), pl. 39:y. This was the tomb of Song Sheng's wife (née Ye), who died in 1418.

No. 137. *Kendi with amber glaze*, Song/Yuan dynasty, ca. 11th–13th century (1986.344). Two amber-glazed, earthenware kendis that were excavated at the Santa Ana site in Manila are ill., Locsin, *Oriental Ceramics Discovered in the Philippines*, pls. 20, 23, where they have been attributed to the Song/Yuan period. • Kendis with green or black glazes from the Cizao kiln complexes in the vicinity of Quanzhou, Fujian Province, are ill., *Kaogu*, 1982, no. 5, pp. 490–98, 489, and pls. 10:1, 11:2, where they have been attributed to the Song/Yuan period. Other vessels with yellow glazes have also been mentioned in the report.

No. 138. *Bottle, Cizhou ware*, Jin–Yuan dynasty, 13th–14th century (18.56.32). Fragments with this type of bold, cut-glaze decoration from several sites in Shanxi Province are ill., Hughes-Stanton and Kerr, *Kiln Sites*, nos. 475–77, 479, 487, 488, 490, 496, where they have been attributed to the Jin dynasty.

No. 139. *Jar, Cizhou ware*, Yuan dynasty, ca. 14th century (1975.1.1664). Exactly where this jar was manufactured is uncertain. A somewhat similar vessel that has been painted with birds and flowers is ill., WBW, *Zhongguo gudai yaozhi*, 1984, pp. 326–38, and fig. 9:9. That jar was found in the 1978 explorations of the Hebiji kilns in Henan Province, and it has been attributed to the Yuan dynasty. Like the jar in the Lehman collection, the one from Hebiji has a dark glaze on the inside; a four-petaled flower in a band on the shoulder of the Hebiji jar has been drawn in much the same manner as the one filling an entire panel on the present piece.

Nos. 141–43. *Bulb bowls and flower pot, "Numbered Jun" ware*, Yuan dynasty, 13th–14th century (26.292.2, 26.292.4, and 16.14.1). A report on a number of kilns—including Juntai and Baguadong—in Yu xian, Henan Province, is published in *Wenwu*, 1975, no. 6, pp. 57–63. Both foliated and stud-decorated "Numbered Jun" bulb bowls are illustrated in this report, figs. 7:1,2,4, 10:1, 11, 12, 15(right), 16. • Fragments of "Numbered Jun" ware from the Yu xian kilns are ill., Hughes-Stanton and Kerr, *Kiln Sites*, nos. 394–402, where they have been attributed to the Song dynasty.

Chapter Eleven: The Ming Dynasty

Color No. 20. *Bowl painted in underglaze red*, Ming dynasty, late 14th century (18.56.35). An underglaze red–painted fragment showing the same lotus-panel design that borders the foot of the Metropolitan's bowl is ill., *Sekai tōji zenshū* [Ceramic Art of the World], vol. 14, *Ming Dynasty* (Tokyo, 1976), pl. 175 (middle). This bit of porcelain was found in 1964 in the bed of the Yudaihe that had surrounded the Inner Palace of the Ming imperial palace at Nanjing, and the fragment has been attributed to the Hongwu period. A report of this find has been published, *Wenwu*, 1976, no. 8, pp. 71–77. • Two views of a fragment of a large blue-and-white plate with the same floral scroll as the one on the outside of the Metropolitan's bowl are ill., *Zhongguo Taoci*, 1982, no. 7, pp. 11–26, and p. 14. This fragment came from what has been identified as an imperial kiln site excavated at Zhushanlu in Jingdezhen; it has been attributed to the early Ming period.

No. 145. *Plate painted in underglaze blue*, Ming dynasty, early 15th century (1978.149). Ten blue-and-white plates with the same decoration are in the Ardebil collection; one of them is ill., John Alexander Pope, *Chinese Porcelains from the Ardebil Shrine* (Washington, D. C., 1956), no. 29.75, pl. 33.

No. 146. *Vase with dark blue glaze*, Ming dynasty, early 15th century (25.13). A blue-and-white, covered, *meiping*-type vase of the same general shape was found in 1970 in the tomb of Yong Wang, in the vicinity of Beijing; it is ill., *Wenwu*, 1972, no. 6, p. 64, and pl. 6:1, where it has been attributed to the Yongle period.

No. 147. *Brick with white glaze*, Ming dynasty, ca. 1412–30 (89.7d). Some white porcelain bricks were discovered under a layer of Xuande material at what has been identified as part of an imperial kiln site found in 1982 at Zhushanlu, in the city of Jingdezhen. The bricks have been attributed to the Yongle period in the report, *Zhongguo Taoci*, 1982, no. 7, pp. 173–75.

No. 148. *Architectural tile with colored glazes*, Ming dynasty, ca. 1412–30 (79.2.789). A tile with a caparisoned elephant supporting a petal-panel plinth from the Baoensita (the Porcelain Pagoda) in Nanjing is ill., J. M. Addis, *Chinese Ceramics from Datable Tombs and Some Other Dated Material: A Handbook* (London and New York, 1978), pl. 34:g. Two of the tiles that Sir John illustrated (including the one with an elephant) are shown in color, *Nankin hakubutsuin ten* [Art Treasures from the Nanjing Museum Collection], exhib. cat. (Nagoya, 1981), pl. 112, where they are said to have been found in 1958 at the site of a *liuli*-ware kiln in Nanjing.

Color No. 21. *Jar painted in underglaze blue*, Ming dynasty, Xuande mark and period, 1426–35 (37.191.1). A large, Xuande-marked, blue-and-white jar with a dragon-and-fungus design is ill., *Zhongguo Taoci*, 1982, no. 7, pp. 171–82, and pl. 23:23. It was excavated in 1982 at Zhushanlu, Jingdezhen, at an imperial kiln site. As has been pointed out in the article (p. 177), this dragon is quite different from the creature on the Metropolitan's jar. There are similarities, however, in the drawing of the claws and certain other features.

No. 149. *Dish painted in underglaze blue*, Ming dynasty, Xuande mark and period, 1426–35 (1975.99). The dragon-and-wave motif can be seen on the exterior of a Xuande-marked, blue-and-white stemcup from the above-mentioned imperial kiln site in Jingdezhen, ill., ibid., pl. 23:25(2).

No. 150. *Bowl painted in underglaze blue*, Ming dynasty, Xuande mark and period, 1426–35 (1982.294). A floral scroll with similar leaves was on the outside of a large, Xuande-marked, blue-and-white bowl that came from the imperial kiln site in Jingdezhen mentioned above; it is ill., ibid., pl. 25:33(2).

No. 151. *Stembowl painted in underglaze blue*, Ming dynasty, Xuande mark and period, 1426–35 (1984.483.1). The interior of the Xuande-marked, dragon-and-wave stemcup from the Jingdezhen imperial kiln site mentioned above is ill., ibid., pl. 23:25(1). On this surface, several characters, described as Sanskrit in the publication, have been painted in underglaze blue. This documents the use of non-Chinese inscriptions on Xuande imperial porcelains. • Four-character Xuande reign marks written in seal script in underglaze blue were on two porcelain fragments found in the same excavations; they are ill., ibid., pl. 22:19(2). The writing of the Xuande mark in seal script—whether in *anhua* or underglaze blue—is uncommon.

No. 153. *Dish with old-rose glaze*, Ming dynasty, Xuande mark and period, 1426–35 (24.80.198). The bottom of a small, red-glazed dish found at the Zhushanlu Jingdezhen kiln site is ill., ibid., pl. 26:42, where it has been attributed to the Xuande period.

Color No. 22. *Dish painted in underglaze blue*, Ming dynasty, late 15th century, Chenghua period (1981.81.1). A parallel dish in the Ardebil collection is ill., Pope, *Chinese Porcelains from the Ardebil Shrine*, no. 29.149, pl. 59.

No. 156. *Bowl with enameled decoration*, Ming dynasty, Zhengde mark and period, 1506–21 (63.175.2). A bowl of this type—with a Chenghua mark—was excavated at the site of the Beijing Hotel; it is ill., Quanguo jiben jianshe gongcheng zhong chutu wenwu zhanlanhui gongzuo weiyuanhui, comp., *Quanguo jiben jianshe gongcheng zhong chutu wenwu zhanlan tulu* (Beijing, 1955), vol. 1, pl. 9:1.

No. 174. *Bowl with blue glaze and gold decoration* (mark: *Wan fu you tong* ["may infinite happiness embrace your affairs"]), Ming dynasty, middle 16th century, Jiajing period (79.2.1122). The German silver-gilt mounts that were manufactured about 1590–1610 help to document the dating of this bowl. • A comparable bowl, which also is in the Metropolitan's collection, has an iron-red glaze on the exterior. In 1910, when it was exhibited at the Burlington Fine Arts Club, this bowl still had a certain amount of its *kinrande* floral design intact, see *Exhibition of Early Chinese Pottery and Porcelain*, exhib. cat. (London, 1911), no. F6, pl. 39. This gold decoration apparently was still intact as late as 1924, when the bowl, described as having "coral-coloured exterior, gilt with leafage," was sold at auction, see Christie, Manson & Woods, *Catalogue of the Renowned Collection of Silversmith's Work . . . Being a Part of The Swaythling Heirlooms*, auction cat. (London, 6 May 1924), lot 115. Unfortunately, only very faint traces of the *kinrande* decoration can be seen today. The bowl was furnished with a silver-gilt lid and high splayed foot in London about 1570–75. It is considered to be the one given to Queen Elizabeth I by "Mr. Lychfelde" in 1588 (A. Jefferies Collins, *Jewels and Plate of Queen Elizabeth I: The Inventory of 1574* [London, 1955], no. 1582). It was presented by James II to his Groom of the Stairs, with whose descendants it remained until purchased by Lord Swaythling, ill., Yvonne Hackenbroch, *Highlights of the Untermyer Collection of English and Continental Decorative Arts*, exhib. cat. (New York, 1977), no. 4; Sir Francis Watson, *Chinese Porcelains in European Mounts*, exhib. cat. (New York, 1980), no. 1.

No. 176. *Vase painted in underglaze blue*, Ming dynasty, Wanli mark and period, 1573–1620 (1979.109). A pair of similar large, covered, blue-and-white *meiping* vases—with dragons on a field of scrolls—found during the 1956–58 excavations of the tomb of the Wanli emperor northwest of Beijing is ill., *China Reconstructs*, March, 1959, pp. 16–19, and accompanying plate. According to an article in *Kaogu*, 1959, no. 7, pp. 358–68, there were six of these large *meiping* vases with dragon designs, all with the Wanli mark on the base, found in the tomb.

No. 179. *Vase painted in underglaze blue*, Ming dynasty, Wanli mark and period, 1573–1620 (19.160). A pair of vessels painted with enamels on the biscuit was found in the tomb of the Wanli emperor mentioned above, ill., *Wenwu Cankao Ziliao*, 1958, no. 10, pp. 23–25, and pl. on p. 20. Although different in proportions, the Metropolitan's vase is quite similar in shape to that of the vessels from the tomb; this shape came from the archaic Chinese bronze *gu*.

No. 181. Kraakporselein *plate*, late Ming dynasty, late 16th–early 17th century (16.93). A repaired *kraakporselein* plate found in 1979–80 in the Ming-dynasty tomb of Zhu Yiyin (died 1603) in Nancheng xian, Jiangxi Province, is ill., *Wenwu*, 1982, no. 8, pp. 16–28, and pl. 5:4,7. This plate is illustrated in color, ZSRMC, *Chūgoku tōji zenshū*, vol. 19, Jingdezhen blue-and-white people's ware (1983), pl. 141. • *Kraakporselein* plates with flattened rims are ill., C. L. van der Pijl-Ketel, ed., *The Ceramic Load of the 'Witte Leeuw' (1613)* [Amsterdam, 1982], pp. 53–82. These plates came from the cargo of the *Witte Leeuw*. The wreck of this ship, a Dutch East Indiaman that sank near St. Helena on its homeward voyage in 1613, was discovered in 1976.

No. 182. *Shallow* kraakporselein *bowl*, late Ming dynasty, late 16th–early 17th century (19.136.13). The Metropolitan's bowl is compared with a very similar one in a still life by Willem Kalf that is dated 1663, see John Carswell, Edward A. Maser, and Jean McClure Mudge, *Blue and White: Chinese Porcelain and Its Impact on the Western World*, exhib. cat. (Chicago, 1985), nos. 51, 52. • Shallow *kraakporselein* bowls from the cargo of the *Witte Leeuw* mentioned above are ill., van der Pijl-Ketel, *Ceramic Load of the 'Witte Leeuw,'* pp. 104–18.

No. 183. *Deep* kraakporselein *bowl*, late Ming dynasty, late 16th–early 17th century (19.136.17). Deep ("high") *kraakporselein* bowls from the same find are ill., ibid., pp. 119–27.

No. 188. *Fragment, "Transitional" ware*, Transitional Period, ca. second quarter 17th century (1979.27.4). This fragment has been identified as coming from the wreck of *Nuestra Señora de la Maravillas*, which sank on the Little Bahamas Bank on 4 January 1656.

No. 198. *Dish, "Swatow" ware*, late Ming dynasty, late 16th–early 17th century (1980.471.5). Blue-and-white "Swatow" dishes with a bird as the main motif were found on the *Witte Leeuw*. They are ill., van der Pijl-Ketel, *Ceramic Load of the 'Witte Leeuw,'* pp. 201–3. • Similar archaic dragons on a blue-and-white "Swatow" dish from the same find are ill., ibid., p. 206(right).

Chapter Twelve: The Qing Dynasty

No. 229. *Deer-shaped vessel with colored glazes*, Qing dynasty, late 17th–early 18th century, Kangxi period (24.80.257). One of a pair of deer-shaped ewers presently at Hampton Court is ill., Arthur Lane, "Queen Mary II's Porcelain Collection at Hampton Court," *Transactions of The Oriental Ceramic Society*, vol. 25 (London, 1949–50), pp. 21–31, and pl. 8:d. The Chinese porcelains now at Hampton Court have been mistakenly associated with those in the "Kensington Inventory" of 1696; however, "two little deare of fine [or five] coloured China" from the Queen's New Bedchamber at Kensington are listed in that 1696 Inventory. (The lid on the Metropolitan's vessel is a replacement.)

No. 284. *Figure of Budai Heshang, Dehua ware*, early Qing dynasty, 17th century (32.100.422). A similar figure of Budai Heshang appears in the Burghley House Inventory of 1688 as "1 ball'd fryor sitting [in] My Ladys Dressing Roome," ill., *The Burghley Porcelains: An Exhibition from The Burghley House Collection and Based on the 1688 Inventory and 1690 Devonshire Schedule*, exhib. cat. (New York, 1986), no. 13.

APPENDIX II:
PINYIN ROMANIZATIONS OF
CHINESE WORDS
AND THEIR WADE-GILES
EQUIVALENTS

The system of transliterating Chinese words used in this book is the *pinyin* system officially adopted in 1979 by the government of The People's Republic of China. Equivalent transliterations of words in the main text, using the Wade-Giles system of romanization, are given below, right (words that are spelled the same in both systems are not listed).

anhua . . . an-hua　暗花

Anhui . . . Anhwei　安徽

An Lushan . . . An Lu-shan　安祿山

Anyang . . . An-yang　安陽

Baguadong . . . Pa-kua-tung　八卦洞

Banpo . . . Pan-p'o　半坡

Banpocun . . . Pan-p'o Ts'un　半坡村

Banshan . . . Pan-shan　半山

Baoensita . . . Pao-en-ssu-t'a　報恩寺塔

Baoji . . . Pao-chi　寶雞

Beijing . . . Peking　北京

Beishouling . . . Pei-shou-ling　北首嶺

Beixin . . . Pei-hsin　北辛

Bianjing . . . Pien-ching　汴京

bise yao . . . pi-se yao　秘色窰

bogu . . . po-ku　博古

Budai Heshang . . . Pu-tai Ho-shang　布袋和尚

canjian hu . . . ts'an-chien hu　蠶繭壺

Caoxieshan . . . Ts'ao-hsieh-shan　草鞋山

Chajing . . . Ch'a-ching　茶經

Changan . . . Ch'ang-an　長安

Changsha . . . Ch'ang-sha　長沙

chayemo . . . cha-yeh-mo　茶葉末

Chenghua . . . Ch'eng-hua　成化

Chengziyai . . . Ch'eng-tzu-yai　城子崖

Chen Jinhou zhi . . .
　　　Ch'en Chin-hou chih　陳覲侯製

Chenliuzhuang . . . Ch'en-liu-chuang　陳劉莊

chi . . . ch'ih　螭

Chongzhen . . . Ch'ung-chen　崇禎

Chu . . . Ch'u　楚

ci . . . tz'u　瓷；磁

Cishan . . . Tz'u-shan　磁山

Cishancun . . . Tz'u-shan Ts'un　磁山村

Cixi . . . Tz'u-hsi　慈禧

Ci xian . . . Tz'u Hsien　磁縣

Cizhou . . . Tz'u Chou　磁州

Dabin . . . Ta-pin　大彬

305

Dadiwan . . . Ta-ti-wan 大地灣

Dadu . . . Ta-tu 大都

Daming Gong . . . Ta-ming Kung 大明宮

Da Ming Xuande nianzhi . . .
  Ta Ming Hsüan-te nien-chih 大明宣德年製

Daoguang . . . Tao-kuang 道光

Datong . . . Ta-t'ung 大同

Dawenkou . . . Ta-wen-k'ou 大汶口

Dawenkouzhen . . . Ta-wen-k'ou Chen 大汶口鎮

Daxi . . . Ta-hsi 大溪

Daxingcheng . . . Ta-hsing Ch'eng 大興城

Dayao . . . Ta-yao 大窰

Dayazhai . . . Ta-ya-chai 大雅齋

Dehua . . . Te-hua 德化

Dehua xian . . . Te-hua Hsien 德化縣

Deqing . . . Te-ch'ing 德清

Ding . . . Ting 定

Dingzhou . . . Ting Chou 定州

dou . . . tou 豆

doucai . . . tou-ts'ai 鬥彩

Duandian . . . Tuan-tien 段店

Erligang . . . Erh-li-kang 二里崗

Erlitou . . . Erh-li-t'ou 二里頭

fahua . . . fa-hua 琺花

falangcai . . . fa-lang-ts'ai 琺瑯彩

Fan Cui . . . Fan Ts'ui 范粹

fencai . . . fen-ts'ai 粉彩

Feng Daozhen . . . Feng Tao-chen 馮道真

Foshan . . . Fo-shan 佛山

Fu fan zhizao . . . Fu fan chih-tsao 福藩製造

Fujian . . . Fukien 福建

Gansu . . . Kansu 甘肅

Ganzhou . . . Kan Chou 贛州

Ge . . . Ko 哥

Gong xian . . . Kung Hsien 鞏縣

gu . . . ku 觚

guan . . . kuan 罐

Guan . . . Kuan 官

Guangdong . . . Kwangtung 廣東

Guangxi . . . Kwangsi 廣西

Guangxu . . . Kuang-hsü 光緒

Guangzhou . . . Kuang-chou 廣州

Guanyin . . . Kuan-yin 觀音

gui . . . kuei 簋

guifu shengong . . . kuei-fu shen-kung 鬼斧神工

Guizhou . . . Kweichow 貴州

Guyuexuan . . . Ku Yüeh Hsüan 古月軒

haima . . . hai-ma 海馬

Hangzhou . . . Hangchow 杭州

Hebei . . . Hopei 河北

Hemudu . . . Ho-mu-tu 河姆渡

Henan . . . Honan 河南

Hongguang . . . Hung-kuang 弘光

Hongwu . . . Hung-wu 洪武

Hongxi . . . Hung-hsi 洪熙

Hongxian . . . Hung-hsien 洪憲

Hongzhi . . . Hung-chih 弘治

Hougang . . . Hou-kang 後岡

Huancui . . . Huan-ts'ui 環翠

Huangbaozhen . . . Huang-pao Chen 黃堡鎮

Huangdao . . . Huang-tao 黃道

huashi . . . hua-shih 滑石

Hubei . . . Hupei 湖北

Hui xian . . . Hui Hsien 輝縣

Hutian . . . Hu-t'ien 湖田

Jiajing . . . Chia-ching 嘉靖

Jian , . . Chien 建

Jian (city) . . . Chi-an 吉安

Jiancicun . . . Chien-tz'u Ts'un 澗磁村

Jiangsu . . . Kiangsu 江蘇

Jiangxi . . . Kiangsi 江西

Jianyang xian . . . Chien-yang Hsien 建陽縣

Jiaotan . . . Chiao-t'an 郊壇

Jiaqing . . . Chia-ch'ing 嘉慶

Jia xian . . . Chia Hsien 郟縣

Jiaxing . . . Chia-hsing 嘉興

jichou . . . chi-ch'ou 己丑

Jin . . . Chin 晉

Jin . . . Chin 金

Jincun . . . Chin Ts'un 金村

Jingdezhen . . . Ching-te Chen 景德鎮

Jingshan . . . Ching-shan 京山

Jingtai . . . Ching-t'ai 景泰

Jing xian . . . Ching Hsien 景縣

Jinhua . . . Chin-hua 金華

Jinsha . . . Chin-sha 金沙

Jiujiang . . . Chiu-chiang 九江

Jizhou . . . Chi Chou 吉州

Ju . . . Chü 莒

Julu xian . . . Chü-lu Hsien 鉅鹿縣

Jun . . . Chün 均；鈞

Junan xian . . . Chü-nan Hsien 莒南縣

Juntai . . . Chün-t'ai 鈞台

Junzhou . . . Chün Chou 鈞州

Kaifeng . . . K'ai-feng 開封

Kangxi . . . K'ang-hsi 康熙

Kexingzhuang . . . K'o-hsing-chuang 客省莊

kongquelu . . . k'ung-ch'üeh-lu 孔雀綠

Kudihuiluo . . . K'u-ti-hui-lo 庫狄廻洛

Lan Caihe . . . Lan Ts'ai-ho 藍采和

Lang Shining . . . Lang Shih-ning 郎世寧

langyao . . . lang-yao 郎窯

Lanzhou . . . Lan Chou 蘭州

Liangzhu . . . Liang-chu 良渚

Li Jingxun . . . Li Ching-hsün 李靜訓

Linan . . . Lin-an 臨安

Lincheng xian . . . Lin-ch'eng Hsien 臨城縣

linglong . . . ling-lung 玲瓏

Linru xian . . . Lin-ju Hsien 臨汝縣

Lintong xian . . . Lin-t'ung Hsien 臨潼縣

Liquan xian . . . Li-ch'üan Hsien 醴泉縣

Liu Bang . . . Liu Pang 劉邦

liuli . . . liu-li 琉璃

Liutian . . . Liu-t'ien 琉田

Li Yuan . . . Li Yüan 李淵

Longqing . . . Lung-ch'ing 隆慶

Longquan . . . Lung-ch'üan 龍泉

Longquan xian . . . Lung-ch'üan Hsien 龍泉縣

Longshan . . . Lung-shan 龍山

Longshanzhen . . . Lung-shan Chen 龍山鎮

Lou Rui . . . Lou Jui 婁叡

luanbai . . . luan-pai 卵白

Luoyang . . . Lo-yang 洛陽

Lushan xian . . . Lu-shan Hsien 魯山縣

Machang . . . Ma-ch'ang 馬廠

Machangyan . . . Ma-ch'ang-yen 馬廠沿

Majiabang . . . Ma-chia-pang 馬家浜

Majiayao . . . Ma-chia-yao 馬家窰

meiping . . . mei-p'ing 梅瓶

Mianchi xian . . . Mien-ch'ih Hsien 澠池縣

Miaodigou . . . Miao-ti-kou 廟底溝

mingqi . . . ming-ch'i 明器

minyao . . . min-yao 民窰

Nanjing . . . Nanking 南京

nianhao . . . nien-hao 年號

Nian Xiyao . . . Nien Hsi-yao 年希堯

Ningbo . . . Ning-po 寧波

Ningyang xian . . . Ning-yang Hsien 寧陽縣

Peiligang . . . P'ei-li-kang 裴李崗

Qi . . . Ch'i 齊

Qian . . . Ch'ien 錢

Qianlong . . . Ch'ien-lung 乾隆

Qicun . . . Ch'i Ts'un 祁村

Qijia . . . Ch'i-chia 齊家

Qikou . . . Ch'i-k'ou 溪口

Qilizhen . . . Ch'i-li Chen 七里鎮

Qin . . . Ch'in 秦

Qinan xian . . . Ch'in-an Hsien 秦安縣

Qing . . . Ch'ing 清

qing . . . ch'ing 青

qingbai . . . ch'ing-pai 青白

Qinghai . . . Ch'ing-hai 青海

Qin Shihuangdi . . .
　　　Ch'in Shih-huang-ti 秦始皇帝

Qionglai xian . . . Ch'iung-lai Hsien 邛崍縣

Qishicun . . . Ch'i-shih Ts'un 奇石村

Quanzhou . . . Ch'üan Chou 泉州

Qujialing . . . Ch'ü-chia-ling 屈家嶺

Quyang xian . . . Ch'ü-yang Hsien 曲陽縣

Raozhou . . . Jao Chou 饒州

Ru . . . Ju 汝

ruancai . . . juan-ts'ai 軟彩

rubai . . . ju-pai 乳白

Ruzhou . . . Ju Chou 汝州

salan . . . sa-lan 灑藍

sancai . . . san-ts'ai 三彩

Shaanxi . . . Shensi 陝西

Shandong . . . Shantung 山東

Shanglinhu . . . Shang-lin-hu 上林湖

Shangyu xian . . . Shang-yü Hsien 上虞縣

Shantou . . . Shan-t'ou 汕頭

Shanxi . . . Shansi 山西

Shan xian . . . Shen Hsien 陝縣

Shaoxing xian . . . Shao-hsing Hsien 紹興縣

Shi Dabin . . . Shih Ta-pin 時大彬

Shilingxia . . . Shih-ling-hsia 石嶺下

Shiwan . . . Shih-wan 石灣

Shouxing . . . Shou-hsing 壽星

Shouyang xian . . . Shou-yang Hsien 壽陽縣

shufu . . . shu-fu 樞府

Shuihu zhuan . . . Shui hu chuan 水滸傳

Shuijizhen . . . Shui-chi Chen 水吉鎮

Shunzhi . . . Shun-chih 順治

Sichuan . . . Szechwan 四川

Sima Jinlong . . . Ssu-ma Chin-lung 司馬金龍

Song . . . Sung 宋

Songze . . . Sung-tse 崧澤

Taian xian . . . T'ai-an Hsien 泰安縣

Taihu (Lake Tai) . . . T'ai-hu 太湖

Taiyuan . . . T'ai-yüan 太原

Tang . . . T'ang 唐

Tang Ying . . . T'ang Ying 唐英

Teng xian . . . T'eng Hsien 滕縣

tianbai . . . t'ien-pai 甜白

Tiandi yijia chun . . .
          T'ien-ti i-chia ch'un 天地一家春

Tianmushan . . . T'ien-mu-shan 天目山

Tianqi . . . T'ien-ch'i 天啓

Tianshun . . . T'ien-shun 天順

Tongan . . . T'ung-an 同安

Tongchuan . . . T'ung-ch'uan 銅川

Tongguanzhen . . . T'ung-kuan Chen 銅官鎮

Tongzhi . . . T'ung-chih 同治

Tunxi . . . T'un-hsi 屯溪

Wan Guifei . . . Wan Kuei-fei 萬貴妃

Wanli . . . Wan-li 萬歷

Wazhaping . . . Wa-cha-p'ing 瓦渣坪

Wuan xian . . . Wu-an Hsien 武安縣

wucai . . . wu-ts'ai 五彩

wujin . . . wu-chin 烏金

Wushan xian . . . Wu-shan Hsien 巫山縣

Wu xian . . . Wu Hsien 吳縣

Xia . . . Hsia 夏

Xian . . . Sian 西安

Xianfeng . . . Hsien-feng 咸豐

Xiaotun . . . Hsiao-t'un 小屯

Xindian . . . Hsin-tien 辛店

Xing . . . Hsing 邢

Xin guan . . . Hsin kuan 新官

Xinzheng xian . . .
          Hsin-cheng Hsien 新鄭縣

Xiuneisi . . . Hsiu-nei-ssu 修內司

xiyang . . . hsi-yang 西洋

Xuande . . . Hsüan-te 宣德

Xuande zhizao . . .
          Hsüan-te chih-tsao 宣德製造

Xuantong . . . Hsüan-t'ung 宣統

yangcai . . . yang-ts'ai 洋彩

Yangjiang xian . . .
          Yang-chiang Hsien 陽江縣

Yangshao . . . Yang-shao 仰韶

Yangshaocun . . . Yang-shao Ts'un 仰韶村

Yangzhou . . . Yang Chou 揚州

Yanshi xian . . . Yen-shih Hsien 偃師縣

yaobian . . . yao-pien 窯變

Yaozhou . . . Yao Chou 耀州

yingcai . . . ying-ts'ai 硬彩

Yinxu . . . Yin-hsü 殷墟

Yixing . . . I-hsing 宜興

Yonghezhen . . . Yung-ho Chen 永和鎮

Yongle . . . Yung-lo 永樂

Yongqing changchun . . .
　　Yung-ch'ing ch'ang-ch'un 永慶長春

Yongzheng . . . Yung-cheng 雍正

yu . . . yü 魚

yu . . . yü 裕

Yuan . . . Yüan 元

Yuan Shikai . . . Yüan Shih-k'ai 袁世凱

Yue . . . Yüeh 越

Yuezhou . . . Yüeh Chou 越州

Yuhang . . . Yü-hang 餘杭

yuhuchun ping . . .
　　yü-hu-ch'un p'ing 玉壺春瓶

Yunnan . . . Yünnan 雲南

Yu xian . . . Yü Hsien 禹縣

Yuxi xian . . . Yü-hsi Hsien 玉溪縣

Yuyao xian . . . Yü-yao Hsien 餘姚縣

Yuzhaoge . . . Yü-chao-ko 玉照閣

Zang Yingxuan . . . Ts'ang Ying-hsüan 臧應選

Zhaili . . . Chai-li 寨里

Zhang . . . Chang 章

Zhang da jia zhen . . .
　　Chang ta chia chen 張大家枕

Zhang jia zao . . . Chang chia tsao 張家造

Zhang Sheng . . . Chang Sheng 張盛

Zhao Kuangyin . . . Chao K'uang-yin 趙匡胤

Zhejiang . . . Chekiang 浙江

zhen . . . chen 枕

Zhengde . . . Cheng-te 正德

Zhengde qinian liuyue zao . . . Cheng-te
　　ch'i-nien liu-yüeh tsao 正德七年六月造

Zheng Rentai . . . Cheng Jen-t'ai 鄭仁泰

Zhengtong . . . Cheng-t'ung 正統

Zhengzhou . . . Cheng Chou 鄭州

Zhonghuamen . . . Chung-hua-men 中華門

zhongwen you . . . chung-wen yu 中溫釉

Zhou . . . Chou 周

Zhu Yuanzhang . . . Chu Yüan-chang 朱元璋

Zibo . . . Tzu-po 淄博

zisha . . . tzu-sha 紫砂

zun . . . tsun 尊

Chinese characters by Joseph Chang

310

GLOSSARY

Anhua. "Secret decoration," or "hidden decoration," which can be engraved into the body of an object or applied in very fine slip. Frequently, it is only possible to see *anhua* decoration by transmitted light.

Biscuit. Unglazed pottery that has been fired.

Celadon. A high-fired green glaze that takes its color from small amounts of iron—and generally titanium—oxides; it is fired in a reducing atmosphere. The term is believed to stem from a French seventeenth-century play in which a character named Céladon was costumed in grayish green.

Ceramics. All objects made from fired clay, whether they are earthenware, stoneware, porcelaneous ware, or porcelain; synonymous with "pottery."

"Cord-marked" pottery. A term used to refer to the relatively crude, utilitarian earthenwares used in ancient China. They may be unembellished or decorated in a simple manner; the surfaces frequently show deep, cordlike markings.

Crackle. A deliberate network of cracks in the glaze brought about by the unequal contraction of body and glaze.

Crazing. An unintentional network of cracks in the glaze brought about by the unequal contraction of body and glaze.

Earthenware. Low-fired pottery made from common clay to which a proportion of other materials may be added to achieve good working and firing properties. Earthenware is porous and permeable; in color, it may range from light buff to tan, red, brown, or black, depending on the clay and firing conditions. Earthenwares are usually fired between about 600° C. and 1100° C.

Enamel. In essence, a glass that has been colored with a metallic oxide. Enamels were used to decorate Chinese ceramics in three ways: they were painted onto the surface of an underlying prefired glaze; they were painted directly onto the surface of a prefired, or biscuit, body; they were used as glazes themselves and could be applied either to the underlying glaze or to the biscuit body. Enamels fuse at low temperatures and are fired in a special enameling kiln.

Glaze. In essence, a glassy coating on the surface of a ceramic. A glaze serves the twofold function of helping to seal the clay body and decorating the object. Most glazes are predominantly composed of silica, with other materials—known as fluxes—added to the silica, primarily to lower its melting point. Alumina is almost always added to increase the viscosity of the glaze. Glazes may be applied to a raw body and fired with the body, or they may be applied to a prefired, or biscuit, body and given a separate firing, known as a glost firing.

There are two basic categories of old Chinese glazes. These are the high-fired glazes that belong to the family of lime glazes (including lime-alkali glazes), in which calcium oxide was employed as the principal fluxing agent; and the low-fired glazes that belong to the family of lead glazes, in which lead oxide was employed as the principal fluxing agent. A few types of glazes do not precisely fit into either of these two categories.

The principal coloring agents used in nearly all Chinese glazes until modern times were the oxides of iron, copper, cobalt, and manganese. (The presence of trace materials—such as titanium—in the raw materials could have a significant influence on the color of the glaze.)

Kaolin. China clay, a white-burning clay that is particularly free of impurities, especially iron. It generally is an important ingredient in the manufacture of porcelain. Chinese kaolin is different in composition from the china clay used in the West.

Lead glazes. A family of glazes in which lead oxide is employed as the principal fluxing agent; lead glazes are fired at relatively low temperatures.

Lime glazes. A family of glazes in which calcium oxide—which is generally referred to as lime—is employed as the principal fluxing agent; this lime can take the form of wood-ash and/or limestone. Lime glazes are fired at high temperatures.

The level of calcia in Chinese high-fired glazes changed considerably over the years. It was highest in the early periods; by the Southern Song period, most earlier high-lime glazes had gradually evolved into a subvariety, lime-alkali glazes. The percentage of calcia became even less in the types of glazes that were developed by the Yuan period and were used throughout the Ming and Qing.

Liuli. A term sometimes used by the Chinese for those lower-fired glazes in the tradition of the Tang "three-color" glazes manufactured from the Song dynasty to modern times. Lead oxide was generally employed as the major fluxing agent in the *liuli* glaze.

Northern and southern wares. The high-fired ceramics that were manufactured in the two primary geographic areas of northern and southern China. These areas are marked by a natural boundary that falls between the Yellow and Yangtze rivers, running on a west-east axis approximately along the crest of the Qinling Mountains and, farther east, the Huai River. In addition to a considerable dissimilarity in the geologies of the two areas, there are numerous ecological differences between the grain-growing northern region and rice-cultivating southern region.

The geological diversity of the two regions manifests itself in the widely varied properties of the local raw materials.

Therefore, the composition of the high-fired ceramics manufactured in northern China differs significantly from that of the wares produced in the south.

Oxidizing atmosphere. A condition achieved by allowing as much air as possible to enter the kiln during the firing; this "clean" firing develops the colors of the body and glaze.

Petuntse. Porcelain stone, a rock that generally is an important ingredient in the manufacture of porcelain. Chinese petuntse is very different from the porcelain stones used in the West, and certain Chinese petuntses—after being suitably crushed and washed—can be used alone to make satisfactory porcelain bodies.

Porcelain. High-fired pottery that, by Western standards, is hard, dense, resonant when struck, impervious to liquid, white, and translucent. Porcelain is fired at a temperature in excess of about 1250° C.

Until a short time ago, it had been believed that all Chinese porcelains were produced by combining white-burning kaolin, or china clay, with suitable proportions of petuntse, or porcelain stone. Recently, however, technical studies of several categories of early Chinese porcelains have revealed that the raw materials used in the production of these porcelains varied among different kiln centers. Furthermore, at certain kiln centers, notably Jingdezhen in Jiangxi Province, the composition of porcelain bodies changed considerably over the centuries.

Porcelaneous ware. Pottery that is superior to the average stoneware; while it approaches the quality of "true" porcelain, it does not have all of the characteristics of "true" porcelain in the Western sense.

Pottery. All objects made from fired clay, whether they are earthenware, stoneware, porcelaneous ware, or porcelain; synonymous with "ceramics."

Reducing atmosphere. A low-oxygen, smoky atmosphere in the kiln that affects the color of the body and glaze.

Sgraffito. Decoration made by cutting away parts of a surface layer to expose a different-colored ground.

Slip. A mixture of clay with water. Chinese potters used a coating of white slip to camouflage inferior bodies in the manufacture of many kinds of ceramics.

Stoneware. Vitrified, high-fired pottery made of clay to which a proportion of other materials may be added to achieve good working and firing properties. Stoneware is fired in excess of about 1200° C. It is dense, hard, resonant when struck, and impervious to liquid; it may be light or dark in color, but it is not translucent.

SELECTED
READINGS

Addis, J. M. *Chinese Ceramics from Datable Tombs and Some Other Dated Material: A Handbook.* London and New York, 1978.

Ayers, John. *The Baur Collection, Geneva: Chinese Ceramics.* 4 vols. Geneva, 1968–74. Vol. 1: *Chinese Ceramics, with Korean and Thai Wares* (1968). Vol. 2: *Ming Porcelains, and Other Wares* (1969). Vol. 3: *Monochrome-Glazed Porcelains of the Ch'ing Dynasty* (1972). Vol. 4: *Painted and Polychrome Porcelains of the Ch'ing Dynasty* (1974).

———. *Chinese Ceramics: The Koger Collection.* London and New York, 1985.

Brinker, Helmut, and Goepper, Roger. *Kunstschätze aus China: 5000 v. Chr. bis 900 n. Chr. Neuere Archäologische Funde aus der Volksrepublik China.* Exhibition catalogue. Zürich, Berlin, Hildesheim, and Köln, 1981.

Carswell, John; Maser, Edward A.; and Mudge, Jean McClure. *Blue and White: Chinese Porcelain and Its Impact on the Western World.* Exhibition catalogue. David and Alfred Smart Gallery, University of Chicago, 1985.

Feng Xianming et al., eds. *Zhongguo taoci shi.* Beijing, 1982.

Fontein, Jan, and Wu, Tung. *Unearthing China's Past.* Exhibition catalogue. Museum of Fine Arts, Boston, 1973.

Gray, Basil. *Sung Porcelain and Stoneware.* London and Boston, 1984.

Harrisson, Barbara. *Swatow in Het Princessehof.* Leeuwarden, 1979.

Howard, David, and Ayers, John. *China for the West: Chinese Porcelain and Other Decorative Arts for Export Illustrated from the Mottahedeh Collection.* 2 vols. London and New York, 1978.

Hughes-Stanton, Penelope, and Kerr, Rose, comps. *Kiln Sites of Ancient China: An Exhibition Lent by the People's Republic of China.* Exhibition catalogue. Oriental Ceramic Society, at the British Museum, London; Ashmolean Museum, Oxford. London, 1980. (See Idemitsu Museum of Arts, below.)

Idemitsu Museum of Arts, ed. *1949–1981 Kinnen hakken no yōshi shutsudo Chūgoku tōji ten* [Kiln Sites of Ancient China: Recent Finds of Pottery and Porcelain]. Exhibition catalogue. Tokyo, 1982. (This is virtually the same exhibition that was held in England in 1980; see Hughes-Stanton and Kerr, above.)

International Conference on Ancient Chinese Pottery and Porcelain, Shanghai, 1982. *Abstracts.*

Jenyns, Soame. *Later Chinese Porcelain: The Ch'ing Dynasty (1644–1912).* 4th ed. London, 1971.

Juliano, Annette L. *Art of the Six Dynasties: Centuries of Change and Innovation.* Exhibition catalogue. China Institute in America, New York, 1975.

———. *Treasures of China.* New York, 1981.

Kaogu. Beijing, 1959—. (Published as *Kaogu Tongxun,* 1955–58.)

Kaogu Xuebao. Beijing, 1953—. (Published as *Tianye Kaogu Xuebao* and *Zhongguo Kaogu Xuebao,* 1936–51.)

Kaogu yu Wenwu. Xian, 1980—.

Kerr, Rose. *Chinese Ceramics: Porcelain of the Qing Dynasty 1644–1911.* London, 1986.

Kilburn, Richard S. *Transitional Wares and Their Forerunners.* Exhibition catalogue. Oriental Ceramic Society of Hong Kong and the Urban Council, Hong Kong, 1981.

Kingery, W. David, and Vandiver, Pamela B. *Ceramic Masterpieces: Art, Structure, and Technology.* New York, 1986.

Krahl, Regina, and Erbahar, Nurdan. *Chinese Ceramics in the Topkapi Saray Museum, Istanbul: A Complete Catalogue.* Edited by John Ayers. 3 vols. London, 1986. Vol. 1: *Yuan and Ming Dynasty Celadon Wares.* Vol. 2: *Yuan and Ming Dynasty Porcelains.* Vol. 3: *Qing Dynasty Porcelains,* with John Ayers.

Le Corbeiller, Clare. *China Trade Porcelain: A Study in Double Reflections.* Exhibition catalogue. China Institute in America, New York, 1973.

———. *China Trade Porcelain: Patterns of Exchange.* New York, 1974.

Lee, Sherman E., and Ho, Wai-kam. *Chinese Art Under the Mongols: The Yüan Dynasty (1279–1368).* Exhibition catalogue. Cleveland Museum of Art, 1968.

Lion-Goldschmidt, Daisy. *Les Poteries et Porcelaines Chinoises.* 3rd ed. Paris, 1978.

———. *Ming Porcelain.* Translated by Katherine Watson. New York, 1978.

Little, Stephen. *Chinese Ceramics of the Transitional Period: 1620–1683*. Exhibition catalogue. China Institute in America, New York, 1983.

Medley, Margaret. *Yüan Porcelain and Stoneware*. London, 1974.

———. *The Chinese Potter: A Practical History of Chinese Ceramics*. New York, 1976.

———. *T'ang Pottery and Porcelain*. London, 1981.

Oriental Ceramic Society, London. *Transactions*. 1921—.

Oriental Ceramic Society of Hong Kong. *Bulletin*. 1975—.

Oriental Ceramic Society of Hong Kong and Fung Ping Shan Museum, University of Hong Kong. *Jingdezhen Wares: The Yuan Evolution*. Exhibition catalogue. Hong Kong, 1984.

Peking Museum of Chinese History et al., eds. *7000 Years of Chinese Civilization: Chinese Art and Archaeology from the Neolithic Period to the Han Dynasty*. Exhibition catalogue (Venice). Milan, 1983.

Pope, John Alexander. *Fourteenth-Century Blue-and-White: A Group of Chinese Porcelains in the Topkapu Sarayi Müzesi, Istanbul*. Washington, D. C., 1952.

———. *Chinese Porcelains from the Ardebil Shrine*. Washington, D. C., 1956.

Rawson, Jessica. *Ancient China: Art and Archaeology*. London, 1980.

———. *Chinese Ornament: The Lotus and the Dragon*. London, 1984.

Satō, Masahiko. *Chinese Ceramics: A Short History*. Translated by Kiyoko Hanaoka and Susan Barberi. New York and Tokyo, 1981.

Second International Conference on Ancient Chinese Pottery and Porcelain: Its Scientific and Technical Insights, Beijing, 1985. *Abstracts*.

Sekai tōji zenshū [Ceramic Art of the World]. 22 vols. Tokyo, 1975–85. Vol. 10: *Chinese Prehistoric and Ancient Periods* (1982). Vol. 11: *Sui and T'ang Dynasties* (1976). Vol. 12: *Sung Dynasty* (1977). Vol. 13: *Liao, Chin and Yüan Dynasties* (1981). Vol. 14: *Ming Dynasty* (1976). Vol. 15: *Ch'ing Dynasty* (1983).

Shangraw, Clarence F. *Origins of Chinese Ceramics*. Exhibition catalogue. China Institute in America, New York, 1978.

Thorp, Robert L., and Bower, Virginia. *Spirit and Ritual: The Morse Collection of Ancient Chinese Art*. Exhibition catalogue. Metropolitan Museum of Art, New York, 1982.

Tichane, Robert. *Those Celadon Blues*. Painted Post, N. Y., 1978.

———. *Ching-te-chen: Views of a Porcelain City*. Painted Post, N. Y., 1983.

Tregear, Mary. *Song Ceramics*. New York, 1982.

Valenstein, Suzanne G. *Ming Porcelains: A Retrospective*. Exhibition catalogue. China Institute in America, New York, 1970.

Van Oort, H. A. *The Porcelain of Hung-Hsien*. Lochem, 1970.

———. *Chinese Porcelain of the 19th and 20th Centuries*. Lochem, 1977.

Watson, William. *Tang and Liao Ceramics*. London, 1984.

Wenwu. Beijing, 1959—. (Published as *Wenwu Cankao Ziliao*, 1950–58.)

Wenwu bianji weiyuanhui, ed. *Wenwu kaogu gongzuo sanshinian*. Beijing, 1979.

Wenwu bianji weiyuanhui, ed. *Zhongguo gudai yaozhi diaocha fajue baogaoji*. Beijing, 1984.

Wirgin, Jan. "Sung Ceramic Designs." *The Museum of Far Eastern Antiquities* (Stockholm) *Bulletin*, vol. 42 (1970), pp. 1–272.

———. "K'ang-hsi Porcelain: Selected Objects from Swedish Collections." *The Museum of Far Eastern Antiquities* (Stockholm) *Bulletin*, vol. 46 (1974), pp. 65–110.

Wood, Nigel. *Oriental Glazes: Their Chemistry, Origins and Re-creation*. London, 1978.

Zhongguo Shanghai renmin meishu chubanshe, ed. *Chūgoku tōji zenshū*. 34 vols. Kyoto, 1981—. Vol. 4: Yue (1981). Vol. 7: Tang "three-color" (1983). Vol. 9: Ding (1981). Vol. 10: Yaozhou (1985). Vol. 12: Jun (1983). Vol. 15: Jizhou (1986). Vol. 16: Song and Yuan qingbai (1984). Vol. 19: Jingdezhen blue-and-white people's ware (1983). Vol. 23: Yixing (1982). Vol. 27: Fujian (1983). Vol. 28: Shanxi (1984).

Zhongguo shehui kexueyuan kaogu yanjiusuo, comp. *Xin Zhongguo de kaogu faxian he yanjiu*. Beijing, 1984.

INDEX

flambé glazes, 253, 255
Fonthill Abbey, Wiltshire, England, 253
Former Han, *see* Western Han
Foshan, 205, 268
Fu, prince of, 203, 209n.18
Fujian Province
    Ming, 187, 203
    Qing, 263
    Song, 103, 109, 112, 114, 115, 121n.19, 138
    Yuan, 126, 138

G

Gansu Province
    Neolithic, 1, 2, 3, 5, 6, 8, 9, 19n.12
    Qin, 39
Gansu Yangshao, *see* Majiayao Yangshao
Ganzhou wares, 117; No. 117
Gao Run, tomb of, 57n.10
Gao Ya and family, tomb of, 57n.8
garnitures de cheminée, 257; Nos. 271–75
Genghis Khan, 123
geometric-impressed pottery
    Han, 36, 47
    Shang, 23, 36
    Zhou, 23, 29, 32, 36–37; Nos. 24, 32, 33
"Ge" wares, 105, 215
gilding
    Ming, 168, 193, 198; No. 174
    Qing, 230, 241, 242, 253, 263; Nos. 224, 227, 243, 253, 254, 277, 278, 283
    Sui, 61, 61n.3
    Tang, 65–66; No. 60
    Yuan, 134, 168
glass paste decoration, 35
glazes, *see* Glossary, 311
    amber, 54, 69, 138
    apple-green, 242
    aubergine, 175, 187, 213, 236, 253; *see also* glazes, purple
    black, 43, 50, 53, 74, 76n.13, 92, 94, 95, 101, 103, 109, 114, 115, 116, 138, 205
    blue, 63, 64, 74, 85, 86, 89, 98, 105, 106, 134, 137, 138, 141, 152–53, 157, 167, 175, 176, 187, 193, 198, 203, 205, 227, 241, 255, 257, 273
    brown, 29, 36, 42, 43, 45, 53, 54, 57n.8, 61, 63, 64, 74, 75, 92, 94, 96, 101, 105, 116, 117, 138, 152–53, 157, 160, 198, 205, 227, 242, 255, 257
    buff, 75, 105
    calcia family, *see* glazes, lime
    celadon, *see* celadons
    chayemo, 255
    clair de lune, 241

colored, 175–78, 187, 198, 213, 255
colored, in the *famille verte* palette, 236
crimson-flushed blue, 253
crystalline, 255
demi-grand feu, 168
enamels used as, 167, 193
famille rose palette of, 253
flambé, 253, 255
green, 29, 32, 36, 42, 43, 45, 47, 50, 53, 54, 63, 64, 69, 74, 75, 92, 96, 98, 105, 157, 160, 168, 175, 187, 193, 205, 213, 236, 253, 255; *see also* celadons; Longquan wares; Northern celadons; Yue wares
hare's-fur, 114
high-fired: Han, 36, 41–43, 45; Ming, 152–53, 157, 160, 167, 168, 175, 193, 198; Qing, 238–39, 241–42, 253, 255, 257; Shang, 22–23, 29, 42; Six Dynasties, 50, 56n.3; Song, 92, 93, 99–100, 120n.6, 121n.13; Tang, 69, 72, 74; Zhou, 29, 32, 36, 37n.1; *see also* Glossary, 311
iron-rust, 255
lead: Han, 45, 47, 47n.11, 53, 63–64, 96, 168; Six Dynasties, 53–54, 56, 57nn.9,10; Song, 93, 95, 96, 121n.9, 138; Sui, 61, 61n.5; Tang, 63–64, 69, 76nn.1,13; 95, 96; Yuan, 138; *see also* glazes, low-fired; Glossary, 311
lime, 23, 42, 56n.3, 75, 99, 106, 121n.13, 168; *see also* glazes, high-fired; Glossary, 311
lime-alkali, 56n.3, 99, 121n.13; *see also* Glossary, 311
liuli, 96, 119, 142, 157, 160, 187; *see also* Glossary, 311
lower-fired, 167–68, 175, 187, 193, 213, 236, 253
low-fired: Han, 45, 53, 63–64, 168; Ming, 168, 175; Qing, 253; Six Dynasties, 53–54; Song, 93, 95, 96, 119, 121n.9; Tang, 63–64, 76nn.1,13; *see also* glazes, lead; Glossary, 311
medium-fired, 168, 175, 209n.9
mirror-black, 242
monochrome, 64, 69, 74, 76nn.1,13; 87, 92, 93, 119n.2, 134, 152–53, 157, 167, 168, 175, 193, 198, 203, 215, 236, 238–39, 241–42, 253, 255, 257, 258
oil-spot, 95, 114
old-rose, 152–53
olive-toned, 32, 43, 50, 74, 84, 89, 137, 141, 205
peachbloom, 239, 241, 242
"peacock feather," 253
pink, 253; *see also* ruby-back porcelains
polychrome, 54, 64, 66, 69, 95, 253, 255; *see also* glazes, *sancai*; glazes, suffused
potassia, 209n.9
"powder-blue," 241, 243
purple, 178, 213; *see also* glazes, aubergine
qingbai, 109, 110, 112, 125
red, 152–53, 157, 167, 193, 203, 238–39, 241, 253, 255

M

Machang, 6, 8, 10, 18–19nn.10,12; Nos. 6–8
Machangyan, 8
magnesium oxide (magnesia), 120n.6, 121n.13
Majiabang, 10, 16, 19n.23
Majiayao, 6, 10; No. 4
Majiayao Yangshao, 5–6, 8, 10, 18–19nn.10,12; Nos. 4–8
"Ma Jun" wares, 141
Manchuria, 211
Manchus, 211, 213, 256
manganese oxide, 75, 121n.13, 238, 242, 311
marbled patterns with Yue wares, 74, 76n.12
marbled wares, 69, 76n.4, 287; No. 296
"Martaban" wares, 205
Master-of-the-Rocks style, 211; Nos. 202, 203
meiping, 125, 134, 157
Mianchi xian, 3
Miaodigou, 4, 5, 10, 11, 18n.8
Miaodigou-II, 10, 11, 19n.15
Ming, 151–209; Nos. 145–200, 290; Color Nos. 19–31
  anhua, 157, 165
  apocryphal reign marks, 157, 165, 167, 200, 203, 287–88; Nos. 191, 195, 202, 214, 223, 297
  archaeological and other documentary comparisons, 302–304
  architectural pottery, 96, 157, 160, 162, 187; Nos. 147, 148
  biscuit-and-white wares, 175; No. 155
  blanc de chine, 203, 263; No. 197
  blue-and-red wares, 167, 220
  blue-and-white wares, 151, 152, 157, 162, 165, 167, 169, 172, 184, 187, 188, 191, 197, 199, 200, 203, 205, 209n.10, 215; Nos. 145, 149–51, 160–63, 166–68, 176–83, 188, 189, 193–95, 198; Color Nos. 21–23, 30
  bronzes, influence of, 197
  brown-and-white wares, 167
  Chenghua, 170, 172, 175, 178, 191, 200, 287; No. 154; Color Nos. 22–24
  Chongzhen, 200, 209n.16; Nos. 193, 194
  Cizhou wares, 203
  cloisonné-style decoration, 175–78; Nos. 158, 159; Color Nos. 26, 27
  colored glazes, 175–78, 187, 198; Nos. 157–59, 186; Color Nos. 25–27
  copies of, 197, 205, 215, 243, 287; No. 297
  Dehua wares, 203, 263; No. 197
  design continuations, 282, 285; Nos. 152 and 290; 184 and 291
  doucai, 172, 175, 179, 191, 198, 243, 287; Color No. 24
  dragon-and-cloud motif, 152–53, 155

  enamels, 152, 153, 155, 157, 167, 172, 175, 179, 184, 187, 191, 193, 197, 198, 200, 205, 227, 285; Nos. 152, 154, 156, 164, 165, 169–73, 175, 184, 185, 190–92; Color Nos. 24, 28, 31; *see also* Ming, *doucai*; Ming, polychrome enamels; Ming, red-and-green family; Ming, underglaze blue and enamels; Ming, *wucai*
  enamels on the biscuit, 198
  enamels as a monochrome glaze, 167, 193; No. 175
  end of, 211
  exportation of Chinese ceramics, 197, 199, 205
  export wares, 191, 197, 199, 200
  fahua, 177
  gilding, 168, 193, 198; No. 174; see also *kinrande*
  green-and-white wares, 175; No. 156
  Hangzhou Guan wares, 106
  high-fired glazes, 152–53, 157, 160, 167, 168, 175, 193, 198
  Hongguang, 203
  Hongwu, 151, 153
  Hongxi, 157
  Hongzhi, 167, 170, 175, 178–79, 184, 282; Nos. 152, 155
  "Interregnum Period," 165, 167, 169, 209n.10
  Jiajing, 175, 187–88, 191, 193; Nos. 166–71, 173–75
  Jingdezhen kilns, 151, 155, 157, 162, 167, 168, 169, 170, 175, 187, 199, 200, 203, 215, 219
  Jingtai, 169
  Jun wares, 203
  Ko-sometsuke wares, 200
  kraakporselein, 197, 209n.14; Nos. 181–83
  liuli glazes, 96, 157, 160, 187; No. 148
  Longqing, 193, 197
  Longquan wares, 99, 137, 167, 203; No. 196; Color No. 19; *see also* biscuit-relief decoration
  lower-fired glazes, 167–68, 175, 187, 193
  low-fired glazes, 168, 175
  "Martaban" wares, 205
  medium-fired glazes, 168, 175, 209n.9
  "Mohammedan" wares, 184, 187; No. 163
  monochromes, 152–53, 157, 167–68, 175, 193, 198, 203, 215; Nos. 146, 153, 175
  pierced work, 198–99, 230; No. 187
  polychrome enamels, 152, 167, 175, 179, 184, 187, 191, 193, 197, 198, 200, 205, 227; Nos. 164, 165, 169, 170, 172, 173, 185, 190–92; Color Nos. 24, 28, 31; *see also* Ming, enamels
  porcelain, 215, 219
  porcelain bricks, 160, 162; No. 147
  Porcelain Pagoda, 157, 160, 162; Nos. 147, 148
  Qing copies of, 215, 243, 287; No. 297
  red-and-green family, 187, 193, 198; Nos. 164, 172; Color No. 28

Y

yangcai, 244
Yangjiang xian, 268
Yangmeiting kilns, 81n.1
Yangshao, 2, 3–6, 8, 9, 10, 11, 12, 14, 16, 17, 18–19nn.6–10; 23, 54; Nos. 2, 3
Yangshaocun, 3
Yangtze River, 32, 51, 72, 74, 109, 311
Yangtze River valley, 12, 16, 17, 23, 32, 36
Yangzhou, 74, 77n.21, 209n.25
Yanshi xian, 21
yaobian, 255
Yao Huren, tomb of, 57n.8
Yaozhou kilns, 64, 74, 76nn.1,4,13; 84–85, 96, 119n.1, 142
yellow-glazed wares: Six Dynasties, 54; No. 46; Tang, 74; No. 71; see also glazes, yellow
Yellow River, 39, 51, 311
Yellow River valley, 2, 3, 4, 5, 9, 11, 12, 15, 21, 23, 29, 32
yingcai, 227
Yinxu, 21–22
Yixing wares, 205, 209n.25, 268, 273, 288; Nos. 285, 286
Yixing xian, 205
Yonghezhen, 115, 137
Yongle, 151, 157, 160, 162; Nos. 147, 148
Yongzheng, 215, 219, 242–44, 247, 253, 255, 256, 257; Nos. 248–58; Color Nos. 36, 38–40
Yuan, 123–49; Nos. 118–44; Color Nos. 16–18
    archaeological and other documentary comparisons, 301–302
    architectural pottery, 96, 142
    blue-glazed wares, 134
    blue-and-red wares, 132; No. 130
    blue-and-white wares, 119, 124, 126, 129–30, 133–34, 137, 149n.14, 151, 152, 197, 288; Nos. 126–28, 133, 134; Color Nos. 16–18
    brown-and-white wares, 124, 126, 133; No. 132
    Cizhou wares, 120n.8, 138, 141; Nos. 138–40
    copies of, 286, 288; Nos. 293, 298
    Ding wares, 142
    enamels, 141; No. 140
    end of, 151
    exportation of Chinese ceramics, 123–24, 138
    Ganzhou wares, 117; No. 117
    gilding, 134, 168
    Hangzhou Guan wares, 106
    Hunan painted wares, 117, 119
    Jingdezhen kilns, 81, 124–26, 129–30, 132–34, 137, 151, 215, 288
    "Jinhua Jun" wares, 137–38, 141
    Jizhou wares, 117, 137; Nos. 111–14, 116
    Jun wares, 87, 89, 98, 141; Nos. 94, 95
    lead glazes, 138; No. 137
    liuli glazes, 96, 142; No. 144
    Longquan wares, 137, 138, 203; Nos. 135, 136; see also biscuit-relief decoration; Yuan, spotted celadons
    "Ma Jun" wares, 141
    Northern celadons, 85, 142
    "Numbered Jun" wares, 138, 141, 149n.25; Nos. 141–43
    qingbai, 110, 124–26, 129, 130, 215, 286; Nos. 118–24
    red-and-white wares, 124, 126, 130, 132–33, 152, 220; Nos. 129, 131
    shufu wares, 124, 126, 129, 130, 152; No. 125
    "Splashed Jun" wares, 87, 89, 98; No. 95
    spotted celadons, 137
    spotted qingbai, 126, 137; No. 123
    turquoise-glazed wares, 141
    underglaze black and polychrome enamels, 141; No. 140
    Yunnan blue-and-white wares, 137
    Zhiyuan reign, 147n.8
Yuan Shikai, 281
Yue, state of, 36, 50
Yue wares
    Five Dynasties, 79; Nos. 72, 72A; Color No. 11
    Han, 50, 56n.2
    Six Dynasties, 50, 51, 56nn.1,3; Nos. 42–44; Color No. 2
    Song, 50, 99
    Tang, 50, 72, 74, 76, 76nn.11,12
    see also brownish black Yue; marbled patterns with Yue; spotted Yue; underglaze-painted Yue
Yuezhou, 50, 74
Yuezhou kilns (Hunan), 56n.5
Yuhang kilns, 50
yuhuchun ping, 125, 130
Yunnan blue-and-white wares, 137
Yunnan Province, 137
Yu xian, 86, 141
Yuxi xian, 137
Yuyao xian, 16, 50, 72, 79

Z

Zang Yingxuan, 199, 215, 219
Zhaili kilns, 53, 54
Zhang family, 94
Zhang family, 105
Zhang Sheng, tomb of, 61, 61n.4; Nos. 53, 54